THE CAMBRIDGE COMPANION TO BRITISH UTOPIAN LITERATURE AND CULTURE SINCE 1945

This *Companion* presents an authoritative study of British utopian literature and culture in the twentieth and twenty-first centuries. Written by leading scholars, it offers a wide-ranging account of utopian thinking in novels, plays, films, TV, fanzines, and poetry. Scholars and students interested in the utopian imagination will find nuanced analyses of British texts, situated within their materialist contexts. With a particular focus on countercultural and subcultural narratives, the book explores how British utopian visions of better societies offer a forceful critique of contemporary inequities such as racism, gender-based violence, class politics, and ecological harm. Blending the utopian with other genres, including the dystopia, the post-apocalypse, and ecocatastrophe narratives, the texts discussed reveal powerful images of utopian possibility. These works offer us vital imaginative and critical resources at a time of ongoing political, economic, and social crises.

PROFESSOR CAROLINE EDWARDS has published widely on contemporary literature, critical theory, and science fiction. Caroline's research has been featured by BBC Radio 4, BBC Radio 3, BBC One South East, the *New Statesman*, *Times Higher Education*, the *Guardian*, *SFX Magazine*, and in a dedicated exhibition at the Museum of London.

A complete list of books in the series is at the back of the book.

THE CAMBRIDGE COMPANION TO BRITISH UTOPIAN LITERATURE AND CULTURE SINCE 1945

EDITED BY
CAROLINE EDWARDS
Birkbeck College, University of London

Shaftesbury Road, Cambridge CB2 8EA, United Kingdom

One Liberty Plaza, 20th Floor, New York, NY 10006, USA

477 Williamstown Road, Port Melbourne, VIC 3207, Australia

314–321, 3rd Floor, Plot 3, Splendor Forum, Jasola District Centre, New Delhi – 110025, India

103 Penang Road, #05–06/07, Visioncrest Commercial, Singapore 238467

Cambridge University Press is part of Cambridge University Press & Assessment, a department of the University of Cambridge.

We share the University's mission to contribute to society through the pursuit of education, learning and research at the highest international levels of excellence.

www.cambridge.org
Information on this title: www.cambridge.org/9781009690492

DOI: 10.1017/9781009690485

© Cambridge University Press & Assessment 2026

This publication is in copyright. Subject to statutory exception and to the provisions of relevant collective licensing agreements, no reproduction of any part may take place without the written permission of Cambridge University Press & Assessment.

When citing this work, please include a reference to the DOI 10.1017/9781009690485

First published 2026

Cover image: City of Brighton in England, UK. Photo: ivetavaicule / DigitalVision Vectors / Getty Images.

A catalogue record for this publication is available from the British Library

Library of Congress Cataloging-in-Publication Data
NAMES: Edwards, Caroline, 1983– editor
TITLE: The Cambridge companion to British utopian literature and culture since 1945 / edited by Caroline Edwards.
DESCRIPTION: Cambridge, United Kingdom : Cambridge University Press : New York, NY, 2026. | Series: Cambridge companions to literature | Includes bibliographical references and index.
IDENTIFIERS: LCCN 2025030887 | ISBN 9781009690492 hardback | ISBN 9781009690508 paperback | ISBN 9781009690485 ebook
SUBJECTS: LCSH: English literature – History and criticism | Utopias in literature | Counterculture in literature | LCGFT: Literary criticism
CLASSIFICATION: LCC PR149.U8 C36 2026
LC record available at https://lccn.loc.gov/2025030887

ISBN 978-1-009-69049-2 Hardback
ISBN 978-1-009-69050-8 Paperback

Cambridge University Press & Assessment has no responsibility for the persistence or accuracy of URLs for external or third-party internet websites referred to in this publication and does not guarantee that any content on such websites is, or will remain, accurate or appropriate.

For EU product safety concerns, contact us at Calle de José Abascal, 56, 1°, 28003 Madrid, Spain, or email eugpsr@cambridge.org

Contents

List of Contributors		*page* vii
Acknowledgements		xi
1	The Utopian Impulse in British Literature and Culture since 1945 *Caroline Edwards*	1

PART I THE DREAM OF IMPERIAL RUINS

2	Cosy Catastrophes: Ambivalent Utopias amidst the Wreckage *Roger Luckhurst*	37
3	The 1960s: New Wave, New Worlds *Tom Dillon*	55
4	Post-Imperial Melancholy in the Long 1970s *Andrew M. Butler*	73

PART II BUILDING NEW COMMUNITIES

5	The British Counterculture, Utopia, and Class *David Wilkinson*	97
6	Staging Utopian Subjects: Contemporary British Theatre beyond the Barriers *Siân Adiseshiah*	119
7	Utopian Communities in Scottish Fiction *Timothy C. Baker*	138

PART III FROM CRISIS TO HOPE: UTOPIAN AESTHETICS

8   Doris Lessing: Surviving Utopia   159
    David Sergeant

9   Utopian Articulations in Experimental British Poetry   178
    Juha Virtanen

10 Utopian Realism and Race   197
    Sara Upstone

PART IV CASE STUDIES

11 Naomi Mitchison's *Memoirs of a Spacewoman*: A Critical
    Feminist Utopia   223
    Katie Stone

12 Ankh-Morpork, Anti-Utopia: Terry Pratchett's *Night Watch*
    and *Making Money*   244
    Jo Lindsay Walton

13 Some Dialectics of Utopia in China Miéville's Bas-Lag Trilogy 270
    Carl Freedman

Index   288

Contributors

SIÂN ADISESHIAH is Professor of Literature, Politics and Performance at Loughborough University. She is the author of *Utopian Drama: In Search of a Genre* (2023) and *Churchill's Socialism: Political Resistance in the Plays of Caryl Churchill* (2009), and co-editor of 'Narratives of Old Age and Gender', *Journal of the British Academy* 11.s2 (2023), *debbie tucker green: Critical Perspectives* (2020), *Twenty-First Century Drama: What Happens Now* (2016), and *Twenty-First Century Fiction: What Happens Now* (2013). She has published widely on contemporary theatre, utopianism, and, increasingly, age studies. She was joint editor-in-chief of the journal *C21 Literature* from 2022 to 2025 and is editor of the Liverpool University Press book series 'Playwriting and the Contemporary: Critical Collaborations'.

TIMOTHY C. BAKER is Personal Chair in Scottish and Contemporary Literature at the University of Aberdeen. He is the author of *George Mackay Brown and the Philosophy of Community* (2009), *Contemporary Scottish Gothic: Mourning, Authenticity, and Tradition* (2014), and *Writing Animals: Language, Suffering, and Animality in Twenty-First-Century Fiction* (2019), which won the British Association for Contemporary Literary Studies prize for Best Monograph in 2019.

ANDREW M. BUTLER is Senior Lecturer in Media and Cultural Studies at Canterbury Christ Church University. He is the author and editor of many books, including (as co-editor) *The Routledge Companion to Science Fiction* (2009) and *Fifty Key Figures in Science Fiction* (2009), *Solar Flares: Science Fiction in the 1970s* (2012) and the Palgrave/BFI handbook on *Eternal Sunshine of the Spotless Mind* (2014). Andrew is one of the editors of the science fiction journal *Extrapolation* and on the editorial board of *Science Fiction Studies*. He is also chair of judges for the Arthur C. Clarke Award.

TOM DILLON is Science Fiction Collections Curator at the University of Liverpool, where they care for a wide array of science fiction materials and aid researchers in accessing the collection. Tom's academic research focuses on the material contexts of science fiction magazines, and they completed a thesis on *New Worlds* magazine at Birkbeck, University of London. Tom is a member of the queer science fiction research collective Beyond Gender and a former co-director of the London Science Fiction Research Community.

CAROLINE EDWARDS is Professor of Contemporary Literature and Culture at Birkbeck, University of London. She is the author of *Utopia and the Contemporary British Novel* (2019) and co-editor of *China Miéville: Critical Essays* (2015) and *Maggie Gee: Critical Essays* (2015). Caroline has published widely on utopian theory, contemporary literature, film, TV and media, science fiction, and the philosophy of time in journals such as *Cultural Politics, Telos, Modern Fiction Studies, Textual Practice, ASAP/Journal, Science Fiction Studies, Utopian Studies, Contemporary Literature, Subjectivity*, and *Foundation: The International Review of Science Fiction*. Caroline's research has been cited in the *New Statesman* and the *Guardian*; featured on BBC One, BBC Radio 4, and BBC Radio 3; and discussed at the Barbican Centre, the Institute of Contemporary Arts, the Academy of Fine Arts in Vienna, and Whitechapel Gallery. In 2017, she curated an exhibition based on her research entitled 'Imagined Futures' at the Museum of London. Caroline is currently writing a book about utopian inhumanism and the elements.

CARL FREEDMAN is William A. Read Professor Emeritus of English Literature at Louisiana State University and the author of many books and articles, including *Critical Theory and Science Fiction* (2000) and *Art and Idea in the Novels of China Miéville* (2015). He has also published extensively on cinema and US electoral politics.

ROGER LUCKHURST is Professor of Modern and Contemporary Literature at Birkbeck, University of London. His many books include *The Trauma Question* (2008), *The Mummy's Curse* (2012), *Zombies: A Cultural History* (2015), and *Corridors: Passages of Modernity* (2019). He is Editor of *The Cambridge Companion to Dracula* (2017) and *Science Fiction: A Literary History* (2017).

List of Contributors

DAVID SERGEANT is Professor of English Literature at the University of Plymouth. He is the author of two monographs, on Rudyard Kipling and the near future in twenty-first-century fiction, three poetry collections, and essays in journals including *Novel, Genre, and Twentieth-Century Literature*. He is co-editor of volumes on Robert Burns and Doris Lessing.

KATIE STONE researches science fiction and utopias, particularly the figures of cyborgs, vampires, and strange children. Katie has completed a PhD in utopian literature at Birkbeck, University of London, and her work has been published in journals such as *Utopian Studies, Science Fiction Research Association Review*, and *Modern Language Review*. Katie is a founding member of the Beyond Gender research collective, a group of researchers, activists, and practitioners who are united by a shared commitment to imagining the world. They are known for their collective close readings of queer, trans, and feminist science fiction.

SARA UPSTONE is Professor of Contemporary Literature at Kingston University, London. She is the author of three monographs, including *Rethinking Race in Contemporary British Fiction* (2016), and has co-edited three collections, most recently (with Len Platt) *Postmodern Literature and Race* (2015). She is currently co-editing a collection on the work of the novelist Hari Kunzru, and another on community in contemporary British fiction.

JUHA VIRTANEN is Senior Lecturer in Contemporary Literature at the University of Kent. His books include *Poetry and Performance During the British Poetry Revival 1960–1980: Event and Effect* (2017), as well as the poetry collections *Backchannel Apraxia* (2014) and *DOOM ENGINES* (2022). His articles on contemporary literature and culture have been published widely and internationally, and his current research focuses on apocalyptic feelings.

JO LINDSAY WALTON is Research Fellow in Arts, Climate and Technology at the Sussex Digital Humanities Lab, University of Sussex, where he currently leads the project Designing Sustainable Digital Futures. Jo has published widely on utopian theory, science fiction studies, contemporary poetry, and the digital humanities in journals including *Science Fiction Studies, Foundation: The International Review of Science Fiction*, and *Finance and Society*. He has co-authored three books, *Communicating Climate Risk* with Polina Levontin (2022); *Serious Game Cookbook: A Beginner's Guide to Using and Designing Serious*

Games with Matthew Whitby, Feng Mao, Katarzyna Stawarz, and Shasta Marrero (2023); and *Visualising Uncertainty: A Short Introduction* with Polina Levontin and Jana Kleineberg. (2020). Jo has edited *Utopia on the Tabletop* (2024), *Poetry and Work: Work in Modern and Contemporary Anglophone Poetry* with Ed Luker (2019), and *On the Late Poetry of J.H. Prynne* with Joe Luna (2015). He is working on his first academic monograph, *Postcapitalism and Science Fiction*, which will be a collection of already published work and is contracted for publication with Lever Press in 2025.

DAVID WILKINSON is Senior Lecturer in English at Manchester Metropolitan University. He is a committee member of the Subcultures Network and the Raymond Williams Society and the author of *Post-Punk, Politics and Pleasure in Britain* (2016). David is currently working on a follow-up, *Days of the Underground*, for Manchester University Press. The book investigates the contested aesthetic and political legacies of the British counterculture, also considering previously neglected working-class and regional contributions.

Acknowledgements

This book has been a long time in the making. It was made possible by the patience and support of friends and colleagues who helped me navigate the Covid-19 pandemic and keep the project on track. I am grateful to Ray Ryan for commissioning the book, Edgar Mendez for his forbearance at my perpetual lateness, and Sherryl Vint, whose friendship and guidance has helped steer the project alongside its sister title, *The Cambridge Companion to American Utopian Literature and Culture since 1945*. The contributors delivered wonderful chapters that confirmed my vision for the volume, as well as exceeding my expectations as to the breadth and variety of utopian literary production in Britain since World War II. They were gracious in their response to my editorial feedback, which was perhaps more 'hands-on' than they might have liked. Iterative drafting with each contributor has helped forge this edited volume into a coherent collection, and I am proud of what we have achieved together.

Over the years, I have been lucky enough to sharpen my ideas about utopianism with a number of brilliant scholars in the field. I have learned a lot from Tom Moylan, Jennifer Wagner-Lawlor, Lucy Sargisson, Phil Wegner, Mark Bould, Ruth Levitas, John Rieder, Veronica Hollinger, Rob Tally Jr., Matthew Beaumont, Jay Telotte, and Raffaella Baccolini. Working alongside colleagues such as Christian Haines, Sean Grattan, Adam Stock, Sarah Lohmann, Heather Alberro, Antonis Balasopoulos, Darren Webb, Charles M. Tung, Emrah Atasoy, Glyn Morgan, Rhys Williams, and Graeme Macdonald has inspired me to keep developing utopian methods, even as we hurtle into the ecocatastrophe of climate emergency. I have been privileged to share dialogues with writers such as China Miéville, Mark Fisher, Jim Crace, Ekow Eshun, Adam Roberts, Sophie Lewis, Season Butler, Sophie Mackintosh, Tade Thompson, Margaret Atwood, Azad Ashim Sharma, Shani Cadwallender, Abi Curtis, and Maggie Gee, which allowed me to explore utopian possibility in the contemporary period. And through PhD supervisions and examining

I have had the unique pleasure of mentoring a generation of utopian scholars and activists, including Raphael Kabo, Katie Stone, Tom Dillon, Amy Brookes (née Butt), Christos Callow, Sasha Myerson, Eleonora Rossi, Laura Kaye, Nora Castle, Joe Davidson, Michelle Clarke, Rob O'Connor, Helena Wee, Heather Goodman, Gabriel Burrow, Lily Taylor, Zhui Ning Chang, Frankie Wakefield, Kae Thomas, and Rolando Travieso. Watching the Beyond Gender collective emerge out of PhD reading groups held originally at Birkbeck has been particularly inspiring and demonstrates the radical potential of resisting the neoliberal university machine when utopian scholars place kindness, care, reciprocity, and collaboration above competitive individualism.

I know my own commitment to utopian practice, and its relationship with utopian methods of textual analysis, owe a great debt to the interlocutions I have shared with such colleagues and friends. These interactions have led to this volume, which I hope might be helpful in your own utopian scholarship and teaching.

CHAPTER 1

The Utopian Impulse in British Literature and Culture since 1945

Caroline Edwards

There is a scene towards the end of British director John Boorman's bizarre 1974 cult classic *Zardoz* where the problem of utopia comes into sharp relief. Who gets to live in utopia and at what cost? One of the elite utopians of 2293, Avalow (played by Sally Anne Newton), summarises how the small community of Vortex 4 sequestered themselves from the apocalyptic wastelands beyond their country house estate. 'The world was dying', she says, 'we took all that was good and made an oasis here. We few, the rich, the powerful, the clever, cut ourselves off to guard the knowledge and treasures of civilisation as the world plunged into a dark age. To do this, we had to harden our hearts against the suffering outside.'[1] Avalow's words are accompanied by slow-motion shots of the immortal figures of Vortex 4 drifting through the rose garden whilst starving 'Outlander' hordes watch from the other side of a periphery shield. These members of the apocalyptic lumpenproletariat appear frozen in time, locked out of the eternal comfort and safety of utopia.

Zardoz was released the same year as the publication of Ursula Le Guin's landmark utopian novel, *The Dispossessed*. As Raymond Williams noted in a review published in 1978, Le Guin's shift to the utopian mode 'is significant, after so long a dystopian interval' and represents a 'renewal of a form of utopian thinking – not the education but the learning of desire – which has been significant among Western radicals since the crises and also since the defeats of the 1960s'.[2] Williams' materialist approach to the agentive process of learning, and enacting, utopian desire is developed in Tom Moylan's influential account, *Demand the Impossible: Science Fiction and the Utopian Imagination* (1986). Moylan suggests that novels such as Joanna Russ's *The Female Man* (1975), Marge Piercy's *Woman on the Edge of Time* (1976), and Samuel Delany's *Triton* (1976) 'reject utopia as blueprint while preserving it as dream'.[3] Their 'critical' utopias interrogate the demands for social justice of the older literary utopias, with

1

protagonists never quite arriving at a settled island of harmony and perfection, but, rather, engaging in an ongoing process of utopian critique.

From Literary Utopian Enclaves to the Utopian Impulse

In *Archaeologies of the Future* (2005), Fredric Jameson reflects upon the formal problem of the utopian enclave within the genre of the literary utopia. As he writes:

> It is a mistake to approach Utopias with positive expectations, as though they offered visions of happy worlds, spaces of fulfilment and cooperation, representations which correspond generically to the idyll or the pastoral rather than the utopia. Indeed, the attempt to establish positive criteria of the desirable society characterizes liberal political theory from Locke to Rawls, rather than the diagnostic interventions of the Utopians, which, like those of the great revolutionaries, always aim at the alleviation and elimination of the sources of exploitation and suffering, rather than at the composition of blueprints for bourgeois comfort.[4]

Jameson's influential theorisation reminds us of a longer tradition that differentiates between the utopian text as a formal or generic set of expectations, and the utopian impulse as a revolutionary instantiation of political desire. In this latter tradition, the utopian impulse operates dialectically, via a process of negation followed by (re-)imagination; like cracking a mirror with a hammer to break it into many fragments that can then be reassembled as a collage, or placed into the furnace to form new globules of molten glass that can be blown into any imaginable shape. The utopian impulse must firstly identify the contemporary source of inequality or exploitation through a process of denaturalising given reality. This ruptural act of critique makes visible the systemic unfairness of the prevailing logic that underpins everyday life under capitalism. Following this critique, the utopian impulse then reformulates the ingredients of contemporary social life *as if exploitation no longer existed*, imagining how we might think, act, feel, and labour under non-repressive conditions. All kinds of new socialities become thinkable in this speculative act of imagination. Taken together, the negative and positive sides of the utopian impulse offer something much more substantive than simply blueprints for a better life in the pastoral and Arcadian tradition of bucolic plenty – beyond scarcity, beyond back-breaking labour, or even beyond death.

This understanding of the utopian impulse owes a debt to the negative dialectics of Theodor Adorno, the Jewish messianic longings of Walter Benjamin's historical materialism, Herbert Marcuse's reorientation of the

1 The Utopian Impulse in British Literature and Culture

utopian impulse as the phylogenetic species memory of freedom, and, most importantly, Ernst Bloch's lifelong commitment to tracing the *Noch Nicht* ('not yet' or 'still not') across culture. It insists on thinking aesthetics and politics together, which illuminates the vital role that subjective formation plays in political change. 'It is all too easy', as Marcuse writes in *The Aesthetic Dimension* (1978), 'to relegate love and hate, joy and sorrow, hope and despair to the domain of psychology, thereby removing them from the concerns of radical praxis'.[5] In a late essay on 'Art and Society' written in 1971, Ernst Bloch argues that works of artistic genius (he has in mind Dante, Giotto, Shakespeare, Goethe, Beethoven, even Hegel) carry with them a utopian surplus that stretches beyond the ideological formations of their historical moment; a Novum 'which is not yet fulfilled'. Rather than justifying the predominant values of their particular age, these artworks rip open historical time through their utopian critique. The violence of the image conveys its revolutionary potential. As Bloch writes: 'I am talking about an anticipatory illumination that could never be realized in an ideology of the status quo but, rather, has been connected to it *like an explosive*, as though it could always engender the most stimulating surplus beyond the ideology.'[6]

Returning to our earlier consideration of *Zardoz*, we might now ask: to what extent can *Zardoz* be understood as a utopian text? Beyond mere bucolic abundance – as signified by the immortal youth and beauty of the pastel-clad inhabitants of Vortex 4 – what kind of utopian critique is at work in Boorman's strikingly odd film? *Zardoz* engages with themes that have been posed by utopian literature since Thomas More's coinage of the term in 1516. Striving for evidence-based perfection in their mirrored labs, the utopian citizens live in communal seclusion as equals. Everyone labours to bake the green bread that sustains them, and all decisions are made collectively. Like More's Utopians, they 'lead a sociable life together' in a moneyless society, 'their mode of dress is the same', and they 'embrace pleasures of the mind'.[7] Despite *Zardoz* revealing the ways in which their utopian way of life is dangerous and exploitative, this, too, responds to a literary tradition that originates in More's complex text. The abundance of More's Utopian commonwealth is attained via colonial conquest and the exploitation of Indigenous communities. The heavily fortified utopian 'island' has, in fact, been constructed by King Utopus who conquered the peninsula nation of Abraxa and 'put ... the natives to work' on a massive engineering project, digging a fifteen-mile-wide channel to sever the new commonwealth from its neighbours.[8] Indeed, the language of imperialism underpins More's text. The utopian life of ease and pleasure is made possible by the fact that 'dirty and more arduous tasks are carried out by slaves', and the citizens of Utopia are protected by a mercenary army composed of their neighbouring Zapoletes, who are described as 'savage, uncouth and warlike, happiest among the forests and rugged mountains where they are reared'.[9] King Utopus' civilising mission to 'cultivate' the brutish Abraxans and exploit the Indigenous Zapoletes mirrors the Tudor political culture that More sought to critique. The same colonial logic was used by Henry VIII after the Wars of the Roses to civilise the *wildehirrishemen* through English husbandry and cultivation; and can be seen in Richard Hakluyt's *Discourse of Western Planting* (1584), which uses the imagery of planting a colony as part of the English imperial project of civilising Virginia to secure investment for colonial economic expansion.[10] The aesthetic, cultural, political, intellectual, and economic achievements of European nations during the sixteenth to eighteenth centuries depended on a de-legitimisation of other cultures; what Damian Tricoire terms the 'enlightened colonialism' of the Age of Enlightenment.[11]

Vortex 4 similarly extracts labour and resources from its colonial outposts in *Zardoz*. Filmed at Hollybrook Hall in County Wicklow (very close to Boorman's own house), the immortals' imposing residence alludes to the English pastoral ideal lauded in the country house tradition. This seventeenth-century literary form linked the new agrarian capitalist class with an older feudal landed aristocracy through refunctioned chivalric ideals,[12] and was contemporaneous with the Tudor plantations cultivated in Ireland as part of England's colonial annexation of its neighbour. *Zardoz*'s lumpenproletariat Outsider hordes provide slave labour to cultivate the wheat required to feed Vortex 4's elite utopians, as well as their dependent population of Apathetics and Renegades. Whilst the Outsiders might be locked out of a life of utopian abundance, these hordes are in fact History in bloody motion. They stamp and shout like the striking British miners with whom they must surely be compared (*Zardoz* premiered at movie theatres in Los Angeles and New York on 6 February 1974, one day before the miners returned to strike and Prime Minister Edward Heath called a snap general election). Anticipating this utopian critical reading, the protagonist Zed spits out the line: 'This place is built on lies and suffering. How could you do what you did to us?'

British Post-War Culture: An Unpayable Debt to an Imaginary Past?

Perhaps the most memorable creative decision Boorman made in *Zardoz*, and certainly the one that attracts the lion's share of critical attention, was casting a scantily clad Sean Connery as the film's leading character Zed. At the time of filming in early 1974, Connery was forty-four years old and had recently been released from a six-picture contract with Eon Productions who tightly regulated the James Bond actor's image. Connery was known for his imposing physique: he had started his career in weightlifting and bodybuilding, before turning to modelling and theatre work in the chorus lines of touring shows.[13] His near-naked appearance in *Zardoz* references Connery's former pin-up status, in a camp futuristic costume that comprises a scarlet loincloth strapped in place by crossed bandoliers. Echoing Bond's tight swimming trunks in *Thunderball* (1965), Zed's skimpy costume is accompanied by thigh-high leather boots, completing the S&M references to Connery's 'phallic power'.[14]

Connery's powerful physical presence in *Zardoz* has certainly contributed to the film's cult status over the years. However, if we read *Zardoz* as a utopian critique of contemporary Britain in the post-war period, Connery's contribution to the film's weird tableaux of class politics, extractivism, and structural inequality becomes clear. In the early 1970s, Sean Connery *was* James Bond. The Scottish actor had achieved global fame as one of Britain's most successful and enduring cultural exports. It is worth recalling how the character of Bond came to exemplify values of discipline, loyalty, and cultural supremacy as uniquely British values. First introduced in Ian Fleming's 1953 spy thriller, *Casino Royale*, the character of Bond drew on Fleming's experiences as a former British intelligence officer and journalist, whose background and education placed him firmly in the English upper class (Fleming was born into a banking family in affluent Mayfair before being educated at Eton and the Royal Military College at Sandhurst, and his father was Member of Parliament for Henley). Umberto Eco's semiotic analysis of the character's fairytale structure is instructive here. As Eco demonstrates, Bond's popularity in the 1950s and early 1960s was dependent on the racial qualities of his villainous counterparts, revealing what Eco calls 'the racist need to show the superiority of the Briton'.[15] Le Chiffre in *Casino Royale* (1953) is part Mediterranean, part Prussian, with Jewish blood; Mr Big in *Live and Let Die* (1954) is Black; Hugo Drax in *Moonraker* (1955) is of German origin; Julius No in *Dr. No* (1958) is half Chinese, half German; Auric Goldfinger in *Goldfinger* (1959) has ambiguous Baltic origins, and is also ethnically Jewish; Ernst Stavro Blofeld, who reappears in *Thunderball* (1961), *On Her Majesty's Secret Service* (1963), and *You Only Live Twice* (1964) is half Polish, half Greek. With their mixed heritage, obscure origins, physical disfigurements, and perverse sexual appetites, Fleming's villains are archetypal fairytale figures that help define Bond as Anglo-Saxon, moderate, loyal to the Service, and disciplined. Fleming's rhetorical strategy of 'middle-class chauvinism', as Eco puts it, thus 'cynically build[s] an effective narrative apparatus' that articulates 'the common opinions shared by the majority of [his] readers'.[16]

National identity, as Benedict Anderson has taught us, is created through imagined communities; as instruments of soft power, literature and culture are at the forefront of this imaginary community formation. In refusing to acknowledge Britain's decline in international influence after 1945, Fleming's simplistic Manichean world of Cold War ideological oppositions allowed readers and audiences to inhabit the fiction of British exceptionalism. Through his defeat of monstrous villains attempting to threaten British security and geopolitical influence, Bond offered readers 'a nationalist fantasy, in which Britain's decline as a world power did not really take place', as James Chapman puts it.[17] Central to upholding this fantasy is the conviction that the decolonisation of former territories only had a minimal impact on Britain's global importance.[18] As scholars have recently suggested, this 'dangerous, imperialist misconception of [Britain's] standing in the world' ultimately resulted in the ongoing civil struggle that is Brexit,[19] a bitter, divided national conversation that was augured by the murder of British MP Jo Cox just a week before the EU referendum in June 2016. As we head into the mid 2020s, the political, economic, and social costs of Brexit become stark and what Michael Gardiner has called 'an unpayable cultural debt to an imaginary past' requires urgent scrutiny.[20] This volume takes as its conceptual starting point the relevance, indeed urgency, of literary and cultural inquiry in the wake of British exceptionalism. As aesthetic and expressive forms, literature and culture can confront the damaging consequences of this unpayable debt to an imaginary past, which persists and calcifies when it is left unexamined and unchallenged. In the chapters that follow, we will explore literary and cultural articulations of the utopian impulse that imagine alternatives to this dominant ideology.

Defining culture, however, is an enormously slippery task. As the Welsh Marxist Raymond Williams once exclaimed in frustration: 'I don't know how many times I've wished that I'd never heard the damned word.'[21] As a founding figure of the British New Left, along with E. P. Thompson, Dorothy Thompson, and Richard Hoggart, Williams' cultural materialism analysed literature and culture as specific historical expressions of bourgeois society within capitalism. For Williams, Marxism intervenes into universalising assumptions about civilised culture by reminding us of 'the full possibilities of the concept of culture as a constitutive social process, creating specific and different "ways of life"'.[22] The radicalism of this conception of culture lies in its sharp differentiation with the previous generation's liberal notion of culture as excellence, 'the best that has been thought and said in the world', as Matthew Arnold put it in 1868.[23] Williams' more anthropological definition of culture as encompassing the largely unrecorded experience of working-class life built on the British adult education movement. The concept was significantly developed by Stuart Hall, who led the Birmingham Centre for Contemporary Cultural Studies (BCCCS), which he founded in 1964 with Richard Hoggart. Hall was inspired by the Italian Marxist Antonio Gramsci, whose concepts of hegemony and organic intellectuals (that is, autodidactic individuals whose intellect is forged in their working-class communities rather than being artificially produced within the 'traditional' academic system) informed the intellectual and institutional practices at the Birmingham School.[24]

British Countercultures: The Explosive Potential of Utopian Surplus

I owe a debt to Stuart Hall's lifelong interrogation of British culture and formations of cultural identity, which underpins my approach in *The Cambridge Companion to British Utopian Literature and Culture since 1945*. The debt is personal. My PhD supervisor Professor Peter Brooker studied with Hall at the Birmingham School (and his external examiner was Raymond Williams). Virtually everything I have written and published on the utopian imagination over the past fifteen years is forged in the theoretical and materialist conjuncture of Hall's acute analysis of British political culture. My aesthetic understanding of utopia's powerful critique has emerged out of the work of Ernst Bloch, Herbert Marcuse, Walter Benjamin, Fredric Jameson, Ruth Levitas, Tom Moylan, and Jack Zipes. This combination of utopian theorisation and materialist critique, which pays particular attention to the unwritten and under-explored subcultures and countercultures from which utopian texts so often materialise, informs my editorial method in this volume. This is an explicitly political volume, in the sense that Hall describes in his influential 1996 essay 'Cultural Identity and Diaspora', where he writes:

> We cannot speak for very long, with any exactness, about 'one experience, one identity', without acknowledging its other side – the ruptures and discontinuities which constitute, precisely, the Caribbean's 'uniqueness'. Cultural identity, in ... this sense, is a matter of 'becoming' as well as of 'being'. It belongs to the future as much as to the past.[25]

The temporality of Hall's understanding of cultural identity references Raymond Williams' tripartite model of the dominant, emergent, and residual valences that make up the unexamined melee of most people's ideological belief-systems. Significantly, it also echoes the Blochian *Vorschein* (forward-dawning) of utopian possibility that unites within its gelid, ephemeral, almost spectral web those historical traces of previous moments of possibility, whose revolutionary power remains undischarged; both 'still not' and 'not yet', as the different translations of *Noch Nicht* express.[26] British subcultures in the twentieth and twenty-first centuries articulate a way of life, as Williams would put it, directly at odds with the dominant culture that Sean Connery's James Bond personifies, and his futuristic Zed satirises. As we shall see in the chapters that follow, the utopian potential within alternative literature and culture discloses its Blochian sense of possibility. Like an explosive, the image Bloch privileges for utopian rupture, the texts, novelists, filmmakers, poets, zine-makers, and playwrights explored in this edited collection rip through the prevailing discourse to reveal a utopian surplus; 'that which is not yet fulfilled'.[27] This surplus interrupts the process of ideological naturalisation through which dominant culture establishes, as well as conceals, its control. As Dick Hebdige, one of Stuart Hall's colleagues at the Birmingham School, argues in *Subculture: The Meaning of Style* (1979), British post-war youth subcultures challenge the hegemony through which dominant classes organise and produce an image of culture that presents itself as legitimate and natural.[28]

Let's take a closer look at how this production of utopian surplus via subcultural resistance plays out. We will start with the British countercultural 1960s, frequently described as the twentieth century's most utopian decade.

London's underground scene was in full swing when the *International Times* launched in 1966. Like New York's *East Village Other* and the *Los Angeles Free Press*, London's *International Times* offered its readers a sense of countercultural community, although it was characterised by its non-committal libertarian values and bringing together of eclectic cultural 'scenes' (the rock scene, the literary scene, the art scene, Bloomsbury intellectualism).[29] The publication's exuberant launch party at London's Roundhouse in Camden set the tone for the shifting cultural politics that followed. In total, 2,500 people danced at the party, including the Italian filmmaker Michelangelo Antonioni and his star actress Monica Vitti, Paul McCartney in disguise, Beat author Kenneth Rexroth, and, according to sources at the time, 'a well-known junkie, a notorious homosexual, and many happy people'.[30] The former site of a railway engine shed, the new Roundhouse became an important London landmark in the 1960s, with

1 The Utopian Impulse in British Literature and Culture 9

bands such as Pink Floyd, Cream, The Who, Led Zeppelin, Jimi Hendrix, and The Doors playing there (later it would become a key venue in the punk scene for bands like X-Ray Spex, The Clash, and Adam and the Ants). Less than a year later, it was chosen as the venue for an ambitious countercultural event, the Congress on the Dialectics of Liberation, which took questions of non-violence and resisting the military-industrial complex much more seriously than simple youthful rebellion. Billed as 'a unique gathering to demystify human violence in all its forms ... and to explore new forms of action', the 1967 congress featured lectures by Herbert Marcuse and the French philosopher Lucien Goldmann, the American civil rights activist Stokely Carmichael, and Beat poet Allen Ginsburg, whose readings and chantings shared the spirit of nascent San Francisco co-operatives. Over the course of the week-long event, young people started living in the Roundhouse, spilling out into local cafes, pubs, and parks to continue debates about revolution and anti-capitalist resistance.[31]

Marcuse began his lecture 'Liberation from the Affluent Society' by reminding the audience that 'flowers, by themselves, have no power whatsoever'. Citing Walter Benjamin's Thesis XV from 'Theses on the Philosophy of History', he underscored the necessity of arresting a capitalist time of repressive productivity:

> Walter Benjamin quotes reports that during the Paris Commune, in all corners of the city of Paris there were people shooting at the clocks on the towers of the churches, palaces, and so on, thereby consciously or half-consciously expressing the need that somehow time has to be arrested; that at least the prevailing, the established time continuum has to be arrested, and that a new time has to begin – a very strong emphasis on the qualitative difference and on the totality of the rupture between the new society and the old.[32]

From the transcript of Marcuse's lecture, published in the 1968 Pelican paperback *The Dialectics of Liberation*, it is easy to imagine the atmosphere in London's Roundhouse. The sense that a 'new time' was emerging, laden with utopian possibility, would have been obvious to the London students attending the conference. Just three months earlier, a high-profile student occupation at the London School of Economics, which had started with a march of 3,000 students, was described by the *Times* as 'unprecedented in British university history'.[33] Over the next couple of years, LSE students would escalate their fight with the smug 'pedagogic gerontocracy' (a more colourful descriptive term for Gramsci's traditional intellectuals), culminating in student leaders smashing their way through campus security gates in January 1969, inspired by world events such the Vietnam War and apartheid in South Africa.[34]

During the 1960s, complacent British middle-class culture came under increasing threat as autonomous spaces such as art galleries, new magazines, and radical bookshops in London, Glasgow, Manchester, Cardiff, and Hull provided a space for challenging cultural hierarchies.[35] Pirate radio stations infuriated politicians and BBC governors alike, flourishing briefly with the launch of Radio Caroline, which began regular broadcasting in 1964 before the Marine Broadcasting Offences Act of 1967 prohibited transmissions from ships.[36] The British establishment was increasingly lambasted, for instance in the satirical current affairs publication *Private Eye*, which launched in 1961, and the late-night BBC television programme *That Was the Week that Was* (1962–3), which became essential Saturday night viewing before it was cancelled by BBC governors who feared its political impact on viewers. The archetypal Englishmen wearing dark overcoats and bowler hats, epitomised by the Whitehall civil servants that ran the country on behalf of their elected ministers, were targeted by John Cleese's 'Ministry of Silly Walks' sketch in *Monty Python's Flying Circus* (1970). As Stuart Ward puts it, 'the end of empire and the steady diminution of British power and prestige also became the source of immense laughter and ridicule'.[37] Beyond mere political satire, this laughter at the expense of the British establishment transmogrified into a vital utopian aesthetic. 'The truth of art', as Marcuse writes in *The Aesthetic Dimension* (1978), 'lies in its power to break the monopoly of established reality . . . . In this rupture, which is the achievement of the aesthetic form, the fictitious world of art appears as true reality.'[38] Perhaps the most iconic example of this ruptural countercultural utopian aesthetic is Heinz Edelmann's direction of the animated film *Yellow Submarine* released in 1968. The film's acid-infused storyline features The Beatles as they womble past psychedelic blue monsters, charging cavalrymen, and live on the titular submarine. The utopian perforation of the British class system is brought to vivid life in the contrast between Liverpool's grim working-class housing, submerged and desaturated beneath the smog spewing from coal-powered chimneys, and the colourful utopian alternative of Pepperland. Here, the circus-like plot splices images and ideas together in a Pop Art picturebook aesthetic in which high and low culture collide through references to the French Surrealists, Japanese graphic art, the medieval epic poem *Tristan and Isolde*, Edward Lear's nonsense poetry, and Edgar Rice Burroughs' Tarzan.[39]

1 The Utopian Impulse in British Literature and Culture

1968, the year of the film's release, has been widely historicised as a utopian conjuncture that culminated in the student–worker protests at the University of Paris at Nanterre and the Sorbonne in May. With their strike food supply committees and municipal buses, the working-class neighbourhoods of Paris and Nantes demonstrated that student–worker solidarity could create forms of local self-government operating outside of the capitalist French state. Inspired by Mao Zedong and Che Guevara, and echoing the demands of the Paris Commune of 1871, graffiti and posters quickly emerged in the city's barricaded Latin Quarter bearing the utopian slogan, '*Soyez réalistes – demandez l'impossible!*' ('Be realistic – demand the impossible!'). This utopian zeitgeist of uprising is also captured in Stanley Kubrick's *2001: A Space Odyssey* on an epic galactic scale. Adapted from a short story by British science fiction author Arthur C. Clarke (who published a novelisation of the same title shortly after the film's release) *2001* had a profound impact on British culture, inaugurating a wave of Astrofuturist iconography within popular art and music. David Bowie's 1969 sci-fi anthem 'Space Oddity', for instance, was released a year later, timed to coincide with the Apollo 11 moon landing.[40] Fusing the heady otherworldliness of space exploration with glam rock personae liberated from the gender binary, Bowie's performances in this period bring to vivid life the proliferant utopian sexualities and genders imagined in New Wave American science fictions by Ursula Le Guin and Samuel Delany.[41] Like many other artists and musicians of his generation, Bowie's utopian fusion of art and politics can be traced to the formative role that art schools played in nurturing the rising stars of the British counterculture.[42] This art school experience shaped a generation of British musicians, who saw their art in contradiction with commerce, forging their outsider status through a curriculum of Romantic philosophy and early twentieth-century avant-garde manifestoes.[43]

The 1960s were also an important time for utopian literary production. Like its North American counterpart, the British 'New Wave' of utopian science fiction generated its own vigorous backlash against a juvenile focus in Golden Age SF, in which male homosocial relations had functioned as 'a necessary precursor to the public passions needed for white manly civilisation', as one critic memorably puts it.[44] Writers such as Brian Aldiss, J. G. Ballard, and Michael Moorcock brought a new literary sensibility to the genre, infusing its outdated (distinctly colonial) utopian tropes of buccaneering space adventures for boys at the galactic frontier, with a strong focus on formal experimentation. When he took over editorial stewardship of *New Worlds* magazine in May 1964, Moorcock set about commissioning countercultural fictions. As he wrote in an early editorial: 'Since SF is growing up ... the form must be reshaped and new symbols found to reflect the mood of the sixties ... '[45] US writers who had relocated to the UK, including Pamela Zoline, Samuel R. Delany, and Thomas Disch, were part of this vibrant scene of writers who became identified by their '"liberated" outburst of erotic expression';[46] as exemplified by Moorcock's defences of William S. Burroughs in a high-profile exchange in the *Times Literary Supplement* in November 1963 against criticisms of Burroughs' obscenity. This formal liberation was not confined to the sexual revolution. At the fringes of this countercultural literary movement was Anna Kavan, whose 1967 novel *Ice* has been read by critics as a loosely fictionalised semi-biographical account of psychic conflict obliquely referencing Kavan's lifelong heroin addiction. Whilst the post-nuclear setting of *Ice* suggests a nightmarish dystopian fable, scholars have recently argued that Kavan's text imbues the nonhuman world with powerful materialist agency, revealing an ecocritical, even utopian, perspectival shift.[47]

As the 1960s gave way to the 1970s, the prevailing affect in British culture marked a sharp distinction from the utopian promise of the 1960s counterculture. After the political defeats of the late 1960s and the increasingly dystopian economic and social problems of the 1970s the mood changed. As John A. Walker notes, British culture shifted from optimism to pessimism, 'prompted by the failure of so many of the hopes of the 1960s, plus the early deaths of so many of its leading figures'.[48] This is encapsulated in the original title to the Sex Pistols' influential 1977 punk anthem 'God Save the Queen', which had originally been titled 'No Future'. Punk's class politics – and I am thinking here not just of the Sex Pistols and the Clash but also female punks like Poly Styrene from X-Ray Spex, Viv Albertine from The Slits, Siouxsie Sioux, The Raincoats, Chrissie Hynde of The Pretenders, and Vivienne Westwood's fashion – were associated with the so-called 'Savage '70s', as the title of Trevor's Sutton's photomontage cover for the December 1979 issue of the *London Illustrated News* framed the decade. Meanwhile, British heavy and doom metal bands such as Black Sabbath, Judas Priest, Bolt Thrower, and Cathedral drew on dystopian and apocalyptic imagery in their cover art. Combining lurid colour palettes with necrotic motifs of machinic power (Judas Priest, *Screaming for Vengeance* (1982), *Jugulator* (1997)), warlike neo-primitive tribalism (Bolt Thrower, *Realm of Chaos* (1989), *War Master* (1991), and *Mercenary* (1998)), and satanic orgies and sacrifice (Black Sabbath, *Sabbath, Bloody Sabbath* (1973) and *Dehumanizer* (1992)), metal bands imagined disturbing sci-fi futures to match the power of their angry lyrics and aggressive sonic distortion. Although British bands were far removed from the American anti-Vietnam War protests and race riots, their immediate environments were grimly dystopian, particularly in the crumbling industrial heartlands of Birmingham and the Black Country.

Whilst British heavy metal undeniably reacts against the music of the 1960s counterculture, woven within the genre's frequently dystopian and apocalyptic imagery lies the glimmer of hope that the disasters they imagine might be averted. This requires more than mere negation, which Bloch argued (in a departure with Adorno's negative dialectics) was in and of itself insufficient to augur a utopian transformation; after all, depicting the dystopian reality may just as easily belie a liberal horror at the loss of bourgeois privilege as a prefigurative glimpse of post-capitalism via apocalypse. The aesthetic framing of the dystopia matters. As Laura Wiebe Taylor argues, such conservatism 'fail[s] to recognize that within metal's images of destruction and despair often lie the seeds of utopian possibility'.[49] The pleasure of heavy metal 'offers its fans an impression of what utopia might feel and sound like' by enacting the power of screamed vocals, extreme speeds and tempo shifts, and intense volume. This British heavy metal and post-punk utopianism took, as David Wilkinson suggests, 'muted but nevertheless vital forms during a moment usually characterised by left historiography as bleak, hopeless and even apocalyptic'.[50]

1970s Science Fiction: Beyond the Colonial Literary Utopia

The 1970s was marked by another surprisingly utopian shift. This is commonly overlooked in historical accounts of English declinism, which focus on the decade's high unemployment, economic stagflation, the 1973 Middle East oil crisis, and industrial disputes culminating in the 1978–9 Winter of Discontent. To discern this utopian shift requires grappling with what Paul Gilroy terms 'postcolonial melancholia'. Gilroy, who had been a doctoral student working with Stuart Hall at the Birmingham Centre in the early 1980s, analysed Black British culture. His landmark 1987 text *There Ain't No Black in the Union Jack* reconsidered the class-based approaches of Marxist British cultural studies (Williams, Hoggart, and Thompson) within the vector of race, drawing on the American Black radical tradition (C. L. R. James, Richard Wright, and W. E. B. Du Bois). Published during the peak of Britain's 'race riots' in the 1980s, which took place in Brixton and Broadwater Farm in London, Toxteth in Liverpool, Handsworth in Birmingham, and Chapeltown in Leeds,[51] Gilroy's text reimagines the relationship between race and class in relation to the contradiction between capital and labour. His later analysis of 'postcolonial melancholy' zeroes in on the 'genteel, common-sense racism' that underpins ordinary definitions of British nationalism; defined by the nation's inability to mourn its loss of Empire.

With Gilroy's analysis in mind, the mixing of utopian and dystopian aesthetic registers by British writers such as J. G. Ballard, Doris Lessing, and Buchi Emecheta starts to look decidedly more utopian than perhaps has been previously recognised. All three were writing back to Empire, to quote the title of Gilroy's co-authored 1982 text, *The Empire Strikes Back: Race and Racism in 1970s Britain*. Ballard spent his childhood in expat Shanghai during the Japanese occupation in World War II, Lessing was born in Iran and grew up in colonial Rhodesia, and Emecheta was raised by Igbo parents in colonial Nigeria (her mother had been sold by the family into slavery as a young girl). Moving to London in her early twenties in 1962, Emecheta raised five children as a single mother (an experience which is recorded in *In the Ditch* (1972) and *Second-Class Citizen* (1974)). She wrote in her spare time, starting with a regular column in the *New Statesman* followed by autobiographical accounts and works of fiction. Breaking with her characteristic realism, her 1983 novel *The Rape of Shavi* is a utopian narrative set in a fictional Sahara. The Shavians are a traditional people whose escape from the ravages of European colonial modernity is abruptly interrupted when a small plane escapes nuclear holocaust, resulting in an alternate history of first contact that confronts the Western colonial gaze through utopian defamiliarisation. Doris Lessing's early years in the United Kingdom provide an interesting comparison to Emecheta's experience. Like Emecheta, her marriage broke down and her experience of motherhood was overshadowed by her energetic involvement in antiracist and antiapartheid activism with the British Communist Party (activities that earned the notice of MI5 and MI6 who kept her under surveillance for twenty years).[52] Lessing's turn away from Marxism towards Sufi mysticism coincided with a move from realist fiction into science fiction in her 'Canopus in Argos' series (five novels published between 1979 and 1983), and standalone novels *Briefing for a Descent into Hell* (1971) and *The Memoirs of a Survivor* (1974). In the latter novel, the unnamed first-person narrator strays into a phantasmagoric, science-fictional 'inner space',[53] retreating from warring gangs of children on the streets outside. Whilst the novel is undoubtedly a dystopian projection of civilisational breakdown, it lacks the rheumy-eyed nostalgia for the recent antebellum past. Rather, despite her middle-class subjectivity, the narrator recognises the freedom to be found in this anarchic

1 The Utopian Impulse in British Literature and Culture 15

new world, which is also a return to the pre-capitalist past: 'all property worries gone; all sexual taboos gone ... all problems shared and carried in common. Free. Free, at least from what was left of "civilization" and its burdens.'[54]

This kind of ambivalent utopianism is also evident in J. G. Ballard's 'concrete trilogy' (*High Rise* (1963), *Crash* (1973), and *Concrete Island* (1974)). The novels are inspired by the futuristic 'Los Angelization' of West London undertaken by the Greater London Council in the late 1960s, culminating in the Westway flyover.[55] Speeding along the Westway at over 70 miles per hour, the middle-class protagonist of *Concrete Island*, Robert Maitland, enjoys the velocity and ease of this American 'automobility',[56] moments before his Jaguar careens off the elevated motorway after a tyre blow-out. Tumbling into the wasteland below, he finds himself trapped in an enclosed 'island' flanked by steep concrete embankments. What follows is a surreal retelling of *Robinson Crusoe*, an oddly utopian Robinsonade of psychic regression as Maitland goes on 'a journey not merely through the island's past but [also] through his own'.[57]

Ballard's use of the colonial utopian literary form to explore the uncharted New World of his protagonists' unconscious continues in an ecocatastrophic vein in his 1962 novel *The Drowned World*. Set some seventy years after a 'succession of gigantic geophysical upheavals' that have devastated the Earth's protective ionosphere, the world is now irradiated in intense tropical heat.[58] The polar ice caps have melted leading to sea level rises and the ascendancy of reptilian megafauna, recalling the planet's distant Triassic past. Kerans, the typically Ballardian white middle-class protagonist, fritters his days in an incongruously 'cosy catastrophe' utopia. Lounging in poolside deckchairs atop a ruined London skyscraper, Kerans and his attractive companion Beatrice read forty-year-old copies of *Vogue* magazine. The modern world has ended and they live in abandoned apartments still lavishly furnished with original surrealist artworks by Max Ernst and Paul Delvaux. The ecocatastrophic future has confined them to a life of pointless luxury – marooned in the upper floors of their flooded high-rise tower, whilst the malaria-infested waters below teem with reptilian life, 'a nightmare world of competing organic forms returning rapidly to their Paleozoic past'.[59] Ballard's next novel, *The Burning World* (1964) (published as *The Drought* in 1965), continues the ecocatastrophic theme with incongruously utopian elements. This time it is the turn of Dr Charles Ransom to navigate a vanished world, accompanied by the river-waif Jordan who is described, in a reference to Shakespeare's *The*

Tempest, as a latter-day Ariel 'rebuilding his world from scratch from the materials of water, wind and sunlight' along the last remaining riverbank as it slowly desiccates into the desert.[60] With its landscape littered with cattle carcases and burned-out cars, human temporality 'appear[s] to be running backwards'.[61] Anthropogenic pollution is the cause of this desert world. Like Crusoe, Ransom builds a makeshift raft and sets off towards the coast, pursued by a grotesque Caliban figure. Here, utopia has shrunk from Thomas More's engineered island (or, rather, peninsula) to the obverse of John Donne's 'No man is an island / Entire of itself'; in this antipodal realm of surrealist regression, each character 'would soon literally be an island in an archipelago drained of time'.[62]

With their British public-school stiff-upper lip, Ballard's male protagonists are not a million miles from Ian Fleming's James Bond. Despite the apocalyptic conditions, each relishes the chance to test his survival skills and revert to a more primitive era of mankind, ultimately surrendering to these devastated landscapes. Kerans in *The Drowned World* wanders off to certain death in the jungle, 'a second Adam searching for the forgotten paradises of the reborn sun'; Ransom in *The Drought* has dissolved all distinctions between himself and the desert so that he 'no longer cast any shadow on to the sand'; and, having survived the mysteriously crystallising Cameroonian jungle, Dr Edward Sanders turns his boat around at the end of *The Crystal World* (1966) to continue the life-threatening search for his 'real identity [which] still moved through the forests'.[63] The utopian element of these novels is not their intertextual regard for Early Modern travelogues such as More's *Utopia*, Shakespeare's *The Tempest*, or Defoe's *Robinson Crusoe* but, rather, their wholesale surrender of the colonial mode of modern subjectivity to the planet's wider atmospheric, nonhuman elements. When European colonial modernity has delivered a historical progress that works, as Joseph R. Winters puts it, 'to rationalize the violence enacted against "less advanced" groups, people who need to be civilized, saved, or brought into the fold of universal history'[64] (note Ballard's reiterated references in *Concrete Island* and *The Drought* to Caliban, Shakespeare's dehumanised Indigenous savage), perhaps the only remaining utopian option is to destroy this model of history altogether – to turn the clock backwards until the elements rule the world once more. In their insistence on the necessity and inevitability of civilisation starting over, Ballard's novels of the 1960s and 1970s outline a properly utopian project of decolonising human history into the unlikely relief of its more-than-human elemental possibility.

Utopian Anachronism as a Weapon, 1980s–2000s

In *Becoming Utopian: The Culture and Politics of Radical Transformation* (2021) Tom Moylan reminds us of the necessity of resisting the 'vampiric practices' of the capitalist present. As he writes, 'they suck radical energy out of all life on this planet', and should be met with a Blochian understanding of utopian praxis as an ongoing *process of becoming utopian* through ideological rupture.[65] Echoing Fredric Jameson's well-known adage, that 'our constitutional inability to imagine Utopia [is] ... not owing to any individual failure of the imagination but [is] the result of the systemic, cultural and ideological closure of which we are all in one way or another prisoners',[66] Moylan encourages us to refuse capitalism's totalising closure even as we labour within the capitalist present. This transformational work of utopian critique draws heavily on Ernst Bloch's legacy, which informed what Moylan calls 'an engaged examination of the revolutionary charge that grows out of humanity's deep and pervasive impulse of hope for a better world'.[67]

One utopian strategy that has been revived in recent years is the excavation of what Bloch called 'the gold-bearing rubble' within art, literature, and culture.[68] In an essay written in 1932, Bloch outlines his concept of *Ungleichzeitigkeit* (translated variously as non-contemporaneity, non-simultaneity, or non-synchronism). The term draws on Marx's notion of *Gleichzeitigkeit* (simultaneity) outlined in the *Grundrisse*, which describes how the commodity can be produced in multiple stages that take place simultaneously, following the division of labour.[69] Bloch's coinage acknowledges the non-simultaneity of historical process and the individual subject's understanding of, and political engagement in, that process. 'Not all people exist in the same Now', he writes. 'Older times than the modern ones continue to have an effect in older strata; it is easy to make or dream one's way back into older [times] here.'[70] This multivalent sense of subjective political temporality helps us understand the anachronistic ideological impulses people often carry unconsciously with them. We can apply this definition of non-contemporaneity to British life under Thatcherism, with its neoliberal revolution of the British state from 1979 until Margaret Thatcher's political defenestration in 1990. During this period there was a pervasive sense of hopelessness among the British left. In tandem with Ronald Reagan in the United States, Thatcher had decisively shifted the British state into its current neoliberal, financialised form. In addition to privatising public utilities, she withdrew government funding from museums, galleries, universities, art councils, and institutions such as the BBC and the British Film Institute. As Roger Luckhurst writes, Thatcher's 'suspicion of culture was of a piece with the hatred of intellectuals in the cultural establishment, apparently stuffed with liberal-left sympathizers who occupied positions of power in theaters, television companies, or the Arts Council'[71] (an ideological assumption, I would add, that returned with a vengeance during the years of Conservative-led austerity from 2010 until 2024). Britain experienced its own 'dark horizon', as Tom Moylan and Rafaella Baccolini described the period in their 2003 study of predominantly North American dystopian literature. Despite the prevailingly dystopian political mood, Baccolini and Moylan argue that critical dystopias emerged in the 1980s, which they describe as 'texts that maintain a utopian impulse. ... allow[ing] both readers and protagonists to hope by resisting closure'.[72]

By the 1990s and into the early 2000s, however, the work of British utopian writers, thinkers, and artists might productively be described as expressing utopian non-contemporaneity in the Blochian sense described earlier; mining previous historical moments for the 'gold-bearing rubble' of utopian possibility. To take just one example, zines rejected the Thatcherite mantra that *there is no alternative*. Emerging out of underground culture, they offered 'a way of understanding and acting in the world that operates with different rules and upon different values than those of consumer capitalism'. This alternative, as Stephen Duncombe writes, was 'fraught with contradictions and limitations ... but also possibilities'.[73] British literature, art, music, and culture produced in the 1990s resisted ideological closure or capitulation to the neoliberal financialisation that confronted it. As Mark Fisher wrote in *Ghosts of My Life* (2014), 1990s dance music constituted *a refusal to give up on the desire for the future*. 'This refusal ... amounts to a failure to accommodate to the closed horizons of capitalist realism.'[74] In literary production, this refusal was expressed by the so-called 'British Boom', which included genre authors such as M. John Harrison, China Miéville, Steph Swainston, Jeff Noon, Justina Robson, Kim Newman, and Hal Duncan. Against a backdrop of anti-Thatcherite techno music, Afrofuturism, and hip-hop, the 'British Boom' offered an energetic period of utopian and speculative genre-blurring that reimagined horror, the Weird, cyberpunk, fantasy, and science fiction. Miéville's early fiction, particularly in the Bas-Lag trilogy (which Carl Freedman considers in Chapter 13), was feted in the early 2000s as part of the wave of New Weird writers whose works garnered critical and popular attention for their energetic revitalisation of Lovecraftian weird. This had its own distinctively English dimensions, which recalled the British eerie tradition and 'haute Weird' (as Miéville termed it) of William Hope Hodgson, M. R. James, and Arthur Machen.[75]

Read in the immediate political context of the squatter's movement, Reclaim the Streets protest parties in London, and the anti-globalisation protests which culminated in the 1999 protests at the World Trade Organisation in Seattle, Miéville's early New Weird fiction is explicitly utopian.[76] Despite Miéville's subsequent abandonment of the term, the British New Weird briefly actualised an aesthetic form that was grounded in overtly leftist, utopian politics.

Another example of this utopian aesthetic can be found in the *Savage Messiah* zines by Laura Oldfield Ford (more recently known as Laura Grace Ford). Originally published between 2005 and 2009, *Savage Messiah* charts the devastation of gentrification, begun during Thatcher's tenure and accelerated in the New Labour years. Composited out of drawings, hand-written notes, annotated photographs, and newspaper clippings, Ford's zines give voice to the vanished struggles of previous generations in the city's filthy, occult landscape of pubs, squats, and estates – across Tottenham, New Cross, Deptford, Elephant and Castle, Ladbroke Grove, and the Lea Valley. Temporality collapses in Ford's zines: it is 1985 and the squatters are back, it is 1992 and punks sprawl on discarded furniture, it is 1981 and the fascists haven't managed to 'terrorise the carnival', it is 2001 and the old bill (police) are injured in a riot, it is 1976 and 'the police presence is overbearing', it is 2004 and the punks are having a party above a co-op. In his introduction to Verso's 2011 collection of Ford's zines (which had very small print runs), Mark Fisher describes how *Savage Messiah* 'deploys anachronism as a weapon.'[77] In resurrecting previous working-class countercultures such as the punks and post-punk movement, the record sleeves and fanzines of the 1970s, even the Parisian *flâneurie* of Baudelaire, Ford conjures a hauntology that recalls 'not so much ghosts from an actual past; they [are] instead the traces of futures that had never arrived but which once seemed inevitable'.[78] As Ford herself has said in interview: 'It seemed important to go back to that moment of the late '70s and early '80s to a point where there was social upheaval, where there were riots and strikes, exciting cultural scenes and ruptures in the fabric of everyday life.'[79] In 2012, Ford took part in a psychogeographical dérive with the writers China Miéville, Iain Sinclair, and Ken Worpole. The group met a few months after the London Riots in August 2011. These riots were incited by the death of Mark Duggan, a young Black man, at the hands of the Metropolitan police on 4 August 2011, which recalled London's race riots in Brixton in 1981 and 1985, and Tottenham in 1985. This was also the brief period in which the Occupy LSX protest camp was in situ, offering a utopian experiment in anti-capitalist liberation as part of the global Occupy movement. Walking across the camp's cobbled paving stones around St Paul's Cathedral (which is owned by the shadowy, private City of London Corporation and the London Stock Exchange), Miéville noted the sense of utopian *Vorschein*, writing in *London's Overthrow* (2012) that the city is 'pre-something'.[80]

In his introductory essay to Verso's edition of Thomas More's *Utopia*, published on the text's 500th anniversary in 2016, Miéville challenges the 'island logic' that underpins the literary utopian form, in which islands at the colonial frontier create sites of social experiment away from the European metropole. As he asks: 'Was More's utopia blueprint, or satire, or something else? As if these are exclusive. As if all utopias are not always all of the above, in degrees that vary as much in the context of their reception as of their creation.'[81] Miéville and Ford, along with Mark Fisher, share a political-poetic gaze that perforates the sleek reflective skin of neoliberal gentrification to reveal a return of the repressed in the form of London's working-class communities – the East End squatters, young counter-culturalists, refugees, ghosts of each immigrant generation's accreted culture, cuisine, music, fashion, life. The anti-capitalist utopianism of Miéville, Ford, and Fisher's resurrection of these Benjaminian traces reminds us of forms and sites of British countercultural struggle that have often been overlooked. As the Spanish historian Julia Ramírez-Blanco argues, the British anti-roads movement of the 1990s and the wider squatting and free party rave movements created 'artistic utopias of revolt'; from Highgate and Camden in North London, and the motorway protest camp in Leyton, East London, to the chalk hills of Twyford Down near Winchester, dockworker parties at the Mersey Docks in Liverpool, and the Greenham Common military base in leafy Berkshire. Combining direct action with artistic practice, these anti-capitalist communities forged intersectional connections between myriad groups via hedonism and pleasure. As Ramírez-Blanco writes: 'Playfulness became a primordial element within a hedonistic environment, where people met their friends and went to parties', filling the streets with music, dancing and barricades.[82]

Into the 2010s and 2020s: A Utopian Turn?

The declension of the vocabulary of utopian hope and possibility during the 1980s and early 1990s, which was undoubtedly overshadowed by the popularity of dystopian and apocalyptic narratives, seems to be making a comeback in twenty-first-century British literature and culture. This can be observed in the activist networks forged during the 2011 Occupy movement, the rapid proliferation of the UK-based Extinction Rebellion

(XR), and the Covid-19 pandemic mutual aid groups, to recent university encampments supporting Palestine (many of which, unlike their American correlatives, have been allowed to remain on university campuses). After fourteen years of Conservative-led austerity, Britons are desperately in need of hope and all too aware of the precarious optimism it promises. As the Australian-born, British activist and scholar Lynn Segal writes in *Radical Happiness: Moments of Collective Joy* (2017), remembering the 'subversive and utopian spirit' of earlier moments of political activism helps 'to keep open spaces of hope'.[83] For more than forty years Segal, close friends with the British socialist and independent MP Jeremy Corbyn, has made her Victorian house in Highbury, North London a commune and feminist stronghold (among its former residents is the writer Marsha Rowe who founded the feminist magazine *Spare Rib* in 1972 with Rosie Boycott and Michèle Roberts). Segal's story reminds us of London's prominent role in the UK squatters' movement, which also spilled out to Bristol, Cardiff, Manchester, and Brighton. Between 1985 and 1992, squatters and travellers occupied buildings in Hackney, East London, transforming the street 'into a vibrant community', replete with its own community garden and city farm. The movement was intersectional, bringing race, class, gender, and sexuality to the forefront of political activism, with groups such as the Brixton Black Women's Group and the Gay Liberation Front building 'an alternative vision of queer urban life' in Brixton and producing the first *Squatters' Handbook* in 1973.[84]

Perhaps the most explicitly utopian moment of the 2020s has been the removal of the statue of Edward Colston, a prominent British slave trader. In June 2020, activists marched with 10,000 protesters, before clambering onto the bronze statue and using ropes to tear it to the ground, then dragging it into the Bristol Harbour. As they did so one protester was pictured with his knee on the statue's neck: a symbolic moment of utopian redemption that referenced the murder of George Floyd who died whilst under restraint by a police officer in Minneapolis in 2020.[85] Another protestor, Jen Reid, jumped onto the statue's empty plinth and held up her clenched fist in a salute that echoed the Black Panthers and Black Power movement. Reid's iconic pose was captured on camera and, after circulating on social media, caught the attention of British artist Marc Quinn who produced a life-size sculpture titled 'A Surge of Power (Jen Reid) 2020'. Cast from black resin, Quinn's sculpture was temporarily placed without permission on the site of Colston's statue, commemorating Reid's 'hope for a better future'.[86] Quinn's artwork, and Jen Reid's powerful assertion of Black agency that inspired it, is a defiantly utopian affirmation of Black futurity. As Tina Campt, a Black feminist theorist of visual culture and contemporary art, puts it, Black futurity is 'not a question of "hope" . . . It strives for the tense of possibility that grammarians refer to as the future real conditional or *that which will have **had to** happen*.'[87] Campt's use of the future real conditional tense to describe Black futurity reminds us that the utopian Novum is a far cry from any teleological understanding of progressive linear time. It requires a leap of faith and imagination; if we are to imagine what life might look and feel like under conditions of real equality (beyond racism, beyond postcolonial melancholia in British culture), we must think *as if* equality has already been achieved and, simultaneously, imagine the prefigurative elements within the present moment that will lead to such liberation. This is not a deus ex machina image of futural utopian abundance or prelapsarian Arcadia; this kind of non-contemporaneity requires, rather, what the French-Brazilian philosopher Michael Löwy called the 'messianic activism' that animated Walter Benjamin's political writings.[88] We can see this kind of utopian non-contemporaneity in the work of the art curator and writer Ekow Eshun, whose 2022 exhibition 'In the Black Fantastic' at London's Hayward Gallery featured the work of artists from the African Diaspora, including Liberian-British artist Lina Iris Viktor, Ghanaian-British artist John Akomfrah, and the British painter Chris Ofili. Merging the spiritual, supernatural, and science fictional, these Black British artists weave non-linear temporalities stretching between African diasporic cultures and futuristic visions of liberated Black subjectivity. Viktor's artworks, for instance, draw on Aboriginal dream paintings and West and Central African cosmologies to rethink the Black utopia of Liberia, established in 1947 by free African Americans. Less a genre than a 'way of seeing', Eshun's theorisation of the Black Fantastic produces what he calls a 'strain of utopianism', as exhibited in a 'productive tension in the two and fro between the everyday and the extraordinary'.[89]

Written just three days after the toppling of Colston's statue, Vanessa Kisuule's poem 'Hollow' also captures this utopian non-contemporaneity. 'You came down easy in the end', the poem begins:

> Each bougie building we flaunt
> haunted by bones.
> Children learn and titans sing
> under the stubborn rust of your name.
> But the air is gently throbbing with newness.
> Can you feel it?[90]

1 The Utopian Impulse in British Literature and Culture 23

The utopian Novum of Kisuule's poem, which gestures towards the tentative feeling of Black British life emerging from the shroud of living 'in the wake', as Christina Sharpe puts it, of slavery and its enduring afterlife of 'blackness's ongoing and irresolvable abjection'.[91] The image in Kisuule's poem of the air 'gently throbbing with newness' expresses the utopian moment in which art and political protest meet: ephemeral yet enduring, gentle yet diluvial in potential, now yet also not-now and gravid with not-yet futurity.

Outline of the Volume

When the commissioning editor at Cambridge University Press approached me to edit this collection, I felt a certain trepidation. Beyond the obvious pre–World War II literary and artistic utopian figures – Thomas More, Francis Bacon, Margaret Cavendish, John Ruskin, William Morris, H. G. Wells, Virginia Woolf, Vanessa Bell, Katherine Burdekin, and Phoebe Willetts-Dickinson – I scratched my head to list British utopian writers or cultural producers in the second half of the twentieth century. So much of utopian scholarship has focussed on American and Canadian authors; notably Ursula Le Guin, Octavia Butler, Samuel Delany, Joanna Russ, Marge Piercy, Margaret Atwood, Suzy McKee Charnas, Toni Morrison, Kim Stanley Robinson, Nalo Hopkinson, Colson Whitehead, Emily St. John Mandel, and Juliana Spahr. I have even been guilty myself of prioritising these writers on courses I have designed and taught on utopian and science fictions. As I began researching the project, I realised how urgently we need a dedicated volume on the utopian impulse in the British literary canon of the twentieth and twenty-first centuries. My own contribution in *Utopia and the Contemporary British Novel* (2019) makes the case for a literary renaissance in the twenty-first-century British novel, exploring the genre-blurring utopian aesthetics of writers such as David Mitchell, Ali Smith, Grace McCleen, Jon McGregor, Joanna Kavenna, Hari Kunzru, Claire Fuller, Maggie Gee, and Jim Crace.[92] What follows is my best attempt at this act of conjuring, made possible by the brilliant contributions of my colleagues. As always, there will be gaps. Some of these are my own literary and cultural blind-spots, some are the result of the Covid pandemic and the ongoing crisis in UK higher education, which made it undoubtedly more difficult to commission chapters from precarious and unemployed academics.

The Cambridge Companion to British Utopian Literature and Culture since 1945 explores these ideas in thirteen chapters divided into four parts. Part One, 'The Dream of Imperial Ruins', examines utopian projections of other spaces and times to reimagine British society outside of imperialist relations: in the 'cosy catastrophes' of the 1950s that exuberantly destroyed the imperial metropolis, 1960s countercultural literary production, and the post-imperial melancholy of 1970s novels, films, and TV programmes. Roger Luckhurst's chapter 'Cosy Catastrophes: Ambivalent Utopias amidst the Wreckage' argues that apocalyptic narratives by writers such as John Wyndham and John Christopher should be read within 'the genre of post-imperial affect'. The uncertain utopian surplus these texts produce lies somewhere between anti-imperial critique and generic pleasure in apocalyptic destruction, hinting at possibilities for political renewal in the depiction of English declinism. Tom Dillon's chapter 'New Wave, New Worlds' explores this declinism in post-war British literature and culture via the metaphor of entropy. Dillon argues that the British science fiction magazine *New Worlds* used entropy as a metaphor for the waning impact of the 1960s counterculture. This dissolution of hierarchies and boundaries offered a utopian critique that can be traced in works by Michael Moorcock, Brian Aldiss, J. G. Ballard, and Pamela Zoline. These writers created important experimental works, Dillon writes, that 'explored the liberatory utopian potential of entropic decay in the midst of postcolonial decline'. Andrew M. Butler continues this theme in his chapter 'Post-Imperial Melancholy in the Long 1970s'. Drawing on scholarship by Roger Luckhurst and Paul Gilroy, Butler traces the utopian impulse in 1970s genres such as the British alternate history, the dystopia, and feminist remediations of patriarchal myths of Albion. In the destruction of a white vision of middle England, works such as Derek Jarman's 1978 cult film *Jubilee* and Daphne Du Maurier's *Rule Britannia* (1972) scrutinise the failed promises of Britain's post-war settlement, offering dystopian visions that 'puncture the boredom of chronic national decline', as Paul Gilroy puts it.[93]

Part Two, 'Building New Communities', draws on contemporary theoretical articulations to reappraise the utopian legacy of the 1970s and 1980s up to the present day. David Wilkinson's chapter 'The British Counterculture, Utopia and Class' examines the post-punk movement of the late 1970s and 1980s 'as a utopian resource of hope in contemporary crisis-ridden conditions.' Wilkinson's analysis of homosexuality and surrealist aesthetics in the visionary BBC 'Play for Today', *Penda's Fen* (1974), demonstrates the degree to which countercultural utopianism persisted into the 1970s along vectors such as class and sexuality, enabling experimental works to perform 'a radical questioning of the contemporary through desires [that are] unfulfillable in present social conditions'. Siân Adiseshiah's chapter 'Staging Utopian

Subjects: Contemporary British Theatre Beyond the Barriers' focuses on affective forms of utopian spectatorship in radical theatre practice. Adopting a Blochian and Brechtian approach, Adiseshiah argues that late twentieth- and twenty-first-century British theatre has created a 'laboratory for constructing the liberated social space of utopia'. London-based Black British playwrights such as debbie tucker green and Mojisola Adebayo, Adiseshiah writes, give us 'powerful articulations of Black, queer, de-colonial forms of intersubjectivity'. Timothy C. Baker's chapter 'Utopian Communities in Scottish Fiction' considers how Scotland's relationship with the idea of utopia is complicated by its role within the United Kingdom. Often conceived of as peripheral to, or oppositional within, the United Kingdom, Scottish literature and culture imagines a space 'both oddly imperial yet strangely subaltern', as Baker cites Caroline McCracken-Flesher. Baker examines how Scottish writers such as Ali Smith, Luke Sutherland, Leila Aboulela, and Jenni Fagan use utopian communities within their fiction to 'look beyond the nation to examine questions of individual and collective desire and identity'.

Part Three, 'From Crisis to Hope: Utopian Aesthetics', explores British works that utilise aesthetic form to appraise revolutionary utopian possibility. David Sergeant's chapter 'Surviving Utopia: Doris Lessing's Prefigurative Fictions' considers Lessing's search for genres and forms appropriate to her own personal utopian vision across a long literary career that spanned six decades. Sergeant evaluates the utopian energies of novels that also tend towards escapist resolutions, for example in *The Memoirs of a Survivor* (1974) and *The Sweetest Dream* (2001). As Sergeant notes, these novels 'sit at odds with the utopian tradition for deserting the idea of societal progress', identifying an anti-modern stance in Lessing's work that recalls the anti-utopianism of Edmund Burke, Aldous Huxley, and George Orwell. Juha Virtanen's chapter 'Utopian Articulations in British Experimental Poetry' traces the shared utopian project of three experimental British poets writing in the 2010s: Sean Bonney, Verity Spott, and Callie Gardner. Experimental poetry presses such as Callie Gardner's DIY magazine *Zarf* (2015–20), the South London-based Asian-led publishing collective the87press, Powys-based Welsh publisher Aquifer, and Manchester-based avant-garde press zimZalla, have built independent community spaces that express an anticapitalist utopian impulse. Composed of gift-based communities, Virtanen argues that the British experimental poetry scene imagines 'something not yet in existence'. Sara Upstone's chapter, 'Utopian Realism and Race' considers utopian novelistic form, extending Upstone's previous theorisation of utopian realism. As

Upstone argues, there is a strong commitment in contemporary British fiction to post-racial and/or multicultural futures in which realism becomes transformed. Rather than mimetically representing the 'here and now', utopian realist authors employ a refracted version of the non-oppressed present to convince readers of the viability of alternative, transformed futures. Black British writers such as Candace Carty-Williams, Zadie Smith, and Bernadine Evaristo offer imagined futures rooted in the experience of Black women, drawing on community responses to the intersectional forces of patriarchy. This contingent and specific utopia, Upstone suggests, reminds us of the imperative 'to overturn existing concepts if one is to reach towards Black justice'.

The final part of this book, 'Case Studies', opens with Katie Stone's chapter 'Naomi Mitchison's *Memoirs of a Spacewoman*: A Critical Feminist Utopia'. Stone's chapter responds to Moylan's influential account of 1970s critical utopian utopias,[94] arguing that Scottish author Naomi Mitchison gives us a fascinating precursor to this predominantly North American phenomenon. Mitchison's 1962 spacefaring adventure *Memoirs of a Spacewoman* predates the American countercultural 1960s and early 1970s, drawing on earlier progressive political traditions. These included her work campaigning as part of the 1930s British birth control movement, involvement in African decolonisation (she covered Ghanaian independence celebrations in Accra for the *Manchester Guardian* in 1957 and campaigned for the British protectorate of Bechuanaland to become the independent nation of Botswana), and her involvement in the Scottish independence movement (Mitchison's 1947 novel *The Bull Calves* portrayed the Jacobite uprising against English imperial rule in Scotland). Stone cautions us against locating utopianism exclusively in what Bloch called the 'Thomas More variety' of literary utopias. Rather, as she cites Bloch, we should search in texts such as *Memoirs of a Spacewoman* for the utopian 'Something that is missing'.[95] Jo Lindsay Walton's chapter 'Ankh-Morpork, Anti-Utopia: Terry Pratchett's *Night Watch* and *Making Money*' offers another compelling case study, examining the utopian implications of Pratchett's much-loved satirical fantasy series, *Discworld*. Although many of *Discworld*'s characters offer a profoundly anti-utopian, often anti-democratic moral outlook, Walton suggests this surface anti-utopianism is at odds with the affective charge of the series, 'which successfully conjures many moments of warmth, kindness, care, and hope'. Read within the European tradition of anti-chivalric satire (in the spirit of Ernst Bloch's analysis of Cervantes' *Don Quixote* as a key example of the utopian 'Venturer Beyond the Limits'), Pratchett's novels invite the reader to laugh at villainy and greed, whilst rooting for what Bloch called 'the little man'.⁹⁶ As Walton demonstrates, the Ankh-Morpork books reimagine the emergence of European political modernity, using satire and laughter to upend the authority of patrician and sovereign figures; laughing, as the English essayist William Hazlitt observed, at 'the difference between what things are, and what they ought to be'. The utopian potential of such laughter undermines the otherwise anti-utopian bent of Pratchett's novels. Carl Freedman's chapter 'The Dialectics of Utopia in China Miéville's Bas-Lag Trilogy' offers a close reading of this trilogy by acclaimed British fantasy author China Miéville, which charts the growth of utopian possibility across the three novels. In the first novel, *Perdido Street Station*, utopian traces are present but sparse within the semi-fascist steampunk Victoriana of New Crobuzon, the city-state at the centre of the fantasy universe of Bas-Lag. The floating pirate city of Armada, in which the second novel *The Scar* takes place, offers a more straightforwardly utopian space modelled on the social organisation of the real-world pirate ships of the eighteenth-century Atlantic. As Freedman illustrates, Armada is revealed to be an *ambiguous* utopia (in Ursula Le Guin's canonical phrase), which contains counter-utopian as well as counter-counter-utopian tendencies. The final novel in the trilogy, *Iron Council*, maps the revolutionary locus of utopian communism in the 'perpetual train' of the novel's title. Far more than *The Scar*, it focuses on the *construction* of revolutionary utopianism and does not overlook the inevitable ambiguities and false starts along the way.

Taken together, the chapters in this volume offer suggestive texts and reading methods that reveal the persistence of the utopian impulse within British utopian literature and culture from the post–World War II period to the present day. As the Black feminist Lola Olufemi writes in her explicitly utopian manifesto *Experiments in Imagining Otherwise* (2021), which was written in the frightening period of social isolation during the Covid-19 lockdowns, we must learn to think otherwise. Whether we call it the communist horizon, or prefiguration, Olufemi's language is unapologetically utopian. The imagination, she writes 'undoes entire epistemes and clears a space for us to create something new. Though this "newness", or the demand for *something else*, can never fully be realised in the realm of the discursive, it exists in other registers: it can be felt, heard, touched, tasted.'⁹⁷

Notes

1. *Zardoz*, dir. John Boorman (John Boorman Productions Ltd., 1974).
2. Raymond Williams, 'Utopia and Science Fiction', *Science Fiction Studies*, 5(3) (1978), pp. 203–14 (p. 213).

3. Tom Moylan, *Demand the Impossible: Science Fiction and the Utopian Imagination* (New York: Methuen, 1986), p. 10.
4. Fredric Jameson, *Archaeologies of the Future: The Desire Called Utopia and Other Science Fictions* (London: Verso, 2004), p. 12.
5. Herbert Marcuse, *The Aesthetic Dimension: Toward a Critique of Marxist Aesthetics*, trans. Herbert Marcuse and Erica Sherover (Boston: Beacon Press, 1978), p. 5.
6. Ernst Bloch, 'Art and Society' in *The Utopian Function of Art and Literature: Selected Essays*, trans. Jack Zipes and Frank Mecklenburg (Cambridge, MA: The MIT Press, 1988), pp. 18–70 (pp. 38, 39, 41) (my emphasis).
7. Thomas More, *Utopia*, trans., and ed. Dominic Baker-Smith (London: Penguin Books, 2012), pp. 89, 63, 86.
8. Ibid., p. 58.
9. Ibid., pp. 71, 102.
10. Arthur F. Kinney and David W. Swain (eds.), *The Routledge Encyclopedia of Tudor England* (New York: Routledge, 2001), p. 155; John Patrick Montaño, *The Roots of English Colonialism in Ireland* (Cambridge: Cambridge University Press, 2011), p. 19.
11. Damian Tricoire, *Enlightened Colonialism: Civilisation Narratives and Imperial Politics in the Age of Reason* (Basingstoke: Palgrave Macmillan, 2017).
12. Nicole Pohl, *Women, Space and Utopia, 1600–1800* (Abingdon: Routledge, 2006), pp. 55–8.
13. In 1953, Connery won a bronze medal in the 'tall men's class' at Mr Universe. Andrew Spicer, *Sean Connery: Acting, Stardom and National Identity* (Manchester: Manchester University Press, 2022), p. 16.
14. Spicer, *Sean Connery*, p. 17.
15. Umberto Eco, 'Narrative Structures in Fleming' in *The Role of the Reader: Explorations in the Semiotics of Texts* (Bloomington, IN: Indiana University Press, 1979), pp. 144–74 (p. 153).
16. Ibid., pp. 151–3, 161.
17. James Chapman quoted in Jeffrey Richards, 'Imperial Heroes for a Post-imperial Age: Films and the End of Empire' in *British Culture and the End of Empire*, ed. Stuart Ward (Manchester: Manchester University Press, 2001), pp. 128–44 (p. 136).
18. As Stuart Ward notes, the 'minimal impact' thesis has dominated British cultural historians writing about the post-1945 era, who barely mention the British Empire. Stuart Ward, 'Introduction' in *British Culture and the End of Empire*, ed. Stuart Ward (Manchester: Manchester University Press, 2001), pp. 1–20 (p. 4).
19. Danny Dorling and Sally Tomlinson, *Rule Britannia: Brexit and the End of Empire* (Hull: Biteback Publishing, 2019), p. 2.
20. Michael Gardiner, *The Constitution of English Literature: The State, the Nation, and the Canon* (London: Bloomsbury, 2013), p. 5.
21. Raymond Williams, *Politics and Letters: Interviews with New Left Review* (London: New Left Books, 1979), p. 154.

22. Raymond Williams, *Marxism and Literature* (Oxford: Oxford University Press, 1977), p. 19.
23. Matthew Arnold, *Culture and Anarchy* [1868], ed. J. Dover Wilson (Cambridge: Cambridge University Press, 1963), p. 6.
24. Stuart Hall, 'Cultural Studies and Its Theoretical Legacies' in *Cultural Studies*, ed. Lawrence Grossberg, Cary Nelson, and Paula Treichler (New York: Routledge, 1992), pp. 277–94 (p. 281).
25. Stuart Hall, 'Cultural Identity and Diaspora' in *Identity: Community, Culture, Difference*, ed. Jonathan Rutherford (London: Lawrence & Wishart, 1998), pp. 222–37 (p. 225).
26. Wayne Hudson's analysis of the complex temporalities contained within Bloch's coinage of the *Noch Nicht* is the most instructive I have read. See Wayne Hudson, *The Marxist Philosophy of Ernst Bloch* (Basingstoke: Macmillan, 1982), p. 20.
27. Bloch, 'Art and Society', p. 38.
28. Dick Hebdige, *Subculture: The Meaning of Style* (New York: Routledge, 1979), p. 16.
29. Simon Rycroft, *Swinging City: A Cultural Geography of London, 1950–1974* (London: Routledge, 2016), p. 88.
30. Elizabeth Nelson, *The British Counterculture, 1966–73: A Study of the Underground Press* (Basingstoke: Macmillan, 1989), p. 45.
31. David Cooper, 'Introduction' in *The Dialectics of Liberation*, ed. David Cooper (London: Penguin Books, 1968), pp. 7–11 (pp. 10–11).
32. Herbert Marcuse, 'Liberation from the Affluent Society' in *The Dialectics of Liberation*, ed. David Cooper (London: Penguin Books, 1968), pp. 175–92 (p. 177). Marcuse is referring to Thesis XV in Walter Benjamin, 'Theses on the Philosophy of History' in *Illuminations*, ed. Hannah Arend, trans. Harry Zohn (New York: Schocken Books, 1968), pp. 253–64 (pp. 261–2).
33. Rand K. Rosenblatt cites *The Times* in 'The Revolution at the LSE', *The Harvard Crimson*, 23 March 1967. Available at: www.thecrimson.com/article/1967/3/23/the-revolution-at-the-lse-plast/ (Last accessed 11 May 2024).
34. John Mair, 'The Agitators', *The Guardian*, 10 July 2003. Available at: www.theguardian.com/education/2003/jul/10/students.uk (Last accessed 28 March 2023).
35. See the 'Radical Bookshop History Project' compiled by Dave Cope and Ross Bradshaw. Available at: https://www.leftontheshelfbooks.co.uk/images/doc/Radical-Bookshops-Listing.pdf (Last accessed 11 May 2024).
36. David Hendy, 'Radio Reinvented: Part One: The Pirates', *bbc.com*, n.dat. Available at: www.bbc.com/historyofthebbc/100-voices/radio-reinvented/the-pirates/ (Last accessed 11 May 2024).
37. Stuart Ward, '"No Nation Could Be Broker": The Satire Boom and the Demise of Britain's World Role' in *British Culture and the End of Empire*, ed. Stuart Ward (Manchester: Manchester University Press, 2001), pp. 91–110 (p. 91).
38. Marcuse, *Aesthetic Dimension*, p. 9.

39. Bettina Kümmerling-Meibauer, 'Mixing Pop Art and Political Criticism: Heinz Edelmann's Artwork for Children', *Dossier thématique*, 13 (2018), n. pag. DOI: https://doi.org/10.4000/strenae.1913.
40. Jason Heller, *Strange Stars: David Bowie, Pop Music, and the Decade Sci-Fi Exploded* (London: Melville House, 2018), p. xi.
41. Indeed, Bowie scholars explore the British star's performance via analytical frameworks such as the Bakhtinian carnivalesque, with its commitment to utopian radicalism. See Alison Blair, '"Oh Man, I Need TV When I Got T. Rex": Bowie and Bolan's Otherworldly Carnivalesque Intermediality', *Celebrity Studies*, 10(1) (2019), pp. 75–88 (p. 79).
42. Virtually every significant artist of the period studied for the Diploma in Art and Design, which had been introduced in 1961: John Lennon studied at the Liverpool College of Art, Pete Townsend attended London's Ealing Art College at the same time as Freddie Mercury of Queen, Ray Davies from The Kinks and Adam Ant both studied at the Hornsey Art College, Eric Clapton was at Wimbledon College of Art, and David Bowie graduated from St Martin's School. Peter Wicke, *Rock Music: Culture, Aesthetics and Sociology*, trans. Rachel Fogg (Cambridge: Cambridge University Press, 1990), p. 95
43. Simon Frith and Howard Horne, *Art into Pop* (London: Routledge, 1987), p. 35.
44. Christopher Leslie, *From Hyperspace to Hypertext: Masculinity, Globalization, and Their Discontents* (Basingstoke: Palgrave Macmillan, 2023), p. 377.
45. Michael Moorcock quoted in Rob Latham, 'Sextrapolation in New Wave Science Fiction', *Science Fiction Studies*, 33(2) (2006): pp. 251–74 (p. 258).
46. Ibid., p. 252.
47. See Laura de la Parra, '"With One Arm I Supported Her: The Other Arm Was the Executioner's": An Ecofeminist Reading of Anna Kavan's *Ice*' in *Avenging Nature: The Role of Nature in Modern and Contemporary Art and Literature*, ed. Eduardo Valls Oyarzun, Rebeca Gualberto Valverde, Noelia Malla García, María Colom Jiménez, and Rebeca Cordero Sánchez (Lanham, MD: Rowman & Littlefield, 2020), pp. 37–48.
48. John A. Walker, *Left Shift: Radical Art in 1970s Britain* (London: I. B. Tauris, 2002), p. 13.
49. Laura Wiebe Taylor, 'Images of Human-Wrought Despair and Destruction: Social Critique in British Apocalyptic and Dystopian Metal' in *Heavy Metal Music in Britain*, ed. Gerd Bayer (London: Routledge, 2016), pp. 89–110 (p. 89).
50. David Wilkinson, '"Pam Ponders Paul Morley's Cat: *City Fun* and the Politics of Post-Punk' in *Ripped, Torn and Cut: Pop, Politics and Punk Fanzines from 1976*, ed. The Subcultures Network (Manchester: Manchester University Press, 2018), pp. 91–109 (p. 91).
51. Anon., 'Race, Policing and the 1980s Riots', Modern Records Centre, University of Warwick Library. Available at: https://warwick.ac.uk/services/library/mrc/studying/docs/racism/1980s/ (Last accessed 16 July 2024).

1 The Utopian Impulse in British Literature and Culture

52. David Caute, *Red List: MI5 and British Intellectuals in the Twentieth Century* (London: Verso, 2022), pp. 86–90.
53. Ballard and Lessing both used the term 'inner space' to describe their fiction during this period. See J. G. Ballard, 'Which Way to Inner Space?' *New Worlds*, No. 118 (May 1962), pp. 2–3, 116–18. Doris Lessing has discussed critics' use of the term 'inner space' to refer to her own work. As she said in a 1982 interview: 'I see inner space and outer space as reflections of each other. I don't see them as in opposition. Just as we are investigating subatomic particles and the outer limits of the planetary system – the large and the small simultaneously – so the inner and the outer are connected.' Lesley Hazleton, 'Doris Lessing on Feminism, Communism and "Space Fiction"', *The New York Times*, 25 July 1982: https://archive.nytimes.com/www.nytimes.com/books/99/01/10/specials/lessing-space.html?_r=1 (Last accessed 12 July 2024).
54. Ibid., p. 147.
55. When it opened in July 1970, the Westway flyover was met by furious local residents trailing protest banners out of their upstairs windows, just feet away from the thundering traffic. Simon Jenkins, 'Concrete Bungle: How Public Fury Stopped the 1970s Plan to Turn London into a Motorway', *The Guardian*, 22 October 2019: https://www.theguardian.com/politics/2019/oct/22/concrete-bungle-how-public-fury-stopped-the-1970s-plan-to-turn-london-into-a-motorway#:~:text=5%20years%20old-,Concrete%20bungle%3A%20how%20public%20fury%20stopped%20the%201970s%20plan,turn%20London%20into%20a%20motorway&text=It%20was%20a%20true,and%20scored%20a%20signal%20victory (Last accessed 12 July 2024).
56. The British sociologist John Urry introduced the concept of automobility in 'The "System" of Automobility' in *Automobilities*, ed. Mike Featherstone, Nigel Thrift, and John Urry (London: Sage, 1005), pp. 25–40. He defines automobility as a 'self-organizing autopoetic, nonlinear system that spreads world-wide and includes cars, car-drivers, roads, petroleum supplies and many novel objects, technologies and signs' (p. 27).
57. J. G. Ballard, *Concrete Island* [1974] (London: Fourth Estate, 2014), pp. 69–70.
58. J. G. Ballard, *The Drowned World* [1962] (London: Harper Perennial, 2008), p. 21.
59. Ibid., p. 19.
60. J. G. Ballard, *The Drought* [1965] (London: Harper Perennial, 2008), p. 21.
61. Ibid., p. 34.
62. Ibid., p. 9.
63. Ballard, *The Drowned World*, p. 175; *The Drought*, p. 233; J. G. Ballard, *The Crystal World* [1966] (London: Flamingo, 2000), p. 171.
64. For an overview of 'enlightened colonialism', see Tricoire (ed.), *Enlightened Colonialism*. Joseph R. Winters, *Hope Draped in Black: Race, Melancholy, and the Agony of Progress* (Durham, NC: Duke University Press, 2016), p. 13.
65. Tom Moylan, *Becoming Utopian: The Culture and Politics of Radical Transformation* (London: Bloomsbury Academic, 2021), pp. 3–5.

66. Fredric Jameson, 'Progress Versus Utopia; Or, Can We Imagine the Future?', *Science Fiction Studies*, 27 (1982): 147–59 (p. 157).
67. Moylan, *Becoming Utopian*, p. 4.
68. Ernst Bloch, *Heritage of Our Times* [1935], trans. Neville and Stephen Plaice (London: Polity Press, 1991), p. 116.
69. Karl Marx, *Grundrisse* [1939], trans. Martin Nicolaus (London: Penguin, 1993), pp. 520–1.
70. Bloch, *Heritage of Our Times*, p. 97.
71. Roger Luckhurst, 'Cultural Governance, New Labour, and the British SF Boom', *Science Fiction Studies*, 30(3) (2003), 417–35 (p. 417).
72. Baccolini and Moylan, 'Introduction', p. 7. I use the phrase 'predominantly North American' because out of the five chapters that focus on a single author in *Dark Horizons*, only one of these (Pat Cadigan) comes from outside the United States.
73. Stephen Duncombe, *Notes from Underground: Zines and the Politics of Alternative Culture* [1997] (Portland; Microcosm Publishing, 2008), p. 10.
74. Mark Fisher, *Ghosts of My Life: Writings on Depression, Hauntology and Lost Futures* (Alresford: Zero Books, 2014), p. 21 [my italics].
75. China Miéville, 'Weird Fiction' in *The Routledge Companion to Science Fiction*, ed. Mark Bould, Andrew M. Butler, Adam Roberts, and Sherryl Vint (New York: Routledge, 2009), pp. 510–15 (p. 510).
76. As Miéville has said in interview, 'the Bas Lag books . . . were a response . . . very directly to the post-Seattle anti-capitalist movement'. China Miéville quoted in Stephen Shapiro, 'Gothic Politics: A Discussion with China Miéville', *Gothic Studies*, 10(1), pp. 61–70 (p. 70).
77. Mark Fisher, 'Introduction: "Always Yearning for the Time That Just Eluded Us"' in Laura Oldfield Ford, *Savage Messiah* (London: Verso, 2011), pp. v–xvi (p. x).
78. Ibid., p. xiv.
79. Laura Oldfield Ford qtd Ibid., p. xi.
80. China Miéville, *London's Overthrow* (London: The Westbourne Press, 2012), p. 14.
81. China Miéville, 'Close to the Shore' in Thomas More, *Utopia* [1516] (London: Verso, 2016), pp. 3–9 (p. 5).
82. Julia Ramírez-Blanco, *Artistic Utopias of Revolt: Claremont Road, Reclaim the Streets, and the City of Sol* (Basingstoke: Palgrave Macmillan, 2018), p. 23.
83. Lynn Segal, *Radical Happiness: Moments of Collective Joy* (London: Verso, 2017), p. 267.
84. Alexander Vasudevan, *The Autonomous City: A History of Urban Squatting* (London: Verso, 2017), pp. 57–8.
85. BBC News, 'Edward Colston Statue: Protesters Tear Down Slave Trader Monument', 8 June 2020. Available at: https://www.bbc.co.uk/news/uk-529 54305%23:~:text=Earlier%2520in%2520the%2520day%252C%2520in,the%2 520city%2520for%2520many%2520years (Last accessed 16 July 2024).

86. Oscar Holland, 'Artist Replaces Slave Trader Statue with One of a Black Lives Matter Protester', *CNN*, 15 July 2020. Available at: https://edition.cnn.com/style/article/edward-colston-marc-quinn (Last accessed 22 March 2024).
87. Tina Campt, *Listening to Images* (Durham, NC: Duke University Press, 2017), p. 17 (italics and bold in the original).
88. Michael Löwy, *Fire Alarm: Reading Walter Benjamin's* 'On the Concept of History' [2001] (London: Verso, 2016), p. 135.
89. Ekow Eshun, *In the Black Fantastic* (London: Thames and Hudson, 2022), pp. 11, 27. Eshun's reference to 'a strain of utopianism' is quoted in Caroline Edwards, 'Reflecting on the Black Fantastic: An Interview with Ekow Eshun', *Foundation: The International Review of Science Fiction*, 52(2) (2023), 64–79 (p. 78).
90. Vanessa Kisuule, 'Hollow' (2020). Available at: www.poetryinternational.com/en/poets-poems/poems/poem/103-30428_HOLLOW (Last accessed 22 March 2024).
91. Christina Sharpe, *In the Wake: On Blackness and Being* (Durham, NC: Duke University Press, 2016), p. 14.
92. Caroline Edwards, *Utopia and the Contemporary British Novel* (Cambridge: Cambridge University Press, 2019).
93. Gilroy, 'Britain's Post-Colonial Melancholia', p. 33.
94. Moylan's analysis in *Demand the Impossible* focused on Joanna Russ, Ursula K. Le Guin, Marge Piercy, and Samuel R. Delany. Subsequent studies have argued that Octavia E. Butler, Sally Miller Gearhart, Suzy McKee Charnas, and James Tiptree Jr. can plausibly be considered associated with this generation of 1970s critical utopians.
95. Ernst Bloch, *The Principle of Hope*, vol. 1, trans. Paul Knight, Neville Plaice, and Stephen Plaice (Cambridge, MA: MIT Press, 1995), p. 309.
96. Ernst Bloch, *The Principle of Hope*, vol. 3, [1959], trans. Neville Plaice, Stephen Plaice, and Paul Knight (Cambridge, M.A: The MIT Press, 1995), pp. 1000–33.
97. Lola Olufemi, *Experiments in Imagining Otherwise* (London: Hajar Press, 2021), p. 34 (italics in original).

PART I

The Dream of Imperial Ruins

CHAPTER 2

Cosy Catastrophes
Ambivalent Utopias amidst the Wreckage
Roger Luckhurst

The 'cosy catastrophe' was the deadly and dismissive term coined by the SF author and critic Brian Aldiss in 1973 to delineate a distinct group of English, ostensibly dystopian disaster fictions written in the years after World War II, usually set in pastoral, post-apocalyptic landscapes of a bucolic England slowly reverting to an earlier, pre-modern age. 'The essence of the cosy catastrophe', Aldiss said acidly, 'is that the hero should have a pretty good time (a girl, free suites at the Savoy, automobiles for the taking) while everyone else is dying off.'[1] The alliterative 'cosy catastrophe' is a neat yoking of opposites, and is surely the model for the later coinage 'cozy crime' or 'cozies', a sub-genre of retro Golden Age crime fiction, where tasteful murders take place in small town or village settings, the whole suffused with nostalgia for a legible regime of crime and punishment. Aldiss's term was harder edged, intended to expose the bad faith of the genre: the reserve of pleasure that curls inside these depictions of the catastrophic erasure of industrial modernity from England's green and pleasant land. Susan Sontag had criticised the infantile pleasures of American B-movie science fiction catastrophe films in very similar terms in her essay 'The Imagination of Disaster' for the high-brow *Commentary* magazine in 1965.

Apocalyptic Writing in England

Cosy catastrophes are mostly identified with the work of John Wyndham, who had major mainstream breakthrough success in England and America with *The Day of the Triffids* (1951), *The Kraken Wakes* (1953), and *The Chrysalids* (1955), so ensuring lots of imitations. Aldiss breezily dismisses these as 'totally devoid of ideas but read smoothly'.[2] Their common assignment for school reading in Britain in the 1970s further marginalised them as merely 'children's fiction'. Wyndham's friend Sam Youd, writing as John Christopher, produced the most sustained body of novels in the genre, from the decidedly un-cosy *The Death of Grass* (1956, now a Penguin Classic), *Wrinkle in the Skin* (1965), and *Pendulum* (1968), via the pioneering young adult dystopia of the 'Tripods' series (1967–8, 1988), all the way to *Bad Dream* (2003), in which England is politically severed from the European Union by the pressure of extreme nationalists.

The cosy catastrophe is embedded in several traditions of apocalyptic writing in England. Wyndham's vision at the opening of *The Day of Triffids*, of a London largely emptied of its population and falling back into savagery and ruin, had echoes of the lone survivor genre started by Mary Shelley's *The Last Man* (1826). This genre endured into the 1950s: Richard Matheson's *I Am Legend* (1954), for instance, exerted a powerful influence on its post-war revival. *Triffids* was also overtly indebted to H. G. Wells's pioneering vision of social collapse in London after the arrival of the Martians in *The War of the Worlds* (1898), part of the substantial foreign invasion genre that peaked before the Great War began in 1914.[3] Wells's vision was harshly underscored by the murderous logic of the social Darwinian imperative of 'survival of the fittest', but cosiness crept into the genre quite early. 'I'm expecting the end of the world today', Professor Challenger announces to his butler in Arthur Conan Doyle's *The Poisoned Cloud* (1913). 'Yes, sir. What time sir?' Austin replies with parodic English phlegmatism. 'I can't say. Before evening.' 'Very good, sir.'[4] This stiff upper-lip survives into the stoicism celebrated in the popular culture of World War II: the Cole Porter or Powell and Pressburger vision of steadfast Englishness. Even more immediately, though, Wyndham's disaster novels were part of the 'ruin literature' written in the wake of the war, when the centres of European civilisation, Paris and London, carried substantial scars of total war, and Berlin had been virtually obliterated by Allied bombing. Wyndham had travelled across Europe and into Germany as a Signals Corps officer in the Allied advance of 1944–5, writing home about the devastation and the vast trail of dead that he witnessed.[5] Youd also served in the Signals Corps in the Second World War, serving in North Africa and Italy. The substantial commentary on the emotions inspired by the contemplation ruins often emphasises the weird mix of horror and delight. In 1953, Rose Macaulay published *The Pleasure of Ruins*, which began with Henry James's confession that many experiences of ruins carry a pleasure that 'shows the note of perversity'.[6] Macaulay ended her study with a short afterword evoking the Blitzed and blasted state of a dreary post-war London in the 1950s, in stark contrast to the splendour of the classical ruins of Greece and Rome.

The *catastrophe* (from the Greek, meaning sudden over-turning) is an *apocalypse* (Greek for uncovering or unveiling) that exists on the limits of possibility. It trembles on the edge of a religious or eschatological revelation (the last book of the New Testament Bible is translated as either the Apocalypse or Revelation of St John). It is a form of writing that asks the impossible: to imagine the end, without aftermath, without remainder, without time, without language, without subjects left to write or read the very account that is composed of it.[7] It is dystopian destruction that also carries an implicit utopian thrust: heaven achieved via a necessary sacrificial burning (the literal meaning of 'holocaust'). Despite the impossible task of what Maurice Blanchot called 'the writing of the disaster', it is persistent and pervasive in many cultural imaginations, not just the Christian tradition.[8] Frank Kermode's influential exploration of this mode in *The Sense of an Ending* suggests that 'we project ourselves ... past the end, so as to see the structure of the whole, a thing we cannot do from our own spot of time in the middle'.[9] The genre's ambivalent investment in the surety of a definitive end can actually be 'a welcome relief from the frustration and anxiety of permanent crisis' in the muddled middle times, Christopher Palmer has argued.[10] These proleptic projections of the end thus always demand to be read as allegories of the present, the time of their composition.

In this chapter, I want to read the post-war English cosy catastrophe through a number of culturally distinct overlapping or overlaid allegorical possibilities. Perhaps most overt is the emergence in August 1945 of the truly remainderless threat of nuclear annihilation inside new and merciless Cold War logics that initially displaced Britain from its prior status as a global power. Nuclear catastrophe, which once stood alone as the dominant interpretation of the genre, might be regarded as an early registration of a wider imagining of ecological catastrophe, a nascent literature of what we now call the Anthropocene. But I want to spend more time with the thesis that the genre emerges from a conservative sensibility of ruination and perceived decline, a figuring of Britain's brutal and definitive displacement from the apex of power in the post-war geopolitical order. The cosy catastrophe arrives in the moment of decolonisation and articulates what Paul Gilroy has termed a 'post-imperial melancholy', which finds its curious pleasures in the masochistic embrace of decline, a paradoxically utopian longing for the dystopian smashing of systems. Needless to say, I do not agree with Aldiss's brisk dismissal of the genre as 'devoid of ideas': the genre teems with them; it is one of the most powerful allegorical articulations of a particularly English post-war sensibility or what Raymond Williams calls 'structure of feeling'.

The Nuclear Imagination

The ambiguous affective economy of the cosy catastrophe genre that was identified by Aldiss was exploited by his fellow iconoclasts in New Wave SF, a movement usually dated as starting in around 1962 (as Tom Dillon discusses in Chapter 3). Subverted or re-routed disaster fiction was a favoured genre for this group. Michael Moorcock in his Jerry Cornelius quartet (*The Final Programme* (1965), *A Cure for Cancer* (1971), *The English Assassin* (1972), and *The Condition of Muzak* (1977)) shows England experiencing an accelerating entropic decline in time and space, disintegrating into multiple alternate realities across the multiverse. Moorcock wrote other works in this mode, such as the episodic *Breakfast in the Ruins* (1972). J. G. Ballard in his important sequence of global disaster novels (*The Wind from Nowhere* (1961), *The Drowned World* (1962), *The Burning World* (1964; published in the US as *The Drought*, 1965), and *The Crystal World* (1966)) and short stories from the same era also actively inverted generic expectations. In Ballard's psychic landscapes, the anti-heroes seemed to embrace the extreme and nihilistic possibilities of catastrophe rather than rue or fight it. This New Wave perversity was continued by Keith Roberts in *The Furies* (1966) or by M. John Harrison in *The Committed Men* (1971) and in his particularly relevant short-story on English decline, 'Running Down' (1975). The 1970s was a period of renewal for these English catastrophes, particularly on television, as in Terry Nation's post-nuclear *Survivors* series for the BBC (1975–7) or the memorable BBC children's TV series, *The Changes* (1975), based on Peter Dickinson's young-adult trilogy (*The Weathermonger* (1968), *Heartsease* (1969), and *The Devil's Children* (1970)), in which everyone above the age of fourteen is overwhelmed by a Luddite rage and destroys every piece of technological modernity before dying off and leaving young adults alone amidst the ruins. In the 1970s, the genre bloomed because it coincided with a period of economic, social, and political disorder as a fragile post-war consensus collapsed. But this was also an era of a further subversion of the form by women writers (as Andrew M. Butler discusses in Chapter 4). Angela Carter's *Heroes and Villains* (1969), Emma Tennant's *The Time of the Crack* (1973), and Doris Lessing's *The Memoirs of a Survivor* (1974) all took aim at the wounded narcissism or masculine melancholia that seemed to saturate the narrative arc of the genre, calling the bluff of its comforting pleasures. Caroline Edwards has also identified the continuation of a 'pastoral post-apocalypticism' in twenty-first-century British fiction, from Maggie Gee's *The Flood* (2004) to Megan Hunter's *The End We Start*

From (2017), which she suggests is notable for 'their remarkably cheerful and demonstrably utopian approach to depicting catastrophic worlds'.[11]

The use of atomic weapons on the Japanese cities of Hiroshima and Nagasaki in August 1945 led precipitately to Japanese surrender and the end of the war in the Pacific theatre. It also, almost immediately, unleashed a sense of profound rupture in history, an existential challenge to the survival of humanity, and a cultural eruption of the apocalyptic imagination. On the day Hiroshima was flattened, the American journalist Norman Cousins penned the famous editorial for the *Saturday Review* 'Modern Man is Obsolete'. Within weeks, *Life* magazine modelled the '36-Hour War', with vivid renditions of the annihilation of American cities. Hiroshima bisected history and the leftist intellectual Dwight McDonald argued: 'Now that we confront the actual, scientific possibility of *The End* being written into human history, and at not so distant a date, the concept of the future . . . loses for us its validity.'[12]

Science fiction had long been complicit in the desire for the ultimate superweapon, as H. Bruce Franklin has documented, and as such entered the nuclear epoch with some advantages.[13] H. G. Wells had predicted the development of nuclear weapons in *The World Set Free* (1914), the book the nuclear physicist Leo Szilard said inspired him to press the American authorities to begin an atomic weapons programme. The proximity of the American SF community to the military-industrial institutions of science resulted, legendarily, in the offices of *Astounding Science Fiction* being raided by the FBI in 1944, as Cleve Cartmill's short story 'Deadline' appeared to hint rather too precisely to elements of the top-secret Manhattan Project building the atom bomb. Robert Heinlein, then serving in the war effort as an engineer, seemed to have the scenarios of nuclear power logics worked out years before the world locked into its Cold War blocs.

After Hiroshima, SF culture blossomed with post-apocalyptic visions: in the elegiac brilliance of Ray Bradbury's 'There Will Come Soft Rains' (1950); in the satirical sequence of post-nuclear visions produced by Philip K. Dick, from *The Man Who Japed* (1956) up to *Dr Bloodmoney; Or How We Got Along After the Bomb* (1965); or in the subtle feminist critique of nuclear war depicted through the domestic front in Judith Merril's short story 'That Only A Mother' (1948), or her novel *Shadow on the Hearth* (1950). The popular embrace of the Japanese monster film *Gojira* (1954), carefully reframed with new footage and released in America as *Godzilla, King of the Monsters!* (1956), unleashed a series of barely allegorical instantiations of nuclear destruction in a B-movie cycle of mutant creature features through the 1950s (these are the films Sontag denounced as queasy spectacles of gormless violence). The American works closest to the 'cosy catastrophe' formula, perhaps, are the post-apocalyptic novels of survival and revival of small-town values in George Stewart's *The Earth Abides* (1949) – a pandemic narrative – or Pat Frank's *Alas, Babylon* (1959). In both, a 'hygienic' disease/war erases much of the sadly fallen state of American modernity and allows the Republic to arise again in small, unfederated frontier communities, free once more to pursue the religious and civic utopia of the founding fathers: 'the shining city on the hill' of biblical prophecy. M. Keith Booker has observed that these texts offer a 'principal vision of escape from the alienation and routinization of the modern world' via 'a nostalgic retreat'.[14] Any fictive shred of comfort in post-apocalyptic fantasies of nuclear war is loudly denounced in the essay prefacing the invaluable extensive bibliographical work Paul Brians has done gathering the hundreds of fictions in this field.[15]

In England, the nuclear imagination is less direct, more elliptical. A rare exception is the telling vision of the state of bankrupted nuclear physics research in the plodding realism of C. P. Snow's *The New Men* (1954). Britain had been locked out of the American development of atomic weapons in 1942, and this exclusion was reaffirmed in peacetime by the Atomic Energy Act (the McMahon Act) of 1946. In Snow's novel, the ramshackle, underfunded state of the British nuclear programme is emblematised by an English physicist dying slowly but inexorably of radiation poisoning after a lab accident. It is part of Snow's vision of England unable to embrace scientific modernity, a case pursued in his famous 'Two Cultures' lecture ten years later. Britain did finally develop an independent nuclear weapon in 1952 (the first atmospheric test was in the Monte Bello Islands off Australia in October 1952), but this belatedness simply underlined the decisive eclipse of Britain as a world power in the immediate post-war period. Wyndham's *The Chrysalids* sets a post-nuclear future in a return to a rural past whose origins have been long forgotten and never represented. Nevil Shute's best-seller *On the Beach* (1957), written after Shute had retired from war service to Australia, renders the slow creep of nuclear radiation from World War III towards the last survivors in the southern hemisphere a horrifying – because entirely passive and grimly inevitable – experience of waiting for a slow death. By the time Ballard wrote 'The Terminal Beach' (1964), setting his story among the ruins of the nuclear test site on the island of Eniwetok, the landscape serves only as a psychic figuration of a guilty post-apocalyptic embrace of the death drive.

Most cosy catastrophes eschew literalism and instead portray global disasters in displaced ways. Wyndham's *Day of the Triffids* takes pains to obscure the origin of the genetically modified plants that seize their evolutionary chance when the human race suffers mass blindness after a meteor shower. The seeds of these killer plants might be the result of the Soviet Union's Lysenkoism, the campaign led by the Soviet agronomist Trofim Lysenko that repudiated orthodox genetics in favour of his own unsubstantiated method for increasing crop yields, which prolonged famines killing millions of people in the 1930s and 1940s. But it might equally be the result of American corporate capitalists competing in nefarious ways for the riches associated with agricultural patents. The key point is that in London and the rolling landscape of the home counties where the action plays out, the *Triffids* shows England caught passively in the middle of larger political powers beyond their limited vision; the origins of the catastrophe are essentially unimportant. Similarly, *The Kraken Wakes* spends much of the novel among characters speculating hopelessly about whether the mysterious underwater attacks are a Western or Soviet conspiracy, leaving it almost too late to orchestrate a response to a global alien threat hiding in the Deeps. In John Christopher's *Death of Grass*, the blight that destroys crops comes out of the East, as pandemics and plagues have commonly been portrayed from the waves of 'Asiatic' or 'Russian' flu in the nineteenth century to the origins of the Covid-19 virus in China in 2019. Once again, the characters picking their way through Christopher's English landscapes are at the mercy of larger geopolitical forces that they cannot control. The Earthquake ruptures that constitute the sudden disaster in Christopher's *Wrinkle in the Skin* (and, more satirically, Tennant's *The Crack* or Harrison's 'Running Down') similarly invite allegorical interpretation of foundational social disturbances registered in exorbitant geological terms.

The Genre of Post-imperial Affect

The tendency of SF criticism has been to read the cosy catastrophe through the lens of nuclear and Cold War contexts. But after Eugene Stoermer and Paul Crutzen influentially fixed the term 'the Anthropocene' in a 2000 paper to name the proposition that human action was starting to transform materially the geological and climate conditions of the whole globe, the fictional eco-catastrophes depicted in these early post-war texts might be productively reassessed as early markers of the 'hyperobject' of climate crisis just lumbering into view.[16] This is what Mark Bould has called 'the Anthropocene unconscious', the register of the slow violence of this emergent catastrophe 'pressing on the present and manifesting in disruptions of discourse' and erupting everywhere across cultural forms.[17] The rising sea levels of *The Kraken Wakes* (1953) or Ballard's *The Drowned World* (1962), the big freeze of Christopher's *The World in Winter* (1962), the deadly heat wave of Charles Eric Maine's *Thirst!* (1958) or Ballard's *The Drought* (1964), or the earthquakes of Christopher's *A Wrinkle in the Skin* (1965), all spew out apparently contradictory visions that are nevertheless united by representing a foundational, epochal shift of humanity in relation to Nature. Here, nuclear power is simply an *acceleration* of ecological changes (with radiation from atmospheric tests stored at the geological level) that might be traced further back to the start of the industrial revolution or even earlier to the rise of agrarian societies. Where critics (including myself) once read Ballard's landscapes of disaster exclusively as objective correlatives of psychical states, they are now retrospectively available as early instances of 'cli-fi'.[18]

The English cosy catastrophe is overdetermined, however, and these frames do not necessarily exhaust their resonances. Central to the curious affect of these books, their utopian/dystopian dyad, is their distinctive flavour of post-war Englishness. They convey a certain sensibility or 'structure of feeling', which Raymond Williams suggested carried all 'the experienced tensions, shifts, and uncertainties, the intricate forms of unevenness and confusion' of social formations yet to emerge fully. If, as Williams contends, 'art and literature are among the very first indications that such a new structure is forming', then it might be worth examining the ambivalences of the cosy catastrophe genre as a marker of that post-war emergence.[19] This ambivalent feeling expresses both sides of the utopian/dystopian dyad, simultaneously, in a kind of *Ruinenlust* that perversely embraces melancholia or hygienic disaster and yet potentially critiques this cluster of post-imperial self-pity.

Although British patriotism is now inseparably fused to a narrative of a lone stand and eventual allied victory over Nazi Germany in 1945, the immediate post-war era was marked by a sudden and brutal eclipse of global status. The total mobilisation of the social and economic order in the war economy left the British state bankrupted and dependent on American loans, whose terms were set in tough negotiations that made it clear that economic power in the West had shifted from Europe to America. One of the conditions of the loans was a dismantlement of protected market around imperial and Commonwealth markets. The British economy had been shored up after the financial crash of 1929 by using colonies and dominions in protectionist ways. The post-war demand for a return to free markets was one key element in the disarticulation of the British Empire, although important too were the anti-colonialist independence and nationalist movements spreading across the imperium, combined with an impossible stretch of the man-power of the British Army to police the imperial status quo.[20] British troops withdrew from policing roles in Greece and Turkey; the British also abandoned the United Nations Palestinian Mandate in 1948, with the state of Israel emerging as a result. Attempts to carefully shift the Indian Empire from colony to dominion status failed with the rise of civil unrest, sectarian violence, and anti-British sentiment in the Indian army. A violent and messy partition into India and Pakistan as independent states in 1948 was the result. Crucial strategic and economic colonies in South-east Asia followed: Malaya and Burma were lost to insurgencies, hard fought because of the valuable economic resources long expropriated from these territories. Loss of oil revenue from Iran and Iraq in the early 1950s, where nationalist governments took ownership, were also major blows to the imperial economy. Winston Churchill returned to the premiership in 1951, his political vision of glorious empire and of Britain as a global strategic power forged in his early career as a reckless journalist in the colonial wars in India, Sudan, and South Africa in the 1890s.[21] But Churchill was also forced to withdraw eighty thousand British troops from the Suez Canal zone in Egypt, for decades the strategic linchpin of the British Empire, the short-cut to the riches of India and South-east Asia. This decision paved the way for the humiliation of Suez in 1956, when the Egyptian government nationalised the canal. The crisis dethroned Churchill's successor as Prime Minister, Anthony Eden. The British were ordered to suspend their military attempt to regain the canal from the Egyptians through the combined pressure of America and the Soviet Union – this, for many, marking the definitive end of Britain as an independent global power. What followed was a phase of decolonisation of African and Caribbean states (running from 1957 to 1964). There had been plans for federations in both regions to retain them as various types of post-colony, but these attempts failed. In 1945, there had been 700 million colonial subjects in the British Empire. By 1968 there were only 5 million (3 million of those in Hong Kong). The formal administrative Empire was dismantled in twenty years, even if new forms of economic neo-imperialism via channels of development and aid emerged out of the ruins of empire.

This phase of British history remains fiercely contested, but there is no doubt that a *persisting after-image* of Empire prevails within British politics.[22] One account of the tone or structure of feeling that emerged as an after-effect of this moment is Paul Gilroy's concept of 'post-imperial melancholy'. Melancholy, unlike healthy mourning, is a monument to the denial of loss or, rather, a pathology of *disavowal* that knows something is lost but steadfastly refuses to accept severance from the loved object. Disavowal was Freud's term for holding simultaneously incompatible ideas: to acknowledge and refuse in the same moment. Gilroy sees post-imperial melancholy as a similar mechanism of defence, a 'comfort of compensation' that gets trapped in a history at once longed for and lost. It is, he says, a conflicted state that is marked by 'a signature combination of manic elation with misery, self-loathing and ambivalence'.[23]

This post-imperial affect corresponds with what Lauren Berlant has termed 'cruel optimism' – an investment in the promise or hope of an object or condition very much in spite of the damage it does. Cruel optimism names the perverse way in which 'people maintain their binding to modes of life that threaten their wellbeing'.[24] Berlant's notion that it is often *genres* that give formal shape to this conflicted affect takes us back very suggestively to the cosy catastrophe. Martin Jay observes a close tie between melancholy and the apocalyptic imagination, writing that 'melancholy may well be the best term to describe the underlying mental condition accompanying fantasies of termination, while mania captures the mood engendered by belief in a rebirth or redemptive unveiling after the catastrophe'.[25] This is the mixed mood of the cosy catastrophe. John Wyndham's post-war fiction, as I have argued elsewhere, is focused very much on the crisis of post-war liberal democracy amidst the ruins of old orders.[26] In *The Day of the Triffids*, this is explored through various models of post-apocalyptic community. The failure of liberalism to respond to a brutal Darwinian struggle between rival species for the same resources gives narrative energy to *The Chrysalids* (which is sympathetic to the new mutants) and *The Midwich Cuckoos* (which is hostile to the new mutants). The global range of *The Kraken Wakes* shows the vulnerability of an empire built on ruling the waves – it is the vulnerable island outposts that are attacked first, an inexorable move from the colonial periphery to the metropolitan centres. The oddly stoical tone of the two protagonists, Mike and Phyllis, is striking: they sit, alone on a diminishing island, amidst rising waters, and toast the end of the world with snatches of T. S. Eliot and Rudyard Kipling poems. These are significant choices, given Kipling's role as a laureate of empire, but also one of its chief mourners, and Eliot's bleak post-war sense of destruction of civilisation, as suggested in his 1949 essay *Notes Towards a Definition of Culture*, with its mood of impending disaster.

Key to this sensibility is an eventual confession of escape or release from the complexities of modern civilisation that the apocalypse has gifted its survivors. As Bill Masen admits early on in *The Day of the Triffids*:

> curiously, what I found that I did feel – with a consciousness that it was against what I ought to be feeling – was release . . . I was emerging as my own master, and no longer a cog. It might well be a world full of horrors and dangers that I should have to face, but I could take my own steps to deal with it – I would no longer be shoved hither and thither by forces and interests that I neither understood nor cared about.[27]

He later sums up his attitude to the obliteration of modernity as 'the sort of gentle melancholy that the eighteenth century thought so estimable'.[28] *The Day of the Triffids* also communicates a clear reinvestment of identity from the imperial city (or post-imperial ruin of a city) to the timeless rhythms of rural England, which will always survive civilisational collapse. Leaving London behind, Bill reflects:

> I began to feel the lightening of spirit . . . The sight of the open country gave one hope of a sort . . . It was not like the towns, sterile, stopped for ever. It was a place one could work and tend, and still find a future . . . As I looked out over the fields I felt my spirits expanding . . . The feeling of release continued to mount as we passed through miles of untouched country.[29]

This is the elegiac solace in English landscape that powers a lot of post-war melancholia, as David Matless has documented.[30] *Triffids* begins to fall into the pastoral post-apocalypticism that becomes typical of the genre. It's an undeniably conservative account of pastoral England, again wrapped up in a sense of the kind of loss articulated by W. G. Hoskins in his classic 1954 account, *The Making of the English Landscape*, which was written with a sense of post-war modernity's catastrophic intervention into the timeless rhythms of rural life. For Wyndham, modernity's dystopian collapse may be an act of utopian rescue that recovers an earlier bucolic England.

There nevertheless remains a sharp edge of ruthless Darwinian survivalism in Wyndham's writing that disrupts too much cosiness (as Rowland Wymer has observed).[31] And it is really the work of Sam Youd/John Christopher that most consistently explores this post-imperial melancholy. His early Realist novel, *Babel Itself* (1951) is set in London in 1947, in 'a dull summer, in the exhausted aftermath of the Second World War'.[32] For contemporary readers, this would have evoked the severe pressure of the hard winter of 1946–7, which had placed food and heating resources under a harsher rationing regime than in war time. 'All these seasons, all these hours, this aftermath and silence; all adding up to a long, grey futility of life', the central character Tenn (short for Tennyson) laments.³³ The use of 'aftermath' here recalls Ross Chambers's definition of an aftermath society, which he defines as 'one regulated by a culture in which collectively traumatic events are denied, and if necessary denied again'.³⁴ In *Babel Itself*, Tenn is caught in a melancholic state of suspended animation that has stretched for years, mourning two brothers, one lost in the Great War, one in the RAF in 1940. The listless bohemian household of room-renters he chooses to hide among exist by living out emptied versions of modernist radicalism or communist politics, and spend their evenings trying to contact the dead in spiritualist séances. 'How I hate the Victorians', one character spits. 'They had the confidence; we have the disillusionment. It all stems from that.' Tenn chimes in:

> It wasn't of themselves that they were confident; they were quite remarkably self-critical. It was the future – it was us they believed in. The millennium was perhaps fifty years away. 1947 would shock them far more than it does us. They really believed in it.³⁵

This finely observed evocation of a post-war sensibility feeds directly into the catastrophe fiction Youd wrote as John Christopher, which he began with *The Death of Grass* in 1956. This portrays a rapid descent from the 'drowsy somnolence' of complacent post-prandial gentleman's clubs in London to the collapse of society into feral rural gangs traversing the English landscape in search of safe havens as a viral blight kills off the food supply. The group that forms around the ex-officer and war veteran of the Italian campaign John Custance constantly debates the necessity of stripping back the compromised virtues of civilised society in order to survive a violent regression to a premodern condition of what Giorgio Agamben calls 'bare life'. It is a similar argument explored in William Golding's *The Lord of the Flies* (1954), a text that for Alan Sinfield offered a kind of universalising apologia for imperial and post-imperial violence and domination by appealing to an intrinsic human condition.³⁶ There is a significant moment of reflection in *The Death of Grass*, focalised through John Custance, as they head north to the promised utopia of the family farm deep in the Westmoreland wilds.

> He wondered: could it all be a bad dream, from which they would awaken to find the old world reborn, that everyday world which already had begun to wear the magic of the irretrievably lost? There will be legends, he thought, of broad avenues celestially lit, of the hurrying millions who lived together without plotting each other's death, of railway trains and aeroplanes and motor-cars, of food in all its diversity. Most of all, perhaps, of policemen – custodians, without anger or malice, of a law that stretched to the ends of the earth.³⁷

This idealised after-image of empire is ruefully projected at a time when bitter wars of English colonial forces against independence movements, for instance in Kenya, were hardly upholding such saintly virtues, but torturing and murdering its opponents. It is a sentiment barely conscious of the roseate glow that is being given to the after-image of Empire. The book is at least clear-sighted enough to engineer a situation in which Custance must commit the murderous violence his group had set out to avoid, hinting that Western civilisation is necessarily underpinned by disavowed acts of violent barbarism.

Cosy Catastrophes in the Era of Decolonisation

Christopher's later catastrophe fiction, *The World in Winter* (1962), was published amidst the complex conjuncture of African decolonisation, anti-colonial struggle on the continent, hard won moments of independence, and a vicious retrenchment of white power in South Africa and Southern Rhodesia, both of whom left the Commonwealth at this time to retain their racist regimes. The novel offers an overt and tendentious rendition of this African moment. The occasion for catastrophic collapse this time is a depression in solar energy, which causes the northern hemisphere and its imperial centres to fall into a sudden ice age. London becomes increasingly unliveable, a frozen waste, while political power shifts to the newly independent African states nearer the Equator. There is a simple satirical inversion in this plot: migrant whites become dispossessed refugees or the servant class routinely abused by their new Black masters. The novel had a queasy echo in the inversion envisaged in Enoch Powell's notorious 'Rivers of Blood' speech in 1968, that in ten or fifteen years ahead 'the black man will have the whip hand over the white man' unless emigration was stopped.[38] In Christopher's story, the protagonist's low point is reached when he is homeless and dispossessed of everything on a beach outside Lagos in Nigeria:

> He was conscious ... of all that he had lost. His job, England itself, seemed unreal when he thought of them ... What he felt was not, he knew, a sense of loss. It was worse than that: a sense of nakedness, of being stripped down to the poor bones of self and circumstance. The things that had gone had been illusions, but he did not see how he would survive without them ... He knelt on the sand, leaned forward. It was an attitude of prayer, but he had nothing to pray to or for. He had nothing to offer, either. All he was aware of was the clinging misery of emptiness.[39]

A little later, after he has been improbably rescued from abjection by a Nigerian he had once been kind to in colonial London, the men list an odd jumble of nostalgic London markers that they toast with a rare brandy:

> Abonitu raised his glass solemnly. They had already toasted that night the Houses of Parliament, the Lyon's Corner House at Tottenham Court Road, Nelson's Column, the Chelsea Flower Show, the British Museum Reading Room, the King's Road, Admiralty Arch, the Samuel Whitbread, Peter Pan's statue, the Imperial War Museum, and Selfridges. The joke seemed less and less funny, but Andrew continued with it compulsively . . .
> Abonitu said: 'I remember going to a Promenade Concert.'
> 'They were *déclassé* in my circle.'
> 'I walked across Hyde Park in a daze afterwards. The music, the excitement . . .'
> 'The fellowship of the arts,' Andrew said. 'And no colour bar.'[40]

These are melancholic fixtures of a vanished kingdom, its alleged lack of colour bar a complete fantasy. In the novel's present, that London is on the verge of being reverse colonised by a group of explorers from Nigeria. When Andrew has the chance to join them, to see London once again, they camp out in the frozen wastes of Parliament Square, once 'the beating heart of empire' and now a territory of low intensity warfare and resistance.[41] They are engaged by guerrilla forces of recalcitrant English cadre, dismissed by the colonisers as 'savages'. This resistance movement is full of men re-energised by their losses, fighting off their own post-imperial melancholy, refusing submission. Andrew hears from the leader of these men that there is rediscovered purpose in this resistance – a fairly outrageous appropriation of the anti-colonial struggle being theorised in Africa by Franz Fanon or Kwame Nkrumah, and a familiar tactic of the formerly powerful embracing victim status. Even a ruined and denuded London offers Andrew a version of cruel optimism: the mirage of Empire gives meaning, still, even as the resistance makes its last stand in its ruins. In Christopher's later take on the student revolution of 1968, *Pendulum*, youth groups and opportunistic 'yobbos' smash the bourgeois sureties of Middle England. In this book, there is another slither of counter-revolutionary utopian possibility amidst the dystopian collapse, a chance for renewal amid the political catastrophe that veers between far left and far right solutions to the crisis. 'A genuine breakdown might shake things up and we might get somewhere', a doctor says, reinforcing a view that the catastrophe had arrived long before in the complacent willingness to be suffocated by the decadent luxuries of modernity. Long before any overt signs of breakdown occur, the rot has set in: 'We were conditioned to slavery before it happened. People's lies regulated by the government. Security the watchword.'[42] Violent counter-revolution is again a form of cruel optimism, a belief that a masochistic acceptance of losses can be the pathway back to restore the active virility of English manhood.

I am arguing, then, that the cosy catastrophe is best understood as a cultural articulation of English declinism. Declinism is an account of post-war England, embraced on both the left and the right, which argues from the starting point that if World War II was won, the peace was lost. The conservative historian Corelli Barnett, a big influence on Margaret Thatcher, blamed the catastrophe that unfolded after 1945 on the liberal establishment and the crazy utopian socialism of the immediate post-war Labour government, who implemented a 'New Jerusalem' dreamworld of state welfarism.[43] Martin Wiener also blamed a cultural elite of classically educated snobs for causing the decline in England's industrial drive, with 1945 just one staging post in a longer decline.[44] Many on the New Left, formed in the long years of Conservative Party rule between 1951 and 1964, used a declinist narrative to attack the sclerotic state of English capitalism and its peculiar institutions.[45] Subsequent economic historians have contested the reality of declinism, but do not doubt its powerful real world effects on British politics.[46] Wyndham and Christopher, even Ballard and Aldiss or the 1970s revisionists of the cosy catastrophe, all share this conflicted, ambivalent sense of a particular disaster that has enveloped England since 1945. And this is the account that starts to be explicitly challenged in the knowing meta-fantasies of post-apocalypse critiqued by Angela Carter, from *Heroes and Villains* (1969) to *The Passion of New Eve* (1977).

That the genre has returned in twenty-first-century fiction and film should not be a surprise. The Brexit vote of 2016 was pushed by supporters with a perfect emblem of cruel optimism: the promise of a return to a grandiose imperial past that would redeem losses and transfigure dystopia into utopia. This project was largely fronted by a Winston Churchill tribute act, who in 2019 was elected as prime minister on the mantra of 'Get Brexit Done'. Brexit was opposed by a rival vision of catastrophe and accusations of self-harm – something dismissed as 'Project Fear'. The phenomenon of 'Left Melancholia' did not especially energise the defence of EU membership either.[47] After the surprise victory and steadily diminishing promises about the positive gains Brexit might bring, the emotional tenor of Brexiters became an avowal of what Fintan O'Toole termed 'heroic failure', a masochistic embrace of defeat and diminishment, diagnosed as something very close to post-imperial melancholy.[48] The links of Brexit to Empire are already an expansive area of study.[49] Appeals to a 'Blitz spirit' or 'Dig for

Victory' British pluck were avowedly nostalgic call-backs to a now entirely imagined war. The after-image of empire did its worst damage here, and, oddly enough, helped ensure that reality was filtered entirely through the cruel optimism of genre. In the moment of de-accession from the European Union, the English rump of Britain had accomplished a perverse realisation: to finally live inside the peculiar fantasy that the cosy catastrophe had been imagining for over fifty years. To quote the graffiti seen on the wall in Danny Boyle's post-apocalyptic film *28 Days Later . . .* (2002), which opens in explicit homage to the early scenes of *The Day of the Triffids* in London: 'The End is Extremely Fucking Nigh.'

Notes

1. Brian W. Aldiss, *Billion Year Spree: The True History of Science Fiction* (New York: Doubleday, 1973), p. 294.
2. Ibid., p. 294.
3. See I. F. Clarke, *The Tale of the Next Great War 1871–1914* (Liverpool: Liverpool University Press, 1995).
4. Arthur Conan Doyle, *The Lost World* and *The Poisoned Belt* (San Francisco: Chronicle, 1989), p. 205.
5. See Chapters 7 and 8 of Amy Binns, *Hidden Wyndham: Life, Love, Letters* (n. p.: Grace Judson Press, 2019).
6. Rose Macaulay, *The Pleasure of Ruins* (London: Weidenfeld and Nicholson, 1953), p. xvii. The same quote from Henry James heads the section on 'Perverse Pleasure' in Christopher Woodward, *In Ruins* (London: Vintage, 2002).
7. For reflections on the aporia or 'impossibility' of post-apocalyptic writing, see Jacques Derrida, 'No Apocalypse, Not Now (Full Speed Ahead, Seven Missiles, Seven Missives)', *Diacritics*, 14(2) (1984), pp. 20–31. For an examination of the resonances of the term 'apocalypse', see also Jacques Derrida, 'Of an Apocalyptic Tone Recently Adopted in Philosophy', trans. J. P. Leavey, *Oxford Literary Reivew*, 6(2) (1984), pp. 3–37.
8. Maurice Blanchot, *The Writing of the Disaster*, trans. A. Smock (Lincoln: University of Nebraska Press, 1986).
9. Frank Kermode, *The Sense of an Ending: Studies in the Theory of Fiction*, 2nd ed. (Oxford: Oxford University Press, 2000), pp. 7–8.
10. Christopher Palmer, *Apocalypse in Crisis: Fiction from* The War of the Worlds *to* Dead Astronauts (Liverpool: Liverpool University Press, 2021), p. 3.
11. Caroline Edwards, *Utopia and the Contemporary British Novel* (Cambridge: Cambridge University Press, 2019), p. 160.
12. Citations from Paul Boyer, *By the Bomb's Early Light: American Thought and Culture at the Dawn of the Atomic Age* (New York: Random House, 1985), p. 236.

13. H. Bruce Franklin, *War Stars: The Superweapon and the American Imagination* (Oxford: Oxford University Press, 1988).
14. M. Keith Booker, *Monsters, Mushroom Clouds, and the Cold War: American Science Fiction and the Roots of Postmodernism, 1946–64* (Westport: Greenwood Press, 2001).
15. Paul Brians, *Nuclear Holocausts: Atomic War in Fiction, 1895–1984* (Kent, OH: Kent State University Press, 1987).
16. Timothy Morton, *Hypberobjects: Philosophy and Ecology after the End of the World* (Minneapolis: University of Minnesota Press, 2013).
17. Mark Bould, *The Anthropocene Unconscious: Climate, Catastrophe, Culture* (London: Verso, 2020), p. 15.
18. See Roger Luckhurst, 'The Genre of Catastrophe' in *'The Angle Between Two Walls': The Fiction of J. G. Ballard* (Liverpool: Liverpool University Press, 1997). In contrast, see, for instance, Jim Clarke, 'Reading Climate Change in J. G. Ballard', *Critical Survey*, 25(2) (2013), pp. 7–21. Continuing Ballard's typical interstitial location, Andrew Milner and J. R. Burgmann see Ballard's work in the 1960s as part of the 'pre-history' of climate fiction in their *Science Fiction and Climate Change: A Sociological Approach* (Liverpool: Liverpool University Press, 2020).
19. Raymond Williams, *Marxism and Literature* (Oxford: Oxford University Press, 1977), pp. 129, 133.
20. Causes and occasions of the end of the British Empire after 1945 remain widely debated. I have used here, John Darwin, *Britain and Decolonisation: The Retreat from Empire in the Post-War World* (Basingstoke: Macmillan, 1988); W. David McIntyre, *British Decolonisation 1946–97: When, Why and How Did the British Empire Fall* (Basingstoke: Macmillan, 1998); and essays in Judith Brown and Wm. Roger Louis (eds.), *The Oxford History of the British Empire: The Twentieth Century* (Oxford: Oxford University Press, 1999). For a more recent discussion which explores the 'decolonial' critique of this period, see Nelson Maldonado-Torres, 'Decolonisation' in *Future Theory: A Handbook to Critical Concepts*, ed. Patricia Waugh and Marc Botha (London: Bloomsbury, 2021), pp. 361–81.
21. See Candice Millard, *Hero of the Empire: The Making of Winston Churchill* (London: Penguin, 2016).
22. See Bernard Porter, 'Epilogue: After-Images of Empire' in *Echoes of Empire: Memory, Identity and Colonial Legacies*, ed. Kalypso Nocolaidis, Berny Sèbe, and Gabrielle Maas (London: I. B. Tauris, 2015), pp. 393–406.
23. Paul Gilroy, *After Empire: Melancholia or Convivial Culture?* (London: Routledge, 2005), p. 114.
24. Lauren Berlant, *Cruel Optimism* (Durham: Duke University Press, 2011), p. 16.
25. Martin Jay, 'The Apocalyptic Imagination and the Inability to Mourn' in *Rethinking Imagination: Culture and Creativity*, ed. in Gillian Robinson and John F. Rundell (London: Routledge, 1994), p. 36.
26. See Roger Luckhurst, *Science Fiction* (Cambridge: Polity, 2005), pp. 130–3.

27. John Wyndham, *The Day of the Triffids* (London: Penguin, 1972), p. 60.
28. Wyndham, *Triffids*, p. 244.
29. Wyndham, *Triffids*, pp. 163–4.
30. See David Matless, *Landscape and Englishness* (London: Reaktion, 1998).
31. Rowland Wymer, 'How "Safe" Is John Wyndham?' *Foundation* 55 (1992), pp. 25–36.
32. Sam Youd, *Babel Itself* (n.p.: Syle Press, 2018), p. 46.
33. Youd, *Babel Itself*, p. 97.
34. Ross Chambers, *Untimely Interventions: AIDS Writing, Testimonial and the Rhetoric of Haunting* (Ann Arbor: University of Michigan Press, 2004), p. xxi.
35. Youd, *Babel Itself*, p. 229.
36. See Alan Sinfield, *Literature, Politics and Culture in Post-war Britain* (Oxford: Oxford University Press, 1989).
37. John Christopher, *The Death of Grass* (London: Penguin, 2009), pp. 96–7.
38. The full text of the speech is available online at https://anth1001.files.wordpress.com/2014/04/enoch-powell_speech.pdf (Last accessed 27 January 2022).
39. John Christopher, *The World in Winter* (London: Penguin, 2016).
40. Christopher, *The World in Winter*, p. 141.
41. Christopher, *The World in Winter*, p. 208.
42. John Christopher, *Pendulum* (n.p.: Syle Press, 2018), pp. 208, 160.
43. See Corelli Barnett's 1986 book, *The Audit of War: The Illusion and Reality of Britain as a Great Nation* (London: Faber, 2011).
44. Martin J. Wiener, *English Culture and the Decline of the Industrial Spirit, 1850–1980*, 1981, new ed. (Cambridge: Cambridge University Press, 2004).
45. See, for instance, Perry Anderson, *English Questions* (London: Verso, 1992), which collects a number of essays first published from 1964.
46. See Jim Tomlinson, *The Politics of Decline: Understanding Post-War Britain* (Edinburgh: Pearson, 2000); and, more recently, David Edgerton, *The Rise and Fall of the British Nation: A Twentieth Century History* (London: Penguin, 2018). Edgerton's explores the debate in David Edgerton, 'The Decline of Declinism', *Business History Review*, 71 (1997), pp. 201–6.
47. Wendy Brown, 'Resisting Left Melancholia', *Verso Books* blog, 12 February 2017. Available at: www.versobooks.com/blogs/3092-resisting-left-melancholia (Last accessed 16 September 2025).
48. Fintan O'Toole, *Heroic Failure: Brexit and the Politics of Pain* (London: Head of Zeus, 2018).
49. See Danny Dorling and Sally Tomlinson, *Rule Britannia: Brexit and the Ends of Empire* (London: Biteback, 2020). A critique of the over-easy conflation of Brexit with imperialism is Robert Saunders, 'Brexit and Empire: "Global Britain" and the Myth of Imperial Nostalgia', *Journal of Imperial and Commonwealth History*, 48(6) (2020), pp. 1140–74.

CHAPTER 3

The 1960s
New Wave, New Worlds

Tom Dillon

Introduction

The English novelist C. P. Snow is perhaps best known for his influential 1959 Rede Lecture delivered at Cambridge's Senate House, 'The Two Cultures', in which he decries the widening gap between the arts and sciences in post-war Britain. As a former chemist, Snow was himself a rare example of a writer who could pass what he considered to be the litmus test of basic scientific literacy: an understanding of the second law of thermodynamics, which states that within a closed system matter tends towards an equilibrium, a process measured by entropy. The British literati of the late 1950s, he noted, were unable to name the content of the law and, what is more, were unashamed of their ignorance. Their response, Snow reports, 'was cold: it was also a negative'.[1] Just a few years later, entropy was everywhere in the arts. The Marxist scholar David Harvey commented on its 'peculiarly pervasive' circulation in the contemporary British arts scene, writing that 'even though many an arts student cannot, according to Snow, state the law precisely, its influence is extraordinarily dominant'.[2] Despite their continued ignorance as to the law's full meaning, the response from artists could no longer be described as cold. In their influential essay 'The Dematerialization of Art' (1968), critics and curators Lucy Lippard and John Chandler spoke of 'the current international obsession with entropy',[3] while the American landscape artist Robert Smithson used the term to describe the new artistic movement of Minimalism in his essay 'Entropy and the New Monuments' (1966).[4] In literature, the American postmodernist Thomas Pynchon explored entropy first in his short story 'Entropy' (1960), and later in his novel *The Crying of Lot 49* (1966).

How did entropy move from irrelevance to ubiquity in the arts in a few short years? What was it about the era of 1960s that seemed to chime so clearly for artists and writers with the theory that described the inevitable dissipation of energy? The British science fiction magazine *New Worlds* is a key agent in this rapid shift towards literary engagement with the idea of entropy. The magazine not only republished Pynchon's short story, but deployed the concept time and again as a key metaphor for understanding the 1960s. As one of the United Kingdom's most exciting and innovative centres for literary experimentation in the 1960s, *New Worlds* encouraged its writers to explore entropy as 'a fit image for the disintegration of society', which the magazine's editors saw as endemic to post-war and post-imperial Britain in the 1960s.[5] Colin Greenland's landmark 1983 study of *New Worlds*, *The Entropy Exhibition*, identifies this preoccupation with entropic decline as symptomatic of the dystopian mood of post-war British literature and culture; a critical assessment that has yet to be challenged.[6] And yet, one of the most influential writers published in *New Worlds*, Thomas M. Disch, wrote that in the 1960s 'utopias proliferated in SF [science fiction], particularly among writers associated with the New Wave, and the London based magazine that published their work, *New Worlds*'.[7]

In this chapter, I will reconsider the important legacy of *New Worlds* magazine on British literary and cultural production in the 1960s. Writing against the grain of prevailing academic criticism, which identifies the editorial direction of *New Worlds* under the editorship of Michael Moorcock to be prevailingly dystopian, I will unearth a latent utopian impulse implied by the key metaphor of entropy. Following Disch's lead, I will re-evaluate the 'Golden Age' of this influential London-based magazine by reading glimpses of hope among the ruins; identifying the Blochian 'forward dawning' of a better world in the ashes of the old.[8] Central to my argument is the contention that the aesthetics of entropy expresses the dissolution of hierarchies and boundaries which, in 1960s Britain, was an undeniably utopian project. I argue that this utopian dissolution found its initial impetus within the wave of decolonisation that swept the world from the late 1950s onwards, which provided a model for those resisting oppression inside the colonial centre of Britain. Beginning with demands for Black rights, these energies would encompass second-wave feminism, gay liberation, and even the resistance to social norms embodied by the 'swinging 60s', with its explosion of music, experimental literature and culture, and outré fashion. Drawing on theoretical work by German art and film theorist Rudolf Arnheim and the influential postcolonialist scholar Homi K. Bhabha, I argue that cultural interpretations of the second law of thermodynamics were as much about utopian possibility as dystopian disintegration. *New Worlds* offers us a window onto this curiously utopian structure of feeling, and I trace postcolonial entropy in the works of central 1960s writers who published work in the magazine, including Michael Moorcock, Brian W. Aldiss, and J. G. Ballard. The chapter concludes with a close reading of Pamela Zoline's short story 'Heat Death of the Universe' (1967). Each of these authors, I suggest, created important experimental works that explored the liberatory utopian potential of entropic decay in the midst of postcolonial decline.

Entropy and Empire

In the popular imaginary of the United Kingdom in the 1960s – which revelled in social upheaval, extravagant fashion, and sexual liberation – the context of anti-colonial struggle is often offstage, taking place *over there* rather than directly touching the events of the decade. However, as Fredric Jameson reminds us, the upheavals of the decade both within and without the colonial centre can be traced to 'the third world with the great movement of decolonisation in British and French Africa' in the late 1950s.[9] The brutal French war in Algeria (1954–62) and the equally brutal repression of the Mau Mau Uprising (1952–60) by the British in Kenya was followed by a string of successful independence movements, which began with Ghana in 1957. Ten years later, in 1968, almost all British territories in Africa had gained independence with the exception of Southern Rhodesia, and Britain began withdrawing from colonial territories in South-east Asia.

Given this context, we might read the decade's cultural obsession with entropy as a metaphor for dissolution – specifically the dissolution of empire. Entropy, with its suggestion of the inevitable decline of order into chaos, expressed an anxiety over the perceived disintegration of world order based on British dominance. Such an anxiety exhibits what Paul Gilroy has diagnosed as post-imperial melancholia (which Roger Luckhurst discusses in Chapter 2), the inability to 'mourn the profound change in circumstances',[10] which developed in the post-war period. Viewed from the perspective of the colonisers, things were falling apart. At the same time, entropy expressed an anxiety that the inverse process was taking place, that Britain was being colonised by a more powerful imperial nation, namely America. Financial support supplied by the United States to Europe in the wake of World War II was attended by an influx of American products, cultural and otherwise. There was a prevalent fear that the United Kingdom was being taken over by American culture. This process of 'Americanisation'[11] was perhaps most clearly expressed in Daphne du Maurier's foray into science fiction, *Rule Britannia* (1972), which imagined Britain subjugated by the US military. Entropy, here, was able to express the movement from separate integral cultures into a homogenised mass determined by the dominant imperial power. At the same time, the imagery of entropy endowed the progressive imagination with visions of postcolonial utopia. The anti-colonial resistance of the 1950s and 1960s was hugely influential on popular resistance movements in the colonial centre, beginning with the Civil Rights movement in the United States and latterly the New Left, second-wave feminism, and gay liberation. The ascension to independence and freedom of postcolonial countries became a model for the ascension to subjecthood by a range of previously oppressed or invisible groups, including people of colour, women, and gay people. Entropy could express the positive dissolution of hierarchies just as easily as perceiving those dissolutions to be negative. Of course, the two visions of entropy here are firmly intertwined. The dissolution of order opens up the utopian potential for establishing new orders that are less hierarchical and more free.

The art critic and gestalt psychologist Rudolf Arnheim penned a short book in 1971, *Entropy and Art*, to address this entropic zeitgeist. Arnheim saw the use of entropy in the arts as moving from seeking 'to diagnose, explain and deplore the degradation of culture', to providing 'a positive rational for "minimal" art and the pleasures of chaos'.[12] For Arnheim, the perception of entropy as negative and destructive was based on a fundamental misunderstanding of the term within the popular imagination. The mistake proceeded initially from the unthoughtful use of language within the sciences, which described entropy as a movement from 'order' to 'disorder'. In actuality, as Arnheim pointed out, entropy measures the movement from highly organised and hence improbable orders to lower organised, and so more probable orders. Matter in the universe is moving from a heterogeneous, improbable, and differentiated state to a homogenous, more probable, and undifferentiated state. At each stage, the change between states appears either as smooth or chaotic depending on whether the change is brought about by 'tension reduction' – the striving of matter and forces to reach equilibrium – or 'catabolic destruction', in which different orders grind into each other to produce new orders. Arnheim argues that scientists speak of entropy as 'disorder when their minds [are] set on the catabolic destruction of form'.[13] If we follow Arnheim, then the positive conceptualisation of entropy might not simply be a nihilistic celebration of the coming of disorder but, rather, frames a recognition of new forms emerging from the catabolic clash of older forms. Entropy can represent then the destruction of borders between hierarchically ordered categories; between coloniser and colonised in the first instance, but also in terms of the hierarchies of race, gender, class, and sexuality.

This model of entropy – understood as a catabolic grinding of order to produce new social forms – is reminiscent of Homi K. Bhabha's formulation of culture in *The Location of Culture* (1994). Bhabha sees culture as emerging from the interstices between existing cultural formations. For Bhabha there are no essential or ahistorical cultures. Instead, each culture is the result of the clash between two or more cultures, a dynamic process of continual cultural production at the boundary between pre-existing orders. By locating culture *between* rather than *within*, Bhabha defines it as an ongoing process rather than by its form or content; a useful formulation that avoids problematic essentialism. This account of culture, however, is in danger of evacuating any agency. Like entropic grinding, cultures simply clash together to create new ones, precluding individual action. Bhabha's answer is to envisage the cultural process as one that takes the individual 'beyond' their accustomed cultural tradition through interaction with another. 'Beyond' here signals both a movement beyond geographical boundaries but also a movement in time. Bhabha's 'beyond' takes the individual into the future 'in order to return in the spirit of revision and reconstruction'.[14] What makes entropic grinding a utopian project rather than an inevitable physical process, as the metaphor might initially suggest, is the movement of the individual beyond themselves as a result of existing at the boundary. As Ernst Bloch puts it, anticipating Bhabha, 'real venturing beyond' can only be achieved through 'the most extreme effort of will' in order to produce the utopian New.[15] This willed movement of the individual beyond the boundary allows a revisionary return that entails the dissolution of the boundary itself. As Bhabha suggests, these 'borderline engagements of cultural difference' go beyond differently positioned cultures in an ecology of power to a number of dearly held hierarchies within Western society, such as 'the customary boundaries between the private and the public, high and low'.[16]

The 1960s was a decade in which these boundaries, especially between high and low cultural forms, were under severe pressure in the United Kingdom. The mixture of popular imagery in fine art came to define the insurgency of Pop Art; music groups such as The Beatles experimented with avant-garde sounds influenced by John Cage and Karl Stockhausen; and the onset of literary postmodernism visible in the works of British and American writers such as Donald Barthelme, Angela Carter, and Thomas Pynchon, mixed popular genres with literary experimentation. Mark Fisher has used the term Popular Modernism to describe this dissolution of popular and avant-garde modes in the United Kingdom in the post-war period; a utopian cultural moment in which the 'elitist project of modernism was retrospectively vindicated'.[17] In a mid 1960s essay entitled 'One Culture and the New Sensibility' (a reference to C. P. Snow's 1959 lecture 'The Two Cultures'), Susan Sontag described just such a merging of high and low as part of a new sensibility that aimed to move beyond bounded cultural categories. In contrast to Snow's insistence that the cultures of art and science stood at either sides of 'a mutual gulf of incomprehension',[18] Sontag insisted that the 1960s was witnessing 'the creation of a new (possibly unitary) kind of culture' out of these supposedly opposing forces.[19] The boundary appeared to be dissolving into a new culture at ease with both scientific knowledge and artistic practice, avant-garde composition, and popular production.

New Worlds for Old

As Roger Luckhurst has pointed out, *New Worlds* magazine is an ideal location in which to examine the fusion of high and low art typical of 1960s cultural production.[20] Established in 1946, the science fiction magazine was handed over to the young fantasy writer Michael Moorcock in 1964. Over the next six years the magazine would pioneer a new form of fiction that fused avant-garde techniques with popular science fiction genre conventions in order to explore a number of burning issues at the time, including advances in technology, the ongoing crisis of colonialism, and the status of individual consciousness. Not only did the magazine determine the future direction of science fiction, ushering in what is known as the 'New Wave' defined by the introduction of new techniques and themes into the genre, it was also a centre of experimental literature. Writers such as J. G. Ballard launched their careers in the pages of *New Worlds* and the magazine influenced a wide range of writers as disparate as Angela Carter and Alan Burns. Covers bore the work of Pop Artists including, Edward Hamilton and Eduardo Paolozzi (listed, tongue in cheek, as the magazine's Aeronautics Advisors); adverts regularly promoted Apple records (The Beatles' label); and reviews praised work from John Cage to Jorge Louis Borges whilst launching broadsides against established science fiction writers such as Isaac Asimov and Robert Heinlein.

From Moorcock's first editorial the direction of travel was made clear. He promised a 'popular literary renaissance' that maintained a broad appeal while using up-to-date literary techniques.[21] Though his editorials did not make direct mention of decolonisation, Moorcock has listed both

3 The 1960s: New Wave, New Worlds

the symbolic 'death of Winston Churchill and the founding of the Kenyan Republic' as well as the intensification of the neo-colonial conflict in Vietnam as important contexts for the new direction of the magazine.[22] Speaking in particular of the '60s optimism' invested in The Beatles, Moorcock writes that 'considerable power was still in new hands; the flow of wealth was moving steadily from capital to labour. The power was diverse, mostly benign and hugely inexpert.'[23] For Moorcock, *New Worlds* partook of the new inexperienced cultural power that flowered in the decade, one that took inspiration from anti-colonial struggle and aimed to redistribute knowledge from the elite to a wide audience. As Tom Moylan has stated, in relation to the critical utopias that appeared within science fiction in the 1970s but which might equally apply to New Wave science fiction of the previous decade, the social upheavals of the 1960s 'significantly awakened subversive utopianism' in opposition to hegemonic Western power structures.[24]

Moorcock's series of books and short stories featuring Jerry Cornelius was at least initially begun as a parody of Sontag's new sensibility. In his first outing in *The Final Programme*, parts of which were serialised in *New Worlds* (1965–6), Jerry Cornelius appears as a hip young man, as comfortable playing the guitar as discussing the latest scientific theories. The novel is set in a Europe that appears to be inevitably slipping into decline. Cornelius is recruited under duress by computer scientist Miss Brunner to restore order by integrating all of human knowledge into a single programme. Europe's decline is couched in the language of entropy. At one point an associate of Miss Brunner's, Mr. Crookshank, comments that 'society hovers on the point of collapse, eh? Chaos threatens!', to which Cornelius replies, 'Entropy, I think Mr. Crookshank, rather than chaos'.[25] The fall from imperial grace is lent the appearance of inevitability and a patina of scientific rigour by the transference of chaos into entropy. However, entropy is depicted as an ambivalent force. Though it explains the process of the dissolution of Europe, Miss Brunner's project to 'save something from the wreckage' brings only more destruction in the novel.[26]

In Moorcock's sequel, *A Cure for Cancer*, serialised in *New Worlds* in 1969, entropy is a far more progressive force. What scant plot there is centres around a fight over a machine invented by Jerry Cornelius called The Shifter, which manipulates the flow of entropy, slowing down or accelerating the inevitable process. A former priest turned journalist, Bishop Beesley, steals The Shifter 'to slow the Cycle in order to preserve the present situation, and, if possible, return to an earlier phase'.[27] Cornelius, by contrast, wants to use the machine to increase 'the entropy rate to maximum'.[28] Though Cornelius wishes to use The Shifter for his own selfish ends, the machine produces new possibilities in the present moment via the entropic clashing of different alternatives. As Cornelius explains, 'one of its functions is a sort of randomizer. It can produce all the alternatives at once ... It breaks down barriers.'[29] The Shifter randomises improbably ordered hierarchies by the introduction of multiple alternatives. This, in turn, breaks down barriers between the separate realities, producing new possibilities beyond the currently existing world. At one point, Cornelius sees himself 'sixteen times – black, white, male, female – and he was dead'.[30] Here we see the dominant white, male, middle-class, universal subject position of colonialism explode into difference across multiple clashing realities.

When characters enter The Shifter the text itself takes on the machine's randomising function. A typical sentence runs: 'Down the middle of the prospekt galloped a brontotherium herd.'[31] A group of extinct rhinoceros-like creatures from the Eocene period stampede down an avenue (known as a 'prospekt' in Russian) in St Petersburg during the Russian Revolution. This clash of realities is mirrored in the newspaper style of the text. It is set out in a double column and broken up by a series of salacious headlines, including 'TRANSVESTITE ORGY IN PARIS HOTEL' and 'OUR NIGHT OF HORROR'. The reader is forced to encounter the narrative not only sequentially but as a media collage of instantaneous news events. Different reports appear to compete with each other across the page, in what Marshall McLuhan, speaking of the newspaper form, called 'front page cubism'.[32] A combination of clashing times and places produce a new narrative reality beyond the confines of the late 1960s present. Though no concrete utopia, the process of stylistic and narrative entropy opens up the possibility of new social formations out of the disintegration of the old. This is not to say that there is any essential utopian form inherent in the media collage adapted by Moorcock; rather, like entropy itself, the collision of disparate elements sets off a process of utopian dissolution.

The explicit postcolonial setting of the novel perhaps gives an indication of the shift from a negative to a positive portrayal of entropy between the first two Jerry Cornelius novels. The dissolution of Europe in *The Final Programme* becomes an explosion into difference in the sequel. During the course of *A Cure for Cancer*, the United Kingdom is invaded by the United States to restore order to a disintegrating polity. If the explicit introduction of American troops were not enough to remind the reader of the Vietnam war, Moorcock adds some heavy-handed references into the mix: London is napalmed, American troops are euphemistically called 'advisors', and

Ladbroke Grove in Notting Hill is daubed with the graffiti tag 'Vietgrove'. However, this is not a straightforward inversion of colonialism, in which the colonised take over the colonial centre, but a displaced one in which a former colonial power is invaded by a new colonial power. We can surmise that Moorcock did not intend this colonial inversion as a lament for the 'Americanisation' of the United Kingdom; rather, his authorial intention was to jolt the reader out of a complacency concerning neo-colonial action in Vietnam by putting them in the position of an invaded populace.[33] Jerry Cornelius' appearance in the novel replicates this uncanny displaced colonialism. His skin is described as being 'as black as a Biafran's',[34] which would have reminded readers of the then-contemporary postcolonial conflict of the Nigerian-Biafran war (1967–70). People generally treat Cornelius as Black, including a racist immigration official and middle-class ladies out for their afternoon tea. However, as the text reminds us, he is not in fact Black but a photographic negative of his white identity in the first novel. Cornelius has Black skin and white hair: 'a very negative appearance'.[35] It is precisely this strange, displaced colonialism – not an inversion but the transformation of the colonial centre by postcolonial energies – which moves entropy from a lament for colonial decline to the utopian possibility enabled by dissolution. Here, the colonial centre is imbued with anti-colonial resistance and postcolonial possibility. Within the displaced colonial context, The Shifter becomes an active tool for moving beyond present circumstances towards a postcolonial utopia based on difference.

Entropic decline bringing about personal or social transformation within a displaced colonial setting was a hallmark of some of the most successful works to emerge from *New Worlds* in the 1960s, including J. G. Ballard's Catastrophe Trilogy and Brian W. Aldiss' Acid Head War stories. Both Ballard and Aldiss, as James Reich has pointed out, brought direct experience of colonialism to their writings.[36] One of Aldiss's formative experiences was serving during World War II with the British army in the British colony of Burma. Ballard spent his childhood in the foreign concession district of Shanghai, before his internment in a Japanese camp in 1941. Ballard's catastrophe trilogy, which comprises *The Drowned World* (1962), *The Drought* (1964), and *The Crystal World* (1966), stages the transformation of the British landscape into an exotic imaginary of the colonies. In *The Drowned World*, seawater rises turn London into a tropical swamp, while in *The Drought* Britain goes through the process of desertification due to disrupted weather patterns. *The Crystal World* is an exception here, set as it is in the actual postcolonial country of Cameroon. However, as with the other two novels, the environmental transformation of the landscape progresses alongside the psychic transformation of Ballard's Western bourgeois characters.

These irruptions of the colonial environment into the landscape and psyche of the colonial centre appear to produce societal decline. And this was in fact the major theme of the sub-genre of science fiction that Ballard was working within in the 1950s, dubbed the 'cosy catastrophe' by Brian Aldiss (as discussed by Roger Luckhurst in Chapter 2).[37] Works such as John Wyndham's *The Day of the Triffids* (1951) and John Christopher's *The Death of Grass* (1956), according to Aldiss, showed the United Kingdom disintegrating under the threat of invasion or disease, only for order to be restored by the close of the narrative.[38] Ballard's catastrophe novels, too, have 'happy endings', as Ballard was keen to stress. However, rather than helping to restore the former order, Ballard's characters embrace the change brought on by the environmental transformation and attendant social dissolution. At the end of *The Drowned World*, the main character Kerans defies rational logic which might dictate he flee north where the climate is cooler and the last vestiges of 'civilisation' cling on. Instead, he heads south into the tropical heat like 'a second Adam searching for the forgotten paradises of the reborn sun'.[39] Though playing into racialised stereotypes of primitivism – the colonial landscape existing as a pre-developmental Eden – Ballard's catastrophe novels suggest that the entropic dissolution of colonial power will not end in disaster. Instead, dissolution is seen as a curiously utopian opportunity for new orders of being to emerge. White Western masculinity is reimagined as accepting this societal transformation, rather than violently resisting it.

Aldiss's Acid Head War stories, all but one episode of which appeared in *New Worlds* between 1967 and 1969 and were published together as *Barefoot in the Head* (1969),[40] similarly stage a psychic revolution in response to a displaced colonial setting. The stories open after Europe has been ravaged by bombs containing a psychoactive agent dropped by Kuwait. These bombs recall various historic contexts. They echo the mass bombing of European cities during World War II and remind the reader of the explosion of psychedelic drug experimentation in the 1960s. Moreover, the conflict is an inversion of colonial power: Kuwait, it should be remembered, was a British protectorate until 1961. The short stories follow a Serbian messiah figure known as Colin Chateris, who preaches of the psychic possibilities opened up by the chemical substance, which appears to dissolve the mind's rational functions. The language of the stories audaciously attempts to mimic the process of dissolution and possibility.

As the book progresses the frequency of puns increases. The result makes difficult reading at points. What to make of 'So he Friends think fuzzed in diseither-organisated for mid-paths'?[41] And yet, as the words dissolve into puns so the number of possible meanings proliferates; each word becomes, in the language of the stories, 'multivalued'. This process of linguistic dissolution, which switches from denotation into connotation, opens Aldiss's narrative to overlapping alternative meanings, and so by implication, new realities. At the beginning of the story titled 'Drake-Man Route' Chateris reflects on the positive outcome of the Acid Head War: 'all paradised by the aerosols until the unclipped hedges of the mind grew their own utopiary'.[42] The process of psychic transformation is imagined through the metaphor of hedge-trimming. The psychoactive aerosols allow the mind to grow 'unclipped', beyond the confines of reason, which then allows the mind to shape itself. The pun 'utopiary' expresses a certain paradox. Topiary is the process of cutting back in order to shape a hedge, but here utopia is created through disordered growth of the mind in many directions. The effect of the war has been to allow the growth of new modes of being made possible by the cessation of psychic trimming.

It appears that Aldiss in fact envisaged these stories as utopian. In a review of Mark R. Hillegas' book *The Future as Nightmare: H. G. Wells and the Anti-Utopians* (1967), Aldiss (using the pseudonym of C. C. Shackleton), notes that Hillegas describes Aldous Huxley's *Island* as a 'psychological utopia' in which individuals reach 'psychic self-actualisation'. Shackleton then asks whether 'Aldiss's Chateris stories come within this category'.[43] Through this subtle link, we can see that Aldiss allies himself to a growing movement of utopian thought within psychiatry and psychoanalysis in the post-war period. In *Eros and Civilisation* (1955) Herbert Marcuse proposed a psychic liberation based on the elimination of 'surplus-repression' to produce a 'psychoanalytical utopia'.[44] R. D. Laing's work of the 1960s similarly explored madness as a lens through which to understand the oppressive structures of society and imagine the utopian construction of liberatory alternatives. As Laing notes, 'madness need not be all breakdown. It may also be break-through.'[45] To return to *New Worlds* writers such as Aldiss, Ballard, and Moorcock, the entropic decline of Europe envisaged in their work and mirrored in the transformation of their characters, is not so much a *breakdown* as a *breakthrough*, revealing utopian glimpses of new psychic structures and new social formations.

'The Heat Death of the Universe': Entropy as a Catalyst for Utopian Anticipation

One story in the entropic oeuvre of *New Worlds* is particularly worthy of close reading: 'The Heat Death of the Universe' (1967) by the American artist and writer Pamela Zoline. Zoline had relocated to London as a student and quickly became associated with Moorcock's Notting Hill circle, contributing illustrations to the publication under his editorship. 'The Heat Death of the Universe' follows a day in the life of a Californian housewife, Sarah Boyle, as she carries out her Sisyphean task of ordering her home. These endless activities are interrupted by a stream of thoughts reflecting on the abstract concerns of avant-garde art, the nature of time, and the inevitable thermodynamic death of the universe. As the story progresses Boyle's household tasks and abstract reflections integrate to a greater and greater degree, creating absurd, humorous, and ultimately tragic subversions of her domestic labour.

Zoline was born in the United States in 1941 and moved to the United Kingdom in 1963 to study fine art where she became an important figure in both New Wave science fiction and underground art scenes centred in London in the late 1960s. Although Zoline was an art curator at The Arts Lab, a formative London countercultural venue, as well as an illustrator for a number of works published in *New Worlds*, she is best remembered for her short story 'The Heat Death of the Universe'. The story has been read by critics as an important work for testing the boundaries between science fiction and other literary forms.[46] Zoline's short story not only dissolves the boundary between science fiction and avant-garde literary experimentation, but also deconstructs a number of other binary categories that were breaking down in this period. The shifting sense of scale between the domestic and the cosmic dismantles the gendered spatial dichotomy of public and private space, while Zoline's use of the scientific concept of entropy as a framework for understanding art and literature straddles the divide between the cultures of science and art, which C. P. Snow had insisted upon.

Zoline's iterative references to entropy in the story draw a clear parallel between the activities performed by Sarah Boyle and the process of thermodynamic decay. The title itself refers to the theoretical endpoint of entropy known as the heat death of the universe, in which all matter will reach a final equilibrium. Inserts spaced throughout the text include encyclopedia-style entries for both Entropy and Heat Death. The small-scale domestic context of Sarah Boyle's struggle to keep the house clean are ironically juxtaposed with the large-scale cosmic process of entropy. At the same time, entropy can be understood to be taking place formally within the text. The discourses of housework and science, of domestic and intellectual labour, are initially organised in the text into separate numbered sections. However, as the narrative progresses, these discrete units are increasingly interspersed within single paragraphs. These two units represent two sides of Sarah Boyle's identity. She is described as 'a vivacious and witty young wife and mother, educated at a fine Eastern college ... only occasionally given to obsessions concerning Time/Entropy/Chaos/and Death'.[47] On the one hand, then, Zoline presents the reader with a self-presentation of the figure of the happy housewife. As Sara Ahmed has put it 'the happy housewife is a fantasy figure that erases the signs of labour under the sign of happiness'.[48] In Zoline's text, Sarah Boyle's domestic labour is invisibilised via apparent self-fulfilment. The image of the 'vivacious and witty young wife and mother' clashes with Boyle's repressed educational ambitions and her desire for an intellectual life, which manifests as a return of the repressed through morbid reflections on entropy and death. This happy housewife persona jars uncomfortably with her pessimistic reflections on the futility and ultimate death of everything. Arnheim spoke of just such an entropic psyche in *Entropy and Art*. He noted that in medical language the term 'disorders' was used to denote 'the lack of coordination among partial systems of the body or the mind'.[49] Arnheim quotes Laing's study of a schizophrenic patient named Julie in his 1960 text *The Divided Self*, in which Laing described Julie's condition as 'the result of a number of quasi-autonomous partial systems striving for expression'.[50] This grinding of quasi-autonomous systems produced such a fragmented psyche that Laing suggested Julie existed in '*a state approaching chaotic non-entity*'.[51] Like Julie, Sarah Boyle can similarly be seen as undergoing a process in which different discourses clash discordantly within a single mind, leading to psychosis. Textually, the result is the increasing interpenetration of the two discourses of domestic labour and abstract reflection; of the happy housewife and the educated woman.

In Zoline's short story, entropy can be read as a deeply ambiguous process. It is a metaphor for the unending labour of domestic life. Additionally, it stands in for the psychic disorder of the individual pulled in two irreconcilable directions. At the same time, the dissolution of boundaries that entropy entails is potentially liberating in the story as well: Zoline's narrative stages the elision of the boundary between the private sphere of domestic drudgery predicated on the division of labour and the public sphere of intellectual labour – implying a potential utopian reality freed from such hierarchically imposed borders. The orientation to the 'beyond' that I spoke of in relation to Bhabha's account of culture is pertinent here. At a number of points in the text, Sarah Boyle daydreams about a future or alternative reality beyond her current circumstances in which her struggle against decay has been overcome. The utopian philosopher Ernst Bloch argued that daydreams are the smallest building blocks of utopian longing, allowing the individual to move beyond their own discrete and bounded subjectivity by imagining the fulfilment of their hopes within a wider collective.[52] As Bloch pointed out, daydreams may be repressive or escapist but many orient us towards a world that is better than our current reality and express, albeit unconsciously, a desire for a more equitable future.

In 'The Heat Death of the Universe' Sarah Boyle's daydreams are variously regressive and potentially liberating. For instance, Boyle 'imagines in her mind's eye, cleansing and ordering the whole world, even the Universe', an unhinged dream of total order.[53] The extrapolation of her domestic role as a reversing of entropic dissolution only works to confine her within her naturalised role of domestic goddess, quite literally in the case of a cosmic Universe-scrubbing housewife. A second set of daydreams within the text involve Boyle imagining a world of entropy completely out of control as another potential solution to the societal constrictions imposed upon her in the form of housework. While dusting, Boyle reflects on Marcel Duchamp's incorporation of dust into his work 'The Bride Stripped Bare by Her Bachelors, Even' (1915–23). This leads to a dream of freedom from housework based on the techniques of Dada:

> The thought of ordering a household on Dada principles balloons again. All the rooms would fill with objects, newspapers and magazines would compost, the potatoes in the rack, the canned green beans in the garbage can would take new heart and come to life again, reaching out green shoots towards the sun. The plants would grow wild and wind into a jungle around the house, splitting plaster, tearing shingles, the garden would enter in at the door. The goldfish would die, the birds would die, we'd have them stuffed; the dog would die from lack of care, and probably the children – all stuffed and sitting around the house, covered with dust.[54]

Taking inspiration from the Dadaist movement, Sarah Boyle daydreams of a paradoxical method of 'ordering' a household which functions by releasing oneself from the task of ordering the house entirely. Giving in to entropic processes becomes a mode of home economics in and of itself. Though it curtails the life of 'the children', the grinding together of different objects produces new possibilities: the canned green beans that have been thrown away 'take on new heart and come to life'; newspapers and magazines become compost for new growth; while the outside and inside of the house merge as 'the garden would enter in at the door'. In this last image of the mixing of garden and domestic interior, we have a metaphor for the entropic dissolution of the boundary enacted in the story between the public and private sphere, and the isolated individual and wider society, as well as the dissolution between the various discourses warring in Sarah Boyle's mind. Zoline's Dada-inspired collage of different objects entropically dissolving is a wonderfully evocative example of Fisher's Popular Modernism. Here, Zoline employs the utopian avant-garde technique of what Bloch called *umfunktionierung* (refunctioning) as the basis for the subversion of the everyday reality of housework, which in turn suggests the utopian overturning of gendered hierarchies in favour of new relations between people (and things) based on freedom.[55]

The final scene of 'Heat Death' enacts just such a utopian daydream with seemingly tragic results:

> The total ENTROPY of the Universe therefore is increasing, tending towards a maximum, corresponding to complete disorder of the particles in it. She is crying, her mouth is open. She throws a jar of grape jelly and it smashes the window over the sink. Her eyes are blue. She begins to open her mouth. It has been held that the Universe constitutes a thermodynamically enclosed system, and if this were true it would mean that a time must finally come when the Universe 'unwinds' itself, no energy being available for use. This state is referred to as 'the heat death of the universe'. Sarah Boyle begins to cry. She throws a jar of strawberry jam against the stove, enamel chips off and the stove begins to bleed.[56]

The discourse of entropy in Sarah Boyle's mind merges here with her domestic labour, both in the form of the narrative and the story's content. Initially separated into numbered paragraphs, the discourses of housework and entropy clash against one another across the sequence of sentences in open typographic conflict. At the same time, Boyle's violent actions appear to accelerate the entropic process, thereby actively carrying out her desired utopian daydream of doing Dadaist housework. The jar of grape jelly breaks the window and so destroys the border between inside and outside. The strawberry jam chips the oven; food and the appliance for cooking food crash into each other with the further confusion of the human body with technology as the oven appears to bleed because of the red jam. However, this is clearly not the utopian liberation of Sarah Boyle's Dadaist daydream. Within the closed system of the house, individual protest appears only as madness. Though entropy provides a model of utopian society free from gendered labour, the story's ending suggests that this can only be achieved if the further boundaries between the individual and society are dissolved. Entropy must therefore lead to the socialisation of resistance if it is to move beyond individual psychosis.

Conclusion: Shreds of Hope Emerging from the Ruins

Hindsight can be as much a handicap as a benefit. The tragic conclusion of Sarah Boyle's narrative appears to undermine her Dadaist daydream of entropic utopia. From our vantage point in the early 2020s, the failures of 1960s utopian politics to coalesce into concrete forms has tended to obstruct our understandings of the utopian imaginings of the decade. Rather than see the utopian possibility within the obsession with entropy, we see only dystopian visions of dissolution and decay that gave way to the 1970s, a time, according to the editors of *The 1970s: A Decade of Contemporary British Fiction*, 'associated by many with decline' due to political strife and economic instability of the decade.[57] Colin Greenland put forward this thesis at the beginning of the 1980s in *The Entropy Exhibition*, at a time of political reaction to the promises of the 1960s and his view was coloured by it. For Greenland, 'the writers of *New Worlds* predicted the mood of the 1970s more accurately, concerning themselves with images of finality, with entropy' than they did the countercultural energies of the time in which they wrote. We are equally as fallible now to reading the present into the past. However, we must try to resist such a backward glance and instead recover, through utopian close readings, the shreds of hope emerging from the ruins of the old.

Notes

1. C. P. Snow, *The Two Cultures and the Scientific Revolution* (Cambridge: Cambridge University Press, 1959), p. 16.
2. David Harvey, 'The Languages of Science', *New Worlds Magazine* (October 1967), pp. 2–4 (p. 4).
3. Lucy R. Lippard and John Chandler, 'The Dematerilization of Art' in *Conceptual Art*, ed. Alexander Alberro and Blake Stimson (Cambridge, MA: The MIT Press, 1999), pp. 46–50 (p. 48).
4. Robert Smithson, 'Entropy and the New Monuments' in *Robert Smithson* (Berkeley: University of California Press, 1996), pp. 10–23.
5. Colin Greenland, *The Entropy Exhibition* (London: Routledge & Kegan Paul, 1983), p. 10.
6. Sherryl Vint, writing of the science fiction 'New Wave', closely associated with *New Worlds* has described the movement as 'providing dystopian views of technologically saturated societies'. Sherryl Vint, *Science Fiction* (London: Bloomsbury, 2014), p. 76. In *The Cambridge History of Science Fiction* Rebecca Evans similarly sees the New Wave as 'oriented towards dystopia'. Rebecca Evans, 'New Wave Science Fiction and the Dawn of the Environmental Movement' in *The Cambridge History*

of Science Fiction, ed. Gerry Canavan and Eric Carl Link (Cambridge: Cambridge University Press, 2019), pp. 434–46 (p. 434).
7. Thomas M. Disch, *The Dreams Our Stuff Is Made Of* (New York: The Free Press, 1998), p. 105.
8. Ernst Bloch, *The Principle of Hope*, vol. 1, trans. Neville Plaice, Stephen Plaice, and Paul Knight (Cambridge, MA: The MIT Press, 1986), p. 77.
9. Fredric Jameson, 'Periodizing the 60s', *Social Text*, 9/10 (1984), pp. 178–209 (p. 180).
10. Paul Gilroy, *Postcolonial Melancholia* (New York: Columbia University Press, 2005), p. 90.
11. Christopher Booker, *The Neophiliacs* (London: Collins, 1969), p. 35.
12. Rudolf Arnheim, *Entropy and Art* (Berkeley: University of California Press, 1971), p. 10. Arnheim was very probably thinking of Robert Smithson's essay 'Entropy and The New Monuments'. Smithson described the 'cosmic joy' that apparently swept the Pacific Northwest after a large power-cut, an event that for Smithson modelled the final state of entropy in which all energy had dissipated known as the heat death of the universe.
13. Arnheim, *Entropy*, p. 25.
14. Homi K. Bhabha, *The Location of Culture* (London: Routledge Classics, 1994), p. 4.
15. Bloch, *Principle of Hope*, p. 4.
16. Bhabha, *Location*, p. 3.
17. Mark Fisher, *Ghosts of My Life* (Alresford: Zero Books, 2014), p. 50.
18. Snow, *Two Cultures*, p. 4.
19. Susan Sontag, 'One Culture and the New Sensibility' in *Against Interpretation* (London: Vintage, 1966), pp. 293–304 (p. 296).
20. Roger Luckhurst, *Science Fiction* (Cambridge: Polity Press, 2005), p. 143.
21. Michael Moorcock, 'A New Literature for the Space Age', *New Worlds Magazine* (May 1964), pp. 2–3 (p. 3).
22. Michael Moorcock, 'New Worlds' in *Into the Media Web*, ed. John Davey (Manchester: Savoy Books, 2010), pp. 436–42 (p. 436).
23. Moorcock, 'New Worlds', p. 436.
24. Tom Moylan, *Demand the Impossible: Science Fiction and the Utopian Imagination* (London: Methuen, 1986), p. 10.
25. Michael Moorcock, *The Final Programme* (London: Fontana, 1979), pp. 62–3.
26. Moorcock, p. 66.
27. Michael Moorcock, 'A Cure for Cancer (4)', *New Worlds Magazine*, June 1969, pp. 4–17 (p. 10).
28. Ibid., p. 16.
29. Ibid., p. 5.
30. Ibid., p. 9.
31. Michael Moorcock, 'A Cure for Cancer (1)', *New Worlds Magazine*, March 1969, pp. 4–20 (p. 20).
32. Marshall McLuhan, *The Mechanical Bride* (London: Routledge & Kegan Paul, 1967), p. 3.

33. Colin Greenland and Michael Moorcock, *Michael Moorcock: Death Is No Obstacle* (Manchester: Savoy, 1992), pp. 89–90.
34. Moorcock, p. 6.
35. Moorcock, p. 6.
36. James Reich, 'Inner Space Odyssey: Suburban Spacemen and the Cults of Catastrophe' in *The 1960s: A Decade of Contemporary British Fiction*, ed. Philip Tew, James Riley, and Melanie Seddon (London: Bloomsbury, 2018), p. ePub p. l. 639.9/905.
37. Brian W. Aldiss, *Billion Year Spree* (London: Corgi, 1973), p. 335.
38. J. G. Ballard, James Goddard, and David Pringle, 'An Interview with J. G. Ballard' in *Extreme Metaphors: Selected Interviews with J. G. Ballard, 1967–2008*, ed. Simon Sellars and Dan O'Hara (London: Fourth Estate, 2012), p. 89.
39. J. G. Ballard, *The Drowned World* [1962] (London: HarperCollins, 2014), p. 175.
40. The first in the Acid Head War stories, 'Just Passing Through' was published in the February 1967 issue of *SF Impulse* (vol. 1, no. 12). A further six stories were published in *New Worlds* between August 1967 and January 1969.
41. Brian W. Aldiss, *Barefoot in the Head* (London: Corgi, 1974), pp. 215–16.
42. Ibid, p. 46.
43. Brian W. Aldiss, 'Dr Moreau Versus the Utopianists (2)', *New Worlds Magazine*, October 1968, pp. 63–64 (p. 63).
44. Herbert Marcuse, *Eros and Civilization: A Philosophical Inquiry into Freud* (Boston: Beacon Press, 1966), p. 131.
45. R. D. Laing, *The Politics of Experience and the Bird of Paradise* (London: Penguin, 1967), p. 110.
46. See Mark Rose, *Alien Encounters* (Cambridge, MA: Harvard University Press, 1981), p. 1; and Sherryl Vint, *Science Fiction* (London: Bloomsbury, 2014), p. 80.
47. Pamela Zoline, 'The Heat Death of the Universe', ed. Michael Moorcock, *New Worlds Magazine*, July 1967, 32–9 (p. 36).
48. Sara Ahmed, 'Killing Joy'. *Signs*, 35(3) (2010), pp. 571–94 (p. 572).
49. Arnheim, *Entropy*, p. 11.
50. R. D. Laing, *The Divided Self* (Harmondsworth: Penguin, 1990), p. 196.
51. Ibid., p. 195.
52. Bloch, *Principle of Hope*, p. 3.
53. Zoline, 'Heat Death', p. 38.
54. Ibid., pp. 35–6.
55. Caroline Edwards discusses Ernst Bloch's use of the technique of *umfunktionierung* in *Utopia and the Contemporary British Novel* (Cambridge: Cambridge University Press, 2019), p. 71.
56. Ibid., pp. 38–9.
57. Nick Hubble, John McLeod, and Philip Tew, 'Introduction: Britain in the 1970s – Controversies and Cultures' in *The 1970s: A Decade of Contemporary British Fiction*, ed. Nick Hubble, John McLeod, and Philip Tew (London : Bloomsbury, 2014), pp. 1–12 (p. 1).

CHAPTER 4

Post-Imperial Melancholy in the Long 1970s

Andrew M. Butler

There is a moment in Derek Jarman's cult 1978 film *Jubilee* when a young punk woman, Amyl Nitrate (played by Jordan Mooney), offers a description of her past and present that hardly sounds utopian: 'It all began with William the Conqueror, who screwed the Anglo-Saxons into the ground, carving the land into theirs and ours', she intones. 'They lived in mansions and ate beef at fat tables, whilst the poor lived in houses, minding the cows on a bowl of porridge – whilst they pushed them around with their arrogant foreign accents.'

At first glance, *Jubilee* might not look like a utopian text. Jarman's title refers to Elizabeth II's Silver Jubilee and her then glorious twenty-five-year reign. The film follows a violent girl gang squatting in East London, spending their endless, unemployed days arguing about music, history, culture, and occasionally rousing enough energy to run off and murder a policeman or make a sexual conquest. The streets are war-torn, strewn with rubble and black smoke, accompanied by the persistent soundtrack of gun fire and Molotov cocktails, which the girls chuck at the men from 'Special Branch', London's new fascist police force. Jarman's film features some of British punk's best-known figures. Jordan Mooney, the English model and actress associated with the Sex Pistols, who worked with Vivienne Westwood and Malcolm McLaren at London's SEX boutique on the Kings Road, stars alongside Adam Ant, whose band Adam and the Ants was managed by McLaren. Female punk bands The Slits and Siouxsie and the Banshees make cameo appearance smashing up cars on the desolate streets of East London. Despite the dystopian, almost apocalyptic visual tone, *Jubilee* is a striking example of the way in which the utopian impulse plays an ambivalent role in cultural production during Britain's turbulent transformation in the 1970s. The horrors of Jarman's alternate punk world relate to its collapsing bourgeois values, which Amyl caustically refers to as the desire for 'one desolate suburban acre and a car, then a TV, fridge and another car'. In Jarman's surreal reimagining of contemporary London, the gentle hippie utopianism that had epitomised the 1960s' era of free love is riotously supplanted by punk's harder-edged assault on political and cultural values. In fact, the film offers its own forcefully utopian energy, particularly in the female-centred narrative and Jarman's casting of British female punk artists and performers. As the journalist and presenter Miranda Sawyer narrates in an episode for BBC Two's *The Culture Show*:

> Female punks played around with ideas of desire, subverting male sexual fantasies through what they wore. They refused to be submissive, they hijacked the perverted. There was something glorious about all these different shapes and sizes of bodies strutting the '70s streets wrapped in rubber.[1]

With its rubber-clad female protagonists, *Jubilee* is a film centrally concerned with the problem of British national identity. Under pressure from Scottish, Welsh, Irish, and Cornish nationalist movements, the union was at a crossroads in the mid-1970s and youth subcultures, especially punk, added fuel to the conflagration of formerly stable values. The film's frame narrative features Elizabeth I (played by Jenny Runacre) who consorts with the English occultist John Dee (Richard O'Brien, best-known at the time for *The Rocky Horror Show*) to travel forwards in time into the 1970s, where Elizabeth is murdered by anarchist gang leader Bod (also played by Runacre, giving the character an air of reincarnated Tudor royalty). In addition to the monarchical continuity between the Tudor queen and Elizabeth II's titular jubilee, the film also prominently displays nationalist signifiers. Bod's gang live in a squat that is festooned with Union Jack bunting, frequent working-class British social spaces such as the chippie and the bingo hall, and saunter past locations of national importance such as Buckingham Palace and the Royal Albert Hall. In one memorable scene, Amyl Nitrate gives a queasily erotic performance of Britannia, which in the film will be Britain's Eurovision entry that year. Jarman's fascination with Britannia as the personification of empire links with his ongoing interrogation of Albion, England's originary mythos. Scholars note that William Blake's personification of Albion as the primeval British man constructs a powerfully utopian legacy in engravings such as *Glad Day* or *The Dance of Albion*. As Gray Watson observed in the exhibition catalogue to the posthumous retrospective 'Derek Jarman: A Portrait' at London's Barbican Gallery in 1996, Blake's vision of Albion 'was most crucial for Jarman and was in fact a key to much of his work... an image of perfection and completeness, who is fallen (broken) and must be redeemed (re-remembered)'.[2] Read within the context of Jarman's remediation of the Blakean mythos of Albion, *Jubilee* can be identified as typical of a range of

4 Post-Imperial Melancholy in the Long 1970s

texts produced during the 1970s that were critical of contemporary English society, whilst also looking nostalgically, if ambivalently, back to happier times. Such depictions feature enclaves, metonymic for England, which are ambiguously utopian.

This chapter explores the ambiguous utopian impulses of literary, filmic, and television works published and produced in the 1970s via the concept of 'post-imperial melancholy'.[3] As Roger Luckhurst argues in Chapter 2 (drawing on Paul Gilroy's work), there is a 'masochistic embrace of decline' within texts that reflect on Britain's former status as a global superpower after World War II, which contains 'a paradoxically utopian longing for the dystopian smashing of systems'.[4] I will trace the utopian contours of these texts' forceful, often shocking, critique of British imperial nostalgia and their fiery anticipations of British society struggling to find its purpose on the world stage, in an era of economic, cultural, and political decline before returning to *Jubilee*. I will focus on particular generic clusters that emerged during this significant decade, including: the British alternate history, which imagines being occupied by Nazi Germany or the United States (Daphne du Maurier's *Rule Britannia* (1972), the BBC's TV miniseries *An Englishman's Castle* (5–19 June 1978), and Len Deighton's *SS-GB* (1978)), the dystopia (the BBC's series *1990* (18 September 1977–10 April 1978), an Orwell-inspired vision of authoritarian bureaucracy in the near-future, and *1985* (1978), Anthony Burgess's novelistic response to Orwell's *Nineteen Eighty-Four* (1949)), feminist remediation of patriarchal myths of Albion (Emma Tennant's *The Time of the Crack* (1973) and Angela Carter's *The Passion of New Eve* (1977)), and explicit reworkings of the classical literary utopia (J. G. Ballard's 'concrete trilogy' (*Crash* (1973), *Concrete Island* (1974), and *High-Rise* (1975)). These three genres critically interrogate the utopian impulse in the 1970s and its possible instantiations in national and transnational imagined communities, as well as the built environment in which the modernity of these communities is expressed.

Post-Imperial Melancholy

Post-imperial melancholy responds to Paul Gilroy's earlier theorisation of 'postcolonial melancholy'. Gilroy sees post-imperial melancholy in the response to the 1999 Macpherson Report on the institutionally racist police handling of the 22 April 1993 murder of Black teenager Stephen Lawrence in Eltham, south-east London. As he writes: 'Britain stays paralysed by the inability to really work through the loss of global prestige and the economic and political benefits that once attended it ... We might tentatively name this ugly formation postcolonial melancholia.'[5] In a lecture first delivered in 2002, he said the attitudes should be called '"postimperial melancholia" in order simultaneously to underline this syndrome's links with the past and its pathological character'.[6] Defending the 'twentieth-century utopia of tolerance, peace, and mutual regard', Gilroy reflects that an openness to racial otherness, such as cosmopolitan dialogue or class-based international solidarity, has been subsumed within a discourse wary of discussing race and racism. As a result, Britain's colonial history 'remains marginal and largely unacknowledged, surfacing only in the service of nostalgia and melancholia'.[7] The real conditions that have contributed to the decline of Britain are ignored and blame is displaced onto 'migrants, their children, their grandchildren or any other permanently strange folk',[8] most have whom have come from the former colonies.

Much British science fiction about alien (read: foreign) invasion, imagines a reborn Englishness that draws on a partly imagined memory of resilience in the face of possible German invasion. This assertion of national identity can be seen as early as H. G. Wells's *The War of the Worlds* (1898), in the artilleryman's impractical plans to rebuild society in drains, tunnels, cellars, and subways, with the occasional above ground-game of cricket. All of the 1950s Quatermass serials – *The Quatermass Experiment* (18 July–22 August 1953), *Quatermass II* (22 October–26 November 1955), and *Quatermass and the Pit* (22 December 1958–26 January 1959) – show British culture coming into contact with aliens, with alien infiltration of the British government featured in *Quatermass II*, perhaps also indicative of an anti-Soviet paranoia. Beginning with 'The Dalek Invasion of Earth' (21 November–26 December 1964), *Doctor Who* repeatedly depicted alien invasions, with the Daleks standing in for Nazis; the Third Doctor (played by Jon Pertwee), exiled to Earth and attached to the British wing of the United Nations Intelligence Taskforce as a scientific advisor, pits an eccentric Britishness of fair play and plucky soldiers against the Nestene Consciousness, which animates plastic objects ('Spearhead from Space' (3–24 January 1970) and 'Terror of the Autons' (2–23 January 1971)), astronauts replaced by aliens ('The Ambassadors of Death' (21 March–2 May 1970), echoing *The Quatermass Experiment*), the Axons ('The Claws of Axos' (13 March–3 April 1971)), and time-travelling Daleks ('Day of the Daleks' (1–22 January 1972)). Whilst the alien invasions fail, these serials assert the intelligence and military prowess of the British in an era when the country was in decline.

4 Post-Imperial Melancholy in the Long 1970s 77

Ian Baucom offers a useful example of this postcolonial, or post-imperial, melancholy. He considers Prince Charles's 'Vision of Britain', which was broadcast in October 1988 on the BBC's *Omnibus* programme. 'Sometime during this century', Prince Charles narrates, 'something went wrong. For various complicated reasons we allowed a terrible damage to be inflicted on parts of this country's unique landscape and townscape.'[9] The Prince's presentation of the architectural wounds inflicted on the British cityscape and countryside, following the postwar reconstruction of Britain's towns and cities in the 1950s and 1960s, expresses a longing for what Baucom calls 'a lost or vanishing country-house England'.[10] This decidedly white vision of middle England was familiar to BBC audiences from Merchant-Ivory's lush productions of E. M. Forster's *A Room With a View* (1985) and *Howards End* (1992), which were filmed on location in Surrey, Chiswick, and Oxfordshire. Edward Said's landmark postcolonial critique 'Jane Austen and Empire' (1993) laid bare the ideological violence that underpins these nostalgic visions of England, with their rose-strewn country homes, leisurely lawn tennis summer days, and rhythms of rural village life. As Baucom notes, Said exposed the dependency of such English country houses and families 'on those distant, all but invisible spaces of empire to which [they are] connected through a perpetual passing of bodies, capital, and commodities, and from which [they derive their] principles of order, stability, and rule'.[11] Colonised nations were viewed not as countries with their own distinctive histories, productive capacities, or cultures, but as outposts of manufacturing and agricultural production, akin to country estates. As Said suggests, citing John Stuart Mill's *Principles of Political Economy* (1848): 'The trade with the West Indies is hardly to be considered an external trade, but more resembles the traffic between town and country.'[12] Since the Elizabethan era, the owners of English stately homes had cultivated this imperial attitude acquiring and building libraries, especially on topics such as mathematics, astronomy, military science, and alchemy. They were patrons to the natural sciences and hosted lively dinner conversations bringing together engineers, industrialists, and aristocrats in organisations such as the Lunar Society of Birmingham (1765–1813).

By the late nineteenth century shifting demographics and the introduction of estate duty (a modern inheritance tax introduced in 1894 to raise money for William Gladstone's government) undermined the country-house economy. Some houses were requisitioned by the British government during times of war – for example, Bletchley Park – some were sold to corporations, and by the 1930s many of the United Kingdom's great country homes were gifted to the National Trust (the National Trust Act 1937 protected families from paying death duties if they donated their property to the Trust). The decline of the country-house economy, as well as the British imperial project that had financed it, was remediated in British fantastic fiction: a lost imagined arcadian, feudal, and utopian past underpins the quasi-gothic settings of shadowy corporate research centres, laboratories owned by lone, wealthy inventors and portals to other worlds – the Newton Institute in the *Doctor Who* episode 'The Time Monster' (20 May–24 June 1973) and Auderly House in the 'Day of the Daleks' episodes, the stately home of Borgia Ginz (Orlando) in Jarman's *Jubilee*, among numerous others – the buildings' roots in slavery and industrial exploitation erased. As Roger Luckhurst observes, works of British New Wave science fiction such as Christopher Priest's *Fugue for a Darkening Isle* (1972) and *A Dream of Wessex* (1977) and M. John Harrison's *The Committed Men* (1971) and *The Centauri Device* (1974) can be read as responses to the final devastation of a particular kind of English middle-class liberalism, sliding into obscurity.[13] As I have noted elsewhere, some 1970s British science fiction writers (including novelists, television programmers, and scriptwriters for film) 'fight a kind of rear-guard action, asserting English's continued significance; others produce obituaries for Englishness or dance upon its grave'.[14] Luckhurst links Britain's post-imperial melancholy to Sigmund Freud's 'Mourning and Melancholia' (1917). As he notes, mourners or melancholics retreat from the external world and their loss becomes psychically processed, which leads to an identification with, and hatred of, what has been lost. For Karl Abraham, an influence on Freud, this introjected loss is a reassurance, with the Ego 'saying' to itself 'My loved object is not gone, for now I carry it within myself and can never lose it'.[15]

The Alternate History: The Hope of British Resistance

In his influential account of the failure of British nationalism, 'The Twilight of the British State' (1977), the Scottish academic and political theorist Tom Nairn argued that post-imperial and post-industrial England had, since the early 1950s, 'fallen into ever more evident and irredeemable decline – the United Kingdom of the permanent economic crisis, falling standards, bankrupt governments, slavish dependence on the United States and myopic expedients'.[16] Inequalities of wealth and economic development could be found in the constituent parts of the United Kingdom and there were growing calls for devolution. Harold Wilson, the Labour prime minister, set up a Royal Commission in 1969 to consider the constitution and the respective positions of Northern Ireland, Scotland, Wales, the Channel Islands, the Isle of Man, Cornwall, and English regions, but the report was not delivered to Conservative prime minister Edward Heath until 1973.[17] By then, the United Kingdom had joined the European Communities, against Labour opposition; reimagined in the *Doctor Who* serial 'The Curse of Peladon' (29 January–19 February 1972), which features intrigues around the planet Peladon's accession to a Galactic Federation. Later episode broadcasts were affected by power cuts caused by the miners' strikes and the ongoing need to conserve electricity led to the imposition of a three-day week at the start of 1974. Heath called a General Election for 28 February 1974; the Conservatives lost seats and the Labour Party, Plaid Cymru, and the Scottish National Party increased them, but Wilson did not have a working majority. The social, political, and economic disruption would have been obvious to writers and producers of science fiction and can be seen in some of the exemplary texts I will discuss in this chapter.

Wilson called a second election for 10 October 1974 and won a majority of three in the election, but there were further nationalist gains.[18] Labour had pledged to renegotiate the terms of the British membership of the European Economic Community (EEC), but a 5 June 1975 referendum confirmed UK membership. The United Kingdom was being pulled in different directions towards Europe whilst being pulled apart from within. Wilson announced his resignation on 16 March 1976 and was replaced by Labour's James Callaghan. Drastic measures were needed to restore the economy; as chancellor of the exchequer, Denis Healey's April 1976 Budget cut borrowing, spending, and value-added tax (VAT) (a newspaper front page for this can be glimpsed in *Jubilee*). The country accepted a loan from the International Monetary Fund, although only half of it was borrowed and it was repaid by May 1979. By then, the referenda for Welsh and Scottish Assemblies had finally been held on 1 March 1979. Wales rejected the motion by a majority of four to one, but even though Scotland was in favour of devolution, turnout was too low for the proposal to pass into law. Callaghan made a pact with the Liberals and struggled to maintain control of the unions; he lost a vote of confidence on 28 March 1979. Margaret Thatcher became Conservative prime minister in the 3 May 1979 General Election and held power until her resignation on 28 November 1990.

Like 'The Curse of Peladon', Daphne du Maurier's final novel *Rule Britannia* (1972) was written in the run-up to Britain joining the EEC and reflects the anxieties of the British people concerning this move. As Aoife Byrne writes, *Rule Britannia* 'is concerned with the construction and manipulation of national identity for totalitarian means'.[19] In du Maurier's near-future, Britain has entered the EEC and, after a referendum, departed. In this turmoil, the United States 'rescues' the United Kingdom, along with Australia, Canada, and South Africa, to form a union of English-speaking peoples that the Americans will dominate. On some levels, the novel imagines the Nazi occupation that would have followed a successful invasion during World War II. Reflecting on the United States–led invasion of the United Kingdom, the focal character Emma thinks 'it can't happen here'.[20] This is perhaps a reference to Sinclair Lewis's 1935 novel or, more likely, to the film *It Happened Here* (dir. Kevin Brownlow and Andrew Mollo, 1964), which imagined a Nazi invasion in 1940. What is a post-apocalyptic dystopia for some is a utopia for others, carving out a comfortable existence. Mad, the novel's septuagenarian protagonist, is a middle-class woman posing as an aristocrat, who has taken up residence with a large adoptive family in a comfortable country-house, that key locale for post-imperial melancholy. She cooperates with neighbouring farmers and labourers but is dismissive of the local professionals and uses the doctor for her own ends. Whilst she is an incomer, she shares some of the attitudes of the Cornish locals when it suits her and demonstrates 'pure bloody-mindedness that refuses to be kicked around'.[21] Mad's selfishness recalls the cosy catastrophe subgenre, which Brian Aldiss unfairly dismisses as 'cosy catastrophes' in which 'the hero should have a good time (a girl, free suites at the Savoy, automobiles for the taking) while everyone else is dying off' (which Roger Luckhurst discusses in Chapter 2).[22] In this sense, *Rule Britannia* follows in the footsteps of British invasion narratives by science fiction writers such as John Wyndham and John Christopher, whose apocalyptic ruination of London and its suburbs returns their middle-class protagonists to a regressive mythic time of pre-industrial agrarianism. Priest claims Wyndham's works depict 'middle-class catastrophe[s]; his characters are of the bourgeoisie, and the books lament the collapse of law and order, the failure of communications, the looting of shopping precincts and the absence of the daily newspaper'.[23] Mad is a character in this tradition, although such narratives tend to be male-centred.

Du Maurier's depiction of Cornwall in *Rule Britannia* can be read in terms of the ongoing Royal Commission on the Constitution and the utopian project of advocating for Cornish self-determination. The establishment of the Duchy of Cornwall in 1337 formalised an English occupation, but there were Cornish rebellions against the state in the fifteenth and sixteenth centuries. Joanie Willett, a British politics scholar and co-director of the Institute of Cornish Studies, notes that Cornish regional identity undermines ethnosymbolic constructions of national identity that are 'inherently overdetermined by an insider/outsider binary'.[24] As she writes:

> Cornwall has a very strong sense of local identity. . . . These boundaries and markers are not necessarily bound up in historical 'facts', but in the ways that they are imagined . . . Celtic, rather than Saxon . . . Methodist rather than Anglican . . . and as a politically Liberal heartland, again, distancing from dominant UK party politics of a Labour/Conservative binary.[25]

Daphne du Maurier's novels and personal politics attest to this strong local identity. Du Maurier was an early member of Mebyon Kernow, the progressive party campaigning for Cornish nationalism, which had been formed as a pressure group for Cornish independence in 1951 and had become, by the 1970s, a centre-left political party. Cornwall in *Rule Britannia* is thus doubly colonised – by the United Kingdom and by the fictional UKUS – and resistance is part of an underlying nationalist agenda as well as representing melancholy. One of Mad's adopted children, Ben, is Black, subjected throughout the novel to racist epithets in an uncomfortable reminder of British imperialism. The potentially successful resistance to the American occupation comes from the Celtic denizens of the former United Kingdom who can transmit radio messages in Cornish, Welsh, or Gaelic, which is not understood by the majority of English-speaking peoples. In the novel, the cohesion of British nationalism is both undermined by, and itself undermines, Cornish, Welsh, Scottish, Irish, and other nationalisms. Willis, a Cornish- and Welsh-speaking activist, for instance, is sceptical of the senseless sacrifice of nationalists, suggesting that 'in a hundred years they may be resurrected as heroes and martyrs, but it's a little late then for the project in hand'.[26] He seems to believe that the current insurgences can defeat the superior military might of America, as was happening in Vietnam at the time of the novel's writing. Emma, by contrast, seems content with the village-scale pastoral utopianism of a new world of 'small communities, sharing each other's work and needs'.[27]

The alternate history was similarly used to explore nostalgia for the British empire in Peter Mackie's three-part BBC television series *An Englishman's Castle* (broadcast on 5–19 June 1978). Set in an alternate version of the 1970s, in which the much-feared Nazi invasion of Britain has successfully taken place, the series begins with a genteel breakfast scene between the writer Peter Ingram (played by Kenneth More) and his son Mark (played by Nigel Havers) discussing how Peter's choice of kedgeree is reminiscent of the days of the British Raj. 'How do you reconcile this nostalgia for Britain's greatness with your craven acceptance of a foreign master?' Mark challenges him. We learn that Paul Ingram had been in the Resistance but surrendered after an amnesty, which left the country run by British politicians on behalf of the German Nazi regime. For now, there are opulent gentleman's clubs, champagne, avocadoes, and kedgeree, echoes of the cosy catastrophe. Mark reminds him of the latter's colonial origins and in an echo of a late 1950s slogan used by Conservative prime minister Harold Macmillan, parrots the lie that the 'ordinary people have never had it so good', but the 'problem' of West Indians, Indians, and Jews has been 'solved'. The title of *An Englishman's Castle* refers to a soap opera of the same name that has made Ingram rich, and depicts earlier British bravery as well as the German-approved virtues of patience, fortitude, and calm acceptance. The soap opera uses Henry Purcell's march 'Lillibullero' (1686) as its theme, familiar to the contemporary audience as a BBC interval theme, but originally popularised during the Glorious Revolution of 1688 when Mary and William were invited to rule Britain. Ingram rejoins the Resistance after he has attempted to add a heroic Jewish character to his scripts. The Resistance ask him to embed dialogue in the soap to trigger an uprising, 'Britons, Strike Home!' – taken from Purcell's incidental music for a 1696 production of John Fletcher's *Bonduca, or the British Heroine*, in which there is a revolution against Roman invaders.

An Englishman's Castle thus dramatises a utopian impulse concerning the continuity of British identity, even though that identity has been threatened both by unwanted and invited invasions. It is not clear how far Britain would have responded to German invasion, but *It Happened Here, An Englishman's Castle*, and Len Deighton's novel *SS-GB* (1978) offer fantasies on the theme. John Sutherland argues that '[t]he popularity of *SS-GB* and *An Englishman's Castle* seem to draw upon a dim national awareness that despite VE [Victory in Europe] and VJ [Victory over Japan], Britain has nonetheless "lost"'.[28] The need to assert British identity is evidence for its very fragility. The bombing of the Caligula Club in the first episode of *An Englishman's Castle* and a letter bomb in the third echo IRA terrorism, but rule from Berlin stands in for a fear of the European Community. The casting of 'stiff-upper-lipped'[29] More brings with it earlier portrayals of Royal Air Force hero Douglas Bader in *Reach for the Sky* (dir. Lewis Gilbert,

1956), and it is in the end he who utters the codewords. As in *Rule Britannia*, it is far from clear that any uprising will succeed.

Deighton offers another alternate history of Nazi occupation in *SS-GB*. Better known for espionage novels, he began writing histories of World War II with *Fighter* (1977). This research helped him imagine a German invasion near Ashford, Kent and the capture of George VI and Winston Churchill. A year later, DS Douglas Archer investigates a homicide in occupied England and uncovers German atomic research, which the Resistance wants to transfer into American hands. There is a power struggle between the Schutzstaffel, the Gestapo, the Abwehr, and the German army and between Germany and a neutral America; the Resistance wants to shift America into becoming allies. If Britain is to win World War II finally, it can only do it with American help. In this alternate history, Britain's resilience and abilities are being demonstrated but also undermined.

Dystopias of Lost Britain

Re-reading speculative visions of occupied Britain in terms of the post-imperial melancholy they express reminds us of the unexpectedly utopian tenor of 1970s literary and cultural production. But the alternate history was not the only sub-genre explicitly engaging with Britain's crisis of national identity at a time of economic decline and the country's declining geopolitical influence on the world stage. The dystopia offers another interesting case study for exploring how British novelists and scriptwriters were intervening into contemporary debate concerning the future role of the United Kingdom. George Orwell's dystopian *Nineteen Eighty-Four* resurfaced as a crucial text in this decade, informing the BBC television series *1990* (1977–8) and Anthony Burgess's novella *1985* (1978).

The BBC's dystopian drama *1990* imagines a near-future that felt alarmingly possible at the time of its broadcast between September 1977 and April 1978. Created by the English television and film writer Wilfred Greatorex, it dispenses with ideas of individualism in favour of the common good, represented by a tentacular bureaucracy and domineering unions. Following national bankruptcy in 1981, Greatorex's dystopian version of Britain strictly controls all areas of life – housing, food, goods, childbirth, and work opportunities are rationed by the state. Industry and culture operate in an expanded public sector that has introduced a three-day week, all of which is under the oppressive bureaucratic management of the Public Control Department (PCD). The show's protagonist Jim Kyle (played by Edward Woodward) works for *The Star*, perhaps the country's last independent newspaper, investigating the cruel actions of the PCD. Kyle also aids the illegal emigration of professionals, echoing both Resistance actions in *Secret Army* (7 September 1977–15 December 1979) – a BBC co-production with the Belgian national broadcaster that Greatorex partly created and wrote for – and post-war fears of a scientific brain drain. Kyle's family only appears in one episode, 'Witness', where his wife, Maggie (Patricia Garwood), and one of his sons, Bevan (Jonathan Scott-Taylor), are threatened by the PCD. Maggie's name may be a nod to Margaret Thatcher, then leader of the opposition, in conjunction with a character called Jim invoking James Callaghan; Bevan is named for Aneurin Bevan, architect of the National Health Service with ambitions to improve upon the housing stock destroyed in World War II. Throughout the episodes of *1990* there is nostalgia for real socialists and a liberal ideal of authentic, lost Britain, where one could do as one pleased and civil liberties trumped collectivisation. The show also references the nostalgic post-imperial motif I have already discussed, the English country house, exploring the collapse of the country-house economy. In this dystopian near-future Britain, aristocratic estates have been appropriated by the government through a punitive wealth tax to be used by the higher-ranking officials as their residences or as treatment centres for political prisoners, and the kind of pub extoled by Orwell in 'The Moon under Water' (1946) has been replaced by status-defined drinking establishments.

In the second series, a cell system of dissidents has been developed to challenge the PCD, and although Kyle opposes the authoritarian bureaucracy, he resists the move to armed resistance. The show makes it clear that whilst Kyle resists the PCD, he also rejects ideological revolution in favour of traditional 'British' standards: 'there is an ordinary decency and an ordinary humanity that does not need a movement'. Kyle retains faith in a legal system over the kangaroo courts, despite the new Home Secretary's suggestion that the PCD is simply 'the unacceptable face of bureaucracy'. Following a self-immolation in Trafalgar Square, echoing similar real-world protests in Czechoslovakia, Vietnam, the United States, and elsewhere, there is a mass destruction of ID cards and hints of rebellion. It may be that the system can only be reformed rather than replaced – Kyle valorises the individual rather than the group, but a system requires a collective to underpin 'ordinary decency' and to police it where it fails. The series is ambiguous as to what any alternative might be aside from some form of neoliberalism.

4 Post-Imperial Melancholy in the Long 1970s

Anthony Burgess's novella *1985* puts unions at the heart of his dystopia. Some critics suspect that Burgess misinterprets Orwell's *Nineteen Eighty-Four*; Richard Cowper writes that 'I had to keep pausing to ask myself whether Burgess and I had read the same book',[30] and Clive James argues that 'Burgess establishes with marvellous thoroughness that he has misunderstood Orwell'.[31] In *1985*, Orwell has died of the neck wound sustained in the Spanish Civil War and Britain has become Tucland (a reference to the Trades Union Congress, Britain's national union centre), where all jobs are controlled by the unions and so citizens can be deprived of the right to earn. The equivalent of Winston Smith is a history lecturer, Bev Jones – named for trade union leader and Labour politician Ernest Bevin, Liberal politician, and economist William Beveridge or Aneurin Bevan.[32] He mourns his wife, killed when an on-strike fire brigade had ignored a hospital fire started by the IRA. Jones loses his right to work and his home for breaking a strike and becomes a vagrant; he is then arrested for shoplifting and sent to a re-education centre. He is eventually expelled from this and joins the resistance of the Free Britons before being arrested again and incarcerated for life.

The novella is misogynistic, homophobic, and anti-unionist, mourning a supposed lost golden age of imperial benevolence and social certainties; here the reader is encouraged to mourn the loss of empire and what post-imperial Britain has become, rather than the horror of political, economic, and legal mechanisms that sustained an empire. In the non-fiction part of the book, Burgess complains that 'the forces of Women's Liberation and Homosexual Liberation [... want] to modify language by fiat, so that if I, a writer, use words that betray even grammatical discrimination, I am in danger of legal punishment'.[33] Burgess seems suspicious of Muslims; just as Arab oil sheikhs are buying London properties in the real world aftermath of the 1973–4 oil embargo by OPEC, the Organization of the Petroleum Exporting Countries. By the end of the novella, 'the Persians ... were going to go to war with the Arabs'.[34] We are left with the likelihood that the American-armed Iranians will assume control of all the Middle Eastern oilfields and economic collapse will ensue. Jones, incarcerated as a political prisoner, retreats into teaching history from Elizabethan times to the present day to fellow inmates, before beginning his lessons again 'to trace the cracks in the structure, to discover where everything began to go wrong'.[35] Like Amyl's historical lecture in *Jubilee*, Burgess's *1985* is a narrative designed to identify the historical hinge moment when utopia slides into dystopia, rather than seeking to justify society as it has evolved. The rise of capitalism and the impact of the British empire is skipped over in Burgess's account of '[a] course on England in the seventeenth century.... The First World War, recovery....'[36] Clive James feels the novella 'sounds like the same union-bashing gone in for by all those members of the British managerial class who are convinced that their entrepreneurial flair is being stifled'.[37] Christopher Priest similarly dismisses it as 'a period piece' and 'the sort of novel one suspect one would be written by a tax-exile who reads right-wing newspapers in his Monte Carlo home'[38] – indeed, we can only note with irony that Burgess was indeed a notorious tax-exile in Monaco at the time of writing the novella.

The Utopian Impulse in the 1970s Critical Dystopia

Whilst Burgess was an expatriate, J. G. Ballard was an immigrant to austerity-era Britain, having been born in Shanghai in 1930 and interned in Japanese prisoner of war camps during World War II. Ballard is thus a child of post-imperial Britain. In the early 1970s, he wrote a thematic trilogy of ambiguously utopian novels, *Crash* (1973), *Concrete Island* (1974), and *High-Rise* (1975). In each, a male middle-class protagonist finds himself in an enclave on the edges of West London, apparently unable to leave. *Crash* features a 'world of expressways, collisions and the protagonists' strange upsurge of sexual activity when they become involved in crashes [within ...] a closed system, setting itself apart from the outside world in the characters' neurotic desire not to leave it'.[39] The narrator James Ballard develops a sexual obsession with car crashes, the sort of distillation of the sexualised and violent media landscape that Jarman was to depict in *Jubilee*. Ballard's forensic examination of the sexualised psychopathology that this modern urban planning makes possible epitomises everything that Prince Charles considers to be wrong with the United Kingdom in his 1988 'Vision of Britain'. With its Americanised concretescape of elevated motorways and dangerous interchanges, Ballard's West London might be read as the dystopian terminus of modernity's project of progress and industrialisation. However, there are perversely liberatory signs here, too, amidst the wreckage of London's older Victorian and Edwardian suburbs, clinging on to the country's last vestiges of traditional village life inside the M25. Ballard's second novel in the trilogy, *Concrete Island*, also begins with a car crash after Robert Maitland's tyre blows out on 'the high-speed exit of the Westway interchange in Central London ... six hundred yards from the junction with the newly built spur of the M4 motorway',[40] trapping him in an urban netherworld; an 'island' of waste ground below the elevated motorway.

As the days progress, he meets a tramp, Proctor, and an acrobat, Jane Sheppard, who seem more concerned with keeping him marooned on this surreal island than aiding his escape and return to civilisation. The island mutates as he explores it – there is an air raid shelter, a civil defence post, an abandoned cinema, and an old churchyard. Having brought Maitland food from an Indian supermarket, Jane notes the Indians 'exploit themselves and their staffs more than the white owners do'.[41]

High-Rise, the third novel in Ballard's trilogy, moves east along the Thames. The novel opens with the arrival of Dr Robert Laing at one of 'five identical [high-rise] units ... set in a mile-square area of abandoned dockland and warehousing along the northbank of the river',[42] presumably somewhere near the Isle of Dogs. The central building of the novel is one of thousands built in the aftermath of World War II to replace Victorian and Edwardian terraces and with the utopian aim of semi-communal living with on-hand facilities. Like Le Corbusier's modern description of the house as a 'machine for living' in his 1927 manifesto *Vers Une Architecture* (*Towards An Architecture*), Ballard's tower block is described as 'a huge machine designed to serve, not the collective body of tenants, but the individual resident in isolation'. Inspired by Ernő Goldfinger's controversial 31-storey Trellick Tower in Notting Hill (1972), the tower block in *High-Rise* opens up 'a different plane of reality'. The Brutalist design of such modernist tower blocks was widely criticised by the popular press at the time, which reported on 'cases of vandalism, sexual violence, drug dealing, burglaries and muggings in the corridors', noting that services such as lifts, lighting, and rubbish chutes were prone to breakdown or vandalism.[43] On 16 May 1968, a few months after opening, a gas explosion at the 22-storey tower block Ronan Point in Newham, East London caused the collapse of the tower block's south-east corner, killing four people.[44] These high-rises, and the estates they were part of, were widely seen as sites of dystopian oppression, their architecture blamed for a range of social problems. But even this dystopia is ambiguous in Ballard's novel *High-Rise*. The protagonist Laing's name recalls the Scottish psychiatrist R. D. Laing, who suggested that schizophrenia might be a rational response to impossible circumstances. Alan Bradshaw and Stephen Brown argue that whilst *High-Rise* is considered one of Ballard's novels where his 'ostensibly utopian settings unfailingly descend into dystopian anarchy',[45] the novel retains a distinctively utopian impulse; it should be read not as 'a journey *into* madness (as the novel is ordinarily understood) but a journey *away* from madness'.[46] Perhaps, the novels in Ballard's concrete trilogy might better be described as *critical dystopias*, which Raffaella Baccolini defines as dystopian narratives that maintain 'the utopian impulse *within* the work'.⁴⁷ Rejecting the traditional dystopia's subjugation of the individual at the end of the novel, the critical dystopia instead 'opens a space of contestation and opposition for those groups ... for whom subjectivity has yet to be attained'.⁴⁸

R. D. Laing's ideas were satirised by Emma Tennant in her comedic reworking of the post-apocalyptic genre in *The Time of the Crack* (1973). As psychoanalyst Joseph Thirsk takes his patients from a Hyde Park funfair through the streets of a London, an enormous crack rips along the Thames, causing widespread devastation across the city. Thirsk and his colleagues believe that '[t]he destruction wrought by the Crack will enable a social "rebirth"' that will allow everyone to regress beyond the womb and be transformed.⁴⁹ In Hampstead, the bourgeois ecologist Jeremy Waters imagines 'a society in which ecology and sociology went hand in hand. A society of brothers, fighting together to preserve the strange and beautiful structures thrown up by the Crack.'⁵⁰ Tennant confronts these masculine power structures with a feminist separatist cult,⁵¹ which presents a satire on media misrepresentations of feminists such as Germaine Greer, Kate Millett, and others as bra-burning women's libbers and media evangelists. Between the two sides lies Baba, a Playboy Bunny, who likes to please men through performance but does not want to be owned by them. At a time when North American feminist utopias were imagining gynocratic societies – Joanna Russ's *The Female Man* (1975), Marge Piercy's *Woman on the Edge of Time* (1977), Suzy McKee Charnas's *Motherlines* (1978), and Sally Miller Gearhart's *The Wanderground* (1978) – British writers such as Tennant and Angela Carter seem more ambivalent about the utopian possibilities thrown up by the feminist movement, and Tennant's critique of patriarchal structures does not progress beyond satire in *The Time of the Crack*.

Carter's dystopian *The Passion of New Eve* (1977) echoes Tennant's satire with the Beulah cult, who kidnap the Englishman Evelyn and force him to undergo gender reassignment surgery; they are thus a rather reluctant visitor to utopia. Evelyn is raped by Zero, who like them is obsessed with a film actress, Tristessa de St Ange. Evelyn finds Tristessa living in a glass mausoleum in the desert and discovers that she is in fact a man. The glass coffin could be a reference to a fairy tale of the same name or to 'Snow White' and it is notable that Carter published her translation *The Fairy Tales of Charles Perrault* in the same year as *The Passion of New Eve* and followed it with her fairy tale reworking *The Bloody Chamber* (1979). If fairy tales emerged, as the Marxist utopian scholar Jack Zipes has argued, from the 'wish fulfilment and utopian projections' of pre-industrial folk consciousness,[52] then Carter's feminist response to the violent subjugation of women in traditional fairytales can be identified within this European context, which is linked to the establishment of national identities. As Nancy A. Walker has suggested, 'in seeking to resist [fairytales'] limiting formulations for women, female writers [like Angela Carter and Margaret Atwood] use the utopian form to address the traditional stories. Conscious, in other words, of the tales' continued power in the present, they imagine the future as the site of alteration.'[53] Here the United States – built upon its own history of slavery and genocide – has broken down into numerous 'self-fashioning tribes who live according to bizarre codes of their own invention'.[54]

Punk: A Space to Change the World

The journey to utopia, which frames the classical narrative structure of literary utopias, resurfaces in Jarman's *Jubilee*. Elizabeth I, her astrologer John Dee, an attendant (Helen Wellington-Lloyd) and Ariel from *The Tempest* (David Haughton) travel from the sixteenth century to a near-future London, where law and order has been abolished. They largely remain outside observers and commentators, although the double casting of Runacre as Bod, the anarchist leader of the violent gang, questions this distinction. Bod shares a squat with Amyl Nitrate, Crabs (Little Nell), Mad (Toyah Willcox), and Chaos (Hermine Demoriane), alongside brothers and lovers Angel (Ian Charleson) and Sphinx (Karl Johnson), as well as aspiring musician Kid (the aforementioned Adam Ant). This largely female gang offers a quasi-feminist inversion of Burgess's male droogs in *A Clockwork Orange* (1962) and Stanley Kubrick's 1971 adaptation. Amyl's alternative history of Britain asks 'Was Churchill a hero? Did he change history for the better?', refusing to condemn Hitler and celebrating Myra Hindley (Mad's references to fascism in the film similarly explore a reactionary strand of punk, which could be homophobic and racist, for example).[55] Mad declares that in her childhood, 'desires weren't allowed to become reality ... so fantasy was substituted for them: films, books, pictures. They called it art. But when your desires become reality, you don't need fantasy, any longer, or art.' The gang do as they please, asphyxiating a lover during sex, brutalising a waitress and the French-speaking maid Chaos, and castrating and petrol-bombing cops. As already noted, Jarman cast figures from the punk scene in the film. Punk was in part a reaction against the milieu of mid 1970s Britain: 'The wrecked economy fuelled an incendiary social situation as racism, xenophobia, and police brutality became the order of the day. Mounting feelings of anger, frustration, and a deepening sense of isolation left much of English youth feeling hopeless. ... Many found a means of expression in punk rock.'[56] The Sex Pistols's 'Anarchy in the UK' (1976) argues for a violent reaction to the contemporary world, but the 'no future' nihilism of their lyrics quickly became commodified through their short career. The Clash's 'White Riot' (1977) responds to the 1975 and 1976 Notting Hill Carnival riots, both showing solidarity with the Black community, but also calling for white rebellion.

Jarman seems sceptical of punk's revolutionary potential as indicated by the co-optation of music within the film. The media mogul Borgia Ginz (Orlando) chooses Amyl's performance as a fetishised Britannia for 'Britain's entry to the Eurovision Song Contest'. Kid and his band are also signed up by Ginz – renamed Scum – and the women are taken to his country house, where Hitler is among the guests. Ginz has the real power in this dystopia, having conquered Britain with his media empire: 'The media, became their only reality, and I own their world of flickering shadows: BBC, TUC, ITV, ABC, ATV, MGM ... KGB ... C of E. You name it. I bought them all, and rearranged the alphabet.' He has purchased Buckingham Palace and Westminster Cathedral, transforming them into a recording studio and a sex club. Much of the film was shot in the dilapidated warehouses and Jarman's own studio/flat in Butler's Wharf, a historic building on the cobbled riverside London street of Shad Thames – a relic of colonial trade – filled with a bricolage of graffitied slogans, posters, and artwork (this area became gentrified from the late 1980s and punk has since been repackaged as alternate heritage). The question of British national identity is reinforced in the final scene of *Jubilee*, which features white cliffs standing in for Dover, the gateway to Europe. Ariel instructs Elizabeth and Dee to 'consider the world's diversity, and worship it. By denying its multiplicity, you deny your own true nature.' Such diversity is reflected in the mixture of heterosexual, gay, and bisexual characters in the film, although it should be noted that almost every character in the film is white. Jarman clearly does not fully endorse this utopia, as the sympathetic treatment of the artist Viv (Linda Spurrier) is at odds with the statements that art and culture is dead.

In 1977, Tom Nairn had written, 'If a progressive "second revolution" still does not take place in England, then a conservative counter-revolution will.'[57] Thatcher ran that counter-revolution. Over the next decade and a half, nationalised industries were privatised and the power of unions such as those of the coal miners, ship builders, steel workers, journalists, and printers were curtailed. Heavy industry was all but destroyed. All aspects of cultural production were affected, particularly the music industry with which Jarman's film *Jubilee* is centrally concerned. As the guitarist for The Slits, Viv Albertine (who briefly appears in *Jubilee*), recollects, 'suddenly we switched into the '80s and it was Thatcherism and capitalism and the music industry became an industry instead of a place to make change and change the world and be rebellious'.[58] Thatcherism came to stand for the freedom of the individual to do as one pleased against the collective threats identified in *1990* and by Burgess in *1985*. Commonwealth countries such as Vanuatu, Zimbabwe, and Belize gained independence in the early 1980s. In June 1980, the Conservative government held secret talks with Argentina to hand over the Falkland Islands, attempting to end a dispute that had begun in 1816, but the Falklanders wanted to stay British. The Argentinians invaded and occupied the archipelago in April 1982 and a convoy of British troops were despatched to liberate the once French and Spanish colonies. British patriotism was reasserted. Jarman's own critique of Thatcherism and its attacks on the welfare state came with his experimental dystopia *The Last of England* (1987). Daniel Humphrey notes that the film is set 'within an apocalyptic postcolonial Britain where the future, past, and present are violently mixed together, [with] something very reminiscent of the Blitz'.[59] Jarman insists on his own 'alliance with a British tradition of middle-class dissent',[60] building on his older idea of Albion, as seen in *Jubilee*, reflecting on his wartime childhood, his relationship with his father, and the traumas of his HIV diagnosis. The film's title points to an 1855 Ford Madox Brown painting which depicts a couple emigrating to Australia from a mid-nineteenth century Britain suffused with economic problems; it is however silent upon the impact of immigrants on Australia and its Indigenous peoples.

The works discussed in this chapter do largely express the post-imperial melancholy created by World War II and the failed promises of the post-war settlement. In the cases of *Rule Britannia*, *An Englishman's Castle*, and *SS-GB*, there is palpable sorrow that an actually invading force was not defeated. In his essay on postcolonial melancholia, Paul Gilroy argues that in English culture 'the melancholic pattern has become the mechanism that sustains the unstable edifice of increasingly brittle and empty national identity';[61] even acknowledging Britain's colonial conquest risks perpetuating that ideology rather than repudiating or making reparations for it. It may even be that the examples here, as well as those cited by Baucom and

Gilroy, offer tragedies which 'punctuate the boredom of chronic national decline with a functional anguish'.[62] Trauma perhaps brings a perverse sense of relief. Utopias and dystopias have continued to be part of British science fiction, with Michael Radford's 1984 adaptation of Orwell's novel *Nineteen Eighty-Four*, Terry Gilliam's satirical and black comic reimagining of Orwell in *Brazil* (1985), and numerous *Doctor Who* serials. But British science fiction all too rarely does the work that Gilroy has called for, even when Britain seeks those sunlit uplands in a post-Brexit context. The cycle of wished-for civilisational collapses and utopian redemptions continues.

Notes

1. 'Girls Will Be Girls', *The Culture Show*, 2014. www.bbc.co.uk/programmes/b048s4tj (Last accessed 19 July 2023).
2. Gray Watson quoted in Mark Douglas, 'Queer Bedfellows: William Blake and Derek Jarman' in *Blake, Modernity and Popular Culture*, ed. Steve Clark and Jason Whittaker (Basingstoke: Palgrave Macmillan, 2007), pp. 113–26 (p. 114).
3. Roger Luckhurst, 'Post-imperial Melancholy and the New Wave in the 1970s', *Foundation*, 93 (2005), pp. 76–88 (p. 79).
4. Roger Luckhurst, 'Cosy Catastrophes: Ambivalent Utopias amidst the Wreckage' in *The Cambridge Companion to British Utopian Literature and Culture: 1945 to the Present*, ed. Caroline Edwards (Cambridge: Cambridge University Press, 2025), page numbers unknown.
5. Paul Gilroy, *Postcolonial Melancholia* (New York: Columbia University Press, 2005), p. 162.
6. Ibid., 90.
7. Ibid., p. 2.
8. Paul Gilroy, 'Joined-up Politics and Postcolonial Melancholia', *Theory, Culture & Society*, 18(2–3) (2001), pp. 151–67 (p. 162).
9. Prince Charles quoted in Ian Baucom, 'Mournful Histories: Narratives of Postimperial Melancholy', *Modern Fiction Studies*, 42(2) (1996), pp. 259–88 (p. 259).
10. Ibid.
11. Ibid., pp. 261–2.
12. Edward Said, 'Jane Austen and Empire' in *Culture and Imperialism* (New York: Alfred A. Knopf, 1993), pp. 80–97 (p. 90).
13. Luckhurst, 'Post-imperial Melancholy', pp. 78–82.
14. Andrew M. Butler, *Solar Flares: Science Fiction in the 1970s* (Liverpool: Liverpool University Press, 2012), p. 107.
15. Karl Abraham, A Short Study of the Development of the Libido, Viewed in the Light of Mental Disorders. In *Selected Papers of Karl Abraham*, trans Douglas Bryan and Alix Strachey (London: Hogarth Press, 1927), p. 437.

16. Tom Nairn, 'The Twilight of the British State', *New Left Review* (1977), pp. 101–02.
17. The report is available at the National Archives, Kew. https://discovery.natio nalarchives.gov.uk/details/r/C2455726 (Last accessed 18 July 2023).
18. A special episode of the children's animation *The Clangers* ('Vote for Froglet') was broadcast that evening, nearly two years after the final episode. *The Clangers* centres on an alien race who interact with extra-terrestrial beings and space debris in a utopia enclave. In 'The Intruder' (28 December 1969) an astronaut lands on their planet with a combined Soviet-US flag.
19. Aoife Byrne, 'Improbabilities Abound': Daphne du Maurier's Rule Britannia and the Speculative Political Future', *Sanglap: Journal of Literary and Cultural Inquiry*, 2(1) (2015), pp. 77–90 (p. 81).
20. Daphne du Maurier, *Rule Britannia* [1972] (London: Virago, 2012), p. 281.
21. Ibid., p. 256.
22. Brian Aldiss, *Billion Year Spree: The History of Science Fiction* (London: Weidenfeld and Nicolson, 1973), p. 294.
23. Christopher Priest 'British Science Fiction' in *Science Fiction: A Critical Guide*, ed. Patrick Parrinder (London and New York: Longman, 1979), pp. 187–202 (p. 194).
24. Joanie Willett, 'National Identity and Regional Development: Cornwall and the Campaign for Objective 1 Funding', *National Identities*, 15(3) (2013), pp. 297–311 (p. 299).
25. Ibid., p. 301.
26. du Maurier, *Rule Britannia*, p. 299.
27. Ibid., p. 282.
28. John Sutherland, *Bestsellers: Popular Fiction of the 1970s* (London: Routledge and Kegan Paul, 1981), p. 243.
29. Ibid.
30. Richard Cowper, '1985', *Vector*, 91 (1979), pp. 13–15 (p. 13).
31. Clive James, 'Look Forward in Mild Irritation' in *From the Land of Shadows* (London: Jonathan Cape, 1982), pp. 104–11 (p. 107).
32. Anthony Burgess, *1985* (London: Hutchinson, 1978), pp. 113–14.
33. Ibid., p. 81.
34. Ibid., p. 218.
35. Ibid., pp. 218–19.
36. Ibid., p. 218.
37. James, 'Look Forward', p. 111.
38. Priest, 'British Science Fiction', p. 58.
39. Ralph Pordzik, 'James G. Ballard's *Crash* and the Postmodernization of the Dystopian Novel', *AAA-Arbeiten Aus Anglistik und Amerikanistik*, 24(1) (1999), pp. 77–94 (p. 86).
40. J. G. Ballard, *Concrete Island* (Frogmore: Panther, 1976), p. 7.
41. Ibid., p. 96.
42. J. G. Ballard, *High-Rise* (London: Triad Granada, 1985), p. 8.

43. Nicola Braghieri, 'The Towers of Terror': A Critical Analysis of Ernő Goldfinger's Balfron and Trellick Towers', *Urban Planning*, 4(3) (2019), pp. 223–49 (p. 246).
44. Ibid., p. 246; Cynthia Pearson and Norbert Delatte, 'Ronan Point Apartment Tower Collapse and Its Effect on Building Codes', *Journal of the Performance of Constructed Facilities*, 19(2) (2005), pp. 172–77.
45. Alan Bradshaw and Stephen Brown, 'Up Rising: Rehabilitating J. G. Ballard's *High-Rise* with R.D. Laing and Lauren Berlant', *Environment and Planning D: Society and Space*, 36(2) (2018), pp. 331–49 (p. 332).
46. Ibid., p. 340.
47. Raffaella Baccolini, 'The Persistence of Hope in Dystopian Science Fiction', *PMLA*, 119(3) (2004), pp. 518–21 (p. 520).
48. Ibid.
49. Maggie Tonkin, 'R. D. Laing, Feminism and the Politics of Birth and Rebirth', *Australian Feminist Studies*, 34(100) (2019), pp. 248–62 (pp. 253–4).
50. Emma Tennant, *The Crack* (London: Faber and Faber, 1985), p. 67.
51. The BBC sketch show *The Two Ronnies* featured a serial, 'The Worm that Turned' (1980) in which the gender hierarchy was reversed in 2012 Britain, starring Diana Dors as the commander of the state police alongside stars Ronnie Barker and Ronnie Barker, who wear skirts. The opening section includes footage of feminists marching and the comedy is decidedly anti-feminist.
52. Jack Zipes, *Breaking the Magic Spell: Radical Theories of Folk and Fairy Tales* (Lexington: The University Press of Kentucky, 1979), p. 6.
53. Nancy A. Walker, *The Disobedient Writer: Women and Narrative Tradition* (Austin: University of Texas Press, 1995), p. 79.
54. Lorna Sage, *Angela Carter* (London: Writers and their Work, 1994), p. 36.
55. Roger Sabin, '"I Won't Let that Dago By": Rethinking Punk and Racism' in *Punk Rock: So What? The Cultural Legacy of Punk*, ed. Roger Sabin (London: Routledge, 1999), pp. 199–218.
56. Antonino D'Ambrosio, 'Let Fury Have the Hour': The Passionate Politics of Joe Strummer.' *Monthly Review*, 55(2) (2003), pp. 34–47 (p. 34).
57. Nairn, 'Twilight', pp. 101–2.
58. Viv Albertine interview, 'The Slits' Viv Albertine on Clothes, Music and Boys', *Channel 4*. Available at: www.youtube.com/watch?v=e3t02TCogc4 (Last accessed 19 July 2023).
59. Daniel Humphrey, 'Authorship, History and the Dialectic of Trauma: Derek Jarman's *The Last of England*', *Screen*, 44(2) (2003), pp. 208–15 (p. 212).
60. Derek Jarman quoted in Lawrence Driscoll, 'The Rose Revived': Derek Jarman and the British Tradition' in *By Angels Driven: The Films of Derek Jarman*, ed. Chris Lippard (Trowbridge: Flicks Books, 1996), pp. 65–83 (p. 66).
61. Gilroy, *Postcolonial Melancholia*, p. 106.
62. Ibid.

PART II

Building New Communities

CHAPTER 5

The British Counterculture, Utopia, and Class
David Wilkinson

Contemporary popular cultural cynicism regarding the utopian potentialities of the British counterculture is now commonplace. In 2019, the parodic adult comic *Viz* featured a comic strip in which British business magnate Sir Richard Branson, fondly recalling the anti-materialistic rhetoric of his 1960s youth, ends up using his vast wealth to annihilate everything and everyone around him to create the meditative, bucolic solitude he desires.[1] This cynicism has long had its scholarly counterparts, too. Leftist thinkers such as Slavoj Žižek have eviscerated the 'countercultural geeks who have taken over big corporations' for their deceitful advancement of a seemingly 'humanitarian ... frictionless capitalism'.[2] Given this, it is easy to neglect the fact that the British counterculture of the 1960s and 1970s engaged in a cultural, social, and political revolt that resonates profoundly with our conflicted present. To trace the persistence of countercultural concerns in the 2020s is to confront a startling array of seemingly 'contemporary' crises: urban policy; ecological destruction and sustainable alternatives; fractured identities of nation and class. The counterculture tracked convulsions in the politics and lived realities of gender, sexuality, and race; it reflected on the uncertain implications of new technologies for work and leisure; and it went about all this with an irreverent lack of faith in existing cultural forms and political institutions, offering alternatives ranging from the local and pragmatic to the expansive and utopian. The British counterculture, therefore, encapsulates not only many of the key concerns of the postwar period; its continuity with the present gives it the potential to provide rich insight into contemporary hopes and fears.

This chapter re-evaluates the contested meanings and legacies of the British counterculture to better illuminate their significance for our troubled times. Its specific focus is the concept of utopia. The chapter therefore develops a theme explored in my previous work, which argues that the post-punk movement of the late 1970s and 1980s may act as a utopian resource of hope in contemporary crisis-ridden conditions.[3]

Yet post-punk also marked the incorporation of the counterculture in various ways, thus teaching harder lessons about the limitations, as well as the possibilities, of countercultural revolt. Here, I return to the historical origins of such post-punk utopianism, further exploring the ways in which what Fredric Jameson has rightly characterised as a 'precious' legacy of the 1960s and 1970s has nevertheless always been a politically fraught and conflicted one.[4] My argument here will be that the ambiguity of the counterculture's utopian possibilities may be explored via an excavation of its class basis. I begin by revisiting what might be thought of as a 'red thread' of utopian thinking in the British cultural materialism of Raymond Williams, tracing its revolutionary lineage back to the European Western Marxism of thinkers such as Herbert Marcuse and Ernst Bloch. This important intellectual milieu frames the utopian significance of the British counterculture. I then critique and develop the cultural materialist-inflected work of the Centre for Contemporary Cultural Studies, founded by Stuart Hall and Richard Hoggart at the University of Birmingham in 1964, to re-evaluate the complex class basis of the counterculture and the significance of this for its utopian potentialities. In the second half of the chapter, I analyse an exemplary countercultural text, the 1974 BBC TV play *Penda's Fen*, which offers the opportunity to make more concrete sense of these complexities and ambiguities. Ultimately, I claim that *Penda's Fen* contains conflicting utopian visions, reflecting the differing class fractions that comprised the counterculture and anticipating the neoliberal present even as it continues to suggest radical unfulfilled possibilities. The utopian function of *Penda's Fen* may be identified as a cultural resource that can help us understand the contemporary moment of crisis. It achieves this by returning our attention to a critical juncture in the post-war period when a heterogenous and heterodox new middle class was first expressing its new-found power, whilst standing at a political crossroads.

Thinking about Utopia

It is not only the legacy of the British counterculture that is ambiguous. This ambiguity extends also to the theoretical frameworks through which we might come to some understanding of the utopian. The British sociologist and utopian theorist Ruth Levitas has pointed to the difficulty of defining utopia as specific cultural content or social function. For Levitas, a more productive way to think about utopia is as *desire that cannot be fulfilled in present social conditions*.[5] Such a notion has been richly developed in Western Marxist and cultural materialist traditions of thought. For

5 The British Counterculture, Utopia, and Class

Ernst Bloch, hope, the future, and the utopian are inseparable. 'The future dimension contains what is feared or what is hoped for', Bloch wrote in the first volume of his neglected magnum opus *The Principle of Hope*.[6] The bourgeoisie, long since past its revolutionary phase, can conceive of the future only in terms of fear – even as it resorts to fraudulent and 'empty promises of the other world' to secure its hegemony.[7] Though Bloch was writing seven decades ago in the wake of fascism and World War II, a cursory observation of the current global spread of reactionary populism and of a dystopia-fixated popular culture would indicate that his position seems as convincing as ever. Yet this nihilism, in the long run, 'is as ephemeral as the class which alone still expresses itself within it . . . . As long as man is in a bad way, both private and public existence are pervaded by daydreams; dreams of a better life than that which has so far been given him.'[8] Bloch is wary of the potential for such hope to be exploited by the 'swindlers' of the capitalist market. He nevertheless defends the utopian possibilities of 'forward dreaming', elaborating the notion of the 'Not-Yet-Conscious' – a kind of chronologically inverted unconscious defined by 'something new that is dawning up' rather than by the archaic and the repressed. Bloch's Marxism means that this 'Not-Yet-Conscious' is not an idealist phenomenon. Rather it is the psychological manifestation of 'objectively real possibility' rooted in current social conditions, in a nod to Marx's theory that capitalism, like all modes of production, contains within it the seeds of its own potential destruction.[9]

For another Western Marxist, Herbert Marcuse, utopia could similarly be identified in the cultivation of a 'new sensibility'.[10] This term captured the preliminary pursuit of alternative ways of life made possible by capitalist economic and technological development – but rendered as yet unattainable on a larger scale by the profit motive and by private ownership of the means of production. It was a strategy that the ageing Marcuse proposed to a countercultural audience at the 1967 Dialectics of Liberation conference held at London's Roundhouse, thus bridging the utopian dreaming of at least two generations. Marcuse, though, conceived of the utopian not only as 'forward dreaming'. In a dialectical twist, there was for him a 'kernel of truth' in otherwise regressive romanticisations of nature and the pre-industrial past; their 'most advanced positions' continue 'to haunt the consciousness with the possibility of their rebirth in the consummation of technical progress'.[11] In other words, the more leisurely and bucolic lifestyle imagined in mythical idealisations of a Golden Age is not inherently naïve or reactionary; rather, something approximating it could actually be possible were current economic and technological resources to be refocused in a socialist and ecological direction. Both these tendencies – Bloch's revelatory 'forward dreaming' and Marcuse's shrewd materialist recovery of romanticism – were present within the British counterculture. We will have cause in the latter part of this chapter to examine how such tendencies play out in *Penda's Fen*.

Doing so will require a consideration not just of the programme's content but also its form. As Fredric Jameson has argued, particular means of representing the world entail both opportunities and limits as to how we are able to imagine that world and what might be possible both within and beyond it.[12] Ultimately, though, the possibilities and pitfalls of utopian cultural forms can only be evaluated by what Perry Anderson has called 'a sense of culture as a battlefield ... the plane of politics'.[13] Here, the theoretical work of British cultural materialism developed by Raymond Williams is useful. From the 1970s onwards, we find Williams considering the history of utopian texts, prompted by a contemporary resumption of the utopian in the writing of countercultural authors such as Ursula le Guin. Central to this work was an emphasis on the social position of cultural producers as one means of understanding the political significance of the cultural texts they made. For Williams, class provided one key frame through which to consider this matter. Thus in his work on utopian form, one of the explanations given for the dystopian turn of writers like Huxley and Orwell is a more broadly 'sour period' of bourgeois thought to which both belonged, in which a common response to social dysfunction was often the desire to 'escape ... both the system and the fight against the system'.[14] Williams's insight here regarding the connections between class and utopian cultural form is a valuable means of understanding the political significance of countercultural utopianism; it will play a key role in my analysis of class in *Penda's Fen*. In order to put it to use, though, we need an explanation of the class basis of the counterculture.

Class, Counterculture, and Utopia

A good place to start is the Centre for Contemporary Cultural Studies (CCCS), a research centre founded in 1964 by Stuart Hall and Richard Hoggart at the University of Birmingham, which became the intellectual heart of British cultural studies. In a 1975 chapter influenced by Raymond Williams's contemporary work, the CCCS characterised the counterculture as a 'profoundly adaptive' middle-class response to post-war shifts in the capitalist productive base.[15] As the culture industry expanded in the post-war period, British consumer capitalism required not just a more flexible, hedonistic consumer base, but also those with the skills to produce and promote it. Middle-class countercultural youth were the vanguard of this production of a particular kind of pleasure-seeking consciousness, shaking up fashion, education, sexual mores, ossified standards of cultural value, working patterns, and more – and facing a predictable backlash from their more straitlaced forebears, perhaps most notably the conservative Christian moral campaigner Mary Whitehouse.[16] Was all the revolutionary rhetoric, then, simply what Jameson has called the 'fantasy bribe', the degraded utopianism of cornucopian consumerist promise whose repugnant underside has been ecological devastation, the super-exploitation of labour and profound social alienation?[17] Not entirely. The CCCS did acknowledge the contested nature of countercultural revolt. They noted that a 'deeper disaffiliation' from the dominant was possible, hinting at the counterculture's attempted alliances with organised labour and the potential for transgression to tip into explicit opposition to the system.[18] Yet they remained ambivalent about the politics of an 'unfinished' cultural trajectory.[19]

It is worth returning to that unfinished trajectory, exploring whether the counterculture may still play a plausible role in contemporary utopian imaginaries and the task of building a collective social agency capable of establishing a more egalitarian and ecologically sustainable future. To do so, the CCCS's analysis requires a degree of rethinking. Its identification of the dissident new middle-class basis of the counterculture is in part persuasive – but it does suffer from a limitation that has been identified time and time again. Can we really locate various youth cultures so neatly within a 'parent' class culture? Against the postmodern drift that has prevailed in the wake of such critiques – especially in the form of the 'post-subcultural turn'[20] – we might instead turn to Raymond Williams's work on cultural formations to deal with this problem. Accounting for the development of dissident middle-class groupings in British cultural and political history, he notes: 'We must remember, first, that a social class is by no means culturally monolithic.' According to this logic, we could characterise the counterculture as the avant-garde of the postwar middle class. But for Williams, cultural formations do not just arise *within* classes: 'Additionally', he suggests, 'there is a basis ... in the changing relations between ... classes.'[21] What if we understood the counterculture in this way? After all, the post-war British working class not only faced transformations of its own as a changing economy reshaped its patterns of labour and culture; it was also far from unaffected by concurrent changes within the middle class. In part this was because of the social mobility enabled by the post-war consensus. It meant that a significant fraction of working-class youth experienced an uneven and often uneasy amalgamation of middle-class culture, education, employment, and expectations with their proletarian roots. 'I had this feeling of not *belonging* anywhere', recalled one of the grammar school participants in Jackson and Marsden's seminal 1966 study of the effects of the 1944 Education Act, *Education and the Working Class*.[22] Given this, it is not difficult to understand why this class fraction might have been drawn to the romantic bohemianism of the counterculture and its immediate precursors. If the counterculture was indeed a formation composed of *both* the dissident new middle class and the displaced working class, it would make sense to consider how this dynamic shaped the ways in which countercultural production dealt with the issue of utopia. This will be my concern in the following analysis of *Penda's Fen*.

Penda's Fen and Utopian Form

The feature-length 1974 television drama *Penda's Fen*, written by David Rudkin and directed by Alan Clarke, was part of the BBC's prestigious and critically acclaimed *Play for Today* series. *Play for Today* ran from 1970 to 1984, generating an immense cultural legacy that was recently marked by a BFI fiftieth anniversary celebration.[23] Rather than rock music, which we might expect to accompany a countercultural narrative, the soundtrack of *Penda's Fen* is taken predominantly from Edward Elgar's oratorio 'The Dream of Gerontius' (1900). Stephen, the troubled protagonist, has lined his bedroom bookshelves with classical Greek and Latin texts, rather than fashionable contemporary Beat literature. At first sight, then, *Penda's Fen* does not appear to be a countercultural text in the way that we might characterise contemporary films such as *Performance* (1970), which featured Mick Jagger, hallucinogenic drug use, and a setting in Notting Hill Gate, a key location of the hippie underground.[24] Yet despite not being 'about' the counterculture, *Penda's Fen* is very much a product of it. *Penda's Fen* is shot through with countercultural enthusiasms and pre-occupations, drawing upon folklore, paganism, and the occult to narrate themes of personal and national identity, social dysfunction, and ecology that culminate in a visionary, utopian transformation. Remarking on the causes for the educational under-performance of Stephen, his headmaster speculates, in an allusion to the countercultural underground: 'I can only assume it's because you've been hankering to join what I term your generation's underside.' As the film critic Jerry Whyte suggests, Rudkin 'mined a rich vein of revolt in a contemporary counter-culture from which he drew and to which he contributed'.²⁵ Meanwhile, 'the mother and father of England' who appear in Stephen's dreams enlisting him to a patriotic Christian conservatism bear more than a passing resemblance to Mary Whitehouse and Malcolm Muggeridge, who co-founded the grassroots Christian movement known as the Festival of Light in the late 1960s to oppose the depiction of violence and sexuality in the mass media.²⁶

It is not just content that renders *Penda's Fen* countercultural but also its material history of distribution. Although produced by a state broadcasting company that enlisted a writer and director with established reputations under the banner of an award-winning series, *Penda's Fen* failed to attract significant viewers. It was repeated only once, in 1990, and was commercially unavailable until a BFI DVD release in 2016, existing before this point only in ghostly VHS recordings uploaded to YouTube. This subterranean history of limited availability has given the programme a 'cult' appeal; former BFI press officer Brian Robinson recalls that in his late 1970s youth, 'to declare your love for it was a special badge that proved you were a radical'.²⁷ It is important to try and be more specific about the nature of such radicalism – and to focus on class as the means of doing so. In what follows, I will treat the creative pairing of writer David Rudkin and director Alan Clarke as an example of the mingled class basis of the British counterculture. Rudkin was a vicar's son who attended an expensive fee-paying public school followed by the University of Oxford, whilst Clarke was educated at a state-run grammar school. The upward social mobility afforded to Clarke as a working-class boy who joined middle-class creative media professionals reminds us of the tensions both within and between British class fractions. Reflecting on Rudkin and Clarke's respective biographical experiences, then, helps us understand the ambiguous utopian vision of *Penda's Fen*, as well as its repercussions in the twenty-first century.

First, though, it is important to consider what kind of a programme *Penda's Fen* is and what possibilities its formal composition thereby enables it to explore. The range of aesthetic resources brought to *Penda's Fen* by Rudkin and Clarke is vast, accounting for its rich and rewarding depth at the levels of dialogue, theme, and visual construction. Significantly, however, many of the formal influences identified are ones with utopian resonance. Matthew Harle and James Machin situate the programme in 'a long British tradition of Christian visionary, ecstatic religious writing from John Bunyan and William Blake to Arthur Machen and Charles Williams'.²⁸ 'British' is highly significant here; *Penda's Fen* is a programme that is deeply focused on the quest for an ideal national identity as much as an ideal personal identity, beginning as it does with serenely shot footage of the Malvern Hills soundtracked by Elgar and Stephen's opening voiceover: 'Oh my country I say over and over – I am one of your sons I say over and over – I am, I am! Yet how shall I show my love?'

Situating *Penda's Fen* within a *visionary* tradition of British religious writing helps uncover some of the programme's utopian aesthetics. An otherwise realist narrative is regularly punctuated from the third scene onwards by Stephen's dreams and fantasies, which come vividly to life in surrealist form. As febrile and erotic as any teenage boy's overheated imagination, these sequences have an added utopian dimension, since they act as signposts for Stephen to a better future. As he relates to various characters in waking life, so these conversations and experiences are processed through dream work. In turn, this facilitates his transformation from a closeted, embittered reactionary into a young gay man with an understanding of his status as an adopted child and of his broader belonging to the world as hybrid, complex, and multifaceted – not to mention equipping him with a critical awareness of late capitalist workaday alienation. In this respect, *Penda's Fen* very much embodies Bloch's notion of 'forward dreaming'; Stephen is guided by the 'not-yet-conscious' towards a potentially brighter future, which in turn is rooted in 'objectively real possibility'. After all, the programme was screened shortly after Edward Heath's Conservative government was toppled by trade union militancy and during the first large-scale blossoming of LGBT activism in Britain, as grassroots groups such as the Campaign for Homosexual Equality and the Gay Liberation Front began to challenge the still prevalent social unacceptability of homosexuality in the wake of the 1967 legalisation of consenting same-sex relations in private.[29] The large-scale immigration of the post-war period, too, had complicated dominant notions of ethnic Britishness, which were anything but straightforward.

Harle and Machin's identification of the visionary qualities of *Penda's Fen* as 'religious' is also vital for understanding its utopian dimensions. Stephen's transformation is not just a matter of 'forward dreaming'. In the programme, a series of oneiric excavations of what Craig Wallace has identified as the 'sleeping king' myth make this kind of forward dreaming possible. Wallace's investigation focuses mainly on the Arthurian legends as embodying the myth of a 'sacred protector' entombed within the land who is fated to return 'following a period of waste, spiritual desolation, and fall' to enact 'revolutionary change', though he acknowledges that Arthur has his precursors and successors.[30] Most notable among those precursors is of course Jesus, though the myth has pre-Christian origins. The multiple unburyings of *Penda's Fen* resonate strongly with Marcuse's hunch that romantic idealisations of the mythic past might be dialectically redeemed for utopian purposes. We see visions of an androgynous angel by a pool; a cracked church floor and a statue of Christ on the cross that hints at the gospel's layering over Anglo-Saxon and Norse mythology through its hallucinatory injunction to 'unbury me, free me from this tree'; and eventually Stephen's encounter with England's last pagan king Penda, who was defeated and killed in battle in 655, in the final scene set on the Malvern Hills at sunset, occasioned by Stephen's discovery of the etymological history of his village's name: Pinvin, Pinfin, Pendefen, Penda's Fen.

Even those visions that do not make obvious use of the 'sleeping king' myth entail a revelatory confrontation with the past, focused on a preoccupation with the relationship between the spiritual and the material. These result in a pagan or heretical affirmation of mystic oneness and a utopian resolution of contradictions, as when Stephen encounters the doleful ghost of Edward Elgar in a ruined barn recalling how he once found musical inspiration in the whine of a hungry dog. Elgar's reminiscence about the inspiration for his orchestral and vocal arrangement of John Henry Newman's 1865 poem ruins Stephen's idealised grammar-schoolboy abstraction of 'The Dream of Gerontius'. A similar effect is achieved by Stephen's dream of reaching for the flaming crotch of school bully Honeybone as 'The Dream of Gerontius' plays in the background, giving an erotic charge to the oratorio's sacred theme. This is a heady brew; a psychedelic assemblage of subversive pastoralism that lingers in the imagination long after viewing. But if *Penda's Fen* is simultaneously 'a bloody political piece' as Rudkin has asserted, what to make of the political significance of its utopian form?[31] At this juncture, we need to return to the idea of 'culture as battleground'; to the fraught social conditions in which culture is produced and received – and the class implications of this antagonism.

'England's Last Hope'? *Penda's Fen*, Counterculture, and Class

One way of thinking through the politics of *Penda's Fen* is to consider the ways in which it articulates an often contradictory jumble of utopian structures of feeling associated with various class fractions. Perhaps most prominently, the programme could be interpreted as a new middle-class utopian vision as a result of the definitive input of Rudkin and Clarke, both of whom had moved into this social location by virtue of their work – though crucially, as we will see, from different initial backgrounds.

Understanding this vision and its political implications requires some definition of the new middle class. For Alex Callinicos, the new middle class of the 1970s was 'a collection of heterogeneous social layers who have in common an ambiguous and intermediate position with respect to the fundamental contradiction between capital and wage-labour'.[32] Val Burris notes that because of this intermediate position of the new middle class, 'nothing definitive can be inferred about their political orientation other than it is likely to be varied and changeable'.[33] We could argue that this diversity and changeability is not only expressed in the potential for the new middle class to side with either the bourgeoisie or the proletariat. Especially in the post-war and contemporary period, it has manifested itself in a distinctive utopianism associated with the new middle class, which is similarly politically uncertain. Difficult to summarise in straightforwardly ideological terms, it is better thought of in Williams's theoretical terminology as a structure of feeling; a useful concept that helps capture the material determinations of that which is usually mystified as amorphous, subjective, and felt.[34]

Of what might this structure of feeling consist, and where can we see it in *Penda's Fen*? To begin with, it is worth confronting the elements of this utopian sensibility that would seem to support a view of the new middle class as ultimately in alliance with the bourgeoisie. In a coruscating critique of the new middle class first published in 1982, Raphael Samuel describes its 'narcissism – the delight which it takes in itself'.[35] The product of an expanded education system, Britain's new middle class dispenses with the snobberies and proprieties associated with pre-war English life. For Samuel, this is in part a historical result of its privileged access to post-war consumerism, revealing the way in which such access has tended to permeate identity and reconstitute it as predominantly a matter of taste, novelty, and sensuous gratification. Thus, as Roger Luckhurst has observed, Rudkin's 'imperative is for his protagonists to *re-author* themselves' – often in ways that focus on the sensuous.[36] This is certainly the case for Stephen, whose journey crucially involves a shift from repressed puritanism to an acknowledgement of his same-sex desires in explicitly physical ways, conveyed by the programme's utopian fusion of the spiritual and material: dreaming of a schoolmate nude and caressing the milkman's arms while emerging from a visionary daze.

The narcissism of the new middle class goes hand in hand with a carefree sense of 'classlessness' – an ideological illusion generated by social mobility and by commonly working within what Samuel calls 'an institutional field of fine gradations but no clear lines of antagonism'.[37] We might add to Samuel's analysis that the ironic result of this sense of 'classlessness' is a classically bourgeois individualism on the part of the new middle class, very much on show in the lonely path of self-discovery taken by Stephen. Formally, this is conveyed in Rudkin's acknowledged debt to filmmaker Carl Theodor Dreyer: a 'psychological realism' intended to convey 'each human creature unalterably alone, each working out (or losing) an individual salvation, in an existential solitude that only love can mitigate'.[38]

This classically bourgeois individualism is not the only residual element of new middle-class utopianism. As Samuel observes, in the lives of the new middle class, 'distinctively working class people' frequently 'have only walk-on parts – like cleaners, porters, maintenance men'.[39] This marginal, haunting presence tends to constitute the working class ideologically as othered; even threatening. Perversely, the new middle-class response to the anxiety it feels in the presence of the working class has often been to marshal its radicalism not in the service of overcoming class inequality but by presenting itself as the collective agent of progressive social change – and the working class as a conservative brake on such progress. Samuel notes: 'As modernisers, heralding the advent of a "post-industrial" society, they see [the] very existence [of the working class] as in some sort anachronistic.'[40] Little surprise, then, that there is something atavistic about every working-class figure who appears in *Penda's Fen*, whether it be the old road worker who 'misspells' Pinvin as its former name Pinfin on a diversion sign and thus reveals its pagan origins, or Joel the milkman and Honeybone as primitive objects of desire, their local accents and exaggerated masculinity contrasting both with Stephen's stiff formality and the casual educated drawl of radical playwright Mr Arne.

A particular moment stands out for me each time I watch *Penda's Fen*. It is an otherwise incidental piece of dialogue that at first glance seems only to serve the purpose of highlighting Stephen's awkwardness when dealing with Joel, upon whom he has an obvious crush. As Stephen fumbles around in military uniform in preparation for a drill at his school, Joel teases him, referring to Stephen ironically as 'England's last hope'. In one possible reading of the programme, Stephen actually turns out to be just this. By eventually rejecting his uptight conservatism in favour of a more expansive, nuanced form of personal identity and national belonging, he becomes an example of the way in which the ascendence of the new middle class aided the reconstitution of capitalism during this era; a flexible, liberalised 'new spirit' that Luc Boltanski and Eve Chiapello have summarised as entailing 'autonomy, spontaneity … conviviality, openness to others and novelty, visionary intuition, sensitivity to differences' and which was particularly concentrated in the counterculture.[41] We can also see the fundamentally ambiguous political loyalties of the new middle class echoed in its romanticisation of ambiguity, contingency, transgression; a sensibility that has become hegemonic with the cultural dominance of postmodernism. 'Child be strange: dark ... impure and dissonant. Our dawn shall come' are King Penda's final words to Stephen in the concluding scene as the latter surveys the town from his commanding hilltop position, embodying the new middle class's sense of itself as occupying a leading social role.

Yet we should not forget that post-war new middle-class radicalism, before its definitive historical 'souring', could and did take a much more explicitly socialist form, revealing the potential for proletarian alliance and a more egalitarian utopian vision. The pivotal character of Mr Arne is a somewhat obvious semi-autobiographical representation of Rudkin himself – and of his New Left dramatist peers such as Caryl Churchill, Trevor Griffiths, and David Hare, whose work embodied the socialist turn of a significant proportion of the new middle class in the post-war period. Arne's views are the most stridently anti-capitalist and ecological on display in *Penda's Fen*, reminding us of a fluke moment in British broadcasting during which such voices briefly had privileged access to a powerful and far-reaching cultural medium.

For all the apparent countercultural irrationalism, too, there are moments when such cultural resources seem to take critical, materialist form. One instance is the motif of unending Manichean struggle that runs throughout both the dialogue and the imagery of *Penda's Fen*, which serves anything but a mystifying function. Rather, when used in discussion between the radical Arne and Stephen's heretical father, it seems to be a metaphor for a materialist understanding of social conflict as a driver of historical change, echoing Marx's dictum that the history of all societies has been the history of class struggle. In this respect, it is at odds with the individualistic, religious, and moralistic focus on the self also present in the programme. Furthermore, that which is buried does not always serve an idealist utopian purpose; sometimes it acts as a stark demystification of the material forces that ruthlessly govern human life and death. Witness Arne's bleak observation of the secret government bunker beneath the village, the purpose of which is never explicitly revealed: 'What is it, hidden beneath this shell of lovely earth? ... Offices, control suites, silent, empty, waiting for The Day? ... Oh, you say, it must be something to protect us. *Us*? When for all we know, the likelihood is our entire civilian population is marked down ... as "strategically expendable".'

Stephen's sexual dissidence, as well, seems bound up with this anti-capitalism in a manner that is strongly reflective of the radical sexual

5 The British Counterculture, Utopia, and Class

politics of 1970s gay liberation, evoking a very different utopian vision of sexual and social egalitarianism. The revelation he experiences concerning his sexual desires is indissoluble from his more general enlightenment concerning the alienation of working life, the ideological function of education and the abuses wrought on the environment by unsustainable urbanism and the military industrial complex. At the time *Penda's Fen* was released, Rudkin viewed 'the gay man' as a figure 'who is ultimately anti-capitalist in his refusal to organise his sexuality in terms of reproduction' evoking the frequent yoking together of sexual dissidence and socialist perspectives during this conjuncture.[42]

Relatedly, although Stephen takes his journey alone, some kind of connection with working-class characters is required for him to experience fulfilment. Here, new middle-class utopianism and a more expressly politicised hint of radical class alliance mingle and overlap; the former's focus on self-realisation and pleasure is conveyed through an eroticised social bond with the latter. This may simply be one more iteration of a familiar fetishism produced by class inequality, in which, as Peter Stallybrass and Allon White have observed, 'social separation' becomes 'constitutive of desire'.[43] Alan Sinfield has further explored the complexities of cross-class same sex desire, pointing out that exploitation, 'indignation and resentment' are likely to threaten romantic and sexual attachment premised on class difference.[44] When Stephen caresses Joel unprompted after he has been helped up from a fall by the latter, Joel responds awkwardly: 'Just help you up, that's all ... That's all.' It is an excruciating moment. Looked at another way, however, Stephen's desires are utopian in that they cannot be fulfilled unproblematically in present social conditions yet hint towards a better world; one in which the overcoming of class divisions may accompany the overcoming of inequalities associated with sexual desires and identities. 'I wish Joel would like me', Stephen remarks childishly to his mother in the second scene – a moment that acquires unexpected poignancy as the narrative unfolds.

Crucially, and finally, there is Clarke's contribution as director. As I noted earlier, though both Rudkin and Clarke had entered the new middle class in respect of their professions, they did so from contrasting initial backgrounds. Clarke, a working-class boy who went to a state-run selective grammar school, inherited the formal language of post-war British social realism, a genre that was at its peak in the fields of drama, film, and literature during his professional training in the late 1950s and early 1960s. From the late 1970s he would go on to develop a distinctive and influential hard-edged take on the genre, which compellingly articulated Britain's collapsing post-war consensus. These uncompromising portrayals of working-class life avoided romanticisation: they include the violence of borstal life in *Scum* (1979); racist social delinquency in *Made in Britain* (1982); and the tensions of cross-class sexual liaisons in *Rita, Sue and Bob Too* (1987).

It would be far too easy, however, to attribute to such work clichéd epithets like 'bleak', 'gritty', and 'hopeless'. It is not always obvious – but at times Clarke's dramas display a loyalty to what Raymond Williams has called 'the basic collective idea' underpinning 'working class culture'; an idea 'embodied in the organisations and institutions which that class creates': for example, trade unions and mutual aid networks; an idea that views social improvement not in individual but collective terms: 'Not the individual, but the whole society, will move.'[45] We may reasonably view such an idea as a kind of working-class utopianism; an impossible desire to universalise so long as capitalism remains the dominant mode of production. This is conveyed not so much via any redemptive elements of plot – Clarke rarely wrote his own screenplays – but by directorial decisions. *Penda's Fen* is an early example of this, despite its decidedly non-realist elements. Spencer Banks, the actor who played Stephen, recalls that Clarke broke convention by insisting on a ten-day rehearsal before shooting, with the effect that the cast and crew were 'a bonded unit' before location filming even began. Christopher Douglas, meanwhile, who played Honeybone, stresses:

> If ever it seemed like a film where in order to be in it or appreciate it you had to be familiar with the Classics and you had to read Ancient Greek, it was dispelled by the position of Alan Clarke; who was so unlike that, though obviously a well-read and highly intelligent man, it didn't feel like you were doing a tweed jacket and pipe BBC classical thing, where everyone went to the same public school and read the same books. It didn't feel intimidating ... [Clarke] would say 'don't act' ... A lot of his work has people offering powerful performances, but there's no 'big acting' going on – it's convincing, realistic, passionate.[46]

Both the solidarity of cast and crew and the unpretentious style of acting encouraged by Clarke lend a deep emotional authenticity to *Penda's Fen*. Importantly, this is particularly evident in scenes that involve characters reaching an understanding of themselves and one another via mutuality – those scenes in which Stephen converses with his adoptive parents, for instance, or with Mrs Arne, who is moved by Stephen's warming to her and wishes him well with his desire to have children after a frank discussion of her own infertility – embodying a tenderly humanistic collectivist utopianism.

Penda's Fen and countercultural utopianism in the present

What, then, of the contemporary political significance of countercultural utopianism as it is articulated in *Penda's Fen*? Placed in historical context, the depiction of Stephen's personal awakening is a brave and beautifully realised move; an instance of the artistic risks that Rudkin and Clarke would continue to take in the pursuit of their political convictions. In the early decades of the twenty-first century, however, we should be wary of any straightforward championing of the programme's radicalism. Rudkin's 'imperative for ... his protagonists to *re-author* themselves', as Roger Luckhurst puts it, and the anti-institutionalism upon which this is premised, is no longer an avant-garde countercultural emphasis or a necessarily liberatory or egalitarian move, if indeed it ever was.

In the intervening decades between 1974 and the present, the new middle class so memorably characterised in Raphael Samuel's 1982 essay made good on its 'progressive' convictions of social and political leadership. Falteringly, at first, via the Social Democratic Party breakaway from Labour in 1981, and then with astounding success via the project of New Labour, whose key figures were all connected with the worlds of education, media, and the professions and whose class origins lay outside the traditional British establishment. In New Labour, it is possible to discern not only the way that the new middle class may ally itself with the bourgeoisie but also the way the former's ambiguous social position may act as a foil, allowing for the famed 'triangulation' by which Tony Blair and his allies appealed to the party's working-class base whilst also attracting the vote of so-called 'Middle England'.[47] The result was a long tenure in office that ultimately embedded the neoliberal policies of Thatcherism as hegemonic common sense. The 'classless', individualistic, and anti-institutional utopianism of the new middle class was saturated into the rhetoric of New Labour; Blair's speech at the 1999 annual Labour Party conference held in Bournemouth was a prime example. In it, he evoked a 'New Britain where the extraordinary talent of the British people is liberated from the forces of conservatism that have for so long held them back'; declared 'not power to the people but power to each person to make the most of what is within them'; and announced, 'the class war is over.'[48] Concurrently, the period between the 1970s and the present has witnessed the cowing of the broader labour movement and, along with it, a counter-hegemonic working-class conviction in collectivism and solidarity. Under the imperialist influence of the United States on Britain, the politics of identity have risen up with a vengeance to fill the void; what Stephen Epstein has called 'the modern

American pluralist myth, which portrays a harmonious competition among distinct social groups'.[49] Andrew Milner has argued that the new middle-class intelligentsia has overwhelmingly and unrepresentatively led new social movements premised on identity rather than class, thus determining the 'developing preference' of such movements 'for individualist ... as opposed to structural solutions'.[50]

Thus, Stephen's *re-authorship* cannot be read as a straightforwardly utopian process. Looked at one way, the lonely journey toward his adoptive identity as a queer, second-generation immigrant is reminiscent of contemporary 'intersectional' identitarian rhetoric, moulded and amplified by the reifications of social media. Fredric Jameson's now decades-old sketch of identity politics as a 'properly interminable series of neighbourhood issues ... invested with something of Nietzsche's social Darwinism', at risk of 'disintegrating into the more obscene consumerist pluralisms' of the dominant culture is still an incisive summary of the way such causes often operate; causes once commonly thought of as inherently leftist.[51] Solidarity is largely alien to contemporary identity politics in Britain; instead 'allyship' has taken its place, a contingent imperative that puts the emphasis on individual conduct rather than collective loyalty. The British employers' organisation Inclusive Employers, for instance, defines an ally as 'someone who is not a member of a marginalised group but wants to support and take action to help others in that group' and proceeds to offer a guide as to how individuals ought to behave in the workplace.[52] Business more broadly has proven only too willing to adapt itself to such rhetoric, as what David Alderson calls a 'diversified dominant' has come to prominence; a hegemonic incorporation of identity politics under the common denominator of the free market.[53]

Sexuality is a case in point. In contrast to David Rudkin's convictions of the 1970s, sexual dissidence has proven to be as commodifiable as anything else in the decades since the first broadcast of *Penda's Fen*. In this respect, gay male subculture in particular – of the sort that Stephen's character might conceivably have gone on to participate in following the acknowledgement of his desires – has historically led the way, though recent years have seen the commercially mediated mainstreaming of a much broader range of sexual and gendered identities. If the utopian is understood to be an anticipatory desire that cannot be fulfilled under present social conditions, then it may well be that the utopian countercultural charge of *Penda's Fen* has been somewhat defused: in part because of its production by members of a class fraction that has gone on to have a significant role in the development of contemporary capitalism.

Much the same could be said of the utopian vision of national belonging offered by the programme. On one reading, its hybrid cosmopolitanism seems infused with a new middle-class enthusiasm for diversity but little else: 'My race is mixed'; 'You are like the English language, you have foreign parents'; 'Even Elgar had some Welsh blood'. As such it offers little explicit resistance to the onset of neoliberal globalisation, naturalised as 'universal' and irresistible by the time of Blair's 1999 speech, and implicitly allied to a celebration of 'multiculturalism' ultimately underpinned by openness to international capital and labour, with the usual power relations between the two still fully intact. More recently, a similar ideology has governed the position of the most fervent defenders of the European Union since Britain's polarising division into 'Remainia' and 'Brexitland' following the United Kingdom's European Union membership referendum in 2016. Presenting themselves as progressive advocates of cosmopolitanism and the rights of immigrants, they have frequently failed to acknowledge adequately the role of the European Union as a bastion of neoliberalism, its failure to deal humanely with the migrant crisis of the past decade and the active persecution of migrants and refugees by the European Union's border agency Frontex, which has only intensified in the wake of the COVID-19 pandemic.[54]

Finally, a comparable judgement might be passed upon the ecological convictions of *Penda's Fen*, so resonant in an era of accelerating climate change and proliferating zoonotic pandemics that epidemiological researchers have increasingly attributed to habitat destruction produced by capitalist expansionism.[55] Towards the end of the programme, Stephen and his father walk along a country lane at dusk in an exquisitely shot and moving scene that signals a new closeness following the revelation of Stephen's biological parentage. His adoptive father, who is the local vicar, takes the opportunity to confess to Stephen his increasingly heretical and dissident views; views that share much more with Arne's perspectives than was initially evident. After identifying the Latin root of 'pagan' as 'belonging to the village', he goes on to say:

> The Village is sneered at, as something petty. Petty it can be: yet it works. The scale is human, people can relate there. Man may in the nick of time revolt and save himself: revolt from the monolith, come back to the Village ... In this day of the mask, this day of Corporation Man – what shall the self do then, poor thing? But curl away in, from the poisoning wind; and dream.

There is something more than simple romanticism to this statement. Discussing the predominantly new middle-class Labour left that formed around Tony Benn in the 1970s and 1980s, Callinicos harshly but accurately sums up 'the preoccupations of this social milieu ... its weird mixture of pseudo-revolutionary rhetoric, parish-pump municipal politics, and feverish sexual experimentation'.[56] The sketch is oddly apposite to *Penda's Fen* too, comprising as it does Stephen's sexual enlightenment alongside a radical oppositionality that sees Stephen's father explicitly evoke Marx at one point, only to propose a parochial and individualist remedy to the profound social alienation he laments. As the attitudes of this milieu diffused and became incorporated into what Raymond Williams terms the dominant,[57] what was once called 'personal politics' has morphed into the convenient fallacy that 'ethical' individual consumer behaviour and 'sustainable' community initiatives may somehow address systemic ecological devastation perpetrated largely by, and in the economic interests of, multinational capital. Even those radical activists who have kept the faith over the years have been convincingly accused of a kind of 'folk politics' by Nick Srnicek and Alex Williams, defined as 'the guiding intuition that immediacy is always better and more authentic ... Folk politics typically remains reactive ... [it] chooses the familiarities of the past over the unknowns of the future ... and expresses itself as a predilection for the voluntarist and spontaneous.'[58]

All this, however, is to discount the key feature of the new middle class: its structural and thus political ambiguity. Recall that just as the politics of the new middle class are uncertain, so too are its utopian visions. We might equally view *Penda's Fen* as retaining a countercultural utopianism that allows for a radical questioning of the contemporary through desires unfulfillable in present social conditions, perhaps accounting for the programme's continuing allure. In this respect it is Marcusean: part of an increasingly mythic 'hauntological' recent cultural past serving as inspiration for Bloch's 'forward dreaming' in the present.[59] Importantly, this is facilitated by the class mixing entailed in its production, resulting at times in a harmonious blending of radical utopian sensibilities into a countercultural class consciousness with more clearly socialist aims.

The portrayal of Stephen's sexuality reminds us of an era in which the most advanced sections of gay liberation argued that true sexual freedom and egalitarianism would only be possible through an overhaul of the economic mode of production. Meanwhile the mythic deep dives of *Penda's Fen* provide cultural resources that might aid the building of a more egalitarian and inclusive national identity – a vital task for the left in an era that has seen a cynical ruling class re-boot the most reactionary notions of Britishness in response to the economic crises of recent years.

And Arne's dark suggestion that in the event of nuclear war, almost the entire civilian population may be considered 'strategically expendable' acknowledges that environmental destruction is in the short-term economic interests of a tiny minority. By implication, it hints that an active, collective consciousness and agency on the part of all those not part of this minority would be necessary to rescue the lovingly captured landscapes of *Penda's Fen* from the plague, plunder, and warfare of unchecked capitalist expansionism. This consciousness might very well be the 'sacred seed' that Arne evokes in nature mystic-cum-materialist terms, 'bedded in some hidden crack' and ready to sprout.

Notes

1. 'Far Out Frolics with Sir Richard Branson', *Viz* no. 289, October 2019, p. 25.
2. Slavoj Žižek, 'Nobody Has to Be Vile', *The London Review of Books*, 28(7), 6 April 2006. www.lrb.co.uk/the-paper/v28/n07/slavoj-zizek/nobody-has-to-be-vile (Last accessed 10 January 2022).
3. David Wilkinson, *Post-Punk, Politics and Pleasure in Britain* (Basingstoke: Palgrave Macmillan, 2016).
4. Fredric Jameson, *Postmodernism, or the Cultural Logic of Late Capitalism* (London: Verso, 1991), p. 160.
5. Ruth Levitas, *The Concept of Utopia* (London: Philip Allan, 1990), p. 8.
6. Ernst Bloch, *The Principle of Hope Volume One* [1959], trans. Neville Place, Stephen Plaice, and Paul Knight (Oxford: Blackwell, 1986), p. 4.
7. Bloch, Ibid., p. 5.
8. Ibid. p. 5.
9. Ibid. p. 7.
10. Herbert Marcuse, *An Essay on Liberation* [1969] (Harmondsworth: Penguin, 1972), p. 31.
11. Herbert Marcuse, *One Dimensional Man* [1964] (London: Routledge, 1991), pp. 62–3.
12. Fredric Jameson, 'Cognitive Mapping' in *The Jameson Reader*, ed. Michael Hardt, Kathi Weeks (Oxford: Blackwell, 2000), pp. 277–87 (p. 287).
13. Perry Anderson, *The Origins of Postmodernity* (London: Verso, 1998), p. 134.
14. Raymond Williams, 'Utopia and Science Fiction' in *Culture and Materialism: Selected Essays* (London: Verso, 2005), pp. 196–212 (p. 207).
15. John Clarke, Stuart Hall, Tony Jefferson, and Brian Roberts, 'Subcultures, Cultures and Class: A Theoretical Overview' in *Resistance Through Rituals: Youth Subcultures in Post-War Britain*, ed. Stuart Hall & Tony Jefferson (London: Hutchinson, 1976), pp. 9–74 (p. 65).
16. Clarke et al., 'Subcultures', pp. 63–5.
17. Fredric Jameson, *Signatures of the Visible* (London: Routledge, 1992), p. 29.
18. Clarke et al., 'Subcultures', pp. 67–8.

19. Ibid., p. 71.
20. See Andy Bennett, 'The Post-Subcultural Turn: Some Reflections Ten Years On', *Journal of Youth Studies* 14(5) (2011), pp. 493–506 for a summary of this tendency. Bennett asserts that any attempt to correlate class and counterculture is 'essentialist', evincing a somewhat utopian faith in youth culture's apparent capacity to 'transcend structural categories'.
21. Raymond Williams, *Culture* (Glasgow: Fontana, 1981), p. 74.
22. Brian Jackson and Dennis Marsden, *Education and the Working Class* (London: Pelican, 1966), p. 110.
23. 'Play for Today at 50'. www.bfi.org.uk/play-today-50 (Last accessed 11 January 2022).
24. *Performance*, dir. Nicholas Roeg (1970).
25. Jerry Whyte, 'Angels and Demons'. www.cineoutsider.com/reviews/bluray/p/pendas_fen_br.html (Last accessed 11 January 2022).
26. Peter Joyce, *The Policing of Protest, Disorder and International Terrorism in the UK since 1945: Britain in Comparative Perspective Since 1945* (Basingstoke: Palgrave Macmillan, 2016), p. 55.
27. Brian Robinson, 'A View from 1974' in *Of Mud & Flame: The Penda's Fen Sourcebook*, ed. Matthew Harle and James Machin (London: Strange Attractor Press, 2019), pp. 141–7 (p. 147).
28. Matthew Harle and James Machin, 'Child Be Strange: Excavating Penda's Fen' in *Of Mud & Flame: The Penda's Fen Sourcebook*, ed. Matthew Harle and James Machin (London: Strange Attractor Press, 2019), pp. 15–22 (p. 17). Notably, Ernest Mathijs and Jamie Sexton have pointed to the connections between the development of cult cinema and utopian desires. See Ernest Mathijs and Jamie Sexton, *Cult Cinema: An Introduction* (Oxford: Wiley-Blackwell, 2011), p. 131.
29. Lucy Robinson, *Gay Men and the Left in Post-War Britain: How the Personal Got Political* (Manchester: Manchester University Press, 2011).
30. Craig Wallace, 'The "Old, Primeval Demon of the Place Opening Half an Eye": Penda's Fen and the Legend of the Sleeping King' in *Of Mud & Flame: The Penda's Fen Sourcebook*, ed. Matthew Harle and James Machin (London: Strange Attractor Press, 2019), pp. 185–95 (p. 187).
31. Adam Scovell, 'And in the Soil, There Be Mirrors: Penda's Fen and Folk Horror' in *Of Mud & Flame*, ed. Matthew Harle and James Machin (London: Strange Attractor Press, 2019), pp. 83–8 (p. 83).
32. Alex Callinicos, 'The New Middle Class and Socialist Politics', *International Socialism* 2(20) (Summer 1983). www.marxists.org/history/etol/writers/callinicos/1983/xx/newmc.html (Last accessed 11 January 2022).
33. Val Burris, 'The Discovery of the New Middle Class', *Theory and Society*, 15(3) (May 1986), pp. 317–49.
34. Raymond Williams, *Marxism and Literature* (Oxford: Oxford University Press, 1977), pp. 128–35.

35. Raphael Samuel, 'The SDP and the New Middle Class' in *Island Stories: Unravelling Britain*, ed. Alison Light, Sally Alexander, and Gareth Stedman Jones (London: Verso, 1998), pp. 256–71 (p. 263).
36. Roger Luckhurst, 'Always Historicise? Penda's Fen in the 1970s' in *Of Mud & Flame: The Penda's Fen Sourcebook*, ed. Matthew Harle and James Machin (London: Strange Attractor Press, 2019), pp. 29–40 (p. 29).
37. Samuel, 'The SDP and the New Middle Class', p. 258.
38. Craig Wallace, 'To Make Visible the Inner State: Penda's Fen and the Films of Carl Theodore Dreyer' in *Of Mud & Flame: The Penda's Fen Sourcebook*, ed. Matthew Harle and James Machin (London: Strange Attractor Press, 2019), pp. 221–30 (p. 224).
39. Samuel, 'The SDP and the New Middle Class', p. 258.
40. Ibid. p. 265.
41. Luc Boltanski and Eve Chiapello, *The New Spirit of Capitalism* trans. Gregory Elliott [1999] (London: Verso, 2005), p. 97.
42. Jerry Whyte, 'Angels and Demons: Review of the BFI Release of *Penda's Fen* on DVD', *Cine Outsider*, 22 May 2016. www.cineoutsider.com/reviews/bluray/p/pendas_fen_br.html (Last accessed 11 March 2024).
43. Peter Stallybrass and Allon White, *The Politics and Poetics of Transgression* (Ithaca, NY: Cornell University Press, 1986), p. 156.
44. Alan Sinfield, *On Sexuality and Power* (New York: Columbia University Press, 2004), p. 141.
45. Raymond Williams, *Culture and Society 1780-1950* (Harmondsworth: Penguin, 1963), p. 313.
46. Christopher Douglas, 'Honeybone: Interview with Christopher Douglas' in *Of Mud & Flame: The Penda's Fen Sourcebook*, ed. Matthew Harle and James Machin (London: Strange Attractor Press, 2019), pp. 197–9 (p. 198).
47. Mark Wickham-Jones, 'Labour's trajectory in Foreign Affairs: The Moral Crusade of a Pivotal Power?' in *New Labour's Foreign Policy: A New Moral Crusade?*, ed. Richard Little and Mark Wickham-Jones (Manchester: Manchester University Press, 2000), pp. 4–33 (p. 26).
48. BBC News, 'Tony Blair's Speech in Full', 28 September 1999 http://news.bbc.co.uk/1/hi/uk_politics/460009.stm (Last accessed 12 January 2022).
49. Stephen Epstein, 'Gay Politics, Ethnic Identity' in *Forms of Desire*, ed. Edward Stein (New York: Routledge, 1992), pp. 239–95 (p. 282).
50. Andrew Milner, *Class* (London: SAGE, 1999), p. 166.
51. Jameson, *Postmodernism*, pp. 320–2, 330.
52. 'What Is Allyship? A Quick Guide', www.inclusiveemployers.co.uk/blog/quick-guide-to-allyship/?cn-reloaded=1 (Last accessed 20 October 2023).
53. David Alderson, *Sex, Needs & Queer Culture: From Liberation to the Post-Gay* (London: Zed Books, 2016), p. 90.
54. Lorenzo Tondo, 'Revealed: 2,000 Refugee Deaths Linked to Illegal EU Pushbacks', *The Guardian*, 5 May 2021. www.theguardian.com/global-development/2021/may/05/revealed-2000-refugee-deaths-linked-to-eu-pushbacks (Last accessed 12 January 2024).

55. John Vidal, 'Tip of the Iceberg: Is Our Destruction of Nature Responsible for Covid-19?', *The Guardian*, 18 March 2020. www.theguardian.com/environment/2020/mar/18/tip-of-the-iceberg-is-our-destruction-of-nature-responsible-for-covid-19-aoe (Last accessed 20 October 2023).
56. Callinicos, 'The New Middle Class and Socialist Politics', n. pag.
57. Raymond Williams, 'Dominant, Residual, and Emergent' in *Marxism and Literature* (Oxford: Oxford University Press, 1977), pp. 121–7.
58. Nick Srnicek and Alex Williams, *Inventing the Future: Postcapitalism and a World Without Work* (London: Verso, 2015), p. 11.
59. I define 'hauntology' here following the work of Mark Fisher, as 'nostalgia for all the futures that were lost' with the onset of neoliberal postmodernity. See Mark Fisher, 'The Metaphysics of Crackle: Afrofuturism and Hauntology', *dancecult: Journal of Electronic Dance Music Culture*, 5(2) (2013), pp. 42–55 (p. 45).

CHAPTER 6

Staging Utopian Subjects
Contemporary British Theatre beyond the Barriers

Siân Adiseshiah

Introduction: Theatre as a Utopian Laboratory

Utopianism registers the prevailing social arrangement as inadequate and unacceptable, and insists that life could, and should, be significantly better. A radical application of utopianism produces opportunities to think expansively about identity, personhood, and subjectivity. It enables movement beyond the familiar liberal humanist fiction of the individual versus the collective, a fiction crucial to anti-utopian rhetoric, which purports that the rights of the individual are undermined in a utopianism focused on the collective.[1] Poststructuralist theory has taught us that the individual is a fiction, and yet, rather than leading to a new politics of affiliation and connectedness, our increased perception of power and difference has only deepened suspicion of collectivity. But if we build on the fictionality of the individual within the framework of utopian thinking, that strengthens the critique of existing structures of power and privilege, whilst simultaneously making visible the possibility for new forms of social relationality. Reimagining selves and others in radically different constellations – as inter-subjectively interlaced within networks of mutual dependency and care – potentially enables routes out of dominant formulations of political identity.

Theatre offers fertile forms and practices for experimenting with the politics of social relationality. An aesthetic mix of multiple sign systems, theatre's dynamic is simultaneously a political demonstration: performers on stage in social scenarios playing roles in front of audiences. It offers, as Diana Knight observes, 'a sort of laboratory for constructing the liberated social space of utopia'.[2] The political potential of the social and practical dimensions of theatre have been harnessed throughout its history, as exemplified in the twentieth century by Bertolt Brecht's deployment of the *Verfremdungseffekt*, which offered audiences a charged fusing of historical critique and revolutionary possibility. Brazilian theatre practitioner Augusto Boal and his Theatre of the Oppressed offered a similarly politically potent dramaturgical methodology, which mined the social character of theatre for its ability to facilitate political consciousness through practical demonstration and role playing. Boal's conception of what he called the 'spect-actor' for instance, conjoins spectator and actor to engender an agentic participant conscious of their role in theatre's ideological production and consumption.

Brecht's project of interpellating audiences into critical spectators, and Boal's coinage of the agentic 'spect-actor', have both had a direct influence on contemporary British theatre. Since the 1970s, British socialist and feminist playwrights have developed innovative dramaturgical and aesthetic strategies for experimenting with politically radical subjectivities. Prominent examples include the work of Caryl Churchill, Timberlake Wertenbaker, Bryony Lavery, Nell Dunn, Pam Gems, Winsome Pinnock, Edward Bond, David Hare, David Edgar, and Howard Brenton, who have variously found innovative ways to critique capitalism, stage hidden histories, and amplify marginalised voices. As part of a wider movement within Britain of alternative theatre making, which sought to challenge mainstream bourgeois theatre conventions and practices, a number of radical touring theatre collectives were formed in the late 1960s, 1970s, and 1980s. For example, with Tony Bicât, David Hare founded the Portable Theatre Company in 1968, which prioritised new work and, as the name indicates, took theatre out of established venues. Aided by the abolition of theatre censorship in 1968, this kind of theatre sought to interrupt mainstream narratives and shake audiences out of ideological complacency. Through the 1970s and 1980s a number of playwrights, including Churchill, Brenton, and Hare worked with Joint Stock Theatre Company, which used what became a distinctive approach of the company, the 'Joint Stock Method': gathering materials from a range of sources, including community testimony, to inform the writing process prior to workshopping the script writing with actors. The radical collective, Monstrous Regiment, was another key initiative: a feminist theatre company that staged productions from the 1970s to the early 1990s, by playwrights such as Churchill and Lavery, of work that put women's lives centre stage. Many of these theatre collectives attempted to practise what they preached, by, for example, pursuing anti-racist and anti-sexist policies in their internal structures, and implementing forms of pay parity.

Despite these experiments in radical theatre practice, utopian theatre has been historically neglected within the fields of both utopian studies and theatre studies. Exceptions include Dragan Klaić's *The Plot of the Future: Utopia and Dystopia in Modern Drama* published in 1991.[3] This was followed by a long hiatus before the publication of Jill Dolan's highly influential *Utopia in Performance: Finding Hope at the Theater* (2005), which analyses a range of contemporary performances in terms of their production of an affective experience of utopian spectatorship. Dolan establishes the potential of performance to prompt utopian feeling in audiences: 'a hopeful feeling of what the world might be like if every moment of our lives were as emotionally voluminous, generous, aesthetically striking, and intersubjectively intense'.[4] She makes a powerful argument for the potential of performance to inspire a collective form of hope for a better future. José Esteban Muñoz's *Cruising Utopia: The Then and There of Queer Futurity* (2009) responds to the critique of reproductive futurism dominant within queer studies (as exemplified by Lee Edelman's *No Future: Queer Theory and the Death Drive* (2004)) with a retheorisation of queer as utopian: his opening lines are 'queerness is not yet here. Queerness is an ideality. Put another way, we are not yet queer.'[5] Muñoz's case studies are aesthetic works that range across theatre, performance, writing, film, dance, nightlife, political activism, and public sex. Pursuing notions of queer temporality and a Blochian theory of critical hope, he tracks the potential of a queer collectivity.

Cross-fertilisation between theatre studies and utopian studies is, thankfully, now beginning to gather pace,[6] but has been strikingly slow to appear in scholarship. This sluggishness is apparent in the *Palgrave Handbook of Utopian and Dystopian Literatures* (2022), which contains fifty-six chapters, not a single one of which is dedicated to theatre. This neglect, I would suggest, is due to two factors: firstly, the hackneyed equation of drama with conflict and utopia with harmony assumes that the politico-aesthetic DNA of drama makes it incompatible with utopian positivity; secondly, the scenographic and bodily limitations of humans on stage in performance is a phenomenological constraint on the utopian propensity to imagine society otherwise. Apparently, the novel's use of the more abstract semiotics of language is better at articulating the otherworldly than the cumbersome sign systems of bodies on stage. These assumptions have led to an under-appreciation of the distinctive affordances of theatre for a utopian politics.

Thus, in this context, I am keen to make visible the ways in which examples from contemporary theatre exploit the distinctive characteristics of drama and performance to interrupt contemporary figurations of the future as either voyeuristically apocalyptic, or as no longer existent (a continuous present with no horizon). I am especially interested in the potential of these theatre examples to register and incite forms of subjectivity and personhood that resist dominant epistemological frames and anticipate alternative systemic arrangements. New writing for the stage, as well as post-dramatic and experimental work includes multiple examples of this: dramaturgies breaking with existing models of the subject, seeking out ways to figure selfhood and social relationality differently, and re-wiring the dramaturgical processes of spectator interpellation.[7]

I have written elsewhere about British contemporary experimental theatre's interest in the New Sincerity: in the ways in which theatre and performance afford opportunities for prompting a post-ironic connectedness amongst performers and spectators over the challenge to imagine different ways of living.[8] For example, the Sheffield-based theatre ensemble, Forced Entertainment, collaborates with artists to make new work that encourages audiences to re-think the world, their location within it, and their relationships with others. Other contemporary British plays we might describe as utopian include Uninvited Guest's performance piece from 2006, *It Is Like It Ought to Be: A Pastoral*, the theatre of Suspect Culture (as eloquently exemplified by Dan Reballato),[9] Joel Horwood's play *This Changes Everything* (2015), and the work of the playwright and theatre maker, Andy Smith. Smith's most recent project is called 'Plays for the People' (2021), plays written to be read by spectator performers – groups of friends meeting in person or online – and designed to be followed by a reflection on the issues contained therein and the experience of participation.[10] These examples are not utopias as such, but they are interested in marshalling the flexibility of experimental theatre to explore utopian ideas and desires.

In the next section of this chapter, I focus on dramatic works by two London-based Black British playwrights who also direct, produce, and perform: debbie tucker green and Mojisola Adebayo. The former is acclaimed as one of the most significant theatre makers of the contemporary period, and has had her work staged at major public venues for new writing: Hampstead Theatre, Royal Court Theatre, National Theatre, and the New Vic. She also writes and makes films. Adebayo's work is increasingly commanding the attention of scholars,[11] students, and theatre audiences, as well as appearing on university syllabi. With an emphasis on solo performances, Adebayo's work has been performed at new writing venues such as the Bush Theatre, the Lyric Hammersmith, the Young Vic, and the Oval House

Theatre (now called Brixton House). Both women produce distinctive work that combines a singular dramaturgy with a transformative politics that shifts the framing of spectatorial perspective. The utopian in tucker green's work is felt through an uncompromising refusal of the prevailing arrangement of social power. Selves and others are stuck in repetitive, circular rhythms and structures that prevent a more equal, just, or productive connectedness. In Adebayo's work, utopian possibility forms part of the affective spectatorial encounter with her theatre: conventional fictions of identity are dismantled as energising and nurturing castings of identification connect, spark, and cross-pollinate in surprising and galvanising ways. Both tucker green and Adebayo are known for making innovative, experimental, and poetical work inspired by music, and at the intersection of aesthetics and politics, but they are at the same time markedly dissimilar to each other: tucker green is known for her stylishly poetic, spare, and rage-full exposure and refusal of the logics of racial capitalism, Adebayo for a fluid storytelling that blends and reshapes identities primed for alternative imaginaries.

Something's Missing: debbie tucker green's Dramaturgy of Refusal

'Something's missing' (*etwas fehlt*) is a phrase spoken by the fictional lumberjack Paul Ackermann (renamed Jimmy Mahoney in later productions) in Brecht's opera *The Rise and Fall of the City of Mahoganny* (1928–9). Mahoganny is a fictional American city, a capitalist paradise – hedonistic and awash with money. In scene 8, Paul speaks the line 'but something is missing' four times. This suggestive phrase is used to form the title of a conversation between Ernst Bloch and Theodor Adorno, originally aired on radio in Germany in 1964, about the contradictions of utopian longing. They discuss ways in which utopian longing has been co-opted by capital through technological innovation and consumption solutions, a process that interpellates human desire as satiated by commodity fetishism, where the pleasures of ownership are prioritised over the substance of existence, or, in other words: *having* is prized at the expense of *being*.

The difficulty of creating utopian content uncompromised by the anti-utopian conditions of the prevailing arrangement of power forms a key problematic in Bloch and Adorno's 'Something's missing' conversation. Elsewhere, Bloch appends 'something is missing' (via analysis of Goethe's *Faust*) with the proposition that 'the fair moment is yet to come', which he locates as part of a 'dialectical journey in which every pleasure attained is defeated by a separate new desire which awakens within it'.[12] However, in the case of Adorno, it is his theory of negative dialectics (fully outlined in his *opus grandis Negative Dialektik* (1966)) that informs his approach to 'something's missing'. The negative dialectic underpins Adorno's reframing of the Marxist-Hegelian dialectic to generalise the logic of the negation of the negation: the positive outcome afforded by the process of negation in the Marxist-Hegelian formulation is figured exclusively in terms of negation by Adorno. This avoids producing a positivistic reproduction of what already exists, whilst at the same time recognising that there is a hole in the whole: something's missing.

One of the most recognisable elements of debbie tucker green's political signature is her unremitting insistence that something is missing. The thing that is absent, lacking, wanting, does not appear in phenomenological form in her plays, but its omittance is seen, heard, felt, and understood, particularly at the level of subjectivity, where her characters are hard – hardened by their inhospitable surroundings – and equally hard to countenance by others, including the audience. Her plays reveal the deadliness of existing society and its histories, and dramatise – through a cruel intimacy – a hard-to-bear encounter with the brutality of our political contemporary. For Adorno, utopia functions as 'the determined negation of that which merely is'.[13] tucker green's work is this disavowal, a rude refusal, of the present in favour of an arrangement that differs categorically from the status quo. tucker green's negation might also be likened to Herbert Marcuse's concept of 'the Great Refusal', which he described as 'the protest against that which is'.[14] Marcuse understood this as a complete refusal of the means of post-industrial capitalist society and its operational practices. To refuse is simultaneously to develop a new sensibility, to pursue the life instinct in place of aggression towards others, the achievement of which demands new forms of subjectivity. tucker green's utopianism is best illuminated as a negation and refusal of what is, a puncturing of the prevailing epistemological frame to get to what ought to be, whose content is undescribed, and whose existence is without guarantee.

tucker green's plays are bracing, abrasive, and impolite: 'Change don't give-a-fuck change gone do its thing with or without you' says a character called Young Adult in her powerful 2018 state-of the-nation play *ear for eye*.[15] A play about the necropolitics of racial capitalism on both sides of the Atlantic, *ear for eye* filled the main stage of the Royal Court of its premier production with Black actors: fifteen of a total cast of sixteen. This itself was a charged, enlivening experience, an encounter whose uniqueness made clear the violent normality of compulsory whiteness. The violence of whiteness forms the material conditions of the play, and is there in the first scene, where an African American mother tries to inculcate her son in ways of diminishing his presence to avoid being shot by police. No hands up (threatening), no showing palms (inflammatory / aggressive), no hands down (belligerent / attitude), no hands in pockets (obscuring / cocky), no hands together (sarcastic / challenging), no hands behind back (arrogance / insolence / ignorance / defiance), no gesturing (antagonistic), no shrugging (ignorant / hostile), no looking at them (confrontational / audacious), no looking away (evasive / elusive / ambiguous), and no turning away (impudence / disobedience / impertinence). The only gesture that might save him, 'looking at the floor', is a deep humiliation that his mother struggles to tolerate: '*hell no,* we didn't raise you to look at no floor, Son'.[16] There is no subject position beyond debased degradation that has a chance of inoculation against white violence, this crushing humiliation fuelling a Black rage that forms the affective economy of much of tucker green's work.[17]

Another of tucker green's works that demonstrates the impossibility of being interpellated as a respected subject within the current political system, particularly for Black people, is her 2016 play *hang*. It includes a cast of three characters, named One, Two, and Three, and in the *dramatis personae* Three is described as a Black woman, and One and Two can be '*of any race*'.[18] It is a one-set play that marshals a heightened realism mixed with tucker green's signature style of pared down poetic and rhythmical dialogue, this combined for the first time in tucker green's *oeuvre* with the temporal dislocation and uncanny estrangement of dystopian science fiction: the play is set '*Nearly now*' and capital punishment is state policy in the United Kingdom.[19] The play presents two intolerable scenarios (for the liberal/left spectator at least): state execution, the horror of which is strengthened through the banality of its bureaucratic processing, and the extreme trauma suffered by Three, who, it is inferred, has been violently sexually assaulted in her own home by a white man, which was witnessed by her disempowered husband and children. She has had to wait three years for her attacker's execution, the method of which she is to decide (hence, the title of the play). The refusal of the play to countenance a negotiable solution within the current structures of power is shown by its making the prospect of justice for Three dependent on the state execution of her attacker.

tucker green's 2005 play *stoning mary*, first performed at the Royal Court, is similarly uncompromising in its radical negation. It is an interweaving of three stories specific to sub-Saharan Africa: a husband and wife fight over one prescription they both need (the inference is it is HIV-related); a mother and father bicker about their child soldier son; and two sisters quarrel on a prison visit where one (the titular Mary) is held whilst waiting for her execution by stoning. We later discover that the child soldier killed the husband and wife of part one; the husband and wife were Mary and her sister's parents; and in revenge Mary killed the child soldier, which resulted in her death sentence. The audacious conceit in the play is that, as the stage directions inform us, '*All characters are white*'.[20] The audience is interpellated as racist: Black narratives from the Global South need to be performed by white people to be legible as crises for white audiences to care about. That the stories are inescapably entangled in a fatalistic drive towards Mary's stoning coupled with a sustained assault on the audience as racist/whites produces a dramaturgy of refusal (of how things are) whose refusal at the same time assumes a critical form of hope as its implication.

This refusal runs through all tucker green's work. It is a wilful negation of what is, or 'willful', as Trish Reid (following Sara Ahmed) writes it – to retain the stubbornly defiant 'will' of the American spelling. Reid reads tucker green as a willful subject and her dramaturgy as a willful practice that 'vehemently exposes uncomfortable connections between the subjective and the social'.[21] Her plays are not only acts of exposure though; they are refusals, categorical rejections or repudiations of the current socio-political frame. The perverse obstinacy of the work's willfulness is felt in its sustained insistence on non-cooperation with the current idiom, and this includes not just non-compliance with the expectations of racial capitalism, but equally a rebuttal of liberal left discourses that are formed from existing political grammars. When Mary is made aware by her sister that 'not even the women' marched for her, she issues forth an explosive invective against all 'bitches': 'feminist bitches', 'black bitches', 'brown bitches', 'rebel bitches', 'underclass bitches', 'overclass bitches', 'political bitches', 'bitches that love to study', or 'the full-uppa-attitude bitches', a speech that runs over three pages.[22] The uncomfortable charge of that speech – the repeated pejorative use of 'bitch' in the white, middle-class space of the Royal Court – would have produced, as Maggie Inchley observes, 'an affective judder'.[23] The decisive blow is to feminism as an inclusive sisterhood. The stinging discomfort of *stoning mary* is felt in the bruising effects of racial capitalism but equally in the play's furious indictment of the absence of (an anti-racist, anti-colonial) feminist solidarity.

tucker green's characters are often spiky, truculent, and confrontational – both to each other and to spectators. This belligerence is in part their refusal

6 Staging Utopian Subjects   127

to be assimilated into pacifying structures and processes. But it is also indicative of a tendency in her work to bring into view the stultifying, distorted, and delimited forms of subjectivity available to her characters, who are frequently working class, often Black, and usually women. In *hang*, the character Three's attempt to hold on to her dignity is legible as awkward and uncooperative, despite her having experienced horrendous trauma and having to endure a protracted banal interview with bureaucrats. Mary's only moment of agency in *stoning mary* – 'I done something. Least I done something. I done something – I did' was her killing the child soldier, an infanticidal act of justice that leads to her own execution.[24] Characters in *ear to eye* are keenly alert to the impossibility of themselves. In scene 3, a Black British woman, relaying her experience of police custody, describes being accused of '"bein aggressive" when I weren't', of '"acting aggressive" when I weren't', and of '"talkin aggressive" which I weren't'.[25] As I have previously written (with Jacqueline Bolton), tucker green's work always withholds resolution at fundamental levels (ethical, political, and ontological), and in doing so produces 'an aggressive but energising demand for a different form of relationality'.[26] Resonant of Marcuse's Great Refusal, the utopianism of tucker green's indignant rebuffing of social discourse is precipitated by what is missing: everything should be different, subjectivity should be entirely otherwise.

   tucker green's radical negation of the political system, its social arrangement and cultural practices, extends to a recognition of the always already compromised toolbox for a politics of liberation. This is resonant of the famous statement by Audre Lorde, 'the master's tools will never dismantle the master's house', which forms the title of one of her short essays.[27] How is the master's house to be dismantled when the tools to undertake it are so conditioned and compromised? This question is as urgent as it is unanswerable. tucker green's dramaturgy sustains two propositions: one, that things are utterly and irremediably fucked, and two, that the damage, pain, and injustice experienced (by the marginalised and racialised in particular) are unbearable and deathly. It is in the interaction between these two propositions that a critical form of utopian hope emerges, a hope that despite the overwhelming power of what is, is inescapably present in expressions of refusal. tucker green's work might be understood in terms of a metaphor Bloch uses of 'clearing the table', the act of ridding existing clutter in turn creates space for a new arrangement, the longing for which is part of the clearing. For Bloch, utopian longing can be 'completely without consideration at all for the content';[28] tucker green's dramaturgy resonates with this: her work does not present audiences with utopian images of potential collectivity, but makes us painfully aware of the irredeemable distortion of available forms of life within contemporary neoliberal capitalism.

Beyond the Barriers: The Transformative Energies of Mojisola Adebayo's Theatre

In Mojisola Adebayo's work, there are glimpses or felt moments of utopian content. For Bloch 'the essential function of utopia is a critique of what is present' but, and this is an important component of this idea, 'if we had not already gone beyond the barriers, we could not even perceive them as barriers'.[29] tucker green rails at the barriers: her work is essentially a radical repudiation of the world as epistemologically and ontologically circumscribed. Adebayo's work, on the other hand, breaks through them – a little at least. Her dramaturgy's transformative energies articulate not an ideal life *per se*, but foretastes of alternative possibilities, transitory previews of powerful articulations of Black, queer, de-colonial forms of intersubjectivity. This is a utopian theatrical experience that is fleeting and oblique, but – following Bloch – there is always a utopian residue that continues to foment, which can lead to transformative change. As Michael R. Ott observes in his discussion of Adorno and Bloch's exchanges on utopian dialectics, 'utopia is not conceived of as a place but a living dialectical praxis through which the possibility of a more utopic society is created'.[30] A living dialectical utopian praxis is a fitting description of Adebayo's theatre.

Where tucker green's dramaturgy animates subjects as stifled, hardened, diminished, and traumatised, Adebayo repurposes different facets of (often marginalised) identities to exploit the potential benefits of collectivity. However, this is not at the expense of difference. Audre Lorde calls for difference to be 'seen as a fund of necessary polarities between which our creativity can spark like a dialectic'. She sees this as having the potential to undo the signification of interdependency as threatening: 'Only within that interdependency of different strengths, acknowledged and equal, can the power to seek new ways of being in the world generate, as well as the courage and sustenance to act where there are no charters.'[31] It is primarily through character, performance, and identity that Adebayo's experiments with utopian castings of subjectivity are politically freighted.

Her subtle, supple investigations of the ways in which theatre can evoke utopian forms of inter-subjectivity is likely informed by Adebayo's identity as a Black South Londoner, mixed race ('London born, Nigerian/ Danish'),[32] and lesbian. A playwright, director, producer, performer, and facilitator, Adebayo prioritises working with people who are 'young, Black, Asian, D/deaf, disabled, HIV+, homeless, slum dwellers, living under occupation, incarcerated, in children's homes, affected by the criminal justice system, female survivors of gender based violence, elders'.[33] She is trained in the Theatre of the Oppressed having worked extensively with Augusto Boal, and she was a performer with Black Mime Theatre. Formed in 1987 by David Boxer and Sarah Cahn as an all-male company, by 1991 Black Mime Theatre had expanded from a small London-based company to a national touring theatre. A Black Mime Women's Troupe was formed in 1990, and in 1992, under the direction of Denise Wong and with the help of Arts Council franchise funding, the two groups were merged. Adebayo does not feel particularly connected to Western theatre traditions, but instead to an African diasporic aesthetic, including call-and-response and other African performance techniques: 'We don't seem to have a dividing line where speech becomes song.'[34] Her work melds a fluid storytelling with poeticism, physical theatre, and use of multi-media to create richly textured performance works.

Moj of the Antarctic (2006) was Adebayo's first major production for the stage. Written and performed by Adebayo, and co-created with the Antarctic Collective, it was first presented at the Lyric Hammersmith in November 2006, and later developed at the Oval House Theatre, London. The play adapts the story of Ellen Craft, an African American enslaved woman who, in 1848, disguised herself as a white man, and escaped slavery in the state of Georgia to come to England. Adebayo queers the narrative of Ellen Craft as recounted in *Running a Thousand Miles for Freedom: The Escape of William and Ellen Craft from Slavery* (1860). She introduces a lesbian love affair with a fellow slave, and a pub scene with Willy Black, a Black Scottish trans man based on a real Black woman who, in 1815, disguised herself as a sailor, called herself William Brown, and served in the Navy for over a decade. The protagonist Moj (a character based on a splicing of Ellen Craft and Adebayo) becomes the first Black woman to travel to Antarctica. The play is a thrillingly anarchic re-telling, where boundary blurring and border transgression inform a fresh dramaturgical adventure.

Moj of the Antarctic is an invigorating mix of Adebayo's solo performance of multiple roles, along with the use of multimedia – film, image, and music. As Suzanne Scafe notes, Adebayo draws on a call-and-response schematic to structure her engagement with the biography of Ellen Craft and the genre of the slave narrative, seeing in Adebayo's approach a purposeful linking of her work 'to the performative elements of those narratives, to the traditions of African American blues performances, and to African diasporic religious practices'.³⁵ The musical roots of call-and-response inform a layering of musical and vocal interventions that together create a conversation: a melody is produced in a phrase that is then replied to by a second phrase, which completes the articulation. This strategy structures *Moj of the Antarctic* in multiple ways, including in its interpellation of spectators, who are written into the script and prompted to communicate with Moj:

> No white or . . . *(She prompts the audience to respond.)* black
> No male or . . . *(She prompts the audience to respond.)* female
> No God or . . . *(She prompts the audience to respond.)* Devil
> Magic!³⁶

This curation positions self and other in a dialectical movement which – whilst not resolved as such – produces a temporary escape from dominant fictions of subjectivity.

The jouissance of this experience culminates in a scene where Moj/Adebayo invites the audience to help her transform into a white man, including putting '*flour on her face*', rubbing '*her chin with a cheese grater to make it rougher*', contemplating (but deciding against) slicing '*her bottom with a carving knife*', ironing '*her hair straight*', and making '*a penis from dough – badly. Gives dough to a female audience member to help her in the task.*'³⁷ This is, as Lynette Goddard notes, 'hilarious in production'.³⁸ Adebayo marks human subjectivity as diminished under racial capitalism – as reduced, squeezed, crushed, distorted in a similar spirit to tucker green – but Adebayo's dramaturgy discovers ways of slipping through the cracks in what seems like an immutable frame. Her refiguration of the subject, subject positioning, and inter-subjectivity produces an exuberant sociality, whose utopian agency gestures beyond the coordinates of our political contemporary.

A more recent play of Adebayo's – *STARS* (2019) – continues this melding of uncompromising critique of the prevailing system with foretastes of utopian subjectivity.³⁹ *STARS* was created in 2016 during a residency with *Idle Women*, a collaborative arts and social justice project formed in 2015 and based in Lancashire that seeks to create 'vibrant and adventurous spaces with and for all women'. Their radical approach to creative practice contains a utopian anticipatory consciousness as they seek to reach 'beyond the horizon' and create 'transformative spaces for women that can't be cut, closed or taken away'.⁴⁰ *STARS* originated as a staged reading downstairs at Ovalhouse Theatre in London (June 2018), followed by work-in-progress at the Unity Theatre, Liverpool (November 2019) as

6 *Staging Utopian Subjects* 131

part of Homotopia Festival (the UK's longest running LGBTQIA arts and culture festival). Having been postponed more than once due to the Covid-19 pandemic, *STARS* (this time appearing with the subtitle '*An Afrofuturist Space Odyssey*') was performed at the Institute of Contemporary Arts (ICA) in London as part of a Tamasha and ICA co-production in April and May 2023.[41] *STARS* is another monodrama: a single performer (Adebayo in the video recording and Debra Michaels in the ICA production) plays a Black octogenarian woman called 'Mrs' who seeks her first orgasm, which leads to her embarking on an extra-terrestrial adventure. As well as playing the character Mrs, the performer plays lots of other roles, and she is joined by a second performer who plays her son, DJ Michael Manners (Adebayo's brother DJ DeboA of Mix 'n' Sync' in the video recording, and Bradley Charles in the ICA production). Michael spins discs (mostly experimental electronic dance music) through the entirety of the performance, and participates in occasional exchanges with his mother. The play is distinctive for its use of multi-media including projection of animation sequences. Issues of access are central to, and integrated with, the play's aesthetics: the published script acknowledges contributions from D/deaf community consultants; the video recording includes an onstage BSL interpreter; and the animation sequences in both productions are accompanied by voiceovers, subtitles, and creative captioning. Arts access workers, FGM consultancy, and an intersex community consultant are also listed in the published text as part of the creative team. The play's anticipatory consciousness of an altogether different personal-political materiality undergirds every element of its production. As Goddard notes, *STARS* 'bridge[s] gaps between art and activism, community and professional theatre, blackness, disability and queerness'.[42] In this way, Mojisola's utopianism is as central to the material conditions of production as it is to its collaborative methods and aesthetics.

The key relationship in the play is between two Black female characters (Mrs and Mary), and is both intergenerational and intercultural. Mary, Mrs' neighbour, is 'of African descent'.[43] Her real name is Maryam, but she uses 'Mary' as a defensive attempt to reduce instances of Islamophobia. She has undergone FGM, and she finds it painful to urinate, and regularly visits Mrs' house to use her toilet. A single actor's performance of both Mrs and Mary breaks the link that binds individual bodies to distinct selfhoods. In her analysis of *Moj of the Antarctic*, Deirdre Osborne states, 'from a single source is created many tributaries. The self-knowledge obtained from the "I"-monologic and the "I"-polyphonic produces a self as correlated with other(s') meanings.'[44] This insight likewise elucidates *STARS*, where multiple modes of subjectivity, affiliation, and sociality break through the delimiting binary of individual/collective. These alternative castings of human relationality produce prefigurations of an alternative sensibility.

The play's disentanglement of bodies and subjectivities is facilitated by the effects of one performer playing multiple roles. Osborne states, 'For black writers, the "I am" of the *cogito* philosophies is not a certain foundation, for, both as citizens and artists, it is fraught with the legacies of "you are".'[45] In *STARS* more than a dozen first-person speaking positions are produced and then disbanded as the performer moves from Mrs with a '*South East London accent*'[46] through Mary's '*RP English but as a second language, with a faint memory of somewhere in Africa – non-specific*',[47] '*the young blood from the estate*',[48] '*an English scholar*',[49] Mrs' mum's '*Jamaican, gentle*'[50] accent, and Terry's '*white, cockney, Jack-the-Lad*'[51] accent via many other subjectivities and accents. The result is a radical loosening of the structure of subject formation, which leads to unanticipated intersubjective encounters in the process. This is further strengthened by the play's deployment of Afrofuturist aesthetics, which, as Alex Zamalin in *Black Utopia* (2019) describes, 'both revise history and imagine impossible trajectories of black freedom'.[52] The published play opens, as the stage directions note, with a ritual: a male performer dressed in '*robes and a hat that resonate with the culture of Dogon, Mali*' and a female performer representing '*the Nommo – an African androgynous anthro-amphibian space traveller*'.[53] These characters are 'extraterrestrial Afro-hermaphrodite anthro-amphibian migrants',[54] which, in their dismantling of binaries, transgressive forms of subjectivity, and traversals of spatial and temporal borders, are similar to Harawayan cyborgs. Indeed, Mrs exhibits her own Harawayan traits: like the cyborg she is an orphan (a 'throwaway baby of a runaway English wife and a black American G.I.'),[55] and she 'does not dream of community on the model of the organic family', but is still 'needy for connection'.[56] The key connection in the play – between Mrs and Mary – replaces the white heteronormative unit of reproductive futurism (famously critiqued by Lee Edelman) with queer Black intercultural and intergenerational kinship.[57] This intervention aligns with a 'politics of regenerative cyborgs' where 'bonds of affinity, solidarity, and kin-making replace those of blood, property, and nation', a utopian praxis proposed by eco-communist collective Out of the Woods.[58]

Conclusion

tucker green's work simmers with indignation in its unremitting insistence that something is missing. Her plays demand attention for their disavowal of conciliation with a terminally unjust system, and for their profound refusal of the way things are. The characters that populate her stage – hurt, recalcitrant, hostile – expound with forceful clarity the warped subject positions available to people under capitalism, the illegibility of marginalised communities (particularly Black people) within current systems of intelligibility, and the subsequent diminished prospects for a liveable life. tucker green's dramaturgy – with resonances of Adorno's negative dialectics – intervenes powerfully and provocatively in public discourse: its radical negation of present circumstances brings with it – in an evocation of Marcuse's Great Refusal – a utopian hope for the potential of something else. This is a critical form of hope, a hope that is, as Bloch proposes, 'the opposite of security' and 'the opposite of naïve optimism', where 'the category of danger is always within it'.[59]

Adebayo's work similarly refuses the current terms of social discourse. Yet her plays experiment creatively with aspects of marginalised identities, figuring subjectivities as adjustable or liquescent, a process that produces a spry and resourceful form of solidarity – what Kodwo Eshun calls '*fluid*arity'.[60] The openness of connection in her plays – the mutability of subject positions as they shift and spark – helps to push through the barriers and allows audiences fleeting previews of alternative ways of being in the world. For Adebayo theatre is 'the art of human relationships in space – in the now, it is the art of being human on planet earth – together, it is the art of dialogue in the sense of working things out with one another (with or without words), it is the art of *ubuntu* – to quote the Southern African philosophy of humanity, empathy, understanding, and compassion, which broadly means 'I am me through you and you are you through me' or to quote Muhammed Ali: 'Me, We'.[61] Adebayo's likening of theatre to the art of *ubuntu* illuminates theatre's capacity to experiment with alternative forms of human connection, its potential to be both sensitive to the diversity of human histories and experiences at the same time as exploring the intersubjective potential of 'me, we'.

Notes

1. See Karl Popper, 'Utopian and Violence', *World Affairs (Washington)*, 149(1) (1986), pp. 3–9; and John Gray, *Black Mass: Apocalyptic Religion and the Death of Utopia* (London: Allen Lane, 2007).
2. Diana Knight, *Barthes and Utopia: Space, Travel, Writing* (Oxford: Clarendon Press, 1997), p. 22.

3. However, Klaić's book, as its title signals, attends to utopias *and dystopias*. In fact, much more attention is paid to dystopias. The book also focuses on male-authored work and pays particular attention to Eastern European playwrights.
4. Jill Dolan, *Utopia in Performance: Finding Hope at the Theater* (Ann Arbor: University of Michigan Press, 2005), p. 5.
5. José Esteban Muñoz, *Cruising Utopia: The Then and There of Queer Futurity*, rev. ed. (New York: New York University Press, 2019), p. 1.
6. A number of books published in the last decade consider the utopian potential of theatre. See Joanne Tompkins, *Theatre's Heterotopias: Performance and the Cultural Politics of Space* (Basingstoke: Palgrave, 2014); Cathy Turner, *Dramaturgy and Architecture: Theatre, Utopia and the Built Environment* (Basingstoke: Palgrave, 2015); Selina Busby, *Applied Theatre: A Pedagogy of Utopia* (London: Bloomsbury, 2021); and Siân Adiseshiah, *Utopian Drama: In Search of a Genre* (London: Methuen Drama Bloomsbury, 2023). From within theatre studies, a conference took place called 'Dystopian/Utopian Theatre in Britain after 2000 and Its Political Spaces' organised by the University of Bielefeld in March 2021, whilst at the Utopian Studies Society Conference (Europe) held at the University of Brighton in July 2022 there were, for the first time, three theatre/performance panels.
7. See Cristina Delgado-García, *Rethinking Character in Contemporary British Theatre: Aesthetics, Politics, Subjectivity* (Berlin: De Gruyter, 2015) for an excellent exploration of the ways in which British playwrights Sarah Kane, Tim Crouch, and Ed Thomas upturn conventional figurations of subjectivity to experiment with character beyond individuality.
8. Siân Adiseshiah, 'Spectatorship and the New (Critical) Sincerity: The Case of Forced Entertainment's *Tomorrow's Parties*', *Journal of Contemporary Drama in English*, 4(1) (2016), pp. 180–95.
9. Dan Rebellato, '"And I Will Reach Out My Hand With A Kind of Infinite Slowness And Say The Perfect Thing": The Utopian Theatre of Suspect Culture', *Contemporary Theatre Review*, 13(1) (2003), pp. 61–81.
10. Andy Smith, 'Plays for the People' currently includes four plays: *A Citizens' Assembly* (in collaboration with applied arts practitioner Lynsey O'Sullivan); *Can we be more antiracist?* (developed in discussion with Aleasha Chaunte); *The Actions* (created in collaboration with director, Sam Pritchard): and *The Rule of Six*. www.andysmiththeatre.com/plays-for-the-people (Last accessed 29 September 2025).
11. See Mojisola Adebayo, Valerie Mason-John, and Deirdre Osborne, '"No Straight Answers": Writing in the Margins, Finding Lost Heroes', *New Theatre Quarterly*, 25(1) (2009), pp. 6–21; Deirdre Osborne, 'Skin Deep, a Self-Revealing Act: Monologue, Monodrama, and Mixedness in the Work of SuAndi and Mojisola Adebayo', *Journal of Contemporary Drama in English*, 1(1) (2013), pp. 54–69; Lynette Goddard, 'Black Lives, Black Words at the Bush Theatre: Art, Anger, Affect and Activism' in *Affects in 21st-Century British Theatre: Exploring Feeling on Page and Stage*, ed. Mireia Aragay, Cristina Delgado-García, and

Martin Middeke (Palgrave Macmillan: 2021), pp. 107–26; Paola Prieto López, 'Black Lives, Black Words: Transnational Solidarity and Collective Artistic Activism', *Atlantis English Studies*, 42(2) (2020), pp. 197–213.
12. Ernst Bloch, *The Principle of Hope*, vol. *3*, trans. Neville Plaice, Stephen Plaice, and Paul Knight (Oxford: Basil Blackwell, 1986), pp. 926–1420 (p. 1014).
13. Theodor Adorno quoted in Ernst Bloch, 'Something's Missing: A Discussion between Ernst Bloch and Theodor W. Adorno on the Contradictions of Utopian Longing' in *The Utopian Function of Art and Literature: Selected Essays*, trans. Jack Zipes and Frank Mecklenburg (Cambridge, MA: MIT Press, 1988), pp. 1–17 (p. 12).
14. Herbert Marcuse, *One Dimensional Man* (London: Routledge, 2007), p. 66.
15. debbie tucker green, *ear for eye* (London: Nick Hern, 2018), p. 49.
16. tucker green, *ear for eye*, p. 9.
17. A seminal essay on the politics of Black rage is Audre Lorde, 'Uses of Anger: Women Responding to Racism' in *The Master's Tools Will Never Dismantle the Master's House* (Milton Keynes: Penguin, 2017), pp. 22–35. See also Michael Pearce, 'Black Rage: Diasporic Empathy and Ritual in debbie tucker green's *hang*' in *debbie tucker green: Critical Perspectives*, ed. Siân Adiseshiah and Jacqueline Bolton (London: Palgrave, 2020), pp. 23–44.
18. tucker green, *hang* (London: Nick Hern, 2015), p. 2.
19. Ibid.
20. tucker green, *stoning mary* (London: Nick Hern, 2005), p. 2.
21. Trish Reid, '"What About the Burn Their Bra Bitches?": debbie tucker green as the Willfully Emotional Subject' in *debbie tucker green*, ed. Siân Adiseshiah and Jacqueline Bolton (London: Palgrave, 2020), pp. 45–65 (p. 49).
22. tucker green, *stoning mary*, pp. 61–2.
23. Maggie Inchley, 'Sticking in the Throat/Keyword Bitch: Aesthetic Discharge in debbie tucker green's stoning mary and hang' in *debbie tucker green*, ed. Siân Adiseshiah and Jacqueline (London: Palgrave, 2020), pp. 171–89 (p. 178).
24. tucker green, *stoning mary*, p. 64.
25. tucker green, *ear for* eye, p. 16.
26. Siân Adiseshiah and Jacqueline Bolton, 'debbie tucker green and (the Dialectics of) Dispossession: Reframing the Ethical Encounter' in *debbie tucker green*, ed. Siân Adiseshiah and Jacqueline Bolton (London: Palgrave, 2020), pp. 67–88 (p. 86).
27. Audre Lorde, 'The Master's Tools Will Never Dismantle the Master's House' in *The Master's Tools Will Never Dismantle the Master's House* (Milton Keynes: Penguin, 2017), pp. 16–21.
28. Bloch, 'Something's Missing', p. 5.
29. Ibid., p. 12.
30. Michael R. Ott, 'Something's Missing: A Study of the Dialectic of Utopia in the Theories of Theodor W. Adorno and Ernst Bloch', *Heathwood Journal of Critical Theory: Power, Violence and Non-Violence*, 1(1) (2015), pp. 1–34 (p. 22).
31. Lorde, 'The Master's Tools', p. 18.

32. Mojisola Adebayo, staff profile (performance page), *Queen Mary University of London* website, n. dat. Available at: www.qmul.ac.uk/sed/staff/adebayom.html (Last accessed 15 September 2023).
33. Ibid.
34. Adebayo quoted in Adebayo, Mason-John, and Osborne, 'No Straight Answers', p. 11.
35. Suzanne Scafe, 'Performing Ellen: Mojisola Adebayo's Moj of the Antarctic: An African Odyssey (2008) and Running a Thousand Miles for Freedom; Or, the Escape of William and Ellen Craft from Slavery (1860)', *The Journal of Commonwealth Literature*, 55(3) (2020), pp. 406–20 (p. 408).
36. Mojisola Adebayo, *Moj of the Antarctic*, in *Plays One* (London: Oberon, 2011), pp. 18–64 (p. 27).
37. Ibid., p. 41.
38. Lynette Goddard, 'Introduction' in *Mojisola Adebayo: Plays One* (London: Oberon, 2016), pp. 12–17 (p. 14).
39. I also discuss *STARS* in my monograph, Adiseshiah, *Utopian Drama*.
40. *Idle Women* website. Available at: https://idlewomen.org/about/ (Last accessed 15 September 2023).
41. I am very grateful to Mojisola Adebayo for generously lending me a video recording of a performance of *STARS*. The recording captures the performance of the play after only three days' rehearsal, and the published script has changed since then.
42. Lynette Goddard, 'Introduction' in Mojisola Adebayo, *Plays Two* (London: Oberon Books, 2019), pp. 13–18 (p. 14).
43. Mojisola Adebayo, *STARS*, in *Plays Two* (London: Oberon, 2019), pp. 187–246 (p. 197).
44. Deirdre Osborne, 'Skin Deep, a Self-Revealing Act: Monologue, Monodrama, and Mixedness in the Work of SuAndi and Mojisola Adebayo', *Journal of Contemporary Drama in English*, 1(1) (2013), pp. 54–69 (p. 57).
45. Ibid., p. 56.
46. Adebayo, *STARS*, p. 193.
47. Ibid., 197.
48. Ibid., 206.
49. Ibid., 211.
50. Ibid., 225.
51. Ibid., 226.
52. Alex Zamalin, *Black Utopia: The History of an Idea from Black Nationalism to Afrofuturism* (New York: Columbia University Press, 2019), p. 10.
53. Adebayo, *STARS*, p. 191.
54. Ibid., p. 212.
55. Ibid., p. 224.
56. Donna Haraway, *A Cyborg Manifesto: Science, Technology, and Socialist-Feminism in the Late Twentieth Century* (Minneapolis: University of Minnesota Press, 2016), p. 9.

57. See Lee Edelman, *No Future: Queer Theory and the Death Drive* (Durham, NC: Duke University Press, 2004).
58. Out of the Woods Collective, *Hope Against Hope: Writers on Ecological Crisis* (New York: Commons Notions, 2020), p. 61. Formed in 2014, Out of the Woods is a transnational political-theoretical-research collective focused on engaging with the challenges of ecological crises. A loose grouping with decolonial, anti-racist, queer, feminist, and communist politics, they have written for *Libcom*, *The New Inquiry*, *Journal of Aesthetics and Protest*, and *Society & Space*.
59. Bloch, 'Something's Missing', p. 16.
60. Kodwo Eshun, *More Brilliant than the Sun: Adventures in Sonic Fiction* (London: Quartet Books, 1998), p. 003.
61. Adebayo, 'Interview' in *Theatre in Times of Crisis: 20 Scenes for the Stage in Troubled Times*, ed. Dom O'Hanlon (London: Bloomsbury, 2020), p. 3.

CHAPTER 7

Utopian Communities in Scottish Fiction
Timothy C. Baker

Introduction: Scottish Utopia on the British Periphery

Scotland's relationship with utopia is complicated by its perceived peripheral identity within the United Kingdom. Like More's Utopia, it is a place apart; an imagined space that only becomes narratable through its relationship with its dominant neighbour. Many key works of literary criticism conceive of the Scottish nation as an inherently separate and utopian community within the United Kingdom, harbouring an oppositional potential to unsettle the union through devolution. Cairns Craig, for instance, has affirmed the value of seeing Scotland as a peripheral nation, divorced from dominant English conceptualisations of history. In much nineteenth- and twentieth-century fiction, he notes, Scotland is presented as 'a world to which narrative, and therefore history, is alien'.[1] Scotland is frequently positioned as the colonised other to English imperialism and Scottish fiction a means through which to critique dominant English narratives and modes. In a survey of the field, Caroline McCracken-Flesher describes Scottish science fiction as an 'oddly imperial yet strangely subaltern literature' that reflects and criticises both national and global ideals.[2]

Given its political union as one constituent part of the UK state, an independent Scottish nation remains a theoretical possibility (as well as a political project that the Scottish nationalist movement seeks to realise), and for many critics Scottish fiction provides utopian imaginative tools through which to conceive of an independent Scotland.[3] Alasdair Gray's landmark novel *Lanark* (1981), for instance, has been read as a response to the unsuccessful 1979 devolution referendum, outlining alternate possible Scottish futures. As Gavin Wallace notes, *Lanark*'s combination of familiar locations with a much wilder utopian ethos can be understood as 'detonat[ing] a cultural timebomb', suggesting ways in which fiction can combine the real with the fantastic in politically productive ways.[4] Indeed, Gray included the injunction to 'work as if you live in the early days of a better nation' on the covers of his novels (paraphrasing a line from the Canadian poet Dennis Lee); a command that was later inscribed on the wall of the Scottish Parliament building in tribute to Gray. Gray's significance to Scottish nationalism demonstrates the extent to which literature has been framed as a vehicle for critiquing the present and imagining a possible future independent from England, in Scotland's ongoing utopian project for self-determination. The American utopian literary theorist Phillip E. Wegner suggests that the most significant utopias in recent British fiction, Ken MacLeod's *Fall Revolution Quartet* (1995–9) and Iain M. Banks's *Culture* series (1987–2012), derive their utopian energy from the writers' Scottish identity, living 'on the contested periphery of the British nation'.[5]

In this chapter, I suggest that twentieth-century Scottish fiction has often been reticent to engage with fully developed utopian paradigms, instead focusing on more quotidian experience. With the notable exception of Neil M. Gunn's *The Green Isle of the Great Deep* (1944), Scottish writers have rarely produced classical utopias or dystopias along the lines of Wells, Huxley, or Orwell, instead focusing on small, and usually geographically isolated, utopian experiments. These utopian communities are often depicted as culturally homogenous, precarious, or subject to abuse. In George Mackay Brown's *Greenvoe* (1972), Margaret Elphinstone's *The Incomer* (1987), Robin Jenkins's *The Missionaries* (1957), Iain Banks's *Whit* (1985), and Ewan Morrison's *Nina X* (2019), apparently utopian communities are revealed as kitsch mockeries, the deceitful stories of power-hungry leaders, or more simply subject to racist, sexist, or classist deprivations. At the same time, however, utopian communities are also positioned as an opportunity to look beyond the nation to examine questions of individual and collective desire and identity. In a less-examined strain of Scottish utopian fiction, traceable to John Buchan's *Sick Heart River* (1941) and Josephine Tey's *The Singing Sands* (1952), utopia is framed in terms of individual desire: the true utopian imaginary is found in the construction of same-sex friendship and, in later texts, love. The most successful utopian communities depicted in Scottish fiction are located mostly or wholly in the imagination: in novels including Ali Smith's *Girl meets boy* (2007), Luke Sutherland's *Venus as a Boy* (2004), Leila Aboulela's *Bird Summons* (2019), and Jenni Fagan's *The Sunlight Pilgrims* (2016), utopia privileges not nation, race, or family ties, but the individual connections made possible through shared texts and stories. This chapter thus traces three main strands of utopian Scottish fiction, beginning with the unusual emphasis on death and cyclical return in a number of key utopian texts, moving to a focus on communal life and homosociality, and concluding with a discussion of storytelling as a utopian act and the importance of queer utopian thinking. One of the most notable features of many of the texts discussed here is that utopia is not located in some far-off future, but instead in continuity and in the bonds created by shared narratives. Examining these themes in conjunction reveals Scottish utopian fiction as more varied than previous accounts have noted.

Utopia and Death: How to Reach the Promised Land

Twentieth-century Scottish fiction frequently presents utopian imagery in relation to ideas of death and myth; the relation between stasis and cyclical return underpins many key novels. This paradigm is clearly represented in Gunn's *The Green Isle of the Great Deep*. *Green Isle* is the Scottish novel that most closely parallels contemporary English utopian fiction; the biographer Francis Russell Hart, for instance, terms it an '"antiutopian" parable' that presents 'a legendary Celtic version of Huxley's *Brave New World*'.[6] Gunn was inspired to write the novel after the novelist Naomi Mitchison criticised his previous novel, *Young Art and Old Hector* (1941), concerning an intergenerational friendship in a Highland community, as overly escapist. The story of a remote place, untroubled by modern crises, seemed politically naïve.[7] In their subsequent correspondence, as well as their fiction, Gunn and Mitchison discuss how socialist and anarchist ideals can be integrated into fiction. Gunn's solution in *The Green Isle*, which returns to the same characters as his previous text but places them in a radically new environment, is to present myth as a counterforce to totalitarianism. At the start of the story Young Art and Old Hector fall into a pool whilst poaching salmon and are transported to a uniquely Scottish utopian land where even fresh grapes are compared to those found in an Inverness shop. It is an Edenic paradise governed by logic, although curiously populated by previous generations from their village, almost as a form of afterlife. The pair immediately sets to disrupting it; by eating the forbidden fruit of the tree of knowledge, they demonstrate the value of free will. Whilst the utopian community takes as its foundational principle a 'change from the individual pattern to the corporate pattern', culminating in the appearance of 'a corporate mind', Old Hector stresses that community cannot be sustained only by knowledge and wisdom, but also requires both magic and love.[8] If the power of individual thought over totalitarian systems is typical of 1940s fiction, Gunn's emphasis on storytelling, including both Biblical and Scottish folktale elements, is distinctive: individual freedom is presented in the ties shared fictions create. Young Art's exploits become the material of legend, and it is these stories, rather than his individual actions, that are presented as a path to liberation.

Green Isle is an unusually death-infused utopia. The pair's initial entry is described as a form of drowning: 'Down went Art, the water gulping into him, choking him, choking him ... until at last the smother of sleep had him and his arms fell away wanly.'[9] The implication that the inhabitants may be ghosts suggests that this is not a land of possibility, but a bureaucratic form of heaven. The connection between utopia and death is clarified and affirmed in subsequent fictions that transport their protagonists to the utopian realm after an apparently watery death. Alan Warner's *These Demented Lands* (1997) is a key example here which, like Gunn's text, is a surreal sequel to a more traditionally realistic previous novel, and suggests that the apparent utopian environment is in fact a form of afterlife. Utopia in these novels is as much the absence of possibility as its presence: it is a form of stasis from which the protagonists must escape. This emphasis on utopia not as a model of how people might live, but how they might die, is more fully developed in *Lanark*. The novel is split between two narratives, the first a semi-autobiographical story of the artist Duncan Thaw, in Glasgow, and the second the story of Lanark, in the anti-utopian, but very Glaswegian, city of Unthank. The Unthank sections, labelled books three and four, begin and end the novel, and it is not entirely clear if Lanark is Thaw, reborn after a possible suicide by drowning – early in the novel Lanark finds shells in his pockets, which are best explained in relation to Thaw's drowning some 300 pages later – and Unthank a future Glasgow, or if Unthank is hell, or something else entirely. Unthank is not a futuristic totalitarian nightmare, but simply and permanently grey: it is a land in which 'dawn' is dismissed as a 'sentimental word', and where art is futile.[10] For the most part Lanark's time in Unthank is depicted as a world without passion or momentum: it is utopia as non-place, or a non-story. The utopian sections of the novel are filled with postmodern narrative experimentation, including the appearance of the author as a god-like figure who boasts of his power to impose his narrative vision on his characters, explaining 'you have no conception of the damage my descriptive powers will wreak when I loose them on a theme like THE END'.[11] The utopian imagination is seen as a willed, individual creation which governs the lives of the characters. Yet the end of the novel, when it comes, is quiet and sad: Lanark becomes involved in government and fails miserably; he likewise fails his family; he ends the novel quiet, alone, and ordinary. The way to resist a conformist vision is not to rebel against it, as in many of the critical utopias produced at the time Gray was writing *Lanark*, but simply individual failure to conform through ineptitude as much as willed opposition.[12] Unthank has many of the hallmarks of dystopian fiction: endless dark, a failed and impenetrable government, and the cannibalisation of the working-class. These are also, of course, hallmarks of much twentieth-century Scottish life. The juxtaposition of two worlds does not point to potential futures but, rather, demonstrates the power of the imagination. In the most famous passage of the novel, Thaw and a friend lament that 'nobody imagines living' in Glasgow: 'Imaginatively Glasgow exists as a music-hall song and a few bad novels.'[13] The utopian act, Gray suggests, lies not in imagining a particular utopia, but in imagining at all. The relationship between the realist and fantastical elements of *Lanark* cannot be resolved: rather, this tension invites the reader to recontextualise their own vision of Scotland.

Lanark's invitation is taken up by a host of subsequent authors, often very literally. Banks's *The Bridge* (1986) utilises a similar structure but translates the action to Edinburgh: the imagined utopian world is a version of the Forth Rail Bridge. Andrew Crumey's *Sputnik Caledonia* (2008) juxtaposes realism with a portrait of an alternate Scotland that is a satellite state of the Soviet Union. Each novel juxtaposes quotidian and utopian settings; in each, the link between the two is not explained, but can be understood as arising from death. Whilst each of these authors depicts totalitarian, socialist, or simply bureaucratic potential Scotlands, their significance is always related to individual stories of grief and loss. As Eleanor Bell influentially argues, literature of this period 'move[s] away from introverted, essential and archaic perspectives of nationhood' towards a more open-ended 'recognition of alternative spaces' that challenge any single final meaning.[14] In this light, a firm separation between 'reality' on the one hand, and utopia or dystopia on the other, would potentially cement a tradition of binary oppositions and essentialist thinking where, for instance, Scotland was always positioned as England's other. Instead, Gray, Banks, and Crumey use utopian spaces, not unlike Gunn, as a way of encouraging more flexible thinking. Utopia is neither here nor there, an imagined future or a familiar present: utopia emerges as what lies between them. Each novel positions not only national but individual identity as fundamentally fluid and always subject to recontextualisation. Rather than positioning Scotland as inherently peripheral, then, these authors challenge centre–periphery relations more broadly.

The values and dangers of peripheral life are examined in a range of postwar novels that address utopian impulses in relation to gender and religion. Jenkins's *The Missionaries* prefigures, in slightly more sedate terms, Robin Hardy's film *The Wicker Man* (1973) in its story of a young Christian man who travels to an imagined island to investigate a new religious community. The community is framed by its inhabitants as a new utopia, and by the local landowners as a nuisance. Andrew Doig, the protagonist, attempts to frame his experience in terms of myth, feeling at times 'not like a modern man at all seeking a buttress for faith, but like the adventurer of fable who needed and obtained the help of the gods'.[15] His investigation of the community should, he believes, be a battle between good and evil, and an enquiry into the nature of religious belief. The reality, he discovers, is instead a world 'where a few narrow-minded, gloomy-souled peasants, greedy for a heaven which itself would be narrow and gloomy, were being dispossessed by authorities who did not believe in any heaven at all'.[16] Like Gunn's Old Hector, Doig finds that a community that has promised an alternative to a materialist present ultimately lacks love, and so is doomed to failure. Utopia promises transcendence and, in this case, spiritual purity, but is subject to the same crises of faith and interpersonal difficulties as quotidian life. Whilst Doig himself is transformed, ending the novel forswearing his previous prudishness and dedicating himself to 'the infinities of life', the community itself is unsustainable.[17] Although Jenkins's novel operates on a much smaller geographical and historical scale than the texts mentioned earlier, the key debate is the same. Utopia cannot deliver what it promises, but neither can a familiar sense of reality. Instead, it is the juxtaposition of utopian ideals and a bland or corrupt world that generates individual change, even as that change is consistently framed in relation to traditional myths and stories. Jenkins's novel is not anti-utopian in a strict sense, insofar as the community's ideals are sympathetically portrayed, even as their power structure is revealed to be selfish and misogynist. Instead, *The Missionaries* suggests that neither myth nor religion, neither individual nor communal life, are sustainable on their own.

If Jenkins is ambivalent about utopias, later writers are far more cynical at times. Banks's *Whit*, depicting the adventures of a missionary from the fictional Luskentyrian community in Stirlingshire, is largely satirical; as much as Banks's Culture novels demonstrate the promise of a utopian future, *Whit* focuses on the dangers of a utopian present. Ewan Morrison's recent novels, however, are far more aggressively anti-utopian. His portraits of failed, and often evil, utopian experiments in *Close Your Eyes*

(2012), *Nina X*, and *How to Survive Everything* (2021) are the most consistently imagined attacks on utopianism in contemporary British fiction. *Nina X* tells the story of a twenty-eight-year-old woman who has escaped from a Maoist commune, never having been exposed to the outside world. She struggles not only with new technology, but language itself: she has, at the novel's opening, no ability to say 'I', and struggles to integrate any personal opinions, including qualifying adjectives, into her writing. The charity workers and NHS staff who attempt to aid her are baffled, and mostly unhelpful; whilst Nina comes to realise 'that Freedom was so lonely', her doctors are quick to diagnose her with various mental health conditions, seeking to medicate her feelings of alienation.[18] At the end of the novel Nina does achieve a form of self-realisation:

> Nina didn't know who this I was. It is a very small thing and so timid and it didn't even have a name and was mostly rubbed out. A thing hiding beneath everything else, that came before words.
> And Nina cried for it and held it tight in my arms.
> And I called it I.[19]

Utopian societies, Morrison suggests, can only exist through the violent erasure of the individual. Utopia, in his novels, is a form of paranoid conformity. In *How to Survive Everything* the leaders are often aware that the society they are creating is predicated on lies; rather than presenting utopias that fail naturally, Morrison focuses on utopian societies that have always been corrupt. Utopian fiction itself, he writes in an essay, is 'unimaginative, repetitious and formulaic', as well as 'an unintended testament to the failure of the utopian imagination'.[20] For Morrison, both utopias and utopian fiction fail to recognise the importance of the individual, and as a result are fundamentally destructive. If the external world in his novels is often little better than that of the intentional communities he depicts, he insists that utopian ideals are inherently harmful.

In many of the best-known Scottish utopian fictions, then, there is a clear divide. Utopia can be, as Banks says in a discussion of his Culture novels, a way to envision the best humanity could achieve; in an interview he bemoans the prevalence of British dystopian fiction that imagines 'another drab, communist future' and emphasises the optimism of his own work.[21] Even as *The Bridge* and *Whit* point to the foibles, and potentially the destructiveness, of utopian societies, they both, like Gray's novels, revel in linguistic invention and sardonic humour. Utopia can also, as seen most clearly in Morrison's novels but also in Gunn's, be positioned in opposition to individual development. If the tension between social conformity and individual freedom, and the concomitant fear that, in Chris Ferns's words, 'we are *already* products of our social environment, and that it is only the unpredictable outcome of competing conditions influences that creates the illusion of individual freedom', is a hallmark of modern and contemporary utopian fiction, Scottish writing of this period adds an additional emphasis on death and myth.[22] Utopia is frequently reached in near-death states, or after death, and is explained, as in Jenkins's work, through mythic frameworks. Criticism of this small cohort of texts often, for better or worse, interprets the utopias as microcosms of the nation; whilst Gray's work, for instance, places far more emphasis on Scottish settings than Morrison's or even Jenkins's, these novels are often interpreted, in Craig's phrase, as depicting the 'doublings of the world [that are] a typical device of Scottish fiction'.[23] The interpretation of texts through a national lens becomes, in effect, a closed loop, where the texts chosen for analysis are those that bear certain structural and thematic hallmarks, which are in turn used as a lens for a particularly national, if not nationalistic, discourse. The readily apparent homogeneity of the authors mentioned, who may differ in political perspectives and class background but are unified in their race and gender, exacerbates the problem: regardless of the strengths of the individual novels, Scottish utopian fiction is too often interpreted as fundamentally representing the Scottish nation, in hope or despair. The question remains one of inclusion and exclusion: the homogenisation of utopian settings often implies that community identity is static and inherently knowable.

Scottish Communal Life and Utopian Homosociality

Yet alternative visions of utopia are available. The novels above rely either on a paralleling of worlds (Gray, Crumey), the appearance of an external narrative agent (Gunn, Jenkins, Warner, Banks's *The Bridge*), or a protagonist's escape from a utopian society (Morrison, Banks's *Whit*). Elphinstone's *The Incomer* and Brown's *Greenvoe* also include external narrative agents but place a far greater emphasis on potentially utopian societies that are whole in themselves. These novels owe less to a utopian tradition than to a prevalent emphasis on the value of communal life that has long been a hallmark of Scottish fiction. For critics such as Hart, depictions of small communities are the common thread of Scottish fiction, whether as a 'compensatory myth' that replaces ideas of a complete and self-sustaining nation or as an echo of the real-world utopian experiments of the nineteenth century, such as Robert Owen's New Lanark.[24] Whilst Owen's belief in 'the path to the salvation of society as the setting up of small self-supporting societies' may, as the utopian sociologist Ruth Levitas argues, have been dismissed by Marx and Engels, Owens's utopian socialist experiment in intentional community in a cotton mill near Glasgow remains a reference point for many Scottish novels, from the title of Gray's *Lanark* to being the site of a field trip in Smith's *Hotel World* (2001).[25] Owen's project suggests the importance of the lived experience of small communities as a way to explore more abstract ideas. Scott Lyall suggests, in a comparison of Gray and Morrison, that the appeal of community as a theme is that it must always be reinvented and adapted to new social and political situations.[26] Throughout the twentieth century especially, remote or rural communities are positioned not simply as microcosms of the nation, but as a way to explore the complexities of human relationships on a small scale. The emphasis on community in Scottish fiction is not, then, parochial in the pejorative sense; novels about isolated communities are not inherently quaint or escapist, as much as those charges have been laid against nineteenth-century communitarian fiction.[27] Instead, small communities are used to explore the precarity of human relations, and the importance of relationships with place. This focus quite easily slips into utopian imagining, as in Elphinstone's and Brown's novels.

The Incomer starts as fairytale: a lone fiddler walks through a dark wood to find a small village and arranges to stay for the winter. Yet soon oddities creep in. The music of Beethoven is not only unrecognised, but dated to centuries past, whilst a volume of T. S. Eliot's poetry is 'an ancient thing' for which '[t]here is no context now'.[28] Like the island of Cailleach in Ellen Galford's feminist satire *The Fires of Bride* (1986), which emerges once every 100 years, Elphinstone's town of Clachanpluck is revealed to be a matriarchal society that owes its peace to its remoteness. Clachanpluck's origin is not fully explained, as much as it seems to be post-apocalyptic. Rather, like Galford's novel, Clachanpluck owes as much to Alan Jay Lerner and Frederick Loewe's musical *Brigadoon* (1947), albeit with very different gender and environmental politics, as it does to stories of global destruction. Clachanpluck is not, unlike the other texts in this chapter, in any way an intentional utopia; whilst it has its own set of traditions and regulations, they are not the outcome of a single authoritative vision but are reinforced by being shared. In combining folklore with more modern sentiments – the novel has striking parallels with Ursula K. Le Guin's *Always Coming Home* (1985) – Elphinstone demonstrates the importance of

7 *Utopian Communities in Scottish Fiction* 147

collective vision in establishing a utopian community, both in terms of the community's political construction and its host of intertextual references. The true utopia, the novel suggests, is one that seems to have always been there. Whereas the other novels in this chapter often depict the clash between a utopian civilisation and its opposite, *The Incomer* is almost entirely contained within a very small geographic radius: utopias can, perhaps, be complete in themselves. As one character claims, '[b]eyond all opposites there is something which is the same'.[29] This principle of similarity, rather than opposition, governs everything in the novel, and gives rise to a relatively early example of homosocial affection (and bisexual desire) in Scottish fiction.

The Incomer is not without conflict. The climax of the novel is a calamitous rape, which is seen not only in terms of sexual violence but violence upon the land itself. If the global apocalypse that seems to predate the novel's action is never discussed, the rape is a true apocalypse, and must be countered with a series of rituals, including the presumed killing of the rapist. Yet if this moment demonstrates that utopian societies are subject to disaster, Elphinstone also emphasises that renewal is still possible. As Fiona, one of the village leaders, says near the end:

> I will create my own village. I will make Clachanpluck, and I will surround it with my forest like the enclosing sea. I will make the forest magical, inviolate, sufficient to itself, impregnable. . . . I will accept what has been handed on to me, and I will allow there to be hope.[30]

Destruction does not end utopia: rather, the hope for collective recuperation is constant in communal life. Utopia is not found in making something new, but in the renewal of traditions that are specific to a particular location. Whilst many utopian and dystopian novels in the Scottish tradition privilege human interactions, Elphinstone's *The Incomer* insists on the primary importance of a close relationship with a specific land.

Whilst *Greenvoe* is in many aspects a very different novel, it too suggests the possibility of utopian renewal through ritual. The majority of the novel portrays the lives of farmers and villagers on the small Orkney island of Hellya, and the destructiveness of an external conglomerate, Operation Black Star. Black Star removes the villagers from the island, but its ambiguous project – most likely mining or oil extraction, but with nuclear overtones – also fails, and the island is left abandoned, covered with concrete. In the final pages, however, a group of men returns to the island, and performs a Eucharistic ritual that brings life to the island: 'The smell of the earth came to them in the first wind of morning, from the imprisoned fields of the island; and the fence could not keep it back.'[31] Hellya, like Clachanpluck, is utopian in the sense that it can always be seen as a place of renewal and growth, even when subject to immediate destruction, whether that destruction is externally imposed or arises from the interpersonal conflicts of the inhabitants. Both novels focus on utopia not as a set of political propositions, but as rooted in a particular place. Remote communities are sustainable, or welcome renewal, because of the close integration of humans and the land. As such, utopia can be found in following the rhythms of the past, rather than looking towards future possibility.

Elphinstone's and Brown's novels thus present a very different utopian imaginary to those discussed earlier. Their focus on homosocial communities is, curiously, also an increasingly significant feature of Scottish utopian writing in this period. Utopia becomes a way to imagine different configurations of gender and sexual identity, including in texts that might ordinarily be seen as heteronormative. The importance of homosocial bonds to utopian imagining is suggested in *Sick Heart River*, Buchan's final novel, which depicts his recurring character Edward Leithen's journey to Canada at the end of his life in search of a geographical utopia. Leithen is, throughout Buchan's work, an enthusiastic supporter of the establishment, and his conservative and explicitly imperialist perspective is never challenged. The titular river valley, which Leithen views as representing his salvation, is a lonely and desolate place, reached only after an arduous journey, yet Leithen initially sees it not only as resembling 'a Highland salmon river', but as 'comforting and habitable': what makes it utopian is that it has been untouched by human corruption, and is newly available to Leithen and his friends.[32] The valley is ultimately, however, a place only of death; at the novel's end Leithen returns south and spends his final days trying to improve the living conditions of the Hares, a local First Nations tribe. His decision to abandon an imagined utopian ideal for a real community comes through his gradual realisation that the close companionship of other men allows for a form of care that transcends both national politics and individual desire: true community comes not from a place, but from the bonds of friendship. Whilst the novel is politically and socially conservative, Buchan creates a template that later writers transform.

Tey's *The Singing Sands*, for instance, is also the final novel in a long series. Her hero, Inspector Grant, finds a dead, unnamed man in a train carriage, and becomes obsessed with tracking down the paradise of singing sands mentioned on a small scrap of poetry written by the dead man. The man, known for much of the novel simply as B Seven, comes to represent both utopia and eros: Grant speaks not only of their 'identity of interests', but his love: he has, he says, 'a thing' for B Seven.[33] The singing sands represent a utopian realisation of a homoerotic desire that Grant cannot quite bring himself to speak. Grant locates the sands in the fictional Hebridean island of Cladda, but finds that this small, isolated community is far too connected to the outside world:

> His first meal in the isles of delight consisted of a couple of bright orange kippers inadequately cured and liberally dyed in Aberdeen, bread made in Glasgow, oatcakes baked by a factory in Edinburgh and never toasted since, jam manufactured in Dundee, and butter made in Canada.[34]

Utopia should be found on this island, and yet the people are as uninteresting and petty as elsewhere. Whilst this view of the unlikelihood or impossibility of utopian island communities is similar to that found in *The Missionaries* a few years later, Tey's approach is somewhat different. That utopia cannot be located in a geographical place is, ultimately, irrelevant. Indeed, Tey's novel, like Jenkins's and Brown's, suggests the difficulties raised by imposing utopian values on real island communities. As the Lewis writer Kevin MacNeil comments, island-based fiction too often elides the marginalised communities on those islands: 'a novel that could be set *anywhere*', he argues, 'might as well *be* set somewhere else'.[35] Whilst the vision of islands as both a microcosm and a place apart has been productive in a variety of Scottish literary contexts, as I have argued elsewhere, it can also lead to the reification of island life MacNeil rejects.[36] Instead of finding a utopian place, in Tey's novel as much as Buchan's imagining utopia becomes a way of connecting with other people, especially in cases where, through gender identity or death, the connection would otherwise be impossible. As much as Buchan and Tey work within an imperialist frame, and provide relatively heteronormative conclusions to their stories, they also suggest utopian ideals as not only personal, but as potentially queer.

Utopian Storytelling and Queer Futures

The importance of utopia not as a place, but as an imaginative relation, is found in a number of subsequent novels that, like Buchan's and Tey's work, are not usually framed as utopian. Ali Smith's *Hotel World* is set in and around a hotel in an unspecified location. The hotel could be anywhere: it is a clear example of what Marc Augé calls non-places.[37] At the hotel's promotional pamphlet puts it: 'It doesn't matter where you are in the world if you're anywhere near a Global Hotel. You could be, literally, anywhere.'[38] The novel presents the stories of five loosely connected women, united by the hotel and by the death of Sara Wilby: the space they share is less physical than textual, as it is only the reader who is able to make connections between all five. The novel explores multiple forms of utopian possibility, from the houseless character Else's memories of Robert Owen and New Lanark to Wilby's own liminal presence between body and spirit in her appearance as a ghost. Wilby, whose name is a nod to possibility (*Que sera sera* [Sara], *whatever will be, will be* [Wilby]) is known through words, even as she must leave the world, and the two terms are consistently confused. Whilst the novel is predominantly read as a story of grief and mourning, or as an example of contemporary Gothic fiction, it is utopian in two different respects, in line with the earlier traditions of utopia as both death and imagination. Firstly, the death of this one character works to create a disparate community, both physically, as characters briefly interact with each other, and more substantially in the reader's own imagination. If the hotel is geographically unmoored, the novel itself becomes a utopian space, just as in Tey's text the true utopia is a scrap of paper. The novel is a space of individual renewal, in bringing a dead character to life, and communal creation, in emphasising links between characters that they themselves are unaware of.

Smith also provides a convincing vision of a present utopia in the final section of the novel, titled 'Present', which critics and readers largely elide. Unlike the other sections, Smith employs a third-person narrative, detailing ghosts who emerge as their names are read. The final ghost is Sara herself, as she is imagined by a salesgirl in a watch shop. The reader knows, as Sara and the clerk do not, that some form of love would have been possible if Sara had lived or been brave enough to speak. The novel, as a utopia, becomes a place where that love can be realised, through the reader's own relation to the characters. This is the fullest expression of a theme that appears more subtly in earlier work: if utopia cannot be achieved, or sustained, in a physical location, its truest form is fictional, because it is there that the reader can enter into a shared imaginative space. Whilst this notion may seem fanciful, it provides a frame to understand the importance in myth and storytelling in all of the texts in this chapter, whether optimistic or cynical. Utopia is known in and through interpersonal relation, of course, but it is also known through storytelling. These are not only stories of utopia, but show that storytelling is itself a utopian act, because it creates a shared space of possibility. The desire for a better world cannot be created through a universal pronouncement on human nature, or even an emphasis on evaluation or radical consciousness, as Ruth Levitas and Tom Moylan discuss.[39] Instead, Smith suggests that utopia is based on personal, immediate interactions, both between individual characters and between text and reader. What makes Smith's writing utopian is not its adherence to a particularly literary tradition, or its setting, but its belief in the power of storytelling to create a more inclusive world.

Smith emphasises the utopian potential of storytelling more clearly in *Girl meets boy*. The novel is largely a retelling of the Ovidian myth of Iphis and Ianthe, set in Inverness, with many allusions both to Shakespeare and contemporary political and cultural events as well as feminist history. The density of intertextual references shows, in part, that '[n]obody grows up mythless': myths and stories have an explanatory power that leads to future choice.[40] Whilst the sexual politics of the novel are very different from Gunn's *Green Isle*, Smith's novel not only uses a similar location, but a similar focus on the power of myth to govern individual action. Here, myth is used to illustrate the uselessness of gender binaries: Ovid's tale provides a way to think past the present to a more hopeful future. The truest utopia is not found in a place, but in acts of storytelling. This is most clearly seen when the two main characters marry at the end, not legally, but truly, and a long paragraph combines myriad wedding traditions, from handfasting to eating kola nuts. Each tradition is a story, and each story is a connection. What happens in a wedding, Smith writes, is:

> Nothing more than what happens when things come together, when hydrogen, say, meets oxygen, or a story from then meets a story from now, or stone meets water meets girl meets boy meets bird meets hand meets wing ... and nothing lasts, and nothing's lost, and nothing ever perishes, and things can always change, because things will always change, and things will always be different, because things can always be different.[41]

The utopian ideal – for there are few paragraphs more utopian in contemporary literature than this one – is found not in a creed or policy. It is not found in a particular place, although it may not be possible without a close relationship to a place. It is not even found in the relationship between individual and community. Instead, utopia is the dissolving of borders in order to make new connections. Utopia, as a space of literary possibility that includes the reader in any new community formation, becomes one of the dominant ways to imagine queer futures. Smith's texts highlight, in José Esteban Muñoz's terms, 'a queer feeling of hope in the face of hopeless heteronormative maps of the present where futurity is indeed the province of normative reproduction'.[42] A queer utopia, in this sense, is a way to find new patterns of relation and interaction within the social, and to imagine new forms of being.

A different formulation of queer utopias can be seen in Sutherland's *Venus as a Boy*, which largely consists of the final notes of a dying young Orcadian called, in later life, Cupid or Désirée. Désirée recalls their childhood on South Ronaldsay, noting that many families 'come to Orkney in hope of finding an island Utopia'.[43] If the island itself is utopian, its human relations are not; Désirée recalls their racist taunting of a young Black boy that could be Sutherland himself, and the island is filled with rape and abuse. Désirée's gift, however, is sex: in touching another person, they can fill them with a level of love they have not experienced. Désirée is one of the first pansexual characters in Scottish literature, as well as an early representation of trans identity, and they love indiscriminately; when they move to London and become involved in sex work, they are able to give this gift of love not only to their clients but to their abusive, former Nazi, Romanian pimp. They are both 'a force of nature' and offer 'knowledge of the divine'.[44] Sex with Désirée offers their clients an 'instant and burning *conviction* their lives can never be the same again'.[45] Like Smith's novels, Sutherland's work positions individual connection as the basis for utopia: it is not a solipsistic version of individual will, as in earlier texts, but instead suggests that connection to one person is connection to all. Like Smith's work, too, the novel's use of mythic elements, including Désirée's forced use of hormones turning them not into a woman, but into gold, combined with place specificity, creates a utopia that is both local and universal. The Orkney of Sutherland's novel is easily recognisable from Brown's work, and that of others, but its use is almost opposed: for Sutherland, renewal is connected to departure, not return.

The combination of displacement and connection as giving rise to new forms of utopia is particularly prominent in two very different novels set in the north-east, Fagan's *The Sunlight Pilgrims* and Aboulela's *Bird Summons*. In Aboulela's novel three Muslim women, struggling to find their place in British society, travel to the grave of Lady Evelyn Cobbold, the first British woman to perform the pilgrimage to Mecca. They are visited by a Hoopoe, who warns them that their journey 'is not a destination but a stage. The stage of consequence where what you do and what you want and what you secretly think will take a tangible shape.'[46] The Hoopoe tells the women different stories, from a variety of folkloric traditions, that help them enunciate their own relation between religious belief and secular life. The monastery they travel to is a utopian

7 Utopian Communities in Scottish Fiction

space in the way it fosters connections not only between the three women, but between different forms of storytelling. Although Aboulela's work is very different from Gunn's and Elphinstone's novels, they are united in their close entanglement of myth, religion, and utopian community. Utopia is not a place apart, but a place of connection, both with other people and larger traditions. Each author, notably, incorporates Scottish storytelling traditions with those from further afield. Whilst Scottish fiction has been criticised for a 'utopian nostalgia for a mythic, independent, self-enclosed Caledonia', these novelists demonstrate the precise opposite: the utopian and mythic combine to create a Scotland that is not self-enclosed, but heterogeneous and outward looking.[47]

The importance of a complex, heterogeneous perspective can even be found in more apocalyptic stories. Whilst the question of reproductive futures is addressed in a number of recent dystopian fictions, including MacLeod's *Intrusion* (2012) and Helen Sedgwick's *The Growing Season* (2017), Fagan's novel takes a much more open approach to bodily autonomy, including a trans protagonist and various polyamorous and non-traditional relationships. The immediate threat of a new ice age is, Fagan suggests, precisely the right time to think about community formation and individual agency. The community formed in the novel is one initially predicated purely on survival in relation to global climate change, which is discussed in both scientific and mythic terms. Like Sutherland's novel, Fagan emphasises the way that small communities are prone to racism, transphobia, and xenophobia: utopia is no panacea. Yet, like Sutherland, Fagan shows that the longing for community is itself a form of connection. The title of the novel comes from a myth, told, notably, by a character named Gunn, who tells of a group of seventy monks who live on an island and go mad, except for one, who survives by 'drinking light'.[48] Yet whilst this story seems to indicate the failure of utopian communities, the characters also conclude, at the novel's end, that '[a]ll humans are sunlight pilgrims'.[49] The desire for community and connection is fundamental to all societies; again, it is by telling stories that utopia is formed. Whilst, as Ferns notes, the 'utopian impulse towards radical change' can rarely be resolved 'by purely *narrative* means', the emphasis these texts place on narrative itself as a means of change remains distinctive.[50] Storytelling is, as in María Puig de la Bellacasa's formulation, a form of 'knowledge as relating' that opens the space for a 'speculative commitment to think about how things could be different if they generated care'.[51] This is one of the key unifying features of the novels discussed in this chapter. The vast majority present death, whether of an individual or a community, as a catalyst for utopian imagining. What remains, they suggest in different ways, is the value of myth or storytelling as a way of creating a better future. Utopia is not what is imposed, and it is not universal: it is here and now, in the narrative act.

Global environmental crises, in particular, are ubiquitous in recent fiction: in texts ranging from Julie Bertagna's Young Adult novel *Exodus* (2002) to Matthew Fitt's experimental Scots-language novel *But N Ben A-Go-Go* (2000) to John Burnside's more classically utopian *Havergey* (2017) utopian communities are frequently juxtaposed with the collapse of global societies. As in Fagan's, Elphinstone's, and Gray's novels, to varying extent, utopia is seen as what survives. The appeal of utopia for modern Scottish writers is that as much as it appears to offer a template to explore possible futures, it can also be used to examine the relation between past and present, and the boundaries that are placed on individual experience. Each of these novels asks, implicitly or explicitly, for whom is utopia intended, and who can access it. Utopia can be geographically placed or far more abstract; it can lead to the repression or liberation of individual will or desire; it can be motivated by particular political or religious ideologies, or seen as representing ideas of a national community. More than this, however, Scottish utopian fiction demonstrates the primacy of community as seen through, and created by, myth and storytelling. Storytelling is a form of relation that creates new possibilities for inclusion. Utopia is not, in the end, a reified vision, nor a simple political allegory, nor an index to the nation. Instead, utopia is a way for fiction to reflect on itself. It is as utopia is imagined, hoped for, and told that it comes into being. As such, utopia holds continued promise not only for new forms of relation, but new forms of storytelling.

Notes

1. Cairns Craig, *Out of History: Narrative Paradigms in Scottish and British Culture* (Edinburgh: Polygon, 2006), p. 37.
2. Caroline McCracken-Flesher, 'Introduction' in *Scotland as Science Fiction*, ed. Caroline McCracken-Flesher (Lewisburg: Bucknell University Press, 2012), pp. 1–14 (p. 2).
3. Thomas Docherty, 'The Existence of Scotland' in *Scotland in Theory: Reflections on Culture and Literature*, ed. Eleanor Bell and Gavin Miller (Amsterdam: Rodopi, 2004), pp. 231–48.
4. Gavin Wallace, 'Introduction' in *The Scottish Novel Since the Seventies: New Visions, Old Dreams*, ed. Gavin Wallace and Randall Stevenson (Edinburgh: Edinburgh University Press, 1993), pp. 1–7 (p. 4).

5. Phillip E. Wegner, 'Detonating New Shockwaves of Possibility: Alternate Histories and the Geopolitical Aesthetics of Ken MacLeod and Iain M. Banks', *CR: The New Centennial Review*, 13(2) (2013), pp. 31–66 (p. 32).
6. Francis Russell Hart, *The Scottish Novel: A Critical Survey* (London: John Murray, 1978), p. 360. For a more extended account, see Timothy C. Baker, 'Scottish Utopian Fiction and the Invocation of God', *Utopian Studies*, 21(1) (2010), pp. 91–117.
7. See J. B. Pick, *Neil M. Gunn* (Tavistock: Northcote House, 2004), pp. 56–7, 79–80; Mitchison's side of the correspondence can be found in the National Library of Scotland, Naomi Mitchison Papers, Acc. 5813.
8. Neil M. Gunn, *The Green Isle of the Great Deep* (Edinburgh: Polygon, 2006), pp. 207, 209, 260.
9. Gunn, *Green Isle*, p. 19.
10. Alasdair Gray, *Lanark: A Life in Four Books* (London: Paladin, 1985), p. 11.
11. Gray, *Lanark*, p. 498.
12. For a discussion of critical utopias, see Tom Moylan, *Demand the Impossible: Science Fiction and the Utopian Imagination* (New York: Methuen, 1986), p. 51.
13. Gray, *Lanark*, p. 243.
14. Eleanor Bell, *Questioning Scotland: Literature, Nationalism, Postmodernism* (Basingstoke: Palgrave Macmillan, 2004), pp. 94, 97.
15. Robin Jenkins, *The Missionaries* (Edinburgh: Polygon, 2005), p. 115.
16. Jenkins, *Missionaries*, p. 116.
17. Jenkins, *Missionaries*, p. 229.
18. Ewan Morrison, *Nina X* (London: Fleet, 2019), p. 137.
19. Morrison, *Nina X*, p. 266.
20. Ewan Morrison, 'Why We Must Walk Away from Omelas: The Problem with Utopias', *Areo*, 27 August 2020. http://areomagazine.com/2020/08/27/why-we-must-walk-away-from-omelas-the-problem-with-utopias/ (Last accessed 15 September 2023).
21. Val Nolan, '"Utopia Is a Way of Saying We Could Do Better": Iain M. Banks and Kim Stanley Robinson in Conversation', *Foundation*, 54(119) (2014), pp. 65–76 (p. 70).
22. Chris Ferns, *Narrating Utopia: Ideology, Gender, Form in Utopian Literature* (Liverpool: Liverpool University Press, 1999), p. 107
23. Cairns Craig, *The Modern Scottish Novel: Narrative and the National Imagination* (Edinburgh: Edinburgh University Press, 1999), p. 165.
24. Hart, *The Scottish Novel*, p. 205.
25. Ruth Levitas, *The Concept of Utopia* (Oxford: Peter Lang, 2011), p. 45.
26. Scott Lyall, '"Tenshillingland": Community and Commerce, Myth and Madness in the Modern Scottish Novel' in *Community in Modern Scottish Literature*, ed. Scott Lyall (Leiden: Brill Rodopi, 2016), pp. 1–24.
27. See Andrew Nash, *Kailyard and Scottish Literature* (Amsterdam: Rodopi, 2007).
28. Margaret Elphinstone, *The Incomer* (London: Women's Press, 1987), p. 55.
29. Elphinstone, *The Incomer*, p. 113.

30. Elphinstone, *The Incomer*, pp. 220–1.
31. George Mackay Brown, *Greenvoe* (Edinburgh: Polygon, 2004), p. 243.
32. John Buchan, *Sick Heart River* (Edinburgh: Polygon, 2007), p. 107.
33. Josephine Tey, *The Singing Sands* (London: Arrow, 2011), pp. 60, 160.
34. Tey, *The Singing Sands*, p. 90.
35. Kevin MacNeil, 'Misty Islands and Hidden Bridges' in *Scottish Writing after Devolution: Edges of the New*, ed. Marie-Odile Pittin-Hédon, Camille Manfredi, and Scott Hames (Edinburgh: Edinburgh University Press, 2022), pp. 163–75 (p. 173).
36. See Timothy C. Baker, 'The Lonely Island: Exile and Community in Recent Island Writing' in *Community in Modern Scottish Literature*, ed. Scott Lyall (Leiden: Brill Rodopi, 2016), pp. 25–42.
37. Marc Augé, *Non-Places: An Introduction to Supermodernity*, trans. John Howe (London: Verso, 2009). See also Caroline Edwards, *Utopia and the Contemporary British Novel* (Cambridge: Cambridge University Press, 2019), pp. 86–94.
38. Ali Smith, *Hotel World* (London: Hamish Hamilton, 2001), p. 180.
39. Levitas, *The Concept of Utopia*, p. 214; Moylan, *Demand the Impossible*, p. 194.
40. Ali Smith, *Girl Meets Boy* (Edinburgh: Canongate, 2007), p. 98.
41. Smith, *Girl Meets Boy*, p. 160.
42. José Esteban Muñoz, *Cruising Utopia: The Then and There of Queer Futurity* (New York: New York University Press, 2009), p. 28.
43. Luke Sutherland, *Venus as a Boy* (London: Bloomsbury, 2004), p. 11.
44. Ibid., pp. 94, 145.
45. Ibid., p. 94.
46. Leila Aboulela, *Bird Summons* (London: Weidenfeld and Nicolson, 2019), p. 82.
47. Monica Germanà, *Scottish Women's Gothic and Fantastic Writing: Fiction since 1978* (Edinburgh: Edinburgh University Press, 2010), p. 6.
48. Jenni Fagan, *The Sunlight Pilgrims* (London: William Heinemann, 2016), p. 145.
49. Fagan, *The Sunlight Pilgrims*, p. 306.
50. Ferns, *Narrating Utopia*, p. 103.
51. María Puig de la Bellacasa, *Matters of Care: Speculative Ethics in More Than Human Worlds* (Minneapolis: University of Minnesota Press, 2017), pp. 28, 60.

PART III

From Crisis to Hope: Utopian Aesthetics

CHAPTER 8

Doris Lessing
Surviving Utopia

David Sergeant

It is not uncommon to see Doris Lessing's writing described as utopian – or as that closely related term, dystopian. On the face of it, this generic categorisation is not hard to understand, given the fierceness of Lessing's critique of contemporary socio-political relations, the visions of a species united and transformed that appear in her texts, of individuals overstepping the boundaries that had restricted them. Equally, however, this is a writer whose 2001 interview with a journal in the latter stages of her career was titled 'Against Utopia'.[1] So, are we looking at someone whose utopian valence shifted over the six decades they were writing? Whilst Lessing's work from the 1980s onwards more frequently attracted descriptors such as 'reactionary', and indeed is more openly provocative regarding issues of political engagement and utopian longing, it is also possible to see this later writing as of a piece with the earlier work in which prospects of radical transformation feature largely.[2] The key, perhaps, is in how we understand utopia. If 'the essence of utopia is a desire for a different and better way of being' as Ruth Levitas has put it,[3] then Lessing's work through the late 1960s and 1970s in particular might reasonably fit the term. However, if we understand utopia as the dream of Enlightenment modernity, in a manner exemplified by a theorist like Fredric Jameson, then Lessing's utopian identity becomes much less stable as a category; as does a reading that places her writing amongst other utopian texts, in what Philp E. Wegner has argued is the 'uniquely modern literary genre of the narrative utopia'.[4]

The fictional experimentation that marks Lessing's writing through the first decade or so of her career – in particular, in the five-volume *Children of Violence* (1952–69) sequence and *The Golden Notebook* (1962)[5] – can be traced to both a personal and an artistic dissatisfaction. Her work through this period sees successive disillusionments – with her parents, colonial society, marriage and romance, as well as Communist politics – becoming yoked to Lessing's increasing disquiet with the abilities of the conventional realist novel to adequately represent this experience. The first three novels of the *Children of Violence* sequence – *Martha Quest* (1952), *A Proper Marriage* (1954), and *A Ripple from the Storm* (1958) – follow the young protagonist Martha Quest, whose maturation follows Lessing's own biographical experience: growing up in Southern Rhodesia, fleeing the constraints of parents, marriage, and motherhood, becoming involved during the Second World War with a Communist group and entering a second marriage with one of them. Chronologically, these novels are followed by what remains Lessing's most famous text, *The Golden Notebook*, in which a young writer, Anna Wulf, tries and fails to write a second novel, becoming increasingly frustrated with everything from the contemporary political scene to the capabilities of the novel form itself. Different parts of Anna's life are divided into four notebooks – black, red, yellow, and blue – before the novel concludes with the eponymous 'Golden Notebook', which is positioned as unifying the fragmented forms and experiences preceding it.

As I have argued elsewhere, for all the brilliance of this final section in bringing *The Golden Notebook* to a satisfying thematic and formal close, the novel nevertheless ended up as another dead-end for Lessing, in her attempt to find a way beyond the biographical and artistic impasse she seems to have reached.[6] Her next novel, *Landlocked* (1965), the fourth in the *Children of Violence* series, can be read as a return to realism that prepares for Lessing's final rejection of it, as romantic relationships – such as the one that had also catalysed the eponymous Golden Notebook – are dismissed as the locus for personal meaning and development.

The Utopian Future, beyond Narrative Representation and Time

The Four-Gated City (1969), the final novel in the *Children of Violence* series, then follows Martha through 1950s and 1960s London, with an increasing interest in a breakthrough into another state that might be best described as mystical – though the novel notes cuttingly that 'mysticism' is just another 'label' that 'will stop the process of thought for a time ... sterilize ... make [it] harmless'.[7] Martha haphazardly ascends onto a 'wavelength', into a 'space' or a 'country' distant from the 'humdrum of ordinary life' but also 'just belong or alongside [it]'; she experiences visions of events that have not yet happened, she reads and reflects on how 'the same processes, the same psychological truths' were visible in everything from 'the poems of St John of the Cross to states of mind described in the Upanishads'.[8] This transfer of focus from politics to mysticism is matched by a generic shift into science fiction in the 'appendix' of *The Four-Gated*

City. In this thirty-five-page conclusion to the preceding 600 plus pages, which is presented as a series of supposedly documentary materials, we glimpse how multiple disasters have destroyed civilisation. The conclusion reveals that Martha has survived and encountered a generation of children on a remote Scottish island who possess the mystical or ESP (extrasensory perception) abilities that she and a few other characters in the novel had only been able to access intermittently and ineffectually:

> There's nothing you can measure or count, but we all feel it, and particularly the other children. For one thing, they are grown up-no, not physically of course, but mentally, emotionally. One talks to them as if they were adult-no, not that; one talks to them as if they are superior to us ... which they are. They all carry with them a gentle strong authority. They don't have to be shielded from the knowledge of what the human race is in this century – they know it. I don't know how they know it. It is as if – can I put it like this? – they are beings who include that history in themselves and who have transcended it. They include us in a comprehension we can't begin to imagine. These seven children are our-but we have no word for it. The nearest to it is that they are our guardians. They guard us.[9]

In certain lights this might appear as a utopian transformation. However, if this is the authentic utopian future, succeeding the imposters to that name – communism, romance, art – that had preceded it, then it is one at odds with the kinds of political and historical progress that have characterised utopias in the twentieth century, particularly following the development of what Tom Moylan has called 'critical utopias' in the 1960s and after: narratives that provide not the blueprint of a transformed society, but that depict the struggle to knit a better world out of the bones of the contemporary.[10] Jay Clayton has described how common the theme of an evolutionary next step for humanity was to the science fiction of the 1950s and 1960s, frequently involving the acquisition of telepathy and the merging into a larger collective mind; and convincingly ascribes this to an 'idealism about a collective society' that has been reassuringly 'stripped ... of its threat to the individual and of its political dimension'.[11] Lessing's utopian move in *The Four-Gated City* and later works seems to resemble this transmuted idealism more than it does the concern with 'minority and gender issues' that Clayton identifies as characterising evolutionary-minded science fiction of the 1970s and 1980s;[12] though he might equally have identified an explicit engagement with political thought and praxis as characteristic of that work.

The perfected future in *The Four-Gated City* is severed from the present by both narrative and history – those conjoined dimensions that have been so crucial to the work of perhaps the preeminent utopian theorist of recent decades, Fredric Jameson.[13] When Martha receives intimations of another state, another world, in *The Four-Gated City*, it is figured as beyond representation – or at least, narrative representation. The city of the novel's title appears in a story told by one of the characters, in which a geometric city figures the holistic completion of both self and society. In the science fiction and other non-realist work that Lessing would go on to write in the decade and a half after *The Four-Gated City*, such geometric figures commonly stand for the state of completion beyond representation and time: from the geometric cities and gardens in *Shikasta* (1979) and *Briefing for a Descent into Hell* (1971), to the 'intricate structures and shapes' and 'patterns of matter' in their 'tenuous though strict dance' at the climax of *The Making of the Representative of Planet 8* (1982).[14]

Equally, as this future is beyond the capabilities of narrative to encompass it, so it is beyond the reach of history and time, in contrast to much twentieth-century utopian fiction, where the trend has been to understand utopia as a process rather than a terminal destination. Such a change can be glimpsed in a complex work like Yevgeny Zamyatin's *We* (1920/1),[15] which mingles dystopian and utopian elements to reveal, as Philip E. Wegner puts it, the 'dialectical nature of [Zamyatin's] concept of infinite revolution'.[16] Ursula Le Guin's *The Dispossessed* (1974) ends poised between what could be either the synthesis of the two poles of its narrative, the anarchist moon Anarres and the earth-like Urras, or the failure of their encounter; with the further implication that this process of departure and return – the 'permanent revolution' – should never cease, in either individual or society.[17] In Marge Piercy's *Woman on the Edge of Time* (1976), the utopian future of Mattapoisett is threatened both by a contemporary enemy and the prospect that it might never come into being if it is failed by the pre-utopian present.[18] More recently, Kim Stanley Robinson's *New York 2140* (2017) ends with the assertion, equal parts rousing and salutary, that 'people are crazy and history never ends, and good is accomplished against the immense black-hole gravity of greed and fear'.[19] In contrast to all of these, the projected future of *The Four-Gated City* is the definitive, teleological end.

One consequence of the crystallisation around a historical future of mystical community is that it definitively severs any possibility of this future being achieved in Lessing's fiction through a secular and stadial progress. It is so distanced from things as they are that the only conceivable transfer to it is via the apocalyptic destruction of the world. This substitution of apocalypse for a secular historical progress that seems impossible is built into the foundations of the apocalyptic tradition, from the Jewish prophetic texts written out of periods of subjugation, enslavement, and foreign rule, to the apocalypticism of the African American tradition.[20] Equally, the prevalence of apocalyptic scenarios in Lessing is obviously part of a wider trend in the Global North in the second half of the twentieth century.[21] What makes the apocalypticism of this tranche of Lessing's work particularly notable, however, is how fiercely and explicitly it becomes part of a turn away from the secular politics that has been such an important part of utopian thought, practice and fiction; and the equal explicitness with which she transfers her commitment into a religious framework, which has self-development at its heart, and which seems to discount any notion of stadial progress or even meaningful societal change. Her excoriating descriptions of colonial and capitalist life possess an energy that might be seen as utopian, perhaps as dystopic in Moylan's sense of that term, work that 'retains a utopian commitment at the core of its formally pessimistic presentation', with the transfer to a dimension of spiritual fulfilment in the science fiction then acting as the consummation of that energy and commitment.[22] However, being stranded beyond history, on the other side of apocalypse, makes that dimension's utopian status extremely problematic.

Lessing's Discovery of Sufism

The turning point in Lessing's life and writing was her discovery of Sufism, as it was propounded by the Afghan thinker and teacher Idries Shah. According to Shah, Sufism is as old as humanity itself, and while it has most visibly found a home and articulation within Islam, it also constitutes the kernel at the heart of all religions – and, equally, does not require a religion for its activity.[23] Between the publication of *The Sufis* in 1964, and his death in 1996, Shah published over thirty works. Given the common association of the 1960s with dubious gurus and cults, it is worth observing, firstly, that Lessing was not alone in her admiration for Shah's work, which received endorsements from a wide range of individuals and public bodies, and, secondly, that Shah's writing explicitly disavows guruism and cultism.[24] For all that Lessing was quite open about her enthusiasm for Sufism, and numerous scholars have explored its influence on her work, it is still easy to underestimate its influence on her writing.[25] It is suggestive, for instance, that there was a gap of four years between *Landlocked* and *The Four-Gated City*, an unusually large break between novels for Lessing; was it explained by her digesting the impact of *The*

Sufis? Both novels have epigraphs from Shah's work, but the latter novel is saturated with Sufi ideas where the former is not – indeed, the eponymous four-gated city has clear echoes of the story 'The Garden' from Shah's *The Way of the Sufi* (1968).[26] Whilst other contacts Lessing had through this period – for instance, with R. D. Laing, the controversial psychiatrist – and other contexts, such as the science fiction New Wave, are no doubt important in her turn to science fiction and 'inner space' in this period, the Sufi influence is paramount and sustained.[27] Similarly, while Allan Hepburn has described how 'miracles and mystical experience figure everywhere in British literature between 1935 and 1965',[28] and James Clements has explored how mid-century writers such as Patrick White, Saul Bellow, William Golding, and Irish Murdoch were united by 'metaphysical concerns'.[29] Lessing's turn to mysticism seems distinct from all these: in part because it is so directly connected to previous political commitments, in part because it operates with reference to a fully-fledged world system, as opposed to a 'mysticism', which in other writers was less coherently that, and more often the product of an elusively heterogenous 'philosophical and intellectual' lineage.[30]

However, for all the impact of Lessing's discovery of Sufism, her writing was not so much transformed as evolved by it, perhaps in one sense completed by it. Crudely put, if through the 1950s and 1960s her writing had been in search of an answer to the question of human purpose and history, that writing had also acted as the litmus test for the candidates it trialled – Marxism, art, love – and then as the final proof of their inadequacy, as they broke down under the scrutiny and scepticism that energised her fiction. Unlikely as it may seem, given the popular association of 1960s spirituality with spaced-out mumbo-jumbo, Sufism not only suggested a new answer to Lessing, but advocated and indeed demonstrated the same scrutiny and scepticism. As she put in in a review of one Shah work, '[the Sufi] sociological and psychological insights are far in advance of our current ideas'; while the registering of 'everything we seem to be' as 'only a mask made by conditioning' is the prerequisite for any form of human advancement.[31] When Lessing's 'realism' – in the sense of an acute observation of the contemporary or historically recent world – becomes the foundation for writing of the possibility of mystical transformation, it matches its role in Sufism. Indeed, one reason Sufism might have been congenial for Lessing is that it has a place for the kind of literature she had always valued – in *Shikasta*, a Sufi-tinted character approvingly identifies Proust as a 'sociologist and anthropologist' – whereas communism, at least in her account of it, did not.[32]

However, if Sufism provided Lessing's realism with the meaningful frame that it had been seeking since the start of her writing career, and science fiction provided the corresponding formal liberation, then both were famously greeted with dislike by many reviewers. It is telling that Ursula Le Guin's scathing review of *Shikasta*, Lessing's heavily Sufistic science fiction novel of 1979, precisely separates the psychologically and socially realist parts of the novel – which, as just noted, had been the foundation of Lessing's earlier writing – from the religious elements. Le Guin singles out the former for praise, whilst damning the latter for being crankish hocus-pocus: 'it all seems to have been inspired by the Velikovsky-Von Daniken school of, as it were, thought'.[33] Notwithstanding Le Guin's criticism, a basic similarity can be detected between a work like *The Dispossessed* – one of the most influential utopian novels of the twentieth century – and Lessing's science fiction through this period. The dialectic between Urras and Anarres in *The Dispossessed* is promised a resolution by the protagonist Shevek's 'chronophysical' insight, which is figured in terms of shapes and patterns in a way that recalls Lessing's work: 'He had seen the Square in his mind a while ago, a design in space like the designs music made in time ... If you saw the numbers you could see that, the balance, the pattern.'[34] Equally, the advanced civilisation of the Hainish are suggestive, in their tutelary-anthropological role in Le Guin's fiction, of the Canopeans; and in *The Dispossessed* they fill, as Philip Wegner has observed, the place of utopian synthesis 'tantalizingly illuminated only in the text's final pages', just as the Canopean-sponsored future does in Lessing's work.[35] The non-trivial difference, however, is that the *Canopus in Argos* universe is driven by cosmic patterns and rhythms rather than any human action, as Le Guin pointed out in her review: 'All great events on earth result from decisions made elsewhere; all our inventions were given us by extraterrestrials; all our religions feebly reflect the glory of an unhuman Founder.'[36] While it would be a mistake to take Lessing's science fiction as a systematic fictionalising of Sufi ideas, these cosmic rhythms seem to be informed by the Sufi emphasis on 'right time, right place, right people' as the underlying requirements for historical progress – not all of which will be subject to human determination.[37] As Lessing herself put it, writing on and quoting Shah: 'There are times when a transmission of Sufi truth is possible, because cosmic influences are in alignment – "... the appropriate wave of the unseen laps upon the shore of possibility ..." – and times when nothing happens because nothing can.'[38] In Le Guin, on the other hand, progress and history are driven by human will and practice.

In *The Four-Gated City* and the *Canopus in Argos* universe we see the historically projected, wholesale transformation of a failing world – one that is loosely suggestive of utopia but is also at odds with its history, which is bound up with secular modernity. But what happens to this concept of transformation in those Lessing works which do not have the evolutionary galactic system of the *Canopus in Argos* series as their framework? For an answer, we might look at two apparently very different novels that Lessing described as versions of autobiography: *The Memoirs of a Survivor* (1974) and *The Sweetest Dream* (2001).[39] They join the diverse array of life-writing forms that Lessing utilised, and underline the consistency and explicitness with which she imbricated her life with her writing as a means of engaging with twentieth-century history and its possible futures. It is striking that for all the forms and genres she experiments with in her career, from the libretto she wrote for Philip Glass's operatic adaption of *The Making of the Representative for Planet 8* in 1988 to her graphic novel collaboration with British comics artist Charlie Adlard in *Playing the Game* (1995), there is not a single work of historical fiction.[40] *The Memoirs of a Survivor* and *The Sweetest Dream* demonstrate the alternative location of something that might be called utopia, in the sense that it involves a positive projection into the future. However, they sit at odds with the utopian tradition for deserting the idea of societal progress, even of meaningful change at that scale. Rather, their creative energies are devoted first, to survival; and, second, to a retreat from history into a unit that might enable this survival. They are utopian only by the minimalist standards of someone who could describe themselves in an interview as an 'optimist', on the grounds that they thought 'the human race will survive because we are good survivors'.[41]

The Memoirs of a Survivor is subtitled *An Attempt at Autobiography*, and was first published by Shah's own publishing house, The Octagon Press – a striking move for an established author contracted to major publishing houses. Her reasons for doing so are unclear, though it is possible she wished to further lend her name to the Sufi cause, or saw the work as particularly apposite to the Octagon list. The novel introduces itself as tracking the elusive zeitgeist – 'that time' – of a world that is recognisable as an occasionally dreamlike version of our own.[42] Cornelius Collins has written eloquently of how the novel 'excels the nonfiction writers most esteemed since the end of the Cold War as visionary thinkers about globalization and geopolitics'.[43] However, the attention to this spirit of the globalised age is in a different key to the kind of attentive sociohistorical charting that had Lessing undertaken in a work like *The*

Four-Gated City. *The Memoirs of a Survivor* echoes the contemporary world but also evades a straightforward identification with it, lacking, as Maureen Howard put it, Lessing's 'old Dreiserian amplitude ... all that apparatus of the old genre'.[44] If we recognise the novel's contemporaneity in its referral to radios, cigarettes, hooligans, and jeans, then its investigations of forces such as sex, tribalism, generational identity, and ageing occur in scenes that blur into something less historically situated, and imply a kind of universalism. It is an intimation of the sense of world history as lacking meaningful change that will become still clearer in Lessing's later writing.

Equally, *The Memoirs of a Survivor* is structured in part by the literal departure of the public world, as the city around the narrator gradually empties out, the population migrating in groups to an unknown destination. Concomitant with this, the non-realist elements of the novel – fable, allegory, myth – become stronger as the novel moves towards its close, and the action tightens around a group of characters with the young girl Emily at their centre. She might be understood as a version or projection of the novel's unnamed first-person narrator, a rerun or repetition of an aspect of themselves. While Emily immerses herself in the external world through the course of the novel, the narrator explores regions inexplicably revealed behind the walls of her flat, which seem to contain fragments and traces of Emily's traumatic childhood. This division of a single character or mind into different parts that are then explored through their narrative dynamic is the stuff of allegory, of course, but in Lessing's usage it is strongly influenced by Shah's use of oral and folk literature, and his explanations of the importance of the teaching story as 'a consistent and productive parallel or allegory of certain states of mind. Its symbols are the characters in the story. The way in which they move conveys to the mind the way in which the human mind can work.'[45] When *The Memoirs of a Survivor* concludes with Emily, Gerald, and a group of feral children coming belatedly together, with the strange cat-dog hybrid Hugo, it is the completion of the journey of the individual soul rather than – or perhaps in the face of – the historical world:

> Both [Emily and Hugo] walked quickly behind that One who went ahead showing them the way out of this collapsed little world into another order of world altogether. Both, just for an instant, turned their faces as they passed that other threshold. They smiled ... seeing those faces Gerald was drawn after them, but still he hesitated in a fearful conflict, looking back and around, while the brilliant fragments whirled around him. And then, at the very last moment, they came, his children came running, clinging to his

hands and his clothes, and they all followed quickly on after the others as the last walls dissolved.[46]

Collins describes this conclusion as the narrator 'find[ing] a way... toward a powerfully expanded consciousness, and lead[ing] a small group of children into a once-hidden Utopian dimension'.[47] The term 'Utopian' slips here into its idiomatic use as a synonym for 'desired' or 'transfigured' – as was noted at the start, not an uncommon tendency when describing Lessing's work. However, when compared to the history of utopias since More's foundational work – in which the dialectic between the individual and the totality, and their mutual transformation, has been a central problem – Lessing's turn to the individual appears as more of a rupture.[48]

In the later novel, *The Sweetest Dream*, even this personal transformation is too much to ask for, and the emphasis falls squarely on the struggle for common decency, sense, and sanity amidst the febrile madness and horror of the world. Read under the aegis of utopia, *The Sweetest Dream* can seem almost comically out of place, being extensively concerned with a dry-eyed dismantling of the sweetest dream of the title, 'a belief in progress, the ever-upwards-reaching escalator to a happier world', with an emphasis on historical movements of the Left – communism, most prominently, though also post-colonial independence.[49] Such deflationary perspectives on utopian-inflected movements of the sixties, including feminism as well as Marxism, saw Lessing commonly described as 'contrarian' in the later years of her life, in some of the more polite assessments (Jeanette Winterson gives a taste of others: 'Is Lessing living on planet Zog, or is it just that she is 81?').[50] In an interview given in the wake of *The Sweetest Dream* – titled 'Against Utopia' by the journal in which it appeared – Lessing comments cheerfully on her earlier communist belief that the world would be transformed into a 'perfect place where there'd be no injustice, no racial prejudice ... Can you *believe* we were so stupid?'[51] In a work like *The Sweetest Dream* Lessing seems to be squarely in what Tom Moylan has described as the anti-utopian tradition. Moylan suggests the term for 'the textual form that critiques and rejects not only Utopia but also the political thought and practice that is produced and motivated by Utopia as a force of societal transformation'.[52] Krishan Kumar locates this specifically British strand of anti-utopianism in Edmund Burke's hostility to the French revolution – often the paradigmatic example of conservative opposition to the utopia of modernity – and traces it forward into writers such as Aldous Huxley and George Orwell. He describes how anti-utopia can originate from both the right and left of the political spectrum and is rooted in 'a fundamental pessimism, or at least scepticism, about the capacities of human beings, and the possibility of attaining more than a moderate degree of happiness in human society'.[53]

The closest thing to a utopian location the novel possesses is a house with multiple occupants in which a few decent and self-sacrificing characters – though each also subject to flaws and failings – support each other and a range of guests. Franklin, who goes there as a bewildered schoolboy from Africa, will later look back, as a complacent and corrupt 'Zimlian' – obviously Zimbabwean – minister, and remember 'that house in London' as having 'more in common with the ease and warmth of his grandparents' huts than anything since'.[54] Sylvia, a character who starts out in the house as a disturbed child unwanted by her mother and ends up working as a doctor in a poverty and AIDS stricken backwater of Zimlia, ends the novel bringing two orphan boys to England in search of a better future for them. When Sylvia dies, the boys are taken in by Frances and her partner Roland: 'a man and a woman daring to love each other so thoroughly – well, it was hardly to be confessed, even to each other'.[55] And so the work of daily and local action, duty, and care goes on, the bulwark against the self-indulgent, self-deceiving, and hugely destructive utopian dreaming of the novel's progressives, whose totemic political movements end up being just as murderous and wicked as the more openly disreputable ones. Indeed, a provocation from the second volume of Lessing's autobiography, *Walking in the Shade* (1997), that 'Hitler's Germany ... was an infant in terror compared to Stalin's regime', is echoed by an incidental character in *The Sweetest Dream* observing that 'Stalin was demonstrably worse than Hitler', before being dismissed by his outraged audience as 'a CIA plant'.[56]

The house or domestic space is an important structure in many Lessing works – it was there in *The Memoirs of a Survivor* as well – and whilst it is possible to read such secluded and delimited social units as prefigurative within the utopian tradition, this relies on them at least implying some kind of return into, and expansion through, the wider social body.[57] A telling comparison for Lessing's use of the utopian enclave in this regard is Octavia Butler's *Earthseed* novels, in which a group of characters in a dystopian near future gather around Lauren Oya Olamina, the founder of a new religion who believes humankind's destiny is to colonise other planets.[58] The first novel, *Parable of the Sower* (1993), concludes with the characters forming the first Earthseed community on a farm, an enclave and secluded community; however, Lauren still believes that they have a historical role to play. The second novel, *Parable of the Talents* (1998), both extends and complicates this belief, plunging Earthseed and Lauren's aspirations into what the science fiction scholar Gerry Canavan has called 'anti-utopian reality'.[59] In Lessing's writing, in contrast, the enclave can prefigure, at best, only the survival of what makes it valuable: it acts as a vessel to preserve humanity's better aspects into another generation, another world situation, in which the species will still face the same problems, in a new context but essentially unchanged from before. To turn to another science fiction work for context, Lessing's sensibility more strongly suggests that of the man in Cormac McCarthy's *The Road* (2006), doggedly carrying the fire – 'It's inside you. It was always there' – through a post-apocalyptic hellscape of barbarity.[60]

For all the anti-utopianism of *The Sweetest Dream,* and its stolid realism, it is possible to see it as partaking of the same world view as had animated earlier works such as *Shikasta* or *The Four-Gated City,* whose science-fictional world transformations apparently come closer to a utopian hermeneutic. If *Memoirs of a Survivor* had provided one alternative form of autobiography for Lessing, then *The Sweetest Dream* was another: the author's note preceding the first page explains how she was unwilling to cover the same period with 'volume three of my autobiography because of possible hurt to vulnerable people'.[61] It is also the case, however, that the switch into fiction coincides with the period when Lessing discovered Shah's writing. Towards the end of *Walking in the Shade* Lessing observed that 'from now onwards – that is, from the end of the fifties – there was a main current in my life, deeper than any other, my real preoccupation ... this was my real life'. However, because the topic 'will mean a great deal to a few people but nothing at all to others ... enough of that'.[62] Notwithstanding the 'possible hurt to vulnerable people', *The Sweetest Dream* also covers the period in which Lessing had embarked on her 'real life', though there is no visible trace of it in the novel; an absence that comes into greater relief if the novel is compared to a work like *The Four-Gated City,* where Martha's investigations into alternative modes of being, amidst the day-to-day life of a household in London, paralleled Lessing's own. Why should this matter? The works by Lessing most commonly identified with the influence of Sufi thought are those which use quotes from Idries Shah as epigraphs (e.g. *Landlocked, The Four-Gated City*) or draw on Sufi ideas about spiritual growth (*Briefing for a Descent into Hell, The Memoirs of a Survivor*).[63] However, we have seen how the explicitly Sufi ideas that entered Lessing's fiction in the 1960s found a ready pairing with her previous work thanks to the Sufi emphasis on an almost anthropological tracing of societal and psychological systems. When a work like *The Sweetest Dream* shows no trace of spiritual activity but continues to track those systems it is still performing what I think

Lessing would have understood as constructive work within a Sufi world system. In this sense her work proceeds in the spirit of a Shah story from *Seeker After Truth* (1982) concerning the Sufi Master of the fourteenth century, Bahaudin Naqshband, who asserts that 'one day everyone will possess' wisdom, 'but in the meantime the work which will be done eventually through the generations has to be performed in one and the same individual'.[64] If the *Canopus in Argos* sequence still takes cognisance of that 'one day', in much of Lessing's other writing, such as *The Sweetest Dream*, the transfer is to the individual and what they can achieve; but it is all part of the same endeavour.

Ecocatastrophe in Lessing's Later Fiction

However, in some of Lessing's later fiction this unchanging need to endure the slings and arrows of human behaviour and historical contingency gains an environmental dimension that puts this position under unique pressure, and also clarifies what might be at stake, in the contemporary moment, in the identification and pursuit of utopian practice. The 1999 novel *Mara and Dann* might be set in a far future in which another ice age has settled over Europe, leaving only Africa temperate – though as the novel starts the climate seems to be changing again – but in many ways it repeats the dynamic of *The Sweetest Dream*.[65] The novel's focalising character, Mara, is fascinated, baffled, and repulsed by the lost civilisation that is ours, and by the recklessness with which it has destroyed human life and the environment. Within this almost traumatic recognition of historical loss, however, there is a recognition that it is merely one instance in a longer, recurring cycle, at the level of both society and planet. A 'new [political] regime' is 'unusual' as it is 'quite new, and still virtuous', though as this newness equates to 'about a hundred years ... the usual rot will set in soon'.[66] The ancient peoples might have been crazed by 'the machines' they invented, and unimaginably destructive, but 'the people alive now were the same as those so clever, but so stupid, ancient peoples' – an assertion whose basic truth Mara immediately recognises.[67] In terms of the planet, 'nothing stays the same ... all the history of Ifrik [Africa] has been that – swings of climate'.[68] The story follows the eponymous characters as they struggle to survive, and as Mara struggles to recover what historical knowledge she can, an effort enabled by her acuity and observational ability in the phenomenological present. It ends with Mara and Dann together in a house with other, broadly sympathetic characters. Notwithstanding the setting, on the shores of a glacial Mediterranean, this is the basic pattern of *The Sweetest Dream* redux.

However, this conception of an unchanging world, punctuated by various scales of disaster, is placed under pressure by climate change, in a way that the twentieth-century world of *The Sweetest Dream* was not – or at least, not so obviously. Put baldly, 'all the history of Ifrik has been ... swings of climate' resembles at best a climate change misconception, and at worst the argument of climate change deniers. As an overview from the Royal Society and the US National Academy of Sciences puts it, 'all major climate changes, including natural ones, are disruptive', but 'the speed of the current climate change is faster than most of the past events, making it more difficult for human societies and the natural world to adapt';[69] and this is before one considers the impact of these changes on an unprecedentedly large human population, equipped with apocalyptic military technologies. It appears to be an exceptional moment in human history, at odds with a historical model based on cycles and recurrences. Lessing's writing of resilience, of the persistence of curiosity and kindness, in the face of cruelty and stupidity and injustice, retains its power and relevance; perhaps all the more so because it is, as Tom Sperlinger has described, unusually preoccupied with the role fiction can play in education, and so in radical individual change.[70] However, its seeming disavowal of the possibility of positive systemic change, of the necessity of utopian hope and striving, is placed into unprecedentedly stark relief by climate change, which for perhaps the first time in human history has put that necessity on the clock. The less positive systemic change that happens, and the slower it happens, the greater the certainty of immense destruction that is either irreversible in fact (e.g. the mass extinction of species) or practical reality (e.g. climate, even if it might change again far into the future). Equally, climate change, like other environmental impacts, is caused by human activity – it is not a case of waiting out the slings and arrows of planetary systems beyond the influence of Anthropos.

Lessing's emphasis on endurance finds a distant echo in more recent work, such as Roy Scranton's *Learning to Die in the Anthropocene* (2016) and *We're Doomed. Now What?* (2018).[71] Scranton accepts as inevitable the disasters that are coming – their mitigation requires too much of humans, the changes are too far advanced – and advocates stoicism in the face of this fact: we must accept the end of civilisation and rethink how to live and value life. While an emphasis on endurance does not automatically equate to disengagement, either ethically or practically, it might nevertheless risk straying inadvertently close to what Kim Stanley Robinson has termed 'cruel pessimism.'

> ... "Although I'm a prosperous person, although I can probably make my child a prosperous person, the world is screwed and therefore I don't need to

worry about it because there is going to be an end." So, there's a sort of apocalyptic end-of-the-world "ism" that says that I don't have to change my behaviour, I don't have to try because it's already doomed.

Some of the most prosperous people on the planet are promulgating this view, which obviously I don't agree with and I feel that it is really dodging the moral imperative. Maybe optimism is a kind of moral imperative, you have to stay optimistic because otherwise you're just a wanker that's taken off into your own private Idaho of "Oh well, things are bad"[72]

Lessing's work remains a powerful expression of the endurance of human knowledge, capability, and decency across hostile stretches of time, and an outstanding dissection of the perverse social and psychological dynamics in which that germ of human positivity must survive and persist. But without hope – a utopian hope – of positive collective and civilisational change, and without the effort to achieve that historical break, does such stoicism and self-knowledge risk also becoming a self-fulfilling acceptance of the worst of the climate change future? This is one challenge that Lessing's work leaves us with, in our crisis-ridden twenty-first century present: how to connect the utopian germ preserved by her characters in the later fiction, with the more expansive hope for societal transformation that has characterised the utopian genre since its inception. And beyond that challenge a further question, one that grows starker with every passing year: at what point do we lose hope – if we haven't already – and what happens to utopia then? How small can it shrink before it is no longer utopia at all?

Notes

1. Doris Lessing quoted in Susan Linfield and Doris Lessing, 'Against Utopia: An Interview with Doris Lessing', *Salmagundi*, 130/131 (2001), pp. 59–74.
2. For scholarly appraisals of Lessing's later work as reactionary see: Margaret Scanlan's description of *The Good Terrorist* (1985) as 'reactionary in its implied politics of quietism and complicity with power'. Margaret Scanlan, 'Language and the Politics of Despair in Doris Lessing's *The Good Terrorist*', *NOVEL: A Forum on Fiction*, 23(2) (1990), pp. 182–98 (p. 196); or Lynne Segal's description of *The Sweetest Dream* (2001) as a 'truly reactionary work'. Lynne Segal quoted in Susan Watkins, 'Remembering Home: Nation and Identity in the Recent Writing of Doris Lessing', *Feminist Review*, 85 (2007), pp. 97–115 (p. 102). Other critics have argued that Lessing's more explicitly utopian texts can be read as reactionary. See, for example, Jeanette King's reading of *The Four-Gated City* as 'a form of reactionary romanticism'. Jeannette King, *Modern Fiction: Doris Lessing* (London: Arnold, 1989), p. 34. It is worth noting that there is no critical consensus on how Lessing's career breaks down in relation to such terms.

3. Ruth Levitas, *The Concept of Utopia* (Oxford: Peter Lang, 2010), p. 209.
4. Philip E. Wegner, *Imaginary Communities: Utopia, the Nation, and the Spatial Histories of Modernity* (Oakland: University of California Press, 2002), p. xv.
5. Doris Lessing, *Martha Quest* [1952] (London: Flamingo, 1996); *A Proper Marriage* [1954] (London: Flamingo, 2010); *A Ripple from the Storm* [1958] (London: Fourth Estate, 2012); *Landlocked* [1965] (London: Fourth Estate, 2013); *The Four-Gated City* [1969] (London: Flamingo, 2010); and *The Golden Notebook* [1962] (London: HarperPerennial, 2007).
6. David Sergeant, 'Fictions of Time and Space: From Realism to Utopia in Doris Lessing's *The Four-Gated City*', *Twentieth-Century Literature*, 67(2) (2021), pp. 139–62.
7. Doris Lessing, *The Four-Gated City* (Boulder: Paladin, 1990), p. 472.
8. Ibid., pp. 50, 537.
9. Ibid., p. 660.
10. Tom Moylan, *Demand the Impossible: Science Fiction and the Utopian Imagination* (New York: Methuen, 1986), pp. 10–11.
11. Jay Clayton, 'The Ridicule of Time: Science Fiction, Bioethics, and the Posthuman', *American Literary History*, 25(2) (2013), pp. 317–43 (pp. 327–8).
12. Ibid., p. 328.
13. For a helpful account of the equivalence of history and narrative in Jameson's work, see Philip E. Wegner, *Periodizing Jameson: Dialectics, the University, and the Desire for Narrative* (Chicago: Northwestern University Press, 2014).
14. David Sergeant, 'Lessing and the Scale of Environmental Crisis' in *Doris Lessing and the Forming of History*, ed. Kevin Brazil, David Sergeant, and Tom Sperlinger (Edinburgh: Edinburgh University Press, 2016), pp. 111–27 (pp. 121–2).
15. Yevgeny Zamyatin, *We* [1924], trans. Clarence Brown (London: Penguin, 1993).
16. Wegner, *Imaginary Communities*, p. 169.
17. Ursula Le Guin, *The Dispossessed: An Ambiguous Utopia* [1974] (London: Gollancz, 2002), p. 274.
18. Marge Piercy, *Woman on the Edge of Time: A Novel* [1976] (London: Random House, 1997).
19. Kim Stanley Robinson, *New York 2140* (London: Orbit, 2017), p. 604.
20. See W. Warren Wagar, *Terminal Visions: The Literature of Last Things* (Bloomington: Indiana University Press, 1982), pp. 46–7; and Maxine Lavon Montgomery, *The Apocalypse in African-American Fiction* (Gainesville: University Press of Florida, 1996).
21. See James Berger, *After the End: Representations of Post-Apocalypse* (Minneapolis: University of Minnesota Press, 1999); and David J. Leigh, *Apocalyptic Patterns in Twentieth-Century Fiction* (Notre Dame: University of Notre Dame Press, 2008).
22. Moylan, *Demand the Impossible*, p. 156.
23. See, for example, Idries Shah, *The Sufis* (London: The Octagon Press, 1964).

24. Nevertheless, some figures – such as Clancy Sigal, Lessing's lover during the writing of *The Golden Notebook* – characterised Shah as a fraudulent guru. See Roberta Rubenstein, *Literary Half-Lives: Doris Lessing, Clancy Sigal, and Roman à Clef* (Basingstoke: Palgrave, 2014), pp. 122–3, 155.
25. For Lessing and Sufism, see Nancy Shields Hardin, 'The Sufi Teaching Story and Doris Lessing', *Twentieth Century* Literature, 23(3) (1977), pp. 314–26; Ann Scott, 'The More Recent Writings: Sufism, Mysticism and Politics' in *Notebooks/Memoirs/Archives: Reading and Rereading Doris Lessing*, ed. Jenny Taylor (New York: Routledge, 1982), pp. 164–190; Shadia, S. Fahim, *Doris Lessing: Sufi Equilibrium and the Form of the Novel* (London: Macmillan, 1994); Müge Galin, *Between East and West: Sufism in the novels of Doris Lessing* (New York: State University of New York Press, 1997); Phyllis Perrakis, 'Sufism, Jung and the Myth of Kore: Revisionist Politics in Lessing's Marriages, *Mosaic*, 25(3) (1992), pp. 99–120.
26. Idries Shah, 'The Garden' in *The Way of the Sufi* (London: The Octagon Press, 1968), pp. 117–19.
27. The frontispiece of Lessing's *Briefing for a Descent into Hell* (1971) reads 'CATEGORY: INNER-SPACE FICTION // *For there is never anywhere to go but in*'. Doris Lessing, *Briefing for a Descent into Hell* (New York: Knopf, 1971).
28. Allan Hepburn, *A Grain of Faith: Religion in Mid-Century British Literature* (Oxford: Oxford University Press, 2018), p. 1.
29. James Clements, *Mysticism and the Mid-Century Novel* (Basingstoke: Palgrave, 2012), pp. 3–4.
30. Clements, *Mysticism*, p. 26.
31. Doris Lessing, 'Conquering Inner Space', *The Times*, Thursday, 5 May 1994, p. 40.
32. Doris Lessing, *Shikasta* (London: Grafton Books, 1981), p. 201. See, for instance, Linfield and Lessing, 'An Interview'.
33. Ursula Le Guin, 'Doris Lessing's First Sci-Fi Book Reads Like a Debut Novel', *The New Republic*, 13 October 1979. Available at: https://newrepublic.com/article/115631/doris-lessing-shikasta-reviewed-ursula-le-guin (Last accessed 13 August 2025).
34. Ursula Le Guin, *The Dispossessed* (London: Gollancz, 2002), pp. 28–9.
35. Wegner, *Imaginary Communities*, p. 177.
36. Ursula Le Guin, 'Doris Lessing's First Sci-Fi Book Reads Like a Debut Novel', *The New Republic*, 13 October 1979. https://newrepublic.com/article/115631/doris-lessing-shikasta-reviewed-ursula-le-guin (Last accessed 2 August 2024).
37. This quotation comes from Shah's *Reflections* (1968) where it appears in a passage titled 'History'. Idries Shah, *Reflections* [1968] (London: The Octagon Press, 1991), p. 82.
38. Possibly Lessing is quoting from memory, as the original quote is in the past tense. See Idries Shah, *Tales of the Dervishes* [1967] (London: The Octagon Press, 1982), p. 122.

39. Doris Lessing, *The Memoirs of a Survivor* (London: Picador, 1976); and *The Sweetest Dream* (London: Flamingo, 2001).
40. See Philip Glass, *The Making of the Representative for Planet 8: An Opera in Three Acts for Orchestra, Small Chorus and Soloists, Music by Philip Glass, Libretto by Doris Lessing Based on Her Novel* (New York: Dunvagen Music Publishers, 1988). The opera premiered on 8 July 1988 at Houston Grand Opera, Texas. For information, see Philip Glass's personal website: https://philipglass.com/compositions/making_rep_for_planet_8/ (Last accessed 2 August 2024). Doris Lessing and Charlie Adlard, *Playing the Game* (London: Fourth Estate, 1995).
41. See Sergeant, 'Scale'.
42. Lessing, *Memoirs*, p. 7.
43. Cornelius Collins, '"A Horizontal, Almost Nationless Organisation": Doris Lessing's Prophecies of Globalization', *Twentieth Century Literature*, 56(2) (2010), pp. 221–44 (p. 223).
44. As Maureen Howard put it, Lessing's 'old Dreiserian amplitude ... all that apparatus of the old genre'. Maureen Howard, 'Doris Lessing Considers Her World and the World', *New York Times*, 8 June 1975. https://archive.nytimes.com/www.nytimes.com/books/97/09/14/reviews/lessing-survivor.html (Last accessed 2 August 2024).
45. Idries Shah, 'The Teaching Story: Observations on the Folklore of Our "Modern" Thought' in *The Nature of Human Consciousness: A Book of Readings*, ed. Robert E. Ornstein (New York: Viking Press, 1974), p. 291.
46. Lessing, *Memoirs*, p. 190.
47. Collins, 'Propehcies', p. 230.
48. Fredric Jameson's mind-bending statement of this dialectic between individual and collective in utopia is as good as any: 'while nature is meaningless, history has a meaning; even if there is no meaning, the project and the future produce it, on the individual as well as the collective basis. The great collective project has a meaning and it is that of utopia. But the problem of utopia, of collective meaning, is to find an individual meaning.' Fredric Jameson, *An American Utopia: Dual Power and the Universal Army* (London: Verso, 2016), pp. 311–12.
49. Lessing, *Sweetest Dream*, p. 110.
50. Jeanette Winterson, 'What Planet Is Doris On?' *The Guardian*, 15 August 2001. www.theguardian.com/books/2001/aug/15/edinburghfestival2001.edinburgh festival (Last accesed 2 August 2024).
51. Lessing quoted in Linfield, 'An Interview', p. 64.
52. Moylan, *Demand the Impossible*, p. 19.
53. Krishan Kumar, *Utopia and Anti-Utopia in Modern Times* (Oxford: Basil Blackwell, 1987), pp. 101–2.
54. Lesing, *Sweetest Dream*, p. 435.
55. Ibid., p. 473.
56. See Doris Lessing, *Walking in the Shade* (London: Flamingo, 1998), p. 57; and Lessing, *Sweetest Dream*, p. 229.

57. For the role of houses in Lessing's work see: Roberta Rubenstein, *The Novelistic Vision of Doris Lessing: Breaking the Forms of Consciousness* (Champaign: University of Illinois Press, 1979); Betsy Draine, 'Nostalgia and Irony: The Postmodern Order of *The Golden Notebook*', *Modern Fiction Studies*, 26(1) (1980), pp. 31–48; and Victoria Rosner, 'Home Fires: Doris Lessing, Colonial Architecture, and the Reproduction of Mothering', *Tulsa Studies in Women's Literature*, 18(1) (1999), pp. 59–89.
58. Octavia Butler, *Parable of the Sower* [1993] (London: Headline, 2019); and *Parable of the Talents* [1998] (London: The Women's Press, 2001).
59. Gerry Canavan, *Octavia E. Butler* (Champaign: University of Illinois Press, 2016), p. 64.
60. Cormac McCarthy, *The Road* (London: Vintage, 2006), p. 279.
61. Lessing, *Sweetest Dream*, author's note preceding p. 1.
62. Lessing, Walking in the Shade, p. 353
63. See, for example, Rubenstein *Half-Lives*, p. 123.
64. Idries Shah, 'Scent and Reality' in *Seeker After Truth: A Handbook* [1982] (London: The Octagon Press, 1992), pp. 10–12 (p. 11).
65. Doris Lessing, *Mara and Dann* [1999] (London: Flamingo, 2000).
66. Ibid., p. 344.
67. Ibid., pp. 381–2.
68. Ibid., p. 374.
69. The Royal Society and the US National Academy of Sciences, *Climate Change Evidence and Causes Update 2020*. https://royalsociety.org/media/Royal_Society_Content/policy/projects/climate-evidence-causes/climate-change-evidence-causes.pdf (Last accessed 2 August 2024).
70. See Tom Sperlinger, 'Radical Pedagogy in Doris Lessing's Mara and Dann', *Critique: Studies in Contemporary Fiction*, 58(3) (2016), 300–11.
71. Roy Scranton, *Learning to Die in the Anthropocene: Reflections on the End of a Civilization* (San Francisco: City Lights Books, 2016); and *We're Doomed. Now What?: Essays on War and Climate Change* (New York: Soho, 2018).
72. José Luis De Vicente, 'Angry Optimism in a Drowned World: A Conversation with Kim Stanley Robinson', *Centre de Cultura Contemporània de Barcelona* website, 31 October 2017. https://lab.cccb.org/en/angry-optimism-in-a-drowned-world-a-conversation-with-kim-stanley-robinson/ (Last accessed 2 August 2024). Robinson is riffing on Lauren Berlant's concept of 'cruel optimism'. Cruel Optimism (Durham: Duke University Press, 2011).

CHAPTER 9

Utopian Articulations in Experimental British Poetry
Juha Virtanen

It is impossible to offer a unified narrative that neatly summarises the utopian positions in modern and contemporary British poetry. Given the complex history of these poetries – as seen, for instance, in the historical divisions between factions of traditional mainstream poets and the radical and experimental poetics of the so-called British Poetry Revival and its present-day legacies – one might even say that it is impossible to offer a unified narrative of modern and contemporary British poetry in general.[1] Nevertheless, this chapter considers what kind of utopian articulations can be glimpsed in contemporary experimental poetry from the United Kingdom. 'Glimpse' is a key term for this chapter, as it primarily focuses on diaphanous filaments that exist between individual objects, spaces, poets, and texts, through which various utopian imaginations can be – however briefly – observed. This chapter is interested in the solidarities and dialogues that exist between different cacophonous parts, and whilst it highlights overlaps between them, it also acknowledges that those overlaps cannot add up to a totalising account. In what follows, I will analyse utopian dimensions in the works of three experimental British poets writing in the 2010s: Sean Bonney, Verity Spott, and Callie Gardner. Responding to our ongoing era of austerity, authoritarianism, and crisis, their respective works offer significant critiques of institutional violence, failures of care, and intellectual abstractions. Moreover, their poetries depict crucial – if ambivalent – utopian glimpses of scandalous joy, leaking care, and concrete community building. These articulations convey anticipatory expressions of, and precursors to, a futurity that is not yet here, but the arrival of which is necessary for our survival.

Zarf and Community Building in Experimental Poetry

Apart from a small number of exceptions, readers are unlikely to encounter experimental poetry in British national media, corporate publishing, or school curricula. These poetries are instead sustained through ecosystems of small-scale publishing, where presses often operate outside of formalised spheres of paid labour. An indicative example of such publications is *Zarf*, a DIY poetry magazine founded and edited by Callie Gardner. In the fifteen of its issues published between 2015 and 2020, *Zarf* was variously based in Cardiff (issues 1 to 4), Leeds (issues 7 to 12), and Glasgow (issues 5, 6, 13, 14, and 15), with each change in location precipitated by the demands of Gardner's postgraduate studies and subsequent employment. Apart from the sixth issue, which was an audio volume comprising mp3 recordings, all *Zarfs* had a roughly similar format: A5 size, paper covers, stapled together. The early issues would even feature a declaration that the '*ZARF* you have in your hands … is printed and made with pride', emphasising that each issue was not simply a collection of poems; more precisely, the production of *Zarf* required poetic, editorial, and physical labour from Gardner and their collaborators.[2] Furthermore, that labour is not framed as alienating; as the specific mention of 'pride' suggests, the labour for *Zarf* is understood as a labour of love. Gardner met the costs of producing the magazine themselves, putting it together with help from friends, and distributing it as widely and cheaply as possible, without any motivation for profit.[3] *Zarf* is therefore a contemporary example of a small press publication that eschews commodification. Like Ken Edwards's description of similar publications in the 1980s, Gardner's editorial ethos centred on producing 'anti-commodities', in which 'the labour that made them retains its visibility'.[4]

The conditions of its production were not the only aspect of *Zarf* that demonstrated such radical potential. The issues often included editorial notes from Gardner, through which they were able to voice some of the politics that informed the publication. Chief amongst them was a continuous dedication to community. The third issue's editorial expressed thanks to fellow poets who had organised a performance event in Canterbury that Gardner read at and found 'transformative', before noting that 'a *zarf* only exists because and for its writer-readers, a community of voracious production'.[5] The reflective editorial included in the final issue likewise states that Gardner started the magazine because they wanted to meet 'other poets', and to have an excuse to go to poetry readings where they might not know anyone in advance.[6] The driving editorial motivation was therefore social: *Zarf* operated as a tool for community building. This operative model coheres with Elizabeth-Jane Burnett's notion of gift exchange.[7] As most experimental poetry is produced without any hope or intention of financial gain, Burnett argues that communities of poets, publishers, audiences, and readers sustain themselves outside of profit-seeking commercial circuits through an exchange of gifts – which might take shape as publications, performances, responses, collaborations, and so on. Whilst such exchanges do not equate to handing out work free of charge, they are still informed by a non-commercial ethos. In each instance – as with the publication of *Zarf* – the gift is about finding ways for individuals to relate with one another, of establishing different social relations which may or may not link with the wider society outside of poetry communities.[8] Indeed, the act of building social relations via publications and poetry events reveals an implicitly utopian ideal: as Burnett notes, the 'alternative economic and social structures' of gift exchange in poetry communities represent, however fleetingly, 'an alternative to capitalism'.[9]

As such, it may be tempting to understand the utopian imaginations of experimental poetry communities in terms of Herbert Marcuse's *An Essay on Liberation* (1969).[10] For Marcuse, the late-twentieth-century innovations in art, music, and literature involve an aesthetic ethos that can 'dissolve the very structure of perception' and therefore allow us to no longer see things in the medium of the 'law and order which formed them'.[11] That is, experimental forms of art can act as tools for imagining or establishing something not yet in existence: art could, in this sense, 'form reality'.[12] While they may not be tantamount to a full revolution, such artworks resist capitalist social structures that coerce individuals to understand themselves in strictly consumerist terms. To borrow from Fredric Jameson's reading of Marcuse, non-conformist art practices might therefore offer a 'concrete acting out of the Utopian impulse'.[13] Applied to the context of experimental poetry, these theories suggest that publications like *Zarf* – and others by presses such as the87press, Aquifer, DATABLEED, Distance No Object, Face Press, Gong Farm, Just Not, Materials, Osmosis, Sad Press, SPAM, Slub Press, Veer/Veer 2, zimZalla, and others – can potentially facilitate a space where comparable utopian impulses are also acted out. The unique circumstances of each press will of course differ: some may benefit from occasional funding, or perhaps a peri-academic connection to a university, whilst others operate on an entirely DIY basis. However, these presses are not explicitly profit-seeking. Publishers dedicated to experimental poetry instead tend to understand their role in social and political terms. That is, by centring around forms of literary production that resist commodification, these poetic communities have the capacity to offer a fleeting glimpse of – or perhaps even an incubating laboratory for – alternative social organisations where resources are distributed in a more syndicalist and egalitarian way.

Yet, it is important to note that Marcuse's essay – which responds specifically to 1960s counterculture – may not seamlessly map onto twenty-first century poetics. Experimental poets in the United Kingdom frequently express suspicions about poetry's supposedly inherent political potential, as Gardner did in many *Zarf* editorials. In the penultimate issue, they noted that is it 'rare' to encounter a poem that not only imagines a world that 'grows differently', but also speaks as though that world was 'already in existence'.[14] These statements challenge an easy application of the Marcusean notion that art can shape reality: experimental forms alone are not sufficient for such a task. Gardner's statement is not, however, a categorical rejection of poetry's utopian potential. Rather, they recognised that while poetry can be a 'resilient technology of love and liberation', it is not inherently so.[15] To avoid negating poetry's capacity for liberation, poets ought to remain vigilant of 'what the world is asking our poems to be and do, and be and do the opposite'.[16] In other words, Gardner proposes that poetry's utopian potential demands an unyielding position of opposition and refusal: 'if they ask you to be simple, be difficult; if they ask you to be articulate, do not bend nor explain; if they want you only as a soothing voice for the evening, screech shatteringly into the still morning'.[17] The positions articulated in *Zarf* are thus closely aligned with Theodor Adorno's aesthetic theories: poetry 'becomes social by its opposition to society'.[18] That is, the oppositional position of poetry does not reside inherently in its formal qualities, but is instead a kinetic force that exists in a constant state of becoming. Its oppositions must be actively produced through vigilance, ongoing critique, and continuous refusal.

Scandalous Utopian Joy in Sean Bonney's Insurrectionary Poetry

Few poets in the United Kingdom articulated these politics of refusal as urgently and compellingly as Sean Bonney. Although Bonney's poetics were always aligned with revolutionary politics, the election of the Conservative–Lib Dem coalition government in 2010 – which ushered in an era of austerity, authoritarianism, and crisis that has continued to the present day – precipitated a radical new direction in his writing. Responding to the student protests and occupations that took place in opposition to the planned spending cuts in further education and the tripling of university tuition fees in November 2010, Bonney's 'Letter on Poetics' – a text that is both an epistolary prose poem and a statement of poetic intent – issued a pressing challenge to easy assumptions about the political force of poetry. 'I turned up and did readings in student occupations', Bonney writes, before confessing that it 'felt stupid to stand up, after someone had been doing a talk on what to do if you got nicked ... to stand up and read poetry.' It was not enough, Bonney felt, to delude himself that his 'poetry had somehow been "tested" because' the audience enjoyed it.[19] In other words, moments of political struggle reveal the ways in which poetry is lacking. It is unable to address the practical needs of such moments and will instead present a weak mimesis of the struggle – for instance, 'a rant against the government' – instead of a direct engagement with it.[20] As a result, poetry might at best become 'an entertaining side show' lost between more pressing political utterances.[21]

Bonney levels these charges at poetry to find an expression that could engage with its political reality in a more active and transformative way. He wonders if there might be a poem that could identify a 'decisive moment' in the 'present conjuncture', and 'exert force' towards it, as a 'concrete analysis' of that contemporary situation.[22] That is, the poem Bonney tries to imagine is an utterance that intervenes in and interrupts its present moment; a poetry that could inform and extend the possibilities of protest, insurrection, and revolution. This is quite likely an impossible task for poetry, and Bonney is clear that such poems may not yet exist. Instead, the poetry of the present is depicted as 'stupid', albeit with a notable caveat: 'stupidity is not the absence of intellectual ability but rather the scar of its mutilation'.[23] The implications of this statement are significant. A scar signifies damage: it is what an injury – or, in this case, mutilation – leaves behind. Long after the act of violence itself, the scar serves as a visible marker of that violence. Since the original act is no longer – and perhaps never was – visible or accessible, its violence can only be understood through the sign of the scar. It thus attests to both violence and vulnerability. To borrow from Sara Ahmed, scars function as a 'trace of where another entity ... has impressed upon the body', and therefore remind us that being in the world leaves us open to receive painful encounters with repressive forces.[24] But at the same time, a scar also contains its own opposite. As the fibrous tissue that replaces normal skin after an injury, a scar is medically understood as the body's natural way of healing. That is, while the scar continues to attest to violence and vulnerability, it also operates as a site of recovery. Although the mutilation will continue to make the echo of itself known through the presence of the scar, it likewise serves as a counterforce that withstands and acts against that mutilation.

It is useful to understand the scar in Bonney's writing from this dialectical perspective. If poetry is the scar of a mutilated intellectual ability, it is a deranged and social utterance that makes both violence and vulnerability visible. At the same time, poetry can – or should – offer a counterviolence that retaliates against that mutilation. Like the Hegelian notion of the Spirit, poetry as a scar does not shrink from death: it endures it and maintains itself in it.[25] That said, the scars that interest Bonney are not just abstract but concrete. The austerity policies he writes against are violent, mutilating, and deadly: there were nearly 335,000 excess deaths in England, Wales, and Scotland between 2012 and 2019, most of which were due to vulnerable people dying prematurely as a result of reduced income, ill health, poor nutrition and housing, and/or social isolation.[26] But because that violence is institutional, it appears ordinary, mundane, and bureaucratic – that is, normalised to the point of obscurity.[27] As Bonney said during an interview in 2012:

> We live in a system of violence. Every time you look at the newspaper and [then Secretary of State for Work and Pensions] Iain Duncan Smith is talking about benefit cuts and blaming the weakest and the poorest of society for all the problems of the bourgeoisie and the very rich, that is ultraviolence.[28]

To extrapolate, the Conservative government's abstract rhetoric of 'benefit cuts' masks the concrete violence that such cuts enact on the vulnerable. As Zoe Skoulding notes, poetry is uniquely attentive to the 'structures of control in language', and therefore it has the capacity to intervene in such structures.[29] In a similar vein, Bonney's notion of poetry as a scar seeks to identify an idiom that reveals Duncan Smith's rhetoric as the ultraviolence it is, and then exerts a linguistic counterforce against it. In this sense, the poetry that Bonney seeks in 'Letter on Poetics' is similar to the Adornian understanding of artworks as socially critical zones of hurt where the 'untruth of the social situation comes to light'.[30]

Consequently, when Duncan Smith appears in Bonney's 2015 collection *Letters Against the Firmament*, he is not words in a newspaper, but instead a 'talking claw' that breaks 'children's teeth with gravel-stones', 'covers them in ashes', and 'blocks out the stars' with his malevolent alphabet.[31] These nightmarish descriptions concretise the point Bonney articulated in the aforementioned interview: as a 'talking claw' Duncan Smith becomes an appendage whose predation is enacted through speech; further, that speech reaches an apocalyptic degree of severity that obscures entire constellations. The deranged imagery thus offers a physical description of the ultraviolence that Duncan Smith enacted with his speeches and policies. The predatory practices of the talking claw depend upon dehumanising others and treating children as objects ready for breaking. Yet, the poem also turns that dehumanising practice against Duncan Smith and through that counterviolence reduces him to an inhuman form. This pattern repeats with other politicians as well. George Osborne, the Chancellor of the Exchequer from 2010 to 2016, is imagined 'lying ... in tatters in the middle of the road'.[32] The collection also includes a poem titled 'The Kidnap and Murder of David Cameron', where the Prime Minister from 2010 to 2016 is depicted howling through the night, 'bloodshot and ridiculous'.[33] In each instance, the institutional violence of these politicians' policies is countered with a deranging and dehumanising violence enacted on their imagined bodies.

Of course, these imagined antagonisms could be dismissed as a vengeful fantasy or a hyperbolic metaphor. However, as the British poet and critic William Rowe points out, such dismissals would be tantamount to allowing 'bourgeois repression ... to have accomplished its own shunting into the imaginary'.[34] In other words, there is something significant about these deranged effigies. Writing about *Don Quixote*, Ernst Bloch noted that there is more to the novel than 'how mad we consider' its titular character to be; we must also consider 'the facts in which and against which he rides'. Bloch reads Cervantes' iconic text as a critique of the 'emerging bourgeois world', and notes that since this world is far from glorious, Don Quixote's rebellion against it is not 'incomprehensible'.[35] Rather, it can be understood as a metaphoric 'guiding light' that imagines alternatives to bourgeois reality.[36] An analogous case occurs in Bonney's imaginary counterviolence. In his analysis of the revolutionary communist Louis-August Blanqui's enigmatic cosmological text *Eternity by the Stars* (1872), Bonney notes that 'revolution tumbles back into poetics' in the moment of defeat, which in turn means that poetry can conceal and sustain such insurgent energies until an insurrectionary moment makes them 'explode outwards into revolution'.[37] Consequently, the deranged forms found in *Letters Against the Firmament* perform a dual function: the violence they depict offers a full and accurate account of British bourgeois reality in the 2010s; but, crucially, the counterforce these poetic forms exert also imagines the possibility of defeating that reality. A comparable moment can be observed in Bonney's epistolary prose poem on the 'strange, negative expression of scandalous joy' he experienced at some of the death parties that took place across the United Kingdom – including in Brixton (which Bonney attended), Bristol, Leeds, Liverpool, and

Glasgow – after the former prime minister Margaret Thatcher passed away in 2013.[38] Contemporaneous reports of such parties, especially those printed in liberal centrist media, tended to frame the events in terms of police presence and arrests, and included eyewitness comments such as 'I would rather that Thatcherism was dead'.[39] Bonney's poem, however, provides a crucial riposte:

> And yes. Every single one of us was well aware that we hadn't won anything, that her legacy 'still lived on', or whatever other sanctimonious spittle was being coughed up by liberal shitheads in the *Guardian* and on Facebook. That wasn't the point. It was horrible. Deliberately so. Like the plague-feast in *Nosferatu*. I loved it.[40]

The death parties share a dynamic with the poetry and poetics in *Letters Against the Firmament*. They might appear like a scene of horror, as the references to 'horrible' and *Nosferatu* indicate. But that scene also reveals something significant about Thatcher and her legacy, which the commentators in the newspapers and social media do not seemingly grasp: how much suffering must a political leader inflict to have their death celebrated in this manner? Bonney loves the death parties because they are a moment of cacophonous solidarity that enables him to glimpse a different political reality where the bourgeois world is – however fleetingly and inadequately – interrupted. In the poem, this interruption is characterised in Benjaminian terms, most notably in the description of the death parties taking place at 'sites of ancient disturbances suddenly blasted wide open'.[41] That is, Bonney's wording recalls Walter Benjamin's observation that a materialist historiography has the capacity to 'blast a specific era' of class struggle 'out of the homogenous course of history'.[42] A similar understanding is also expressed in Bloch's utopian theories, where a tendency towards futurity can 'open up even the No-Longer-Conscious' of the past.[43] In a Blochian sense, then, Bonney's link between the death parties and 'ancient disturbances' animates this radical past to highlight what is missing in the present: a 'Not-Yet-Conscious ... forward dawning' into a future where the violence of capitalism is not just interrupted, but defeated.[44] The scandalous joy Bonney experiences at these revelries might indeed 'be fleeting', but it holds a utopian promise precisely because 'it gives rise to new types of political perceptions and possibilities'.[45] In the context of everyday life where 'no-one can even *think* revolt', such experiences should not be dismissed.[46] It is because of the experience of scandalous joy – which the poem about the death parties subsequently sustains – that Bonney is able to imagine a time where 'we marched on Parliament, burned it to the ground'.[47]

Corporeal Leaking: Verity Spott's Utopian Praxis of Care and Response

Bonney was not the only British poet who articulated such antagonisms in the 2010s. Despite the doubts in 'Letter On Poetics', his readings – whether performed at protests, squats, picket lines, lecture halls, or rooms in various pubs – had a significant impact on other poets. As Luke Roberts recollects, hearing Bonney's work in the early 2010s made younger poets in particular experience an 'electric' new 'permission' to 'say what [they] wanted'.[48] Given the politics in Bonney's work, it seems inappropriate to interpret Roberts' comments as suggesting a hierarchical genealogy of influence. Instead, this sense of permission is better understood as an expression of solidarity, where other poets feel newly emboldened by the scandalous joy and cacophonous collectivity that emerges in Bonney's poetry.

Verity Spott's contemporaneous work frequently articulated such solidarities. Her 2014 pamphlet *Gideon* was framed as a hex against George Osborne. The title of the poem is derived from the name Osborne was given at birth, and some of its lines – such as 'thus we may now call as one for the head / and intestines of George Osborne' – express sentiments that clearly overlap with those found in *Letters Against the Firmament*.[49] Similarly, Spott's 2017 pamphlet *We Will Bury You* contains the names of all the members of parliament (MPs) who voted against a proposed end to the cap for public sector pay on 29 June that year. The text responds to this austerity-driven act of institutional violence with hexes of counter-violence: in the early stages of the poem, Lucy Allan MP is told that 'whilst you lie dutifully on the ground your gut will wrench and prickle. You will shit in your bed.'[50] As Jennifer Soong has noted, whilst politicians may often remove themselves from the people and places their policies affect, there is no such escape in *We Will Bury You*; instead, it is 'the politicians' own bodies that turn against them'.[51] Like Bonney's depiction of Duncan Smith as a talking claw, Spott's poem turns the actions of the MPs back on themselves. At the same time, it is important to note that Spott felt compelled to write *We Will Bury You* due to intense feelings of 'helplessness' and 'political impotence'.[52] Whilst the poem's hexes are potently phrased, they are also expressed through a complex and conflicting positionality. A key part of Spott's poetry is therefore the way in which it exists both within and against: the counterforce her work exerts arises from, and co-exists with, a position of empathy and vulnerability.[53]

Spott's 2017 book *Click Away Close Door Say* articulates these complex positions. The book was composed between 2014 and 2016, and documents the experiences of working as a carer in a 'specialist support service that looks after young adults with high functioning autism', or other related 'mixed diagnoses'.[54] The period depicted in the book coincided with the service provider 'transitioning from one company to another', and the poems therefore reflect the lived experiences within and against the 'inner contradictions of private care'.[55] That is, the context of UK austerity haunts *Click Away Close Door Say* as well. Because roughly 50 per cent of the spending cuts enacted during Osborne's chancellorship targeted the welfare system and local government, austerity 'decimated' the social care sector.[56] Meanwhile, the private service in *Click Away Close Door Say* – where working life was characterised by understaffing and the resultant failures of care – was first purchased by a private equity firm, and then sold for £500 million profit to Acadia, a US-based healthcare group.[57] In other words, austerity and profit margins lead to a withdrawal of care. Whilst Spott insists that the poems in her book are not 'protests' per se, her responses to the material harm of private care nevertheless recall the Adornian socially critical zones of hurt where the untruth of our social situation comes to light.[58]

'Elegy', the final section of the book, features multiple representations of such hurt. One of these is the recurring reference to the act of leaking. Such imagery appears earlier in the book, but the final section uses it with unsettling frequency: 'You were leaking'; 'burned and leaking skin'; 'When you're leaked upon your total care'; 'where you found yourself still rocking / gently, your whole skin a leaking tatter of wounds'; 'My skin / never leaked like yours does. Your skin leaks everyday'; 'We are both and all leaking, our entire worlds are sprained'; and 'Whether it can be said or not that I leaked I did'.[59] There is some ambiguity regarding the identity of the second person ('you') in these lines, but the final page suggests that their name is 'Dan', and they are presumably one of the residents at the care service.[60] For Danny Hayward, the motif of leaking represents this resident's 'fantasy that structures their sense of reality', and thus it serves as a 'voice of patient tenderness' and vulnerability.[61] But whilst the leaking is certainly an expression of tenderness and vulnerability, there is scope to interpret it further. Considered via Julia Kristeva – a theorist Spott lists as an 'obsessive' figure for the composition of the book – the act of leaking approaches the abject.[62] In Kristeva's analysis, bodily fluids such as blood, sweat, and excrement are understood as a 'defilement' that recalls the border between the living and the dead; that is, in order to 'extricate' oneself from that border – and thus exist as a living body – one must expel and repel such fluids. More succinctly, corporeal leaking is culturally coded as something that we must 'permanently thrust aside in order to live'.[63] It approximates 'death infecting life', and is thus 'the upmost abjection'.[64] In this context, the leaking skin in Spott's poem signifies marginalisation to the point of social death. The imagery of the building entrance – another recurring reference throughout the book – specifies that its 'uncoded door' leads to an 'airlock' where a code must be entered to progress further.[65] Thus sealed from the outside world, Dan and their fellow residents have been metaphorically thrust aside by society. Furthermore, since the 'care of vulnerability' within the facility itself is compromised by the profit-seeking sale of the company, the residents are cast aside internally as well.[66] The vulnerability that the leaking represents is therefore produced and compounded by abjection.

However, Donna Haraway imagines leaking not as abjection, but instead as something more utopian. For her, leaks 'might help open passages for a praxis of care and response'.[67] That is, whilst leaks might be construed as socially unacceptable, bodies – which tend to ooze from every pore – are not sealed containers: the abjection of bodily fluids reprimands the body for simply existing corporeally. Haraway therefore considers leaking as evidence of how 'bodily ethical and political obligations are infectious'.[68] Admittedly, her arguments are made specifically with reference to multispecies companionship, but they also apply to human sociality. Leaking is vulnerable because it implies infection: the same pores that release fluids outward can also leave our interiority open to the world. The leaking skin is therefore a site of sharing; it potentially offers a meeting point between subjectivities, through which care and solidarity might be formed. This pattern can also be observed in the motif of leaking at the end of *Click Away Close Door Say*. In the earlier iterations, it is only Dan – the 'you' – who leaks: their skin is the leaking tatter of wounds, whilst the speaker's skin has never leaked in that manner. Yet, in the latter iterations, the pronouns shift: instead of the second-person addressee ('you'), it is the collective first-person plural ('we') who are leaking. The speaker ultimately insists that their skin is leaking as well. Leaks thus become an act of shared vulnerability. They facilitate a shared tenderness and a shared caring. Moreover, since membership of the collective 'we' in the poem is ambiguous and therefore capacious, this shared caring can be expansive. Spott's leaking praxis of care and response is, in other words, promiscuous, insofar as it designates 'an ethics that proliferates outwards to redefine caring relations from the most intimate to the most distant'.[69] As such, its collectivity highlights a utopian promise. To borrow from the utopian queer theorist José Esteban Muñoz, the 'we' in Spott's poetry is a Blochian not-yet-conscious 'future society that is being invoked and addressed at the same moment'; its shared tenderness and care indicate a possible description of what a 'larger social order could be' and 'what it should be'.[70] The significance of this should not be overlooked. Whilst Spott's imagery carries a more melancholic tone than the scandalous joy that Bonney finds at the death parties, her shared acts of leaking nevertheless leave open the possibility of a forward dawning into the new.[71] The book concludes with the following fragment:

> The whole establishment, the institution,
> pouring out into the little street; to the right the sea,
> to the left the main road. Ahead, houses.[72]

The concluding image suggests that the pores have subsumed the establishment. While the airlock at the entrance was designed as a sealed container, its occlusions have been covertly breached, and the leaking has intensified into outright pouring. In some ways, this conclusion reverses the culturally encoded abjection of leaking bodies, as now it is the bodies that must extricate themselves from the institution. Their re-entry into the public sphere may still be tentative and not without risks: the street outside is only little, and the urban development that crowds the landscape leaves the sea as the only open space in the vicinity. Nonetheless, the final adverb 'ahead' indicates that the poem concludes with a view towards a new futurity; perhaps one where 'multiple forms of belonging in difference' may simultaneously adhere to 'a belonging in collectivity'.[73]

Callie Gardner and Concrete Utopianism

The futurity that the end of Spott's book anticipates – and that Bonney's poetry at times envisions – can be related back to Gardner. In the notes to their 2018 book *Naturally It Is Not*, Gardner makes an explicit claim on utopian thought: 'truly utopian positions can't be theorized into existence', they write, before stressing that such positionalities must 'be imagined out of life as it is lived and language as it is used'.[74] What is shared in the utopian imaginations that these three poets articulate, in other words, is a commitment to concrete analyses of concrete situations. The possibility of utopia begins with a negation of the present, and consequently, utopian articulations may initially assume the form of critique. In Bonney's writing, this is partly enacted through a radical and self-reflexive interrogation of political struggle and poetry's relationship to it. For Spott, this approach requires a complex negotiation of existing both within and against the realities of privatised care. One of Gardner's key techniques for this utopian process is satire. In the first section of *Naturally It Is Not*, they outline a satirical account of what appears to be an academic conference or a comparable meeting of delegates. These occasions can inspire 'subtheorising' about how 'every body is a utopia', but such declarations are tantamount to a meeting of an 'unmobilisable force' and 'an unmakeable object'.[75] What theoretical discourse lacks, as the terms 'unmobilisable' and 'unmakeable' suggest, is concrete action. Pronouncements about utopian bodies will simply strike an overly 'easy pose' if those bodies cannot also be mobilised.[76] The critique that Gardner articulates is therefore not anti-intellectual or anti-academic; rather, their poem suggests that theoretical positions are lost unless they are also translated into lived daily practice.

Gardner's position echoes Bloch's distinction between abstract and concrete utopias. That is, the satirical critique in Gardner's poem is directed at abstract utopianism, which – in Bloch's words – is without a 'solid subject behind it' and thus 'without relation to the Real-Possible'.[77] Whilst potentially useful for its function as critique, an abstract utopia is ultimately unmobilisable because it is 'without contact with' historical consciousness, and as a result lacks 'a real forward tendency into what is better'.[78] By contrast, a concrete utopia is one that is truly 'anticipatory'.[79] As per Muñoz's reading of Bloch, concrete utopias are 'relational to historically situated struggles' and 'a collectivity that is actualised or potential'.[80] A concrete utopia, in other words, is engaged with a lived situation. It can be glimpsed in the cacophonous collectivity and scandalous joy that Bonney experiences at the death parties. It exists in the promiscuous care of leaking in *Click Away Close Door Say*. And it is also articulated in the poetics of Gardner's poem. *Naturally It Is Not* consistently draws upon intertextuality, and whilst Gardner makes use of a dizzying range of materials, it is the quotations from writers such as Nat Raha, an Edinburgh-based poet and activist-scholar whose books include 2018's *Of Sirens, Body & Faultlines*; Jennifer Cooke, a London-based theorist, poet and academic whose publications include the 2015 pamphlet *Apocalypse Dreams*; Amy De'Ath, a London-based poet and academic whose works include 2016's *ON MY LOVE FOR gender abolition*; Anthony (Vahni) Capildeo, a Trinidadian-Scottish poet, professor, and writer-in-residence whose collections include 2016's *Measures of Expatriation*; and Peter Manson, a Glasgow-based poet whose publications include 2009's *Adjunct: An Undigest*, that appear especially noteworthy.[81] Each of these writers is an active member of the poetry communities in which Gardner participated, and as such they are not simply authors consulted as research materials for *Naturally It Is Not*. They are individuals Gardner will have met at poetry readings and related events, perhaps published in *Zarf* and, in some cases, counted as friends. The inclusion of such voices in the poem is therefore a gesture of solidarity that mirrors Gardner's ethos as an editor: in both instances, the reading and writing of poetry contains a promise of community building. The politics of Gardner's poem are utopian because they ceaselessly reach out to others. By thinking through and alongside multiple comradely voices, *Naturally It Is Not* seeks to form collectivity and hopes to actualise those collectives through poetic dialogue and critique.

To the extent that it is possible to offer a summary of utopian articulations in British experimental poetries, the examples from Gardner, Bonney, and Spott suggest that poetry speaks in anticipation of concrete utopias that are not yet here. But what does it mean to read poetry from such a perspective in late 2023, when this chapter was first drafted? In the years that followed the publication of *Letters Against the Firmament*, the institutional violence described in the book has only grown more acute. Spott followed the publication of *Click Away Close Door Say* with 2020's *Hopelessness*, which in part addresses the ideological divisions that have become entrenched in the United Kingdom since 2016.[82] Tragically, both Bonney and Gardner have passed away, the former in 2019 and the latter in 2021. Is it possible to speak of utopian articulations in poetry when the contemporary moment seems so devoid of hope?

Perhaps hope continues to exist in concrete acts of promiscuous and radical care. Recent years have seen the emergence of the Poets' Hardship Fund (PHF), a volunteer-run and donation-reliant initiative that seeks to offer funds of £50 per month to UK poets suffering from financial hardship. PHF eschews means-testing and is instead organised on a simple principle: 'give when you can and take when you can't'.[83] The fund was initiated as a response to a 'decade of punitive austerity' as well as the 'brutally mismanaged' government response to the Covid pandemic, and whilst the organisers readily admit that the scale of these problems is far beyond their individual and collective capacities for creating change, they hope that the PHF is at least 'a start'.[84] This sense of 'a start' is crucial. The PHF could thus be understood as an act of radical care, which in turn means that its mutual aid also offers a further 'radical promise through a grounding of autonomous direct action and non-hierarchical collective work'.[85] These types of collective action are crucial examples of social organisation where resources are distributed in a syndicalist and egalitarian way, and they thus contain a utopian promise.

Poetry is steeped in that promise as well. Nat Raha's *Of Sirens, Body & Faultlines* (2018) includes a line composed of three terms separated by spaces and colons.[86] It reads: 'love : necessity : anti-fa'.[87] This unusual punctuation establishes a network of relations. A common grammatical use of colons involves the separation of two independent clauses, especially when the second clause explains or illustrates the first. The three terms in Raha's line could thus be read as definitions and extensions of one another: love is necessity is anti-fascism. However, the line's colons are not placed directly after each preceding word but are instead separated by an additional space. They are therefore placed at an equidistance from both the preceding and the subsequent word, which in turn removes a sense of hierarchy between them. In effect, this equidistance also allows the terms to be understood in a reverse order: anti-fascism is a necessity, and this type of resistance is an act of love. In her critical work, Raha has observed that 'desire and need and love emerge only through the inauguration of worlds that do not yet exist'.[88] In other words, the 'struggle against the world that breaks us', and the struggle for a 'world of mutuality and support . . . is always in progress'.[89] A true sense of collectivity is therefore always at a point of emergence. It is anticipatory and produced continuously through incremental acts and transitional demands. Like the Blochian understanding of utopia, it is always in process, intervening in, and reconstructing, reality. That is, the collective actions that Raha identifies as a necessity are necessary precisely because they are an expression of, and a precursor to, a more loving society. This is also true for the respective forms of collectivity that are found and anticipated in *Letters Against the Firmament*, *Click Away Close Door Say*, and *Naturally It Is Not*. These poets, and other writers like them, recognise that the present moment is wholly unliveable. Moreover, in articulating this, they demand a better world: one that may not yet be here, but upon which our survival depends.

Notes

1. The British Poetry Revival, whilst not an uncontested or an unproblematic term, generally refers to poetries emerging in the 1960s and especially the 1970s, when poets in the United Kingdom – influenced by, amongst others, the poetic innovations of modernism, as well as Donald Allen's 1960 anthology *The New American Poetry 1945 to 1960* – rejected the conservatism of the Movement poets (such as Philip Larkin), and began to incorporate a range of experimental and innovative practices within their poetics. The poetry discussed in this chapter can be seen as a continuation of these experimental practices. A more detailed account of these histories is beyond the remit of this chapter, but there are several accomplished studies available. See, for example: Peter Barry, *Poetry Wars*

(Cambridge: Salt, 2006); Robert Hampson and Peter Barry (eds.), *New British Poetries: The Scope of the Possible* (Manchester: Manchester University Press, 1993); Robert Hampson and Ken Edwards (eds.), *Clasp: Late Modernist Poetry in London in the 1970s* (Bristol: Shearsman Books, 2016); David Kennedy and Christine Kennedy, *Women's Experimental Poetry in Britain 1970–2010: Body, Time & Locale* (Liverpool: Liverpool University Press, 2013); Robert Sheppard, *The Poetry of Saying: British Poetry and Its Discontents 1950–2000* (Liverpool: Liverpool University Press, 2005); Robert Sheppard, *When Bad Times Made for Good Poetry* (Bristol: Shearsman Books, 2011); Juha Virtanen, *Poetry and Performance During the British Poetry Revival 1960–1980: Event and Effect* (Cham: Palgrave Macmillan, 2017).
2. Callie Gardner, 'Back Matter', *Zarf*, 1 (2015), p. 32
3. Callie Gardner, 'Editorial', *Zarf*, 15 (2020), p. 2.
4. Ken Edwards, 'Writing and Commodities', *Association of Little Presses Catalogue 1985* (London: ALP, 1985), n. pag.
5. Callie Gardner, 'Editorial (Foot)note', *Zarf*, 3 (2016), p. 1.
6. Gardner, 'Editorial', p. 2.
7. Elizabeth-Jane Burnett, *A Social Biography of Innovative Poetry Communities: The Gift, the Wager, the Poethics* (Cham: Palgrave Macmillan, 2017).
8. Burnett, *Social Biography*, p. 1.
9. Ibid, p. 6.
10. Robert Sheppard makes similar arguments regarding experimental poetry from the 1960s (in particular) and 1970s. See Sheppard, *The Poetry of Saying*, pp. 47–8.
11. Herbert Marcuse, *An Essay on Liberation* (London: Allen Lane, 1969), p. 39.
12. Ibid, p. 24.
13. Fredric Jameson, *Marxism and Form* (Princeton: Princeton University Press, 1971), p. 111.
14. Callie Gardner, 'And the EDITORIAL Is', *Zarf*, 14 (2020), p. 1.
15. Ibid.
16. Ibid.
17. Ibid.
18. Theodor Adorno, *Aesthetic Theory*, trans. Robert Hullot-Kentor (London: Bloomsbury, 2013), p. 308.
19. Sean Bonney, *Letters against the Firmament* (London: Enitharmon Press, 2015), p. 140.
20. Ibid.
21. Jennifer Cooke, 'Sean's Four Letter'd Words' in *Four Letters Four Comments*, ed. Sean Bonney et al. (Scarborough, ME: Punch Press, 2011), n. pag.
22. Bonney, *Letters Against the Firmament*, pp. 140–1.
23. Ibid, p. 141.
24. Sara Ahmed, 'Collective Feelings or, the Impressions Left by Others', *Theory, Culture and Society*, 21(2) (2004), pp. 25–42 (p. 27).
25. G.W.F. Hegel, *Phenomenology of Spirit*, trans A.V. Miller (Oxford: Oxford University Press, 1977), p. 19.

26. David Walsh, Ruth Dundas, Gerry McCartney, et al., 'Bearing the Burden of Austerity: How Do Changing Mortality Rates in the UK Compare between Men and Women?' *Journal of Epidemiology & Community Health*, 72 (2022), pp. 1027–33.
27. Vickie Cooper and David Whyte, 'Introduction: The Violence of Austerity' in *The Violence of Austerity*, ed. Vickie Cooper and David Whyte (London: Pluto Press, 2017), pp. 23–6.
28. Sean Bonney, 'Sean Bonney in Conversation', *Damn the Caesars*, 22 June 2012. www.youtube.com/watch?v=uHkj96Vlo8c (Last accessed 13 October 2023).
29. Zoe Skoulding, *Poetry & Listening: The Noise of Lyric* (Liverpool: Liverpool University Press, 2020), p. 62.
30. Adorno, *Aesthetic Theory*, p. 323.
31. Bonney, *Letters against the Firmament*, p. 111.
32. Ibid, p. 104.
33. Ibid, p. 94.
34. William Rowe, 'Notes Towards a Commentary on Sean Bonney's Letters Against the Firmament', *Journal of British and Irish Innovative Poetry*, 14(1) (2022). https://doi.org/10.16995/bip.4736.
35. Ernst Bloch, *The Principle of Hope*, vol. 3, trans. Neville Plaice, Stephen Plaice, and Paul Knight (Oxford: Basil Blackwell, 1986), p. 1048.
36. Ibid, p. 1046.
37. Sean Bonney, 'Comets & Barricades: Insurrectionary Imagination in Exile', *Mute Magazine*, 9 January 2014. www.metamute.org/editorial/articles/comets-barricades-insurrectionary-imagination-exile (Last accessed 13 October 2023).
38. Bonney, *Letters Against the Firmament*, p. 99.
39. Alexandra Topping, 'Police Make Arrests at Thatcher Death Street Parties in Bristol and Brixton', *The Guardian*, 9 April 2013. www.theguardian.com/politics/2013/apr/09/police-arrests-thatcher-death-parties (Last accessed 19 October 2023).
40. Bonney, *Letters Against the Firmament*, p. 99.
41. Ibid.
42. Walter Benjamin, *Selected Writings Volume 4: 1938–1940*, ed. Howard Eiland and Michael W. Jennings, trans. Edmund Jephcott et al. (Cambridge, MA: Harvard University Press, 2003), p. 396
43. Ernst Bloch, *The Principle of Hope*, vol. 1, trans. Neville Plaice, Stephen Plaice, and Paul Knight (Cambridge, MA: MIT Press, 1996), p. 141.
44. Ibid, p. 77.
45. Lynne Segal, *Radical Happiness: Moments of Collective Joy* (London: Verso, 2018), p. 260
46. Sean Bonney, *Happiness: Poems After Rimbaud* (London: Unkant Publishing, 2011), p. 43.
47. Bonney, *Letters against the Firmament*, p. 117.
48. Al Fireis, Anna Strong Safford, Luke Roberts, and Steve Willey, 'PoemTalk 122 Full Video: On Sean Bonney's Happiness', PennSound, YouTube video, 8 March 2018. www.youtube.com/watch?v=K8RwQ9zf_JU&t=55s (Last accessed 13 October 2023).

49. Verity Spott, *Gideon* (London: Barque Press, 2014), p. 8.
50. Verity Spott, *We Will Bury You* (London: Veer Books, 2017), n. pag.
51. Jennifer Soong, 'Escapist Poetry', *Chicago Review*, 66(02) (2022). www.chicagoreview.org/escapist-poetry/ (Last accessed 13 October 2023).
52. Verity Spott, 'Keston Sutherland and Verity Spott Discuss *We Will Bury You*', YouTube video, 3 December 2020. www.youtube.com/watch?v=6NXURFEBA8Y (Last accessed 13 October 2023).
53. The phrasing of 'within and against' is indebted to Fred Spoliar. See Fred Spoliar and Verity Spott, '(FEATURE) A Conversation with Verity Spott – Part 1', *SPAM Plaza*, 23 March 2021. www.spamzine.co.uk/post/feature-a-conversation-with-verity-spott-part-1 (Last accessed 13 October 2023).
54. Verity Spott, *Click Away Close Door Say* (London: Contraband Books, 2017), p. 101.
55. Ibid.
56. Cooper and Whyte, 'Introduction: The Violence of Austerity', p. 21.
57. Danny Hayward, *Wound Building: Dispatches from the Latest Disasters in UK Poetry* (Earth: punctum books, 2021), p. 75.
58. Spott, *Click Away Close Door Say*, p. 101.
59. Ibid, pp. 87, 88, 89, 93, 95, 96.
60. Ibid, p. 97.
61. Hayward, *Wound Building*, p. 81.
62. Spott, *Click Away Close Door Say*, p. 101.
63. Julia Kristeva, *Powers of Horror: An Essay on Abjection*, trans. Leon S. Roudiez (New York: Columbia University Press), p. 3.
64. Ibid, p. 4.
65. Spott, *Click Away Close Door Say*, p. 96.
66. Ibid, p. 93.
67. Donna Haraway, *Staying with the Trouble: Making Kin in the Chthulucene* (Durham, NC: Duke University Press, 2016), p. 105.
68. Ibid, p. 115.
69. Andreas Chatzidakis, Jamie Hakim, Jo Littler, Catherine Rottenberg, and Lynne Segal, *The Care Manifesto: The Politics of Interdependence* (London: Verso, 2020), p. 41.
70. Jose Esteban Muñoz, *Cruising Utopia: The Then and There of Queer Futurity* (New York: New York University Press, 2009), p. 20.
71. Bloch, *The Principle of Hope*, vol. 1, p. 77.
72. Spott, *Click Away Close Door Say*, p. 97.
73. Muñoz, *Cruising Utopia*, p. 20.
74. Callie Gardner, *Naturally It Is Not: A Poem in Four Letters* (London: 87 Press, 2018), p. 143.
75. Ibid, p. 7.
76. Ibid.
77. Bloch, *The Principle of Hope*, vol. 1, p. 145.
78. Ibid.
79. Ibid, p. 146.

80. Muñoz, *Cruising Utopia*, p. 3.
81. Gardner, *Naturally It Is Not*, pp. 147–50.
82. Spoliar and Spott, '(FEATURE) A conversation with Verity Spott – Part 1', n. pag.
83. A, D & T, 'The Poets' Hardship Fund', n. dat. https://poetshardshipfunduk.com/ (Last accessed 13 October 2023).
84. Ibid.
85. Hiʻilei Julia Kawehipuaakahaopulani Hobart and Tamara Kneese, 'Radical Care: Survival Strategies for Uncertain Times', *Social Text*, 38(1) (2020), pp. 1–16 (p. 10).
86. I offer a more extensive analysis of this line in Juha Virtanen, '"love : necessity : anti-fa": Hostile Environments and Necropolitics on Nat Raha's Of Sirens, Body & Faultlines and Jay Bernard's Surge', *ANGLICA: An International Journal of English Studies*, 32(3) (2023), pp. 47–65.
87. Nat Raha, *Of Sirens, Body & Faultlines* (Norwich: Boiler House Press, 2018), p. 42.
88. Nat Raha, 'Transfeminine Brokenness, Radical Transfeminism', *South Atlantic Quarterly*, 116(3) (2017), pp. 632–46 (p. 633).
89. Ibid, p. 643.

CHAPTER 10

Utopian Realism and Race

Sara Upstone

Introduction: White Statues and Black Lives

In June 2020, I found myself organising an online reading group for doctoral students at Kingston School of Art, London, where I work. I live a five-minute walk from the campus, but had not been there since March, when I hastily left most of my books to enter a period of isolation that was designed to protect both myself and my mother, both of us clinically vulnerable to Covid-19 as a result of chronic illness. Intensely grateful to work in a profession that allowed me to protect myself and those I loved, I set up the group as an impromptu response to the situation and to create a communal space for those of us trying to make sense of what was happening.

As the UK news reported a higher mortality rate in Black and minority ethnic victims of the virus, the response to the pandemic became the latest manifestation of the disturbing re-emergence of deeply entrenched structural racism within Europe and the United States. Just a month before the group met, the murder of African American George Floyd by a White police officer had reignited the Black Lives Matter movement, the hideous images of Floyd's arrest and the brutality he experienced precipitating an outpouring of anger; mass protests across the United States and beyond opened the way for many others to speak their stories and for renewed calls for institutions to act decisively against racism. My choice of text for the reading group, Homi Bhabha's *The Location of Culture* (1994), was motivated by the collision of these events. I had initially read Bhabha's text when I had myself been a postgraduate. Now, more than twenty-five years after its initial publication, I was intrigued to discover whether it might still speak to the urgent questions of race, community, and social justice that were being either implicitly or explicitly raised by the stories dominating our newsfeeds and social media.

In that meeting, which for many was the first academic opportunity to discuss the unfolding situation, our discussion turned to the statue of

Edward Colson, which less than two weeks earlier had been pushed into Bristol Harbour by Black Lives Matter protestors. In the midst of our conversations we found ourselves identifying strongly with Bhabha's own reading of a moment two decades earlier, his identification of the turn of the century as 'the moment of transit where space and time cross to produce complex figures of difference and identity, past and present, inside and outside, inclusion and exclusion'.[1] Our view of events in Bristol brought to life Achille Mbembe's argument in *A Critique of Black Reason* (2013) that the statue exists as the 'subject who outruns death';[2] the memorialisation of a temporal disruption that brings the colonial past into the present and, within it, the authority of the memorialised White subject. In stone and marble, that subject is again made 'real'. This reality evokes the absence of the Black subject, and with it thus also the continued evocation of the unreality of that subject within the racist past. The racist past is thus also the racist present, and the immortality of the statue a promise of a racist future. This destruction of the subject reaches back to slavery. Mbembe invokes the slave master's leash to illuminate how the dehumanisation of the Black subject is woven into the materiality of slave experience:

> The leash is that kind of rope attached to a person who is not free. And the one who is not free is the same as the one to whom you cannot extend a hand, and who therefore must be dragged around by the neck. The leash is the ultimate signifier of slave identity, of the slave condition, of the state of servitude. The experience of servitude means being placed forcefully in the zone of undifferentiation between human and animal, in those zones where human life is seen from the posture of the animal – human life taking on the shape of animal life to the point that the two can no longer be distinguished, to the point where it is no longer clear what part of the animal is more human than the human and what part of man is more animal than the animal.[3]

As we read Bhabha and experienced the news, we encountered the visceral and jarring juxtaposition of these events – of Black bodies impermanent, dehumanised, and threatened, and of White bodies immortalised and elevated in their individualised subjectivity. As the statues were torn down, we watched as the media gaze fell on those obscured by an English heritage industry of museums, artefacts, and country houses that have historically been implicated in the whitewashing of national identity,[4] revealing 'the peculiar temporality whereby the subject cannot be apprehended without the absence or invisibility that constitutes it – "as even now you look/but never see me" – so that the subject speaks, and is seen, from where it is not'.⁵ We were a multiracial group of artists, filmmakers, literary scholars, philosophers, and designers. Many of us were making work that celebrated our commitment to the articulation of difference and the power of intersectional dialogue to create change. How, we wondered, could so much possibility – our reflection of the growing diversity of British arts and affirmation of its centrality 'to the excellence of Britain's artistic output'⁶ – continue to survive conterminously with so much prejudice and despair?

As we continued our reading, our group found that Bhabha offered us a provocation, to embrace this messy relation between past, present, and future within our artistic practice. His work challenged us to consider how we might connect to history not as melancholy or nostalgia, but rather as an interruptive force of the present, because 'art does not merely recall the past as social cause or aesthetic precedent; it renews the past, refiguring it as a contingent "in-between" space, that innovates and interrupts the performance of the present. The "past–present" becomes part of the necessity, not the nostalgia, of living'.⁷ For Mbembe it is the novelist in particular that is engaged in this disruptive temporal practice. Writing on the Black novel he declares: 'The present, as present, draws on both the sense of the past and that of the future or, more radically, seeks to abolish both, hence, in novelistic writing, the predominance of a time that might be called paradoxical, since it is never fully anchored in the present, nor is it ever completely cut off from the past or the future.'⁸

In this chapter, I examine the 'peculiar' utopian temporality of the contemporary moment as it is represented in three novels by Black British female writers: *Queenie*, by Candace Carty-Williams (2019); *Swing Time* (2016), by Zadie Smith; and *Girl, Woman, Other* (2019), by Bernadine Evaristo.⁹ These novels, I suggest, represent a particular incarnation of what I have identified in previous work as *utopian realism*.¹⁰ The idea of utopian realism identifies in contemporary fiction a strong commitment to post-racial and/or multicultural futures in which realism is not about mimetically representing the 'here and now', but rather uses the present to convince readers of the viability of alternative, transformed futures. Novels such as Monica Ali's *Brick Lane* (2003), Diana Evans's *26a* (2005), and Zadie Smith's *NW* (2012) create ostensibly realist worlds that are spatially and historically situated, yet combine these identifiable worlds with outcomes that in their positivity encourage readers to imagine socio-political circumstances beyond the current state of relation.¹¹ In particular, utopian realists foreground a relationship between utopian thinking and models drawn from both personal and historic experience, forming what might be seen as examples of *design fictions*. In design practice, a design fiction is the term given for the development of future designs that are based on functional prototypes. Such futures must therefore work, but they must also be situated within a specific narrative context. What emerges is a possibility that, although separate from the present, is identifiable: 'The design fiction relies on the diegetic prototype along with the context to present these cues. While an audience may be able to suspend their disbelief by relating to the work as fiction, the elements presented in the story must also contain a certain logic in order to be effective.'[12]

Speaking of her literary success, Evaristo has often noted in interviews that in 1994 she began writing affirmations, 'envisioning the future I wanted for myself and writing it down as if it had already happened'.[13] If we transfer this concept to utopian realism, then we identify contemporary set narratives that not only recreate the present to speculate on the future, but also use both the present and the past to situate those possibilities. Shaped in relation to the long history of Black experience, but also in relation to gender and queerness, these novels impress upon the reader the need to consider the future not as a free or fanciful exercise in speculative thinking, but rather as an opportunity to construct a realisable plan for how we might live. Such thinking complicates ideas of the post-racial or planetary humanism; for whilst this may be an ultimate ideal it is not one, these fictions suggest, that is either close at hand or to be achieved without a radically revised acceptance of difference.

Queenie: Discordant Temporalities of Black and White British Experience

To begin, however, it is useful to lay out the territory upon which such futures rest. The publication of Candace Carty-Williams's *Queenie* is itself an event that might have been utopian a decade earlier. As novelist Diana Evans points out in her 2019 review, the radicalism of *Queenie* is its 'highly entertaining' quality.[14] The events of Black Lives Matter and racial politics in contemporary Britain serve as a backdrop rather than taking centre stage in a narrative focused instead on a young woman's romantic adventures. Comparisons with *Bridget Jones's Diary*, first published in 1996, draw attention to the struggle of Black British women to find narrative representation of their everyday lives. The twenty-three years between the two publications marks the discordant temporalities of Black and White experience. Whilst the publishing industry responds with novels like

Queenie to claims of White cultural hegemony, the novel itself explores this issue alongside Queenie's love life struggles. Queenie works as a journalist at a fashionable online magazine called *The Daily Read*, and the novel depicts her repeated attempts to get the story of Black Lives Matter on to its pages, her meticulous research rejected for not having enough of a 'hook'. As Queenie scans the pages of Tumblr in her free time and reads about the violence unfolding in the United States, her editor asks her to write about the best black dresses worn by advocates of the #MeToo movement. Alongside this, the novel is filled with instances of a popular culture in which Black lives have been obscured – for example the lack of Black characters in the iconic TV show *Friends*.[15]

These popular references ask how one can build a more inclusive future if access to knowledge continues to reflect White authority. The cultural products are the contemporary equivalent of the White statue. Their pervasive presence, the endless re-run of shows on streaming services, keeps White subjectivities alive beyond their normal lifespans, just as the deaths of young Blacks are either unreported or relegated to the small print. For Mbembe the history of Blackness is one of simultaneous materiality and fantasy, what he calls a *vertiginous assemblage* divided into three phases: the advent of slavery, the period from abolition to the end of apartheid, and then finally a twenty-first-century moment defined by globalisation and neoliberalism.[16] In this third phase subjects are not exploited but rather abandoned, time is condensed in the service of profit, and the human is stripped of individuality. What was once the Black experience of dehumanisation is also a universal condition, that itself risks doing violence to the specificity of racism.[17]

Queenie illustrates that while these digital 'monuments' survive, in physical space the bricks and mortar presence of the Black community is under erasure. Marching in support of Black Lives Matter, Queenie walks through Brixton in South London. That Brixton is historically a primary site of Black community commemorated in 1998 with the creation of Windrush Square and cited as the centre of an alternative counter-discourse of British heritage,[18] locates the novel specifically in relation to the evolving spatial politics of urban Black identity in Britain. Queenie finds that the Caribbean bakeries and fabric stalls have been replaced by vegan bars and boutiques, asking, 'When had that space that I had known like the back of my hand, the only area I'd ever been to that I felt like I could be myself in, the place where so many people looked like me, talked like my family, when had it gone?'[19] In asking not *where*, but *when*, Queenie disrupts the idealistic teleology of 'improvement' inherent in

London's gentrification. In the wake of Black Lives Matter, her experience of the erosion of Caribbean spaces in Brixton declares the untimely nature of a post-racial discourse of the present that must rather be rightly located in a possible future. The gendered aspects of this temporal dislocation are heightened by Brixton's specific importance to the Black women's movement, its position as the site of the Black Women's Group founded in 1979 where key figures in the Black arts movement such as Joan Riley, Dorothea Smartt, Su Andi, Valerie Mason-John, and Jackie Kay would meet.[20] In the novel Queenie's pitch to report on the march is met by a White male colleague's claim that '*All* lives matter', so that these intersecting questions of race and gender are conterminously placed under erasure. But it is also a disjunction that disrupts bonds of friendship and gendered community, as she finds that her White female friends are silent in response to her attempts. In this moment, those 'friends' are themselves stripped of the unreality that Queenie has placed on them to facilitate their friendship, 'with what I'd been trying to pretend hadn't always been a room full of white not-quite-liberals'.[21]

Yet Queenie not only observes this erasure, she experiences it for herself. A matter of both gender and race, as the romance plot continues the reader sees Queenie repeatedly disavowed by men she believes are committed to her, all of them White. Most notably, her long-term boyfriend exists as an absence for the majority of the novel. Having left her for a 'break', it emerges at the end of the text that he has been living with another (White) woman for several months. This literal absence is foreshadowed by his unwillingness to be fully present in Queenie's reality throughout their relationship, failing to speak out when his relatives are racist. This absence is itself a silencing of Queenie's own subjectivity, her own reality as an individual absented by his refusal of recognition. In this moment, Queenie directly confronts the consequences of this erasure for the future, asking, 'What would happen in ten years' time when his uncle was saying that word, making racist jokes to our children?'[22] Later, in therapy sessions, Queenie directly confronts the unreality of her subjectivity, declaring 'I can't wake up and not be a black woman' before listing the stereotypes that this entails.[23] She is subject to what Mbembe calls the 'codified madness'[24] of Blackness, its presence as that which is seen when 'one sees nothing', beyond the edge of reason. Mbembe turns from Fanon's being looked at, and the subsequent alienation of the Black subject from itself,[25] to what is looking, to remind us that 'racism consists, most of all, in substituting what is with something else, with another reality', the failure of the racist who in looking does not realise that what they see does not exist.[26]

Black Belonging: Knocking on the Door That Does Not Exist

At stake in Mbembe's description is the very nature of reality. As Queenie struggles to get Black experience represented in the magazine, but also to get herself seen, she strives for the future in the expectation of a recognition that is repeatedly frustrated. In this respect, Queenie's endeavours reflect those of the Black individual in society as they are outlined so poetically by the Mbembe:

> To be Black is to be stuck at the foot of a wall with no doors, thinking nonetheless that everything will open up in the end. The Black person knocks, begs, and knocks again, waiting for someone to open a door that does not exist.[27]

How, Mbembe asks, does one perceive of a future when the fundamental reality needed to make that future possible is uncertain? The defining feature of the master–slave relation is for Mbembe the hold that the master has on the future. The slave, he argues, is given no future of their own, and even the positive future is one of a gift of emancipation that it is the master's privilege to confer.[28] The struggle is ultimately thus a struggle for the right to one's own, freely determined future, and the power of Black British communities and collective political action to foreground this in resistance of any definition in terms of this absence or lack. As such, Queenie's battle for visibility through her journalism operates within the much longer history of Black civil rights in Britain, in a continuum that reaches back to the Windrush generation and their demands for racial equality, but more explicitly to the Black British activism of the 1980s, in which much-commented upon rioting and protest was accompanied by 'Black women writers [who] were at the forefront of the Black arts movement, very much innovating and working at the cutting edge, bringing important debates and contentious issues to the fore'.[29]

In this context, Black British female utopian realist novels are concerned not so much to open doors, as to find a creative means to establish the reality of the door that does not exist, pulling from a transatlantic Black civil rights movement, but embedding this in the specificities of Black British activism. Utopian realism rests upon the ability to hold the present in a state of simultaneous imagination and reality; it must present the reader with a present that is imagined beyond its current level of optimism, but with a realism that prevents it from becoming an alternate world. What the author enacts in this regard, however, is not only a fictive strategy, but also a reflection of the commitment to possible futures that sustains the

Black community. At the end of *Queenie*, the eponymous protagonist is portrayed as in a moment of relative success: she has confronted her mental illness, faced her cheating boyfriend, and written a list of why things are 'definitely better'.[30] Queenie's 'better' final reality does not include the opportunity to write political articles; she is instead given a music column. Her disappointment with this recognises that the solution to Queenie's situation is not a post-racial ideal in which her race becomes invisible. Indeed, just before her final list Queenie gives her cousin Diana the reminder that people who do not see race are lying but also, crucially, that 'people *should* see it. We're different and they need to accept our difference.'[31] Despite everything, Queenie succeeds. Like the cover of *A Critique of Black Reason*, which cites French journalist Maria Malagardis describing Mbembe as 'one of those paradoxical optimists who predict the worst without ever losing their faith in the future',[32] Carty-Williams maintains an unwavering commitment to possibility.

Girl, Woman, Other: Revising the Black British *Bildungsroman*

In this respect *Queenie* has much in common with Bernadine Evaristo's *Girl, Woman, Other*. The novel is striking for its persistent, unfailing commitment to success – the Booker prize–winning novel tells the interwoven, inter-generational stories of Black British women, and while they are a mosaic of cultural, sexual, and ethnic diversity, they are united by the fact that each of them undergoes a journey that brings them ultimately to a place of relative triumph. Opening with a theatre first-night, and ending with the unlikely discovery of a long-lost mother, these moments of unlikely triumph, both professional and personal, frame the other women's stories.

Evaristo's novel can be seen in this regard as a twenty-first-century example of what Mark Stein defines as the Black British *bildungsroman:* a novel of transformation in which multiple protagonists look back on their earlier lives from the position of maturity.[33] Yet it also acts as a powerful critique of that form in the service of laying the foundations for thinking about Black British futures. Evaristo's female protagonists come to triumph, but their stories are not so much about the learning of lessons that typify the nineteenth-century form as about a powerful and dynamic refusal to be defeated by a system that is frequently both racist and sexist. It is in this revised format that success is specifically located within a context of resistance. The paperback cover of *Girl, Woman, Other* is impressed with the words 'It is future, it is past. It is fiction, it is history. It is a novel about who we are now.' Yet the 'present' of the novel is directed towards a political activism concerned for the future – Amma lives in London in a commune called Freedomia attempting to create a Marxist alternative to London's exclusionary capitalist culture; Yazz's father is an author of a trilogy of books entitled *How We Lived Then, How We Live Now*, and *How We Will Live in the Future*.[34] Success in this context is framed as possible because of a collective strength, with the Black British female community in a battle against institutional oppression and wider societal bigotry, including patriarchy. There is the recognition here that the future thinking of both men and White society is not in the service of Black women, as revealed in Amma's reflection that her father's socialism means desire for 'a revolution to improve the lot of all mankind. literally.'[35] This is a repetition of the classical awareness that the ambivalent space of utopia is rarely in the service of those without access to power, brought to the fore in Amma's negative experience of the competing ideologies of Freedomia and later in Dominique's experience of the American commune Spirit Moon, where her lover manipulates the site's separation from society to isolate and mentally abuse her. Yet Dominique is rescued by the wider community of women, who help her to escape. As racism makes that which does not exist the centre of a new reality, so the collective demand for recognition presents the unravelling of this unreality which makes (false) appearance into reality.

Evaristo's Black women, then, exceed the structures that act to oppress them, and they do so via an intersectional collectivity. Whilst the novel upholds the power of difference, it also suggests that the power of differences as conveyed dialogically in conversations between protagonists produces counter-cultural strength. Evaristo was a founding member of the Theatre of Black Women, established in Dalston in 1982 and – until it was disbanded in 1988 – creating work with the remit to specifically represent the lives and stories of Black British women.[36] The theatre was a key player in the 1980s Black British Arts movement, which interrogated the racist values propagated during the decade by Margaret Thatcher's Conservative government, and the novel reflects this collective action in the celebration of women's communal solidarity. For example, whilst at university Yazz finds herself in a discussion with a White girl, Courtney, who quotes Roxanne Gay and the danger of 'privilege Olympics' resulting in a moment described as #whitegirltrumpsblackgirl.[37] Megan dreams of a gender-free world, and her girlfriend Bibi, whilst declaring this unlikely, nevertheless asserts that 'dreaming wasn't naïve but essential for survival'.[38] Whilst larger utopian projects in the novel, such as the commune at Spirit

Moon, ultimately fail because of their isolationism, it is within society, and in spaces of encounter, that the novel's women find contentment. Bummi's dream of the future is to start a cleaning company staffed by women from across the world; she goes to bed and dreams of them cleaning up the damaged and polluted environment, millions of women cleaning up the planet, captured on international media, and unstoppable because of 'superhuman powers'.[39] When she starts the real company, it is indeed multinational, a real fragment of her future dream.

The women in *Girl, Woman, Other* recognise the continued need for Black feminism to produce, in Mbembe's terms, a Blackness that might exist where it is 'not thought',[40] re-imagined outside of a Western consciousness and its reasoning of a Blackness falsely presented as truth. As such, it invokes a Black utopian tradition that, as Alex Zamalin has argued, can be traced back to the commitment of slave communities to a 'utopian hope' in the wake of the dystopian horrors of subjugation, and yet is frequently obscured in a thinking of utopia through White imaginaries.[41] Thinking this Blackness, however, only works within the context of a cultural exchange, Mbembe's own awareness in terms of the signifier 'Black' that 'we must conjure with the term in order to reaffirm the innate dignity of every human being and of the very idea of a human community, a same humanity, an essential human resemblance and proximity'.[42] Mbembe in this regard has much in common with a Black British sociological tradition that has its origins in the moment of 1980s activism. This begins with the work of Stuart Hall, which transformed the Birmingham School of Cultural Studies into a key shaper of British thinking on race and gender and continues through the writings of Paul Gilroy and his seminal anti-Thatcherite treatise *There Ain't No Black in the Union Jack* (1987), which has in the post-millennial period translated its earlier discourse on racial justice into an explicit concern for definitions of humanity.[43] Gilroy's ideas of planetary humanism promote an ideal state of post-racialism that he is very clear can only be achieved, ironically, through the recognition of both race and gender, but also through contemporary Black feminism's intersectionality, which is based on a need 'to hold on to our strategic multiplicity and celebrate our "differences" within a conscious construction of "sameness"'.[44] It is in keeping with this intersectional call for recognition that Evaristo suggests that it is the right of these women to be conceived not only in relation to identity categories but as individuals. This is a simultaneously modest and ambitious desire for the future, a demand encapsulated in Winsome's wish for her granddaughter to see her as a 'person in her own right' only to recall that 'she never has been, first she was a daughter, then a wife and mother, and now also a grandmother and great grandmother'.⁴⁵ Winsome's moment of individuality in this respect comes when she begins a sexual relationship with her son-in-law, prompting her to ask 'who was this woman', repeated three times for emphasis.⁴⁶ Her expression of her sexuality, doing things she would never have done with her husband, identifies the space of desire versus need that Bhabha, via Fanon, sees at the centre of claims for subjectivity, the awareness that:

> As soon as I desire I am asking to be considered. I am not merely here-and-now, sealed into thingness. I am for somewhere else and for something else. I demand that notice be taken of my negating activity [my emphasis] insofar as I pursue something other than life; insofar as I do battle for the creation of a human world – that is a world of reciprocal recognitions.⁴⁷

The future, then, is to be one of the connected individual, together and yet each with their own named story, no longer the shadow of a White, male statue.

The Design Fiction in the Wake

In *Girl, Woman, Other*, Evaristo's women find the strength to triumph not in spite of their negative experiences, but in relationship with them. The novel begins with Amma's play about to open at the National Theatre and this moment precipitating her recollection of when her theatre career began and the racism she has experienced, setting up a recurring situation in which a present experience of success is the catalyst for the character's remembrance of connected past experiences. Such remembrances come in a reworked stream of consciousness prose that hovers at the boundaries of poetry, unfinished yet rhythmic sentences and broken paragraphs that resonate with the stylistic experimentations of Evaristo's previous novels. This experimental quality connects Evaristo most obviously to the early Windrush generation pioneers of Black British literature such as Samuel Selvon and Wilson Harris, but perhaps more interestingly to the 1980s Black Arts scene in London of which Evaristo was an integral part. The majority of the texts from Black women writers and artists associated with this movement – fictions such as Ravinder Randhawa's modernist-styled *Wicked Old Woman* (1987) and Barbara Burford's magical realist stories in *The Threshing Floor* (1987)⁴⁸ – have not achieved widespread critical attention, yet Evaristo's implicit dialogue with these earlier works reinforces the novel's focus on communal creativity. In *Girl, Woman, Other*, fragmented remembrances are presented largely without reflection, drawing readers instead into the material realities of earlier moments in which experiences of racist exclusion, male violence, and trauma are commonplace. Such representation has the effect of constructing an equivalence between past and present – both are equally 'present' in the narrative moment. History, therefore, becomes a crucial defining feature of the present, but also of the future. Near the end of the novel, this is made explicit when Yazz and her father look out over the London skyline. Discussing the growth of the skyscraper her father reveals that 'the concept wasn't new at all', 'indebted to the various high-rise precedents ... of Egypt ... the Renaissance ... the five-hundred-year-old mud-brick constructions of Shibam'.[49] At the same time, however, there is a consciousness, most explicit in Waris's mother's recollection on the impact of 9/11 on British Muslims, 'viewed with a blatant hostility that gets worse every time a jihadist blows white people up', that movement towards equality is not linear.[50] It is a disjunctive temporality that in part has the effect of resonating with the novel's Black Lives Matter context and reminding the reader of the continued presence of racism in Britain, yet at the same time a statement of resistance focused on the defiance of a community who refuse to be suppressed by prejudice.

In tracing this line between future and past, Evaristo's women construct what Carolina Sánchez-Palencia reads as the novel's queer, Black, feminist temporality. For Sánchez-Palencia, the women in the novel – the majority of whom are lesbian – are examples of queer alternatives to Elizabeth Freeman's ideas of chrononormativity and reflect her definition of erotohistoriography, producing in their intersecting timelines 'an overlapping of diverse chronologies', where non-linear histories are recounted through corporeal encounter.[51] Alongside these queer disruptions, she identifies the simultaneous critique of chononormativity by Black studies scholars including Achille Mbembe and Johannes Fabian.[52] I want to suggest that in these latter terms Evaristo's characters might also be thought of as reflecting what Christina Sharpe defines as the Black experience of living in the wake: the never present and yet always present history of slavery and Black exploitation which, she argues, must always be a part of thinking, and of care.[53] For Sharpe, this is an act of remembrance, but it is also an act of bringing into being: to 'insist Black being into the wake' and demand recognition.[54] Mbembe constructs this relation in his own terms in his analysis of the nineteenth century African American minister Alexander Crummell:

> Against memory deployed as an irrepressible appetite for death, he opposed two kinds of capacities and practices: hope and imagination. Crummell

distinguished between the memory of slavery and permanent reference to a history of misery and degradation. The passage from slavery to liberty required not only a subtle treatment of memory but also a reworking of dispositions and tastes. The reconstruction of oneself at the end of slavery consequently involved a tremendous amount of work on the self. The work consisted of inventing a new interiority.[55]

Mbembe weaves this source into the more recent work of Fabien Eboussi Boulanga, who he argues presents 'difference anew, as a vigilant form of memory, a critical model of identification, and a utopian project, all at once.'[56]

So it is that in *Girl, Woman, Other*, the women are connected to a continuum of Black experiences, as a utopian project where reference to the past is the route to success. Throughout, Evaristo fuses imagined elements with real-world references, and a number that fall in-between: the Bush Women's Theatre group is a loosely renamed version of the Bush Women's Theatre Group, the bookshop Sister Write where they launch their feminist *samizdat* is real, while the plays they put on are imagined. Freedomia itself is a thinly veiled imagined representation of Frestonia, a West London collective based in Freston Road, Hammersmith, that in the 1970s attempted to secede from the United Kingdom and establish itself as an independent state based on principles of collective ownership and communal living. Frestonia was one of a number of communities that evolved in the 1970s, most notably as part of the London Squatters Campaign. Frestonia became a cultural hub for writers, artists, and musicians, and although it disbanded in the 1980s the attention it received means it continues to be invoked as a model of utopian alternatives to capitalist property ownership, most recently the subject of a 2021 musical by Sarah Woods, *The Ruff Tuff Cream Puff Estate Agency*, which is based on a story by one of the original Frestonia inhabitants, poet Heathcote Williams.[57] Alongside this, there is frequent reference to Black feminists, authors, and critics. Yazz interrogates her father on his exclusive reference to White, male sources, demanding instead he cite the work of bell hooks, Angela Davies, Frantz Fanon, Julia Kristeva, and 14 other figures given specifically by name; Amma lists the films that inspired her radical theatre, including the Black Audio Film Collective's *Handsworth Songs* and the work of Pratibha Parmar; Bummi is reading Buchi Emecheta's *The Joys of Motherhood*.[58] Through these references the novel serves to educate readers on the rich Black cultural history available – not a generalised statement, but a specific reading and viewing list of writers and films. Reference to the Black Audio Film Collective, which was established in Dalston in 1982,[59] points again towards the specific manifestations of a 1980s Black British tradition of cultural activism and its pioneering experimental work: filmmaker John Akomfrah's *Handsworth Songs* (1986) is not only a pivotal piece of Black filmmaking exposing institutional police racism, it is also integral to a debate surrounding the burden of representation placed on Black artists, played out in an exchange of letters between Salman Rushdie, Darcus Howe, and Stuart Hall.[60] Amma's reference thus evokes the contested terrain of experimental, speculative work within this context of realist representation. More widely, Evaristo's reference contributes to a larger discourse within Black British feminism that has focused on the reconstruction of a Black feminist historiography, particularly 'memory work' that aims to construct a methodological 'braiding' that works as a feminist counternarrative.[61] The novel's authorial responsibility in this regard also situates the novel within broader trends in contemporary literary fiction, what myself and Kristian Shaw have defined as *transglossic* literatures that renew the position of the author as public figure in order to contribute to social justice and equality.[62]

Yet the novel is also clear that, like authors and filmmakers, ordinary Black women are the foundation for the futures of those who come after them. This is most evident in the narrative of Shirley, a schoolteacher, who counters the racism in her classroom by teaching the Holocaust, and about lynchings in the American South.[63] Her star pupil is Carole, one of the other women in the novel; as such, the interconnections between the narratives traces a line not only between one woman's experience and her future, but between those experiences and the future of the generations of women to come. Carole's own story becomes one which plays out her teacher's example, yet within the confines of her own life she becomes her own lesson. Carole's narrative begins by showing the reader a moment of success; she is a businesswoman in London, 'in her perfectly-tailored city clothes, the balletic slope of her shoulders, straightened hair scraped back into a martial topknot, eyebrows plucked with calligraphic flair, her discreet, no-nonsense jewellery of platinum and pearls'.[64] It is only after this introduction that readers are given the story of Carole, aged thirteen and a half, at her first party, raped by a boy that she likes and trusts. As the narrative returns us to the present, Carole is looking across the city, watching the people stream across the Millennium Bridge. Its futuristic design, its association with a new century, prompts her to think about an article she has read in which the future is filled with technologically altered humans, their brains implanted with nano-electronics, 'cyborgs ... primed to behave in socially acceptable ways'. Which leads her to think: 'perhaps it will stop vile men raping drunken little girls (and getting away with it)/perhaps it will stop little girls feeling it's their fault (and never telling a soul)'.⁶⁵

Carole imaginatively constructs a feminist future which draws from the horror of her own experience, critiquing the liberal resistance to the curtailment of male freedoms, but also the idealised, socially unaware future-thinking of the popular science magazine, which decouples its enthusiasm for technological advancement from the imperatives of social justice. Her utopia becomes, instead, what might be called a *design fiction:* a plan for the future that is specifically rooted in the iterative processes of her own experience, a humanised equivalent of design modelling. This notion of a design fiction, produced in the wake, is woven into Mbembe's thinking, when he outlines how 'on the basis of a critique of the past, we must create a future that is inseparable from the notions of justice, dignity, and the *in-common*'.⁶⁶

Swing Time: The Tempo the World Wants to Dance To

At the centre of the *design fiction in the wake* is Mbembe's reading of history as a memory that holds the power of renewal through an eschewal of repetition, a variegated process of becoming.⁶⁷ It is to this process that Zadie Smith's novel *Swing Time* (2016) is to some extent devoted. The story of an unnamed narrator and her childhood friend Tracey and their experiences growing up as mixed-race girls in the 1980s is intersected with the narrator's later life in the employment of a Madonna-esque pop star named Aimee. The two girls are consumed in their childhoods by the world of amateur dance – Tracey a burgeoning performer; the narrator fascinated by the early Hollywood musical. The title of the novel is a reference to the Fred Astaire film of 1936, notorious for the dancer's performance in blackface, but also to the notion of the intersection of past and future: not a moment for swinging rhythms in music, but rather a temporality of artistry which moves across time. It is revealed in a scene where Tracey and the narrator watch the iconic performance of Al Johnson in *Ali Baba Goes to Town* (1937) – Al's singing to the Africans 'a verse that seemed to swing time itself' so that the Arabian scene is the promise of 'a thousand years in the future where they would set the tempo the world wants to dance to, in a place called Harlem'.⁶⁸ The structure of the novel mimics this movement: backwards and forwards between past and present in alternating chapters it follows, as Kaitlyn Greenidge notes, 'the pattern of storytelling that one follows when one is relating a trauma – the eerie experience of the past as a continuous event'.⁶⁹

This temporal movement can also be seen as the temporality of Black utopia. In *Black Utopias: Speculative Life and the Music of Other Worlds* (2021), Jayna Brown draws on José Esteban Muñoz's theorisation of queer utopia as spatio-temporal disruption in *Cruising Utopia: The Then and There of Queer Futurity* (2009), re-thinking this for a narrative of Black speculative fiction that reveals how utopia 'is not accessible in standard linear time or in normative spaces'.[70] Brown distinguishes her work from Muñoz's in the contention that such Black utopias exist not in visions of the future, but rather 'a spatial/temporal fold within the here and now' that resonates with the concept of utopian realism as a narrative of present-day speculation.[71] *Swing Time* foregrounds how such utopian realism rests upon a manipulation of temporality within a present-day foundation, the folding together of different historical and future moments into a conterminous present. Like Queenie, the narrator undergoes a narrative of development, here focused on her movement past the influence of her friend Tracey towards the lesson offered by her mother. The first description of the narrator's mother is of a woman 'dressed for a future not yet with us but which she expected to arrive', describing Tracey as a girl for whom, in contrast, 'the present is all she has'.[72] Yet the narrator's mother roots her focus on the future in a commitment to the past, which the narrator herself attempts to resist. The narrator's mother attempts to address her daughter's cultural education by bringing her the riches of the Black artistic presence – *Gone with the Wind* as a way to the NAACP, the Harlem Renaissance, Paul Robeson, Langston Hughes.[73] The narrator, aged eleven, is uninterested: her preference instead for 'rhythms and song ... the red silk of Mammy's underskirt or the unhinged pitch of Prissy's voice' represents a space of enchantment untouched by a history of racist experience, a dream in which 'we had never graced the sad pages of the history books my mother bought for me'.[74] In classic *bildungsroman* style, she looks back on her early identification with the dancer as 'a man from nowhere' and recognises she should have loved Bill 'Bojangles' Robinson, who danced 'for the Harlem dandy, for the ghetto kid, for the sharecropper – for all the descendants of slaves';[75] yet instead she watches Judy Garland pretending to be a Zulu and dancing the cakewalk in *Meet Me in St Louis* (1944), and Fred Astaire in blackface in *Swing Time*. Later, as an adult, the narrator is given an opportunity to perform and the notion of a continuum between her own artistry and her Black predecessors comes to her, her own relation to what is labelled jazz as in fact 'Black Classical Music'.[76] As she leaves the performance, the rain falls on to her hair, which curls up from its straightened form. Yet when this is again disavowed, this time by Aimee, it is the narrator's mother who again reminds her that people 'have roots ... you've let this woman pull yours right out of the ground'.[77]

The narrator's mother attempts to disenchant her daughter and Tracey from their supposed illusions; she recognises that the dream of genuine happiness rests not on an enchanting denial, but rather on a re-enchantment that is only possible in a future that has arisen in dialogue with the past. The narrator becomes aware of moves 'back from the future'[78] in the iconic performances she watches, aware that the way Tracey dances traces a line not only to her father through to Michael Jackson, but back through a history of Black performers, from Prince to James Brown and all the way to the Nicholas Brothers. Smith has said in interview that the trauma Black people face is the violence of having been removed from time, having been lifted from the history that might have been theirs.[79] In this moment, the narrator enacts a radical reclamation of that time, but also a repurposing of a disrupted chronology. Meanwhile Tracey is too damaged to see the connection. She remains traumatically out of time, only hears the narrator mentioning her father, caught in the violence of her own experience and unable to see the wonder that the narrator feels so that the words end up 'turning to ash'.[80]

To evoke a design fiction is to both look to the future and to warn against the unfettered utopia. Implicit in this viewpoint is the danger of a future thinking unmarked by history. Like Shirley's instruction of the children in *Girl, Woman, Other*, the narrator's mother wrestles against an optimism that is divorced from the past. When Tracey uses a racist word and is challenged with a lecture from the narrator's mother she is met with the statement 'It's just a word'.[81] Tracey represents both the ideal, post-racial future, and the barrier to its realisation. She is simultaneously both a marker of the denial of Black experience and the dangers of naïve or ignorant unawareness of racism's present reality, but also a utopian realist glimmer of a next generation future that could be. The narrator's encounter with another White friend, Lily, reinforces this point – a short chapter just two pages long that interrupts the main narrative as a vignette in which Lily declares the unfairness of an all-Black film because in England 'everyone was equal anyway'.[82] The narrator is left questioning who the 'we' is to which Lily refers in her outburst, made to feel the disjunction between the reality for Black lives and the utopian view of these lives from White perspectives. As an adult, the narrator experiences such a dangerous optimism in the work of Aimee, who is 'uncontained by space and time',[83] a representative of artistic freedom, but also an unawareness of inequality. Aimee involves herself in a philanthropic project in an unnamed African country, and yet her White privilege obscures the need to build her endeavours on an awareness of the past; she sees differences as 'never structural or economic but always essentially differences of personality'.[84]

There is a 'truth' to this resistance in synchronicity that announces its radicalism in the refusal to submit to a straightforward realism. Whilst events may be rationally impossible, the folded temporality of utopia constructs a sense of veracity which defies definitions of falsehood and replaces historical proof with an affective authenticity – a reality based on what feels true, rather than what is ostensibly accurate. Such alternative versions of reality speak to the narrow confines of official histories, and, like the countercultural reference points of *Girl, Woman, Other*, act to address a Black British history formed in the wake of both slavery and historic racisms. When Tracey declares that her absent father is a backing dancer for Michael Jackson the narrator accepts it as 'a fact ... at one and the same time absolutely true and obviously untrue'.[85] When she finally meets him, she does not attempt to reconcile the reality with the stories, declaring this 'impossible' and so they remain 'facts' in inverted commas, never quite true, and yet also never disavowed.[86] The first generation to have home video, the narrator interprets this as being 'the first generation to have in our own homes, the means to re- and forward-wind reality',[87] to put the people on film exactly where they want them. Tracey gets Fred Astaire's 1935 musical comedy *Top Hat* to the scene she chooses, and reads it intently, the minutiae revealed in a scene played over and over. This childhood prepares the narrator for a life in which she is able to simultaneously face the harsh realities of contemporary life and yet also re-write circumstances to facilitate her own survival, never allowing herself to be completely subsumed by the experiences of racism and sexism she encounters, the traumas of her life remembered always as both 'the fiction and the reality'.[88]

Dance in this respect has a particular function. When the narrator's father tells her a story of Astaire asking Jackson to teach him to moonwalk, it leads to the conclusion that while art is temporal, dance has 'no time, no generation'.[89] Resisting the notion of movements or genre, dance exists for the narrator as Mbembe's repetition: each dancer evokes memory in a spirit of renewal that does not repeat the past but constructs a future. When the narrator finally sees Tracey's father dance, she declares that 'watching him I felt I understood now what Tracey had meant by placing her father and Michael Jackson in one reality, and I didn't find that she was a liar, exactly, or at least I felt that within the lie there was a deeper truth. They were touched by the same inheritance.'⁹⁰ Like the statue thrown into the water, the revelation of the presence within the dance is where the encounter with the real is revealed. It is thus no surprise that time and memory for Mbembe are ultimately experienced through the senses, a process of reaching for that which exceeds the limits of language, and by extension has the ability to communicate across cultural boundaries.⁹¹ Indeed, it is explicitly dance and music that are identified as where the 'real' is revealed,⁹² precisely for these sensory qualities: writers and theorists together acknowledging that the past must not only be re-told, it must also be re-performed, if we are to enact as well as dream our radical futures.

Conclusion: Towards Black Justice

The narrator of *Swing Time* does not merely internalise her mother's viewpoint. At the novel's conclusion she wonders if there is not a possibility for reconciliation with Tracey: 'something else I could offer, something simpler, more honest'.⁹³ What she adds to her mother's lesson in this moment is a desire that springs from the shared experience of being a woman that is able to encompass difference, the girl she imagines when walking through the African village with Aimee who 'lives everywhere and at all times in history ... looking over you with a secret she can't tell'.⁹⁴ There is in this desire a common ground formed between the three novels I have discussed: a commitment to the future that is rooted in a Black experience, but also that is intimately associated with belonging to a community of women for whom that Black experience has also been shaped by the intersectional forces of patriarchy. In this chapter I have attempted to trace a web of associations between Mbembe and Bhabha in their shared connection to the work of Fanon, and between these critics and the three authors I have chosen, each of whom in different ways uphold Mbembe's project to construct an 'alternative genealogy' of the term 'Black'.⁹⁵ Both Mbembe and Bhabha are concerned with what they see is the fundamental (and denied) place of Blackness in the development of European modernity – as a delirium.⁹⁶ In each of the three novels explored here, this absence is confronted in the spirit of a renewal, powerfully intersected by gender, to produce a very contingent and specific utopia – *a design fiction from the wake* – that is testament to the imperative to overturn existing concepts if one is to reach towards Black justice.

Notes

1. Homi Bhabha, *The Location of Culture*. New York: Routledge, 1994), p. 2.
2. Achille Mbembe, *A Critique of Black Reason* [2013], trans. Laurent Dubois (Durham, NC: Duke University Press, 2017), p. 126.
3. Ibid., p. 153.
4. Mike Crang and Divya P. Tolia-Kelly, 'Nation, Race, and Affect: Senses and Sensibilities at National Heritage Sites', *Environment and Planning A: Economy and Space*, 42(10) (2010), pp. 2295–548.
5. Bhabha, *Location*, p. 67.
6. Global Future, 'Stretching the Flag: Measuring and Celebrating the Diversity of British Culture', June 2019. https://nousthinktank.wpengine.com/wp-content/uploads/2022/09/NOUS_StretchingtheFlag_compressed.pdf (Last accessed 29 September 2023), p. 16.
7. Bhabha, *Location*, p. 10.
8. Mbembe, *Critique*, p. 122.
9. Candace Carty-Williams, *Queenie* [2019] (London: Trapeze, 2020); Zadie Smith, *Swing Time* (London: Hamish Hamilton, 2016); Bernadine Evaristo, *Girl, Woman, Other* [2019] (London: Penguin, 2020).
10. Sara Upstone, *Rethinking Race in Contemporary British Fiction* (London: Routledge, 2016).
11. Monica Ali, *Brick Lane* (London: Doubleday, 2003); Diana Evans, (2005) *26a* (London: Chatto and Windus, 2005); Zadie Smith, *NW* (London: Hamish Hamilton, 2012).
12. Davis Levine, 'Design Fiction', *Medium*, 13 March 2016. https://medium.com/digital-experience-design/design-fiction-32094e035cd7 (Last accessed 1 October 2021).
13. Annabel Kemp, 'Author Bernardine Evaristo on Her Award Wins, Activism, and What Inspires Her Writing', *Woman and Home*, 7 November 2021. www.womanandhome.com/life/books/author-bernardine-evaristo-interview/ (Last accessed 31 July 2024).
14. Diana Evans, '*Queenie* by Candace Carty-Williams Review: Timely and Important', *The Guardian*, 12 April 2019. www.theguardian.com/books/2019/apr/12/queenie-candice-carty-williams-review (Last accessed 1 October 2021).
15. Carty-Williams, *Queenie*, p. 18.
16. Mbembe, *Critique*, p. 3.
17. Ibid., pp. 3–4.
18. Rodney Harrison, 'Heritage as Social Action' in *Understanding Heritage in Practice*, ed. Susie West (Manchester: Manchester University Press, 2010), pp. 240–76.
19. Carty-Williams, *Queenie* p. 210.
20. Su Andi, Dorothea Smartt, and Carol Leeming, 'Women, Black Arts, and Brixton in the 1980s: A Conversation', *Contemporary Women's Writing*, 11(2) (2017), pp. 137–48.
21. Carty-Williams, *Queenie*, p. 213.

22. Ibid., p. 44.
23. Ibid., p. 325.
24. Mbembe, *Critique*, p. 3.
25. Frantz Fanon, *Black Skin, White Masks* [1967] (London: Pluto, 1986).
26. Mbembe, *Critique*, p. 32.
27. Ibid., p. 152.
28. Ibid., p. 153.
29. Su, Smartt, and Leeming, 'Women, Black Arts, and Brixton', p. 144.
30. Carty-Williams, *Queenie*, p. 386.
31. Carty-Williams, *Queenie*, p. 377.
32. Mbembe, *Critique*, n. pag.
33. Mark Stein, *Black British Literature: Novels of Transformation* (Columbus: Ohio State University Press, 2004).
34. Evaristo, *Girl*, p. 46.
35. Ibid., p. 10.
36. Anon., 'Theatre of Black Women', Hackney Museum website, n. dat. https://museum-collection.hackney.gov.uk/names/AUTH5788 (Last accessed 31 July 2024).
37. Evaristo, *Girl*, p. 66.
38. Ibid., p. 327.
39. Ibid., p. 171.
40. Mbembe, *Critique*, p. 28.
41. Alex Zamalin, *Black Utopia: The History of an Idea from Black Nationalism to Afrofuturism* (New York: Columbia University Press, 2019), p. 7.
42. Mbembe, Critique, p. 173.
43. Paul Gilroy, There *Ain't No Black in the Union Jack: The Cultural Politics of Race and Nation* [1987] (New York: Routledge, 2002).
44. Paul Gilroy, *Between Camps: Nations, Cultures and the Allure of Race*. London: Routledge, 2004); Heidi Safia Mirza, '"Harvesting Our Collective Intelligence": Black British Feminism in Post-Race Times', *Women's Studies International Forum*, 51 (2015), pp. 1–9 (p. 7).
45. Evaristo, *Girl*, p. 257.
46. Evaristo, *Girl*, p. 272.
47. Bhabha, *Location*, p. 12.
48. Ravinder Randhawa, *A Wicked Old Woman* (London: The Women's Press, 1987); Barbara Burford, *The Threshing Floor* (London: Firebrand Books, 1987).
49. Evaristo, *Girl*, p. 416.
50. Evaristo, *Girl*, p. 58.
51. Carolina Sánchez-Palencia, 'Feminist/Queer/Diasporic Temporality in Bernardine Evaristo's *Girl, Woman, Other* (2019)', *The European Journal of Women's Studies*, 29(2) (2022), pp. 1–15 (p. 3). Elizabeth Freeman, *Time Binds: Queer Temporalities, Queer Histories* (Durham, NC: Duke University Press, 2010).
52. Sánchez-Palencia, 'Feminist', p. 3.
53. Christina Sharpe, *In the Wake: On Blackness and Being*, Durham, NC: Duke University Press, 2016), p. 5.

54. Ibid., p. 11.
55. Mbembe, *Critique*, p. 93.
56. Ibid.
57. Sarah Woods, *The Ruff Tuff Cream Puff Estate Agency* (musical), Belgrade Theatre, Coventry, 9–16 October 2021. Information available at: www.steinplays.com/news/the-ruff-tuff-cream-puff-estate-agency-adapted-by-sarah-woods-belgrade-theatre-9th-16th-oct/ (Last accessed 31 July 2024).
58. Evaristo, *Girl*, pp. 46–7, 31, 156.
59. Anon., 'Black Audio Film Collective', Tate website, n. dat. Available at: www.tate.org.uk/art/art-terms/b/black-audio-film-collective (Last accessed 31 July 2024).
60. Diagonal Thoughts, 'The Handsworth Songs Letters', *Diagonal Thoughts Blog*, n. dat. Available at: www.diagonalthoughts.com/?p=1343 (Last accessed 29 September 2023).
61. Joan Anim-Addo, 'Activist-Mothers Maybe, Sisters Surely? Black British Feminism, Absence and Transformation', *Feminist Review*, 108 (2014), pp. 44–60.
62. Kristian Shaw and Sara Upstone, 'The Transglossic: Contemporary Fiction and the Limitations of the Modern', *English Studies*, 102(5) (2021), pp. 573–600.
63. Evaristo, *Girl*, p. 221.
64. Ibid., pp. 114–15.
65. Ibid., p. 145.
66. Mbembe, *Critique*, p. 177.
67. Ibid., p. 94.
68. Smith, *Swing Time*, p. 191.
69. Kaitlyn Greenidge, 'Shaken Out of Time: Black Bodies and Movement in Zadie Smith's *Swing Time*', *The Virginia Quarterly Review*, 93(1) (2017), pp. 196–9 (p. 197).
70. Jayna Brown, *Black Utopias: Speculative Life and the Music of Other Worlds* (Durham, NC: Duke University Press, 2021), p. 8.
71. Ibid.
72. Smith, *Swing Time*, pp. 10, 31.
73. Ibid., p. 100.
74. Ibid.
75. Ibid., p. 24.
76. Ibid., p. 117.
77. Ibid., p. 155.
78. Ibid., p. 192.
79. Zadie Smith quoted in interview, Jeffrey Eugenides, 'The Pieces of Zadie Smith', *New York Times Style Magazine*, 17 October 2016. www.nytimes.com/2016/10/17/t-magazine/zadie-smith-swing-time-jeffrey-eugenides.html (Last accessed 1 October 2021).
80. Smith, *Swing Time*, p. 101.
81. Ibid., p. 82.

82. Ibid., p. 117.
83. Ibid., p. 73.
84. Ibid., p. 111.
85. Ibid., p. 36.
86. Ibid., p. 38.
87. Ibid., p. 16.
88. Ibid., p. 146.
89. Ibid., p. 38.
90. Ibid., p. 186.
91. Ibid., pp. 121, 123.
92. Ibid., p. 131.
93. Ibid., p. 453.
94. Ibid., p. 408.
95. Mbembe, *Critique*, p. xiii.
96. Ibid., p. 2.

PART IV

Case Studies

CHAPTER 11

Naomi Mitchison's Memoirs of a Spacewoman
A Critical Feminist Utopia

Katie Stone

Feminist utopianism has come to be defined by what Tom Moylan terms the 'critical utopias' of the 1970s.¹ In his 1986 monograph, *Demand the Impossible: Science Fiction and the Utopian Imagination*, Moylan argues that the interlocking movements for gay and women's liberation, civil rights and black power, decolonisation, and an end to the war in Vietnam provided a context within which 'utopian writing was given new life' in the novels of Joanna Russ, Ursula K. Le Guin, Marge Piercy, Samuel R. Delany, and others.² These writers sought to reveal what Russ has called the 'gross and ghastly fact' that 'so much of what's presented to us as "the real world" or "the way it is" is so obviously untrue'.³ They demonstrated that the creation of fictional worlds that were radically divergent from, but importantly connected to, their historical moment was an effective means of producing such revelations. By imagining societies structured around presumed gender fluidity, queer and polyamorous sexualities, liberatory reproductive technologies, and collectivised childcare, Moylan's critical utopians denaturalised gendered relations in 'the real world'. As Moylan puts it: 'The oppositional ideology of this critical utopian form is one of combative engagement with ... the ideological claim that a social alternative to what currently exists is impossible.'⁴ To create a critical utopia is to refute this claim, to demand the impossible.

Naomi Mitchison's Critique of Utopianism and Feminism

Since the publication of *Demand the Impossible* many utopian scholars have taken up the task of elaborating on who the 'others' to whom Moylan refers might be. Joining Moylan's four key feminists, writers such as Octavia E. Butler, Sally Miller Gearhart, Suzy McKee Charnas, and James Tiptree Jr. have since been firmly associated with what Russ terms 'the mini-boom of feminist utopias' published in the 1970s.⁵ Scottish author Naomi

Mitchison, who published her first science fiction (SF) novel, *Memoirs of a Spacewoman*, in 1962 at the age of sixty-five, initially seems an unlikely addition to this list. Mitchison is obviously not writing in response to the global protest movements that crystallised in May 1968. Nor is she immersed in the same culture of American feminist consciousness-raising groups which was integral to later feminist utopians. Her tales of a sexually adventurous space farer seem to align more with New Wave characters such as Jean-Claude Forest's erotic SF adventuress Barbarella (serialised from 1962–78 in the French glamour publication *V Magazine*) than Le Guin's anarchist syndicalists, whilst her interest in biology and genetics connects her to an older generation of decidedly non-feminist British SF authors including her personal friends Aldous Huxley and Olaf Stapledon.[6] Much like Pamela Zoline's 'The Heat Death of the Universe' (1967) (discussed by Tom Dillon in Chapter 3) – another example of feminist SF published in the United Kingdom in the 1960s – *Memoirs* is easy to write off as an anomaly within the genre; a fledgling attempt at the kind of feminist dreaming that would take over a decade to fully flourish.

Nevertheless, I intend to argue that *Memoirs of a Spacewoman* can usefully be read as a critical feminist utopia, one that touches on many of the genre's foundational tensions and ambiguities. If one examines what Rick Altman might term the '*semantic* elements' of feminist utopianism – that is, the 'common topics, shared plots, key scenes, character types [and] familiar objects' of the genre – this reading of *Memoirs* is relatively uncontroversial.[7] The society that Mitchison depicts shares many of the features of Piercy's Mattapoisett or Delany's Triton. Mitchison's protagonist Mary lives in a world of freely accessible abortions, inter-racial and multi-gendered parenting teams, queer and alien sexual practices, and universal, child-led education. And yet, this is not where Mitchison's focus lies. Instead of providing a detailed study of this utopian society, Mitchison uses it as the backdrop for Mary's adventures to numerous alien worlds, populated by sentient creatures who variously resemble centipedes, caterpillars, dinosaurs, and starfish. In this chapter, I argue that this is not a move away from utopianism. I follow the utopian philosopher Ernst Bloch in his contention that 'to limit the utopian to the Thomas More variety ... would be like trying to reduce electricity to the amber from which it gets its Greek name'.[8] Bloch locates utopianism not only in the 'Thomas More variety' of literary texts, which precisely delineate a better world, but also in all works that dwell upon what he calls 'the Something that is missing' – the elusive ingredient whose absence prevents our world from becoming a utopia.[9] By creating a utopian society and then immediately leaving that society behind to focus on other, stranger, and perhaps even better alien worlds, I suggest that Mitchison is able to maintain her focus on that missing ingredient even as she depicts a feminist utopia. What *Memoirs*' narrative structure offers in this reading is a means of testing out the utopian-ness of Mary's society through contact with other worlds. Mitchison takes her liberated, feminist space woman and forces her to confront her underlying assumptions about, for example, whether feminism necessitates an embrace of femininity over masculinity; or, whether a person's genetic makeup determines their gender, or their character, or their political allegiance. Here, Mitchison presents a critical approach not only to utopianism but also to feminism. Her writing demonstrates that replacing space men with space women, or even choosing feminism – which has so often been embroiled with imperialism, eugenics, and transphobia – over patriarchy, is insufficient if one seeks a utopia of full gender liberation.[10] And yet, the possibility of finding a feminist utopia, on the next planet, or in the next moment of communication with a many-gendered alien, remains open. Far from acting as an immature, not-quite-feminist utopia, then, I see *Memoirs* as a critical study of feminist utopianism in which the genre's many pleasures and dangers are laid bare.

This chapter is structured around two of Mary's expeditions. I begin by discussing an expedition in which she collaborates with a government ministry responsible for extracting minerals from alien worlds. I read this episode as a commentary, both on the clash between patriarchal and feminist forms of scientific exploration, and on the impossibility of mapping this clash onto diametrically opposed models of masculinity and femininity. I then turn to Mary's first expedition, to a world where the people resemble starfish, where I discuss the tension between Mary's professed gender essentialism on the one hand and the radical transformation she experiences through contact with the starfish on the other. In each of these episodes I argue that Mitchison raises important questions about the relationship between gender and feminism, feminism and utopianism – questions to which she frequently responds with multiple answers. By producing this reading, I hope to underline the fact that, as Tom Dillon has demonstrated in Chapter 3, British feminist SF of the 1960s does not merely act as an inferior precursor to the great US utopias of the coming decade. The activism that infuses Mitchison's writing includes her work in the British birth control movement of the 1930s, her close relationships with members of the Communist Party in Britain, her dedication to Scottish independence and the rights of Highlanders, and her interest in the decolonisation of Botswana.[11] Whilst I will not produce a detailed study of the influence of these activist movements on Mitchison's utopianism here, their diversity of both focus and tactics, along with their international outlook, clearly demonstrate that utopian writing founded in political struggle cannot be confined to scholarship that focuses only on the United States or the 1970s. It is true to say that Mitchison does not fit neatly into the feminist utopian tradition. As Sarah LeFanu, the editor of the Women's Press Science Fiction series in which *Memoirs* was republished, puts it, Mitchison's writing questions 'the very possibility of the existence of utopia'.[12] However, I suggest that this only makes her work more relevant to a properly critical feminist utopianism, founded upon an 'awareness of the limitations of the utopian tradition', as much as on the possibilities offered by envisioning a feminist utopia.[13]

Sea Urchins and Femininity

The utopianism of the society depicted in *Memoirs* begins simply, with the absence of misogyny. Mary is a woman, she is sexually active, she is a mother, *and* she is an astronaut. Mitchison depicts this as the norm in Mary's society where there is no suggestion that Mary's gender has negatively impacted her life. Critics have noted the historical significance of Mitchison's decision to feature a female protagonist in her first SF novel. For example, LeFanu describes *Memoirs* as 'an extraordinary book, not least because it is a science fiction novel that centralizes a woman's sexual and emotional experiences at a time when female characters barely appeared in science fiction'.[14] Moreover, not only is Mary a female protagonist, she is also depicted as a leading scientific expert in the field of non-human communications – a hybrid science composed of biology, linguistics, and psychology. The exclusion of women from scientific study was a subject with which Mitchison, who was raised alongside her brother Jack who became the noted geneticist 'J. B. S.' Haldane, was all too familiar. In the early twentieth century even women such as Mitchison, who grew up in elite, upper-class British families and showed early interest in and aptitude for experimentation – Mitchison co-authored her brother's first paper in genetics – faced barriers that prevented them from pursuing scientific careers. Mitchison's biographer Jenni Calder describes how, although both Jack and Naomi attended the prestigious Dragon School 'which catered mainly for the sons of academics' whilst growing up in Oxford, Jack went on to Eton while Naomi's education was brought to an abrupt halt when she began menstruating.[15] As Calder notes, despite her family's relatively liberal attitudes to women's education, once Mitchison had entered puberty, 'no one ... could close their eyes to her gender'.[16] In her study of Mitchison's self-professed 'love-hate relation with science', Susan Merrill Squier notes that scientific study in the Haldane household and beyond was shaped by 'a variety of spoken and unspoken cultural codes far more constraining for women than for men'.[17] Living in a family of leading British scientists and thus enjoying far more access to science than the vast majority of women, Mitchison still came up against the fact that, as Squier puts it, 'scientific investigation is gendered male, thus excluding women from scientific practices'.[18] To write a novel about a female scientist in this context is a defiant political act.

However, the goal of greater female representation either in science or in science fiction remains far more modest than the demands for the impossible voiced in the critical utopias of the 1970s. Writing of the transformative potential of feminist utopianism in a symposium on women and SF published in 1975, Charnas states: 'Through science fiction I can see the same drab realities illuminated with the brilliance of the strange; everything becomes transmuted, fresh, newly-meaningful.'[19] This goal, of transforming 'everything' through a newly feminist way of looking, is not effectively addressed by simply writing about women. Mitchison's inclusion of female characters in the exploitative scientific institutions that dominated British society during her lifetime, frequently buttressing the apparatus of capitalist extraction and colonial domination on which the British empire relied, falls far short of Charnas's radical transmutation of reality.[20] Or it would fall far short if Mitchison's only innovation was to represent her scientists as women. In fact, in *Memoirs* Mitchison produces a far more robust reconfiguration of what a feminist science might look like. A key element of this reconfiguration is the fact that Mary and her fellow scientists are governed by a rule that prefigures *Star Trek*'s prime directive: to communicate but never to interfere. As Mary explains: 'Before the codifying or [sic] rules for space explorers, there were constant examples of deliberate interference with other life, almost always ending disastrously and making communication less easy for several generations.'[21] In contrast, the science of communication that she practises is one which expressly seeks to avoid the kind of harm historically perpetrated by British scientific institutions. As Lucile H. Brockway has argued in her study of the ties between botany and colonial expansion, the efforts made by British scientists to taxonomise and collect 'foreign' plant life were inextricably linked to what she calls 'a comprehensive system of energy extraction and commodity exchange which for a time, in the nineteenth and early twentieth centuries, made Britain the world's superpower'.[22] Mitchison seeks to intervene in this history and imagine in its place an anti-colonial, feminist science. Donna J. Haraway has argued that Mitchison's efforts to reimagine science in this way, by 'foregrounding the problem of imperialism', reflect the many competing influences that made up the British intellectual scene of the early twentieth century including 'sexual experimentation; political radicalism; unimpeded scientific literacy; literary self-confidence; [and] a grand view of the universe from a rich, imperialist, intellectual culture'.[23] In *Memoirs* Mitchison draws on each of these strands but also highlights the tensions between them. For example, rather than attempting to perform what Haraway has elsewhere called 'the god-trick of seeing everything from nowhere', and thus enjoying the imperialist 'grand view of the universe', Mary communicates with the extraterrestrials she encounters by making herself visible and vulnerable to them, and involving her whole being in the act of communication.[24] She describes 'communicating all over with ... tongue, fingers, toes, and sexual organs' when communing with Martians, for example, and risks 'having the whole stability of [her] personality altered and shattered in an irreversible way' through these acts of intimate communication.[25] What Jane Donawerth terms the 'utopian vision of science' that Mitchison has produced is thus shown to involve far more than 'the participation of women in science'.[26] As Donawerth argues, for Mitchison '"good" science' is 'subjective, relational, holistic and complex' – a science which attempts to break ties with not only the misogyny which would exclude women from scientific study, but also the variously gendered violences of ecological extraction, colonial conquest, and capitalist growth.[27]

Mitchison tests out the relationship between this 'utopian vision of science' and gender in one of Mary's briefest expeditions. Awakening from the time blackout that explorers experience while in transit, Mary finds herself 'in orbit round a world which seemed to consist on its surface of evenly convex hills thickly wooded'.[28] Acting as part of a team of explorers, Mary's mission is to study the fauna and flora of this hilly planet and to communicate with any sentient lifeforms, as always, without interference. In the process of their investigation the team discovers three different kinds of leafy, coraline, and feathery organic growth emerging from the hills, but no sign of sentient life. Despite this apparent absence, the explorers conduct their investigation with typical delicacy. Speaking of the feathery growths, Mary states: 'I felt that these were definitely animal, to use a rather archaic classification, and was prepared to watch carefully before making any observations which would result in destroying or injuring one of them.'²⁹ She also draws attention to the precautions taken on landing to avoid harm to the planet and notes sadly that despite warnings given using sound and heat there remains some risk to slow moving life and vegetation; writing: 'It was routine, but always makes me uncomfortable.'³⁰ Set against these tentative approaches to contact are the actions of the employees of the Minerals Ministry. Unlike the enquiry undertaken by the explorers, who seem to have no requirements to produce profitable, or even measurable outcomes from their investigations, the mineralogists are explicitly searching for 'valuable materials'.³¹ This is one of the least utopian aspects of Mary's society in that it is directly reminiscent of the British culture of imperial extraction in which Mitchison grew up.³² In Mitchison's future world the remaining inhabitants of Earth, now known as Terra, still 'use up minerals too fast'.³³ Their hunger for minerals has led the ministry employees to adopt scientific practices that Mary and her team deem to be both unwise and unethical. For example, Mary notes that the mineralogists 'always take far too little acclimatisation time' on reaching the planet and describes how they 'immediately chopped off specimens' of the growths which Mary had observed.³⁴ This extraction escalates as the chapter progresses. The mineralogists fail to heed the mission lead's warning that 'we had better first find out what these objects were, what their use was, and to what or whom' before cutting into them.³⁵ They continue to extract the valuable minerals from the coraline growths until the 'hill' they have landed on begins to tremor, prompting a recognition in Mary: 'Suddenly I realised that this landscape of columns and snappers was exactly what one sees under a low power microscope looking at a sea urchin. These hills were simply enormous echinoderms.'³⁶ This insight gives the scientists just enough time to escape from the back of the urchin they have mutilated before it dives into the surrounding waters, drowning two ministry employees who ignored Mary's warning.

This episode functions as a direct, feminist critique of the scientific culture in which Mitchison grew up. John Rieder has famously argued that 'science fiction comes into visibility first in those countries most heavily involved in imperialist projects – France and England'.³⁷ Mitchison, then, can be understood as following in the tradition of British writers such as H. G. Wells whose early SF 'exaggerates and exploits [the] internal divisions' of colonialism by staging the encounter between humans and aliens as a distorted inversion of the relationship between imperial scientist and colonised subject.³⁸ Indeed, by juxtaposing the mineralogists' hasty, short-sighted and greedy approach to mining with Mary's feminist science, Mitchison explores what Rieder has called 'one of the enduring dichotomies in the developing genre of science fiction', which he locates in Wells's *First Men in the Moon* (1901).[39] In this scientific romance Wells depicts two astronauts, one who sees the moon as a site of 'knowledge for its own sake' and one for whom, as Rieder puts it, 'the most interesting thing about the lunar underground is the apparent abundance of gold'.[40] Mitchison supplements Wells's critique of this extractive attitude to alien minerals with a focus on the gendered dynamics of colonial mining practices. Whilst women always played a role in British science – notable among them Margaret Cavendish who attended meetings of the Royal Society as early as 1667 and who published an important precursor to later British utopian SF in the form of *The Description of the New World, Called the Blazing World* (1666) – scientific extraction was frequently gendered male. As Donawerth has argued, 'feminist science theorists have shown that male scientists from the seventeenth century on have conceived of nature as a potentially unruly woman to be mastered and penetrated for her secrets'.[41] In Mitchison's narrative the connection between men's mastery of the non-human world on the one hand and their domination of women on the other is made in the form of Ministry employee Quinag: 'a smoothy, but what a delicious smoothy'.[42] Quinag spends his time seducing Mary in a way which distracts her from her task. She tries to 'continually change [her] focus' in order to see the lifeforms before her in a 'fresh, newly-meaningful' light, to use Charnas's terminology, 'but, while changing it, accidentally meeting Quinag'.[43] Not only does Quinag and the ministry he represents risk distracting Mary, he also explicitly denigrates the mission lead in misogynistic terms; describing her as 'a bossy old mum' and suggesting, even after they know the nature of the sea urchins, that 'it was surely unreasonable to talk about interference'.[44] This refusal to take seriously the non-interference policy that lies at the core of Mary's feminist utopian science is punished in *Memoirs of a Spacewoman* by death. Quinag ignores the orders to leave, sneaks off with a young, female member of the expedition, and is ultimately drowned. Mary cries at the news of his death but ultimately agrees that 'it was his fault really', and that 'there is nothing to be done but forget it', or at least to try.[45] A patriarchal science is left to drown as a feminist, utopian one takes off into the starry sky.

Whilst this feminist critique of the underlying presumptions that structure scientific praxis is clearly more sophisticated than demands for rectifying misogyny solely through greater female representation, Mitchison's utopianism still risks falling into a reductively binary model of gender relations. Commenting on the critical utopias of the 1970s, Russ argues that 'few of these societies ... examine gender stereotypes to see if they are true, or argue against them. We merely see that they are not true and do not apply.'[46] In contrast, Mitchison *is* interested in including gender stereotypes in her utopia. In her depiction of this expedition, for example, 'the logic of mastery', which Julietta Singh argues drives both ecological devastation and colonial domination, is firmly tied to masculinity whilst femininity offers a soft and nurturing alternative approach to scientific investigation.[47] However, by including these stereotypes in her utopia, Mitchison is also able to interrogate them. Under further examination, the apparently straightforward relationship of masculinity to the ministry on the one hand and femininity to the explorers on the other begins to slip. In part this is due to the fact that both parties include people of different genders, with Peder Pedersen, a man who on a previous mission was unable to comfortably fit into the explorers' quarters due to his large stature, among the explorers, and Soo, a young woman described as a 'poor little girl' who drowns alongside Quinag, among the mineralogists.[48] More significant than this, however, is the fact that the biologists' feminist ethics do not imply an exclusively soft femininity. This is most evident in Mitchison's description of the mission lead, 'that strange woman who called herself 513 because she had been one of the group that had discarded names – and indeed a great deal else'.[49] 513 is a female explorer who continually counsels against interference and yet her numeric 'name' evokes the calculated dispassion of the Numbers of Yevgeny Zamyatin's dystopian novel *We* (1924), in which the replacement of names by numbers is accompanied by a wholesale rejection of both femininity and emotion. 513 relates to others 'a little coldly' and when she has to make the decision to leave Quinag and 'poor little Soo' behind in order to ensure the safety of the others she does so immediately and seemingly without qualms.[50] Meanwhile, 'the senior Ministry man' meets the news of their deaths by screaming 'half hysterically'.[51] This mission, then, is in no sense a clear-cut battle of the sexes.

Even Mary, who aligns herself most directly with femininity, frames her life as an explorer as an escape from the work of mothering. Before embarking on this expedition, she had 'had a delicious year' in which she 'felt just like a twentieth-century Mum', dedicated exclusively to raising her children.[52] Whilst she enjoys this work and sees it as complementary to the work of a communications expert – one of the things she teaches her children is how 'to handle bees and spiders gently and understandingly' – she knows that she is not in fact maternal in a way that a twentieth-century audience would recognise.[53] As she puts it: 'I could get away, that was the difference.'[54] The femininity of these independent, itinerant explorers is inevitably a complicated one that does not stand in polar distinction from a rigidly defined masculinity. It does involve delicate approaches to feathery alien life forms, but it also involves a break from motherhood and an opportunity to sit 'in a ship among ... instruments and tables, thinking intently and uninterruptedly'.[55] Mitchison's utopian science is here shown to be precisely that: a science, indicative of what Squier has called 'the initially uncomfortable, disruptive notion that feminists may not need to renounce science wholly'.[56] The complexities of Mitchison's relationship to the dream of an ethical, feminist science have been repeatedly emphasised by critics. Indeed, in her study of Mitchison's time as a Voluntary Aid Detachment nurse serving in Britain during World War I, Anna McFarlane refuses to separate out Mitchison's dedication to scientific practice from her commitment to a feminist care ethic. As McFarlane puts it, Mitchison is 'someone who overturns the assumption that humanity comes from the humanities by bringing empathy from her medical training to her writing rather than the other way around'.[57] In *Memoirs*, Mitchison draws on this wartime experience as a nurse, where her role was both feminine and scientific, to present a vision of science practised by people of all genders and combining both empathy and harsh decisions, subjectivity and data, femininity and masculinity.

By complicating the gendered dynamics of these two visions of science, Mitchison distinguishes herself from those feminists who appeal to a benevolent, naturalised femininity untouched by the supposedly inherent violence of male-ness. In her influential 1985 essay 'A Cyborg Manifesto', Donna Haraway notes that many feminists writing in the 1960s 'insist on the organic, opposing it to the technological'.[58] In this formulation of gender relations, femininity is organic, masculinity is technological, and utopianism is accessible through a return to Nature via 'female embodiment', which, as Haraway points out, 'seemed to mean skill in mothering and its metaphoric extensions'.[59] This nostalgic version of feminist utopianism does not, however, dominate the critical utopias produced in the United States in the 1970s. Haraway has described feminist SF authors such as Russ, Delany, Butler, and Tiptree as 'theorists for cyborgs' and argues that cyborg feminism – which centres the indeterminate boundaries between men and women, humans and animals, organisms and machines – is predicated upon the 'non-innocence of the category "woman"'.[60] As Haraway puts it: 'There is nothing about being "female" that naturally binds woman ... a highly complex category constructed in contested sexual scientific discourses and other social practices.'[61] This is the kind of feminism that can be observed in *Memoirs*. Indeed, Mitchison's affinity with cyborg feminism draws attention to the fact that, in her manifesto, Haraway mentions a number of key cyborg theorists who do not hail from the United States, including British writer Mary Shelley. Just as Shelley's Dr Frankenstein seems to embody the epitome of an overreaching masculine mode of scientific inquiry that plunders a feminised Nature, but in fact succeeds in birthing a Creature who defies any preconceived model of gender, Mitchison imagines a scientific practice that appears to reify the gender binary only to subsequently undermine the fixity of all gendered markers.[62] By raising the spectre of gendered stereotypes – the soft mother worried about killing plants, the misogynist miner gleefully drilling for rare minerals – Mitchison is able to denaturalise them and leave the reader with a complex web of differently gendered beings who alternate between conventionally masculine and feminine conduct. Mitchison's feminism does not offer an easy escape into an anti-scientific, feminised Nature. In *Memoirs*, even the feminist policy of non-interference is not a panacea for all previous scientific malpractice. As Haraway has argued in her reading of Mitchison's novel, Mary's adventures beg the question: 'How could conversation occur, in any form, if the rule of noninterference were to be strictly interpreted?'[63] There is no pure, safe, entirely feminine form of (non-)contact offered here. In the next section, I discuss how Mitchison retains her commitment to the horizon of feminist utopianism despite the failure of femininity to offer a clean escape into utopianism; despite the fact that, as with so many of Haraway's cyborg theorists, in her utopia 'it's not just that "god" is dead; so is the "goddess"'.[64]

Starfish and Essentialism

Those familiar with *Memoirs* may be surprised at my insistence on reading Mitchison's novel as an example of anti-essentialist feminism and indeed it is important to note that my assessment of the novel's denaturalisation of womanhood is directly at odds with Mary's professed beliefs about gender. When introducing herself as a communications expert, Mary makes the claim that the science of communication is not only intrinsically feminine but, moreover, is best practised by women. She states: 'I may be out of date, but I always feel that biology and, of course, communication are essentially women's work, and glory.'[65] This, as many critics have noted, is the aspect of Mitchison's work that most distances her from the queer feminism of Haraway and her cyborg theorists. In his study of empathy in *Memoirs*,

Gavin Miller argues that 'the text tends to essentialize the capacity for nurture and empathy as *female*, and not merely feminine'.[66] For this reason he suggests that 'despite the striking parallels between Mitchison's novel and contemporary ideas of a feminine ethics, one should not exaggerate the affinity of *Memoirs* with modern feminist thought'.[67] I believe that Miller is correct to highlight Mary's essentialist statements as being at odds with what feminist utopianism must be if it is truly to break with the oppressive logics which have consistently governed gender relations. However, I also believe that Mitchison's text does not necessarily endorse Mary's interpretation of the essential womanliness of her utopian science. In other words, it is not so much that Mitchison's politics are made to seem outdated when compared with the younger generation of US writers who would go on to champion queer politics in their utopias in the following decade. Rather, it is Mary who is proven to be out of date. I will return briefly to the story of the sea urchins to examine how Mary's biologically essentialist views are challenged through the very act of communicating, which she views as inherently feminine.

As an examination of the conduct and characteristics of the exploration personnel makes clear, the communications science upon which *Memoirs'* utopianism rests is neither exclusively practised by women nor defined by its femininity. However, I have yet to address the most significant obstacle to mapping this expedition onto a binary model of gender. It is the sea urchins themselves, those 'identical rounded hills, each of which ... had the same covering', who most profoundly challenge the notion that life can be neatly divided into opposing male and female beings.[68] These life forms seem not to be divisible along gendered lines or, at least, gender differences are not reflected in their outward appearance in any way. The mystery of both their biological reproductive systems and the relationship structures which facilitate their social reproduction render any statement about their gender absurd. They demonstrate that a utopian politics predicated only on gender, in isolation from all other structures of power, is utterly insufficient when faced with anything other than a society of men and women whose gender is the only presumed difference between them. However, this is not to say that the sea urchins are impervious to a feminist politics. In fact, it is precisely their lack of adherence to a binary gender system that evokes what Haraway has called 'cyborg "sex"' – something that she locates in feminist SF from Shelley's *Frankenstein* (1818) to Butler's *Lilith's Brood* (1987–9).[69] Speaking of the 'lovely replicative baroque of ferns and invertebrates', Haraway discusses how creatures without binary sex act as 'such nice organic prophylactics against heterosexism'.[70] In *Memoirs*, the subversive potential of this cyborg sex can be felt in the obvious tension between the sea urchins' apparent sexlessness on the one hand and Mary's essentialism on the other. This tension has led Miller to argue that 'Mitchison fills in the supposed metaphysical and ethical abyss between human and animal, only to excavate an (empirically unsubstantiated) naturalized gulf between male and female'.[71] However, I contest the idea that it is Mary's essentialism which is given the last word in Mitchison's novel. To trust in the naturalness of fixed, binary sex in *Memoirs* is – as Mitchison's human characters do at their peril – to ignore the transgressive presence of the sea urchins beneath their feet. The moments in which Mary is most confident in her understanding of sex and gender are those in which she is most likely to fail in her task of communicating with non-human beings. While Quinag may be a masculine distraction to Mary's communications, her real failure on the planet of the sea urchins lies in her inability to remember the lessons she learned from another world of echinoderms, on her very first expedition.

The destination of Mary's first expedition is 'lambda 771 in the Q series'.[72] She describes the planet as having 'not an impossible atmosphere', but notes that 'communication had not been established'.[73] The sentient life on lambda 771 is descended 'from a radial form, something like a five armed starfish, itself developing out of a spiral'.[74] Mary identifies this evolutionary path, and its difference from the evolutionary path taken by humanity, as the reason for previous failures in communication. She states: 'It is only in circumstances like this that we realise how much we ourselves are constructed bi-laterally on either-or principles. Fish rather than echinoderms.'[75] To communicate with these starfish, Mary must work against not only her genetic identity as a cisgender woman, but her identity as part of the huge number of bilaterally symmetrical animals found on Earth. In their co-written book *The Science of Life* (1931), designed as an introduction to the biological sciences, Julian Huxley, H. G. Wells, and G. P. Wells explicitly state that this kind of communication is impossible. They write: 'One cannot imagine oneself a starfish or a sea-urchin however hard one exerts one's mind.'[76] And yet, in what Squier has argued may well be a deliberate reference on Mitchison's part to Huxley, Wells, and Wells, Mary does just that. She describes how the 'radiates', as she calls them, 'never thought in terms of either-or', and how she took on this way of thinking; stating: 'It began to seem to me very peculiar that I should do so myself.'[77] As Squier suggests, by depicting Mary's transformative communication with these starfish-like beings, 'Mitchison challenges Huxley's dogmatic assertion that there are distinct limits to the empathetic and epistemological reach of the human species.'[78] Mary does what was deemed impossible by those intent on maintaining the separation between the white, British, colonial scientific subject and the passive, non-human, alien object of study and learns to communicate with a truly alien being, transforming herself in the process. In this way she accesses what Moylan terms 'the revolutionary potential of the utopian imagination', in which he locates the possibility of that 'radical rupture that is necessary for the constant striving of humanity for a world free of oppression and full of satisfaction'.[79] For Squier, this utopian moment of rupture involves a complete transformation of how scientific knowledge is conceptualised; moving from a male-dominated scientific epistemology 'purged of all subjective feelings' to a feminist science 'that acknowledges, builds in, and corrects for, the existence of subjective feelings'.[80] In my reading of this episode, however, this transformation is less about rejecting masculinity than it is about refusing binary logics altogether. What Mary is expressly rethinking here is the fact 'that so many of [her] judgements were paired; good and evil, black or white, to be or not to be', and, one might add, male or female.[81] Rather than conforming to Mary's own assessment of communication as an essentially feminine science, the starfish offer a vision of communication that leaves binary gender behind.

It is notable that Mary is aware of her own shortcomings when it comes to fully comprehending the starfish. For example, she remembers how she 'made a most ludicrous mistake about their sex life' which was 'all due to [her] own anthropomorphising'.[82] It is in this context that one can identify Mary's most confident assertion of biological determinism. A mere two paragraphs after describing this self-confessed error, Mary states: 'I believe communication science is so essentially womanly. It fits one's basic sex patterns.'[83] Despite Mary's confidence, her professed beliefs about womanhood begin to seem increasingly questionable when put in such close proximity to her other, sex-based, 'ludicrous mistakes'. Moreover, her mistakes are not reserved to Mary's assessment of these strange creatures with their mysterious bodies. One might argue that whilst starfish and sea-urchins defy binary models of gender, humans remain neatly categorisable – raced and sexed. However, in *Memoirs*, Mitchison also casts doubt on those human identity markers which are ascribed to genetics. The society depicted in Memoirs *is* anti-racist, to the extent that there are many Black and Indigenous people and people of colour among the explorers, and Mary highlights the fact that her society has been forged by 'Changers' of all races.[84] In spite of this professed anti-racism, however, Mary herself retains an essentialised and fetishistic attitude towards race. She obsessively details her racial difference from both T'o – the man with whom she is romantically involved on the starfish expedition – and their 'curly, coffee-coloured daughter' Lil-burn[85]; writing of T'o that he 'had the delicious springy hair of his father's ethnic group', and aspiring to have 'a pale brown baby' with him.[86] And yet, as with Mary's gender essentialism, hers is not the only understanding of race presented within the text. T'o himself continually rejects Mary's essentialised view of race. Mary describes how he 'would never let [her] touch' his hair, and he objects to her focus on genetics when naming their daughter.[87] Mary states: 'I wanted her to have one of those delicious polysyllabic African names, but T'o begged me to call her by one of the old names – the names of the Changers.'[88] T'o here refuses Mary's understanding of himself and his daughter as being defined by their race and instead turns his daughter's naming into an act of political alliance with the anti-racist history that the Changers represent. When Mary ascribes her failure in successfully understanding the sexuality of the starfish to the fact that her 'subconscious drive was firmly fastened on [her] self and T'o', therefore, it is possible to read this as an indicator of Mary's excessive reliance on not only sex but also on race as essentially determining characteristics.[89] In *Memoirs*, to commune with an alien is to see all of the myths that are habitually used to buttress conservative, scientific ideology through alien eyes and in so doing to open up the possibility of forging a new, utopian mythology.

Conclusion: Feminism and Utopianism

What I have endeavoured to demonstrate in this chapter is that many of Mary's stated beliefs do not align with the politics of critical feminist utopianism exemplified in US SF in the 1970s *and* that it is for precisely this reason that *Memoirs* provides such an important text for the student of feminist utopias. For Mary, utopianism may lie in a wholehearted embrace of femininity as opposed to masculinity, but for Mitchison the path to utopia is not so simple. Again and again, Mitchison offers the reader the possibility that the solution to the conflicts that Mary encounters lies in femaleness, or femininity, or an otherwise inherent, naturalised genetic identity, and again and again that possibility is ultimately refused. In one episode, Mary recounts the story of an all-female expedition to a world in which butterflies terrorise their own larval forms in a conflict based on sex and reproduction. Here, the women explorers are not united by their gender but, rather, are deeply divided, ultimately leading one of them to commit the novel's only act of direct and deadly interference. In another episode, Mary details the birth of a 'haploid' child, developed exclusively from the genetic information contained in one of her eggs.[90] Rather than depict this child as in some way doubly womanly, due to her lack of a father, Mary names her Viola, after Shakespeare's cross-dressing heroine, who she views as 'as near a two-sexed person as we get on earth'. Later, Viola proceeds to defy her genetic similarity to Mary by performing an act of communication that Mary herself had deemed impossible.[91] Perhaps most telling of all is the episode in which Mary communes with the starfish. The prompt used to snap her out of the starfish way of thinking and back into the 'either-or's of human thought is 'baby or not baby'[92]; in other words, she is supposed to decide on the spot whether or not to have a baby with T'o. However, whilst this choice is initially presented as the definitive binary that will jerk Mary back into appropriately bilateral, genetically determined, human thought, Mitchison spends the remainder of the novel undermining this binary. Mary, after all, lives out both of these possibilities. As Lesley A. Hall has argued in her study of Mitchison's relationship to the politics of reproduction, Mary realises 'Mitchison's ideal of women having meaningful work and motherhood'.[93] She responds to this 'either-or' question by demanding 'both'. Moreover, the children that Mary goes on to birth are variously alien, haploid, and surrogate. Her role as a mother evokes less the '"universal" (trans-erasive) feminist solidarity' of a politics securely grounded in shared wombs, than those 'utopian traditions' in which, as the critical utopian scholar Sophie Lewis describes, writers 'have speculated about what babymaking beyond blood, private coupledom, and the gene fetish might one day be'.[94] The fact that Mary opens her narrative by stating that she thinks 'less about [her] four dear normals' – the children produced through heterosexual, human reproduction – than she does about the strange gelatinous aliens grafted onto her body as part of an experiment, serves to denaturalise and de-essentialise pregnancy. Lewis has argued that 'there can be no utopian thought on reproduction that does not involve uncoupling gestation from the gender binary' and, despite Mary's protestations about her essential womanliness, her experiments in babymaking open the way to just this kind of queer, reproductive utopianism.[95]

By drawing attention to the anti-essentialist elements of *Memoirs* I do not mean to suggest that Mitchison ever fully resists the allure of the gender binary or that of genetic determinism. As Natasha Periyan discusses in her study of Mitchison's evolving understanding of genetics, the Scottish writer had a complicated relationship with the science of eugenics, which 'spurred her commitment to intelligence and spurned her progressive feminist and class politics'.⁹⁶ My intention is not, then, to claim that Mitchison is straightforwardly satirising Mary's essentialism in *Memoirs*. Rather, I suggest that what Ashley Maher has called the deliberate 'looseness' of the novel's structure – which moves from episode to episode without implying any progressive development of either Mary's character or of the utopian society in which she lives – provides a means of continually interrogating the notion of an essentially benign femininity and the promise of utopia that it tantalisingly dangles.⁹⁷ By keeping the tensions that lie at the heart of feminism at the forefront of her utopia, Mitchison shines a light on the genre's continuing ties to eugenics, racism, and transphobia in a manner reminiscent of the recent critical turn made by scholars such as Alison Kafer, Asha Nadkarni, and Trish Salah.⁹⁸ And yet, as with these scholars' work, this turn does not entail a descent into anti-utopian nihilism in *Memoirs*. Despite her obvious suspicion of both, Mitchison's commitment to utopianism and feminist politics instead prompts a recognition of the fact that although the political movements that informed feminist utopianism are 'coded around the year 1968' they did not begin in the United States in the 1960s.⁹⁹ This recognition in turn prompts an exciting expansion of the generic boundaries of the critical utopia, suggesting possibilities for reading Mitchison's work alongside that of, for example, her South African acquaintances Doris Lessing and Bessie Head, or earlier British utopian writing such as Lady Florence Dixie's *Gloriana; or the Revolution of 1900* (1890).¹⁰⁰ As well as creating a more internationalist approach to critical utopianism, this expansion makes way for an important reckoning with the genre's strong and ongoing ties with early eugenic and imperialism feminisms – ties that shaped Mitchison and that she in turn reshaped. Ultimately, to include *Memoirs* within the genre of the critical, feminist utopia is to acknowledge that creating a feminist utopia is not enough. In Mitchison's novel it becomes clear that it is only once society has been restructured to eliminate gendered inequalities that the real task, of working out what happens when you use gender as the basis of a radical, utopian politics, begins.

Notes

1. Tom Moylan, *Demand the Impossible: Science Fiction and the Utopian Imagination* (Oxford: Peter Lang, 2014), p. 1.
2. Ibid., p. 10.
3. Joanna Russ, *To Write Like a Woman: Essays in Feminism and Science Fiction* (Bloomington: Indiana University Press, 1995), p. xv.

4. Moylan, *Demand the Impossible*, p. 141.
5. Russ, *To Write*, p. 133. For critical discussion of these and other post-1960s feminist utopian creators, see Angelika Bammer, *Partial Visions; Feminism and Utopianism in the 1970s* (Oxford: Peter Lang UK, 2015); Jayna Brown, *Black Utopias: Speculative Life and the Music of Other Worlds* (Durham, NC: Duke University Press, 2021); and Peter Fitting, 'Recent Feminist Utopias: World Building and Strategies for Social Change' in *Mindscapes: The Geographies of Imagined Worlds*, ed. George Edgar Slusser and Eric S. Rabkin (Carbondale: Southern Illinois University Press, 1989), pp. 155–63.
6. For a study of Mitchison's relationship to Huxley's writing, see Maria Aline Ferreira, '"The Malediction of the Clones"?: Huxley, Mitchison, Haldane' in *Biotechnological and Medical Themes in Science Fiction*, ed. Domna Pastourmatzi (Thessaloniki: University Studio Press, 2002), pp. 186–207.
7. Rick Altman, *Film/Genre* (London: Bloomsbury Publishing, 2019), p. 89. Emphasis in original.
8. Ernst Bloch, *The Principle of Hope, Vol One*, trans. Paul Knight, Neville Plaice, and Stephen Plaice (Cambridge, MA: MIT Press, 1995), p. 15.
9. Ibid., p. 309.
10. For a discussion of British feminist literature and imperialism, see Gayatri Chakravorty Spivak, 'Three Women's Texts and a Critique of Imperialism', *Critical Inquiry*, 12(1) (1985), pp. 243–61. For feminist utopianism's ties to eugenics, see Asha Nadkarni, *Eugenic Feminism: Reproductive Nationalism in the United States and India* (Minneapolis: University of Minnesota Press, 2014); and for a discussion of transphobia in feminism, see Serena Bassi and Greta LaFleur, 'Introduction: TERFs, Gender-Critical Movements, and Postfascist Feminisms', *Transgender Studies Quarterly*, 9(3) (2022), pp. 311–33.
11. For more details on Mitchison's varied activist career, see Jenni Calder, *The Burning Glass: The Life of Naomi Mitchison* (Sheffield: Sandstone Press, 2019).
12. Sarah LeFanu, 'Difference and Sexual Politics in Naomi Mitchison's Solution Three' in *Utopian and Science Fiction by Women: Worlds of Difference*, ed. Jane Donawerth and Carol A. Kolmerten (Syracuse: Syracuse University Press, 1994), pp. 153–65 (p. 163).
13. Moylan, *Demand the Impossible*, p. 10.
14. LeFanu, 'Difference and Sexual Politics', p. 153.
15. Calder, *The Burning Glass*, p. 24.
16. Ibid, p. 33.
17. Mitchison cited in Susan Merrill Squier, *Babies in Bottles: Twentieth-Century Visions of Reproductive Technology* (New Brunswick: Rutgers University Press, 1994), p. 170; and Squier, *Babies in Bottles*, p. 173.
18. Ibid., p. 175.
19. Charnas in Suzy McKee Charnas et al., 'Women in Science Fiction: A Symposium', ed. Jeffrey D. Smith, *Khatru*, 3–4 (1975), pp. 4–125 (p. 9).
20. For a discussion of the relationship between British colonialism and scientific study, see Lucile H. Brockway, *Science and Colonial Expansion: The Role of the British Royal Botanic Gardens* (London: Academic Press, 1979).

21. Naomi Mitchison, *Memoirs of a Spacewoman* (London: The Women's Press, 1962), p. 16.
22. Brockway, *Science and Colonial Expansion*, p. 6.
23. Donna J. Haraway, 'OTHERWORLDLY CONVERSATIONS, TERRAN TOPICS, LOCAL TERMS' in *Material Feminisms*, ed. Stacy Alaimo and Susan Hekman (Bloomington: Indiana University Press, 2008), pp. 157–87 (p. 180).
24. Donna J. Haraway, 'The Persistence of Vision' in *The Visual Culture Reader*, ed. Nicholas Mirzoeff (Abingdon: Routledge, 1998), pp. 677–84 (p. 678).
25. Mitchison, *Memoirs*, pp. 58, 17.
26. Jane Donawerth, 'Utopian Science: Contemporary Feminist Science Theory and Science Fiction by Women', *NWSA Journal*, 2(4) (1990), pp. 535–57 (p. 535).
27. Ibid., p. 535.
28. Mitchison, *Memoirs*, p. 73.
29. Ibid., p. 75.
30. Ibid., p. 74.
31. Ibid.
32. For a study of the impact of ecological imperialism on nineteenth and twentieth century British literature, see Serpil Oppermann, 'Ecological Imperialism in British Colonial Fiction', *Journal of Faculty of Letters*, 24(1) (2007), pp. 179–94.
33. Mitchison, *Memoirs*, p. 74.
34. Ibid., pp. 74, 75.
35. Ibid., p. 75.
36. Ibid., p. 79.
37. John Rieder, *Colonialism and the Emergence of Science Fiction* (Middletown: Wesleyan University Press, 2008), p. 3.
38. Ibid., p. 7.
39. Ibid., p. 75.
40. Ibid.
41. Donawerth, 'Utopian Science', p. 548. Mitchison's formulation of a feminist scientific praxis is discussed at more length in Katerina Kitsi-Mitakou, 'None of Woman Born: Colonizing the Womb from Frankenstein's Mother to Naomi Mitchison's Clone Mums' in *Biotechnological and Medical Themes in Science Fiction*, ed. Domna Pastourmatzi (Thessaloniki: University Studio Press, 2002), pp. 208–24.
42. Mitchison, *Memoirs*, p. 74.
43. Ibid., p. 78.
44. Ibid., p. 80.
45. Ibid., pp. 81, 82.
46. Russ, *To Write*, p. 138.
47. Julietta Singh, *Unthinking Mastery: Dehumanism and Decolonial Entanglements* (Durham, NC: Duke University Press, 2018), p. 3.

48. Mitchison, *Memoirs*, p. 81.
49. Ibid., p. 74
50. Ibid., pp. 79, 81.
51. Ibid., p. 81.
52. Ibid., p. 71.
53. Ibid.
54. Ibid.
55. Ibid.
56. Squier, *Babies in Bottles*, p. 198.
57. Anna McFarlane, '"Becoming Acquainted with All That Pain": Nursing as Activism in Naomi Mitchison's Science Fiction', *Literature and Medicine*, 37(2) (2019), pp. 278–97 (p. 293).
58. Donna J. Haraway, *Simians, Cyborgs, and Women: The Reinvention of Nature* (Abingdon: Routledge, 2013), p. 174.
59. Ibid., p. 180.
60. Ibid., pp. 173, 157.
61. Ibid., p. 155.
62. For a discussion of gender subversion in Shelley's novel, see Susan Stryker, 'My Words to Victor Frankenstein above the Village of Chamounix: Performing Transgender Rage', *GLQ: A Journal of Lesbian and Gay Studies*, 1(3) (1994), pp. 237–54.
63. Haraway, 'OTHERWORLDLY CONVERSATIONS', p. 181.
64. Haraway, *Simians*, p. 162.
65. Mitchison, *Memoirs*, p. 18.
66. Gavin Miller, 'Animals, Empathy, and Care in Naomi Mitchison's *Memoirs of a Spacewoman*', *Science Fiction Studies*, 35(2) (2008), pp. 251–65 (p. 263.) Emphasis in original.
67. Ibid., p. 262.
68. Mitchison, *Memoirs*, p. 76.
69. Haraway, *Simians*, p. 150.
70. Ibid.
71. Miller, 'Animals', p. 264.
72. Mitchison, *Memoirs*, p. 20.
73. Ibid.
74. Ibid.
75. Ibid.
76. H. G. Wells, Julian S. Huxley, and G. P. Wells, *The Science of Life*, 3 vols. (New York: Doubleday, Doran & Company, 1931), p. 218.
77. Mitchison, *Memoirs*, p. 26.
78. Squier, *Babies in Bottles*, p. 180.
79. Moylan, *Demand the Impossible*, p. 20.
80. Squier, *Babies in Bottles*, p. 180.
81. Mitchison, *Memoirs*, p. 26.
82. Ibid.
83. Ibid.

84. Ibid., p. 127.
85. Ibid., p. 71.
86. Ibid., pp. 21, 30.
87. Ibid., p. 21.
88. Ibid., p. 127.
89. Ibid., p. 26.
90. Ibid., p. 64.
91. Ibid., p. 66.
92. Ibid., p. 30.
93. Lesley A. Hall, 'Send in the Clones? Naomi Mitchison and the Politics of Reproduction and Motherhood' in *Naomi Mitchison: A Writer in Time*, ed. James Purdon (Edinburgh: Edinburgh University Press, 2023), 73–88 (p. 77).
94. Sophie Lewis, *Full Surrogacy Now* (London: Verso Books, 2019), pp. 13, 20.
95. Ibid., p. 22.
96. Natasha Periyan, 'Naomi Mitchison, Eugenics and the Community: The Class and Gender Politics of Intelligence' in *The 1930s: A Decade of Modern British Fiction*, ed. Nick Hubble, Luke Seaber, and Elinor Taylor (London: Bloomsbury, 2021), pp. 91–122 (p. 119).
97. Ashley Maher, '*Memoirs of a Spacewoman*: Naomi Mitchison's Intergalactic Education', *Textual Practice*, 34(12) (2020), 2145–65 (p. 2154).
98. Alison Kafer, *Feminist, Queer, Crip* (Bloomington: Indiana University Press, 2013); Nadkarni, *Eugenic Feminism*; Trish Salah, 'Narrating Trans Genres: Transgender Chronotopes in *Woman on the Edge of Time* and *The Deep*', keynote lecture, *Trans/Queer Gender and Narrative Form: A Symposium on Gender and Narrative*, Newcastle University (online conference), 15–29 April 2021. Unpublished transcript shared with the author.
99. Moylan, *Demand the Impossible*, p. 9.
100. For a utopian reading of Bessie Head's writing, see Modhumita Roy, 'Utopia in the Subjunctive Mood: Bessie Head's *When Rain Clouds Gather*' in *The Politics of the (Im)Possible: Utopia and Dystopia Reconsidered*, ed. Barnita Bagchi (New Delhi: SAGE Publications India, 2012), pp. 179–96. For a comparative reading of Mitchison and Dixie's work, see Grace Borland Sinclair, *Fractal Fictions and Feminist Futures: The Speculative Fiction of Lady Florence Dixie and Naomi Mitchison*, MPhil thesis, University of Glasgow, 2022.

CHAPTER 12

Ankh-Morpork, Anti-Utopia
Terry Pratchett's Night Watch *and* Making Money

Jo Lindsay Walton

'Who knew what evil lurked in the hearts of men? A copper, that's who.'[1] Within recent Anglophone literary history, the English author Terry Pratchett looms large both as a writer of speculative fiction, and as a satirist and moralist. His immensely popular Discworld series relates the rapid transformation of the fictional Ankh-Morpork from a medieval to a modern city-state. Pratchett's Discworld series can be classed as comic high fantasy – it features witches, trolls, dwarfs, werewolves, and so on – though it is really *sui generis*, a one-of-a-kind postmodern transmedia screed, drawing together various modes of satire, parody, pastiche, allegory, homage, spoof, remix, allusion, plagiarism, pasticcio, unofficial sequel-writing, 'lampshading', steampunk, alternative history, and metafiction.[2] Pratchett is keenly interested in how his characters' lives are shaped by larger historical forces, and inspects numerous social institutions of liberal modernity through the lenses of comedy, satire, and fantastical estrangement. The expansive worldbuilding of Ankh-Morpork lends itself to being read as an exercise of the critical utopian imagination, casting the world around us in fresh light and revealing its latent possibilities. Such perspectives appear in the emerging scholarly literature on Pratchett, which has sometimes incorrectly presented the Discworld as politically radical, or as playfully unruly in ways that hint at radical possibilities.

Although the Discworld's politics are heteroglossic, by recognising their strong continuities with the longer history of liberal anti-utopian polemic, and specifically British liberal centrism of the late 1990s and 2000s, we can more accurately position the Discworld in relation to contested histories of enlightenment, industrialisation, empire, globalisation, and financialisation. In this chapter, I will offer a close examination of key works like *Night Watch* (2002) and *Making Money* (2007) to reveal that utopian thinking is primarily invoked pejoratively in the Discworld books, employed by Pratchett to cast doubt upon alternatives to capitalist modernity, and upon collective action as a means of generating social change.

12 Ankh-Morpork, Anti-Utopia

The Discworld is remarkable for combining its postmodern artifice with worldbuilding of great strength and solidity. While Pratchett borrows elements from many sources, he tends to make them his own, partly through serious consideration of their interaction with the Discworld's established elements.[3] Extrapolative reasoning within a fairly cohesive fantasy world underlies a sociological turn in the later Discworld books, in which various institutions such as policing, the press, and the money system, take their turns in the spotlight. This sociological turn places the Discworld in dialogue with utopian and dystopian literary traditions. As the British utopian theorist Ruth Levitas writes: 'If sociology embeds utopia, literary utopias similarly embed sociological analysis.'[4] Such sociological analysis requires, above all, a capacity to place personal narratives within their wider public and systemic contexts. This type of imagination is evident in the Discworld books of the 2000s, although the practice of isolating a social institution for observation and analysis is prefigured in earlier books. *The Colour of Magic* (1983) introduces modern insurance to the medieval city-state of Ankh-Morpork. *Guards! Guards!* (1982) looks at the shift from personal authority to rule of law, and *Small Gods* (1992) at the relationship of church and state.[5] In books like *Men at Arms* (1993), *Soul Music* (1994), *Feet of Clay* (1996), and *Jingo* (1997), Ankh-Morpork emerges from the chrysalis of Fritz Lieber's medieval-esque city of Lankhmar (the setting for swords-and-sorcery tales such as *The Swords of Lankhmar* (1968)), and comes more to resemble a fantasy London of the eighteenth and nineteenth centuries – albeit a Big Smoke blended with the mists of many metropoles, from New York and Seattle, to Venice, Tallinn, Paris, and Prague.

Throughout the 1990s, as Ankh-Morpork's distinctive spaces and places sprouted details with the publication of each new work in the Discworld series, so too did the city-state's distinctive temporalities. From its amorphous early sketches, Ankh-Morpork was maturing against the backdrop of Cool Britannia and Britpop, a cultural moment that Mark Fisher skewered for 'drawing on off-the-peg cliches of Englishness', for its 'deep pessimism about the present' and its 'implicit assumption that all great cultural moments lie in the past' based on 'a perceived incommensurability between English culture and "the future"'.[6] This was the era when Francis Fukuyama's most infamous thesis – in Jacques Derrida's scathing description, 'the advent of the ideal of liberal democracy and of the capitalist market in the euphoria of the end of history' – could be seriously entertained and debated.[7] It was formative for Pratchett's worldbuilding in Ankh-Morpork, where liberalising attitudes around race and gender from the United Kingdom's previous decades were overlaid with urbanisation and industrialisation from its previous centuries. Crucially, in Ankh-Morpork, progressivism *in* the present tended to be superimposed on progress *to* the present. Levitas suggests that 'sociological observation and utopian aspiration are combined in the identification of tendencies within the real'.[8] Although Ankh-Morpork invoked an impression of dazzling, dizzying possibilities, its trajectories had a fixed destination. The future to which it was hurtling had already happened in the real world of Pratchett's 1990s readership.

As the Discworld's sociological turn intensified through the 2000s, this sense of truncated utopian aspiration deepened. Pratchett satirically inspected many major institutions of liberal modernity, from workers' unions and international trade in *The Fifth Elephant* (1999) to the printing press and journalism in *The Truth* (2000), protest and popular assembly in *Night Watch* (2002), the postal service and communications networks in *Going Postal* (2004), capitalist banking and finance in *Making Money* (2007), and sports and mass entertainment in *Unseen Academicals* (2009).[9] Books like *Jingo* (1997), *The Fifth Elephant* (1999), *Night Watch* (2002), *Thud!* (2005), and *Snuff* (2011) also continued Pratchett's exploration of policing and rule of law begun in *Guards! Guards!* (1989). In addition to revealing how such institutions function, might the Discworld's estrangements have allowed us to imagine radical alternatives? On the whole they did not. In a 2002 interview, Pratchett suggested that the role of fantasy is 'to take that which is commonplace and therefore no longer seen and lift it up and turn it around and present it to the viewer from a completely new direction'.[10] The emphasis on revelatory defamiliarisation is commonplace within utopian studies; Pratchett's remark resonates with the thoughts of critics and creators such as Bertolt Brecht, Samuel R. Delany, Ursula K. Le Guin, Darko Suvin, Fredric Jameson, Tom Moylan, and Seo-Young Chu.[11] Tellingly however, Pratchett's reference point is the English author G. K. Chesterton, whose notion of estrangement places less emphasis upon emancipation, than upon a private spiritual practice of meditative marvelling. Chesterton's open-hearted theodicy re-enchants the status quo principally for its protection, not for its dissection.[12] In this chapter I want to make similar claims for Pratchett's work. The Discworld's characteristic patterns of defamiliarisation operate to disguise the contradictions of liberal capitalist modernity, and to sharpen the invective against its alternatives. As I argue, this anti-utopianism is more *concrete*, in a Blochian sense, than any utopianism that might be excavated from the Discworld.

Utopian Villains, Anti-Utopian Heroes

The Discworld is funny. Its anti-utopianism operates less through direct argument, and more through the depiction of social types: what sorts of

12 Ankh-Morpork, Anti-Utopia

people exist on the Discworld, what they do, whom we are expected to laugh at, or laugh with, and why. In itself, the fact that the Discworld does not deal in moral absolutes is not especially noteworthy. The Discworld's heroes and villains are constructed, like many heroes and villains, partly through dismantling simplistic notions of heroism and villainy that few readers are likely to seriously entertain. What are more interesting are the details: *which* specific shades of moral grey are condoned, castigated, or made ambiguous, and how.

In his characterisation of heroism and villainy, Pratchett participates in a long tradition of anti-chivalric satire, including Cervantes's *Don Quixote* (1605, 1615), Shakespeare's *Troilus and Cressida* (c. 1602), Voltaire's *Candide* (1759), and even contemporary grimdark fantasy.[13] This tradition celebrates pragmatism, experience, and local contextual knowledge. We are invited to take pleasure when Pratchett's old hands, figures such as Sam Vimes and Granny Weatherwax, educate naïfs and zealots whose heads are stuffed with lofty notions. By contrast, political radicals are likely to be dreary annoying misfits like the young Reg Shoe,[14] eccentric do-gooder chins like Adora Belle, or nasty villains like Lupine Wonse and Grag Ardent. Other major sources of Discworld villainy fill out a standard rogue's gallery of British centrist social commentary: foreign ultraconservatives; religious fundamentalists; stodgy, insufficiently eccentric aristocrats; officious officials; incredibly overt racists; and the bioessentially mentally disordered.

We are asked to root for Discworld heroes sometimes despite their despicable acts, and occasionally because of those acts. In *Night Watch*, for example, when Vimes encourages junior City Watch officers to purchase illegal weapons for everyday policing, the novel invites us to revel in Vimes's seasoned realism, not ruin the joke by identifying with his victims.[15] The Discworld frequently represents police corruption and brutality, but in ways far removed from any anti-carceral critique. Instead, these comic narratives gently normalise, apologise for, or even celebrate the acts that they depict. As Vimes boasts in *The Fifth Elephant*: 'We don't kill people in Ankh-Morpork just because they're accused. Well, not on purpose. And not because someone tells us to.'[16] Here Pratchett beautifully captures the senior police officer's slight unease with his own sentiment. But Vimes's unease has a place in the overall structure of feeling that the Discworld communicates, whereas the implications of that unease – for instance, the final thoughts of an Ankh-Morporkian teenager restrained to death by Sergeant Fred Colon or Corporal Nobby Nobbs – has no place whatsoever.

It is worth spoiling the fun a little, since the Discworld's ideological centre remains somewhat at odds with the Discworld's reputation within the emerging body of scholarly literature. For instance, the many interesting and useful essays in *Discworld and the Disciplines* (2014) and *Terry Pratchett's Ethical Worlds* (2020) nonetheless manage to be curiously apolitical.[17] One exception, by Janet Brennan Croft, offers a bold and optimistic reading of Pratchett's golems to argue for a 'socialist and communist' strain to his work.[18] Essays in the earlier *Terry Pratchett: Guilty of Literature* (2004) actually include more precise descriptions of Pratchett's political ideology, yet also perpetuate the now untenable rumour that Pratchett is difficult to pin down. For instance, Edward James suggests that 'Pratchett's own political views do not necessarily emerge very clearly' in the City Watch books.[19] Farah Mendlesohn persuasively excavates Pratchett's moral individualism, but leaves his political individualism to be inferred, and suggests (in *Jingo*, for example) that 'we are not even allowed to assume that we have identified the good guys'.[20] In 2004 there may have been an element of tactful intervention in the still-unfolding story of the Discworld.[21] Two decades on, we can safely say that political views emerge quite clearly in the Discworld books – whether or not to call them Pratchett's own is another conversation – and that the Discworld's heroes and villains are quite clearly distinguished.

One potential problem is that the Discworld's liberal anti-utopianism is somewhat at odds with the affective charge of the series, which often growls with heartfelt bitterness at social injustice. Throughout the series, there are many moments of warmth, kindness, care, and hope that we might associate with what Bloch termed the 'warm stream' of utopian thinking: the dreams of fairytales and wishful images that accompanies the rational 'cold stream' of analysis.[22] This tension might be contextualised, if not resolved, by remembering that British liberalism in the late 1990s and 2000s clung to a somewhat ambiguous, oppositional, and underdog status. This was certainly the case for parliamentary liberalism, disrupted by New Labour's soft neoliberalism and seeking a new identity. Not long after New Labour took power in 1997, the Liberal Democrats under party leader Charles Kennedy edged away from a rapprochement with the new governing party and sought a role familiar to any literary satirist: opportunistically jabbing critiques in many directions, wherever opportunities for advantage arose. The Liberal Democrats certainly were not in a position to articulate any grand alternative to the parliamentary neoliberal consensus, and in the late 2000s, under Nick Clegg's leadership, grew even more skilfully ambiguous. Joining with Conservative attacks on New Labour's 'nanny-state', they were able to appear more credibly concerned with individual liberty and collective prosperity than the Conservatives. By the end of the

12 Ankh-Morpork, Anti-Utopia

decade, the time of books like *Making Money, Unseen Academicals,* and *Snuff,* the Liberal Democrat party was mostly associated with strong progressive policies on education and the environment, and opposition to the Iraq war. In short, a left-wing voter in the UK 2010 General Election could be forgiven for believing the Liberal Democrats were marginally their best option.[23] This is a politics that has dated disastrously, however, in the still short time since Pratchett's death in 2015. The decade has been dominated by precisely the kind of illiberal authoritarian populism that liberal anti-utopianism claims as its chief antagonist, yet has shown itself singularly ineffective at tackling in practice: *I'll take the guy on the right: or do I mean the guy on the left?* Some indicators of Britain's illiberalism over the past decade include stark reductions in legal aid and further erosion of equality before the law; the expansion of surveillance, disciplinarity and the outsourcing of carceral infrastructure to for-profit providers; the repeal of the Human Rights Act; regressive welfare cuts and degrading and punitive sanctions on the disabled and unemployed; the hostile environment policy and racist deportation of UK citizens stripped of citizenhood on bureaucratic technicalities; haphazard militarism abroad including moral cover and practical assistance for genocide; and, of course, restrictions on freedom of movement and trade following a chaotic and protracted withdrawal from the European Union.[24]

Satire can easily be excused for failing to foresee the future, except where the pattern of omissions actually begins in the past. Whilst comic fantasy has no strong obligation to draw even-handedly from the history which inspires it, to the extent that Ankh-Morpork is telling a story of industrialisation and modernity, the story has at least two conspicuous omissions. One is empire. Ankh-Morpork is a multicultural, cosmopolitan metropolis, the major inspirations for which include London and New York. Yet aside from a few brief allusions ('It is no longer considered ... nice ... to send a warship over there to, as you put it, show Johnny Foreigner the error of his ways'),[25] there are no good Discworld correlates for the imperial histories of these cities. Trolls, dwarfs, werewolves, and other immigrants regard their squalor as an acceptable price to pay for more socially liberal attitudes and for commercial opportunities. Empire is touched on in *Interesting Times* (1994) and *Jingo* (1998), but for the most part Pratchett's interest is displaced to *Nation* (2008), a one-off non-Discworld book. There are consequences to denying the Discworld any equivalent to the proto-colonialism of enclosure in the Atlantic archipelago, to the British Empire, the settler-colonial genocide of North America, or wars of national liberation and other anti-colonial movements. Downplaying colonialism entails downplaying colonialism's role in essentialising differences as racial differences. The origin of the golems, who intermittently allegorise chattel slavery, is lost in the primordial past, rather than being entangled with the ongoing enlightenment and industrial revolution. The same is true of the ethnic enmity between trolls and dwarfs in works such as *Thud!*[26]

The second and connected absence is democracy. Throughout the series, and despite Ankh-Morpork's several constitutional crises, the city-state's system of government does not alter much. Ankh-Morpork is ruled by a Patrician, and in most books, this office is filled by the same man, Lord Havelock Vetinari. Vetinari is a tyrant who is the best of all possible tyrants. Ankh-Morpork, after suffering under the rule of men like Homicidal Lord Winder and Mad Lord Snapcase, and dallying with other forms of government, now has 'a form of democracy known as One Man, One Vote. The Patrician was the Man; he had the Vote.'[27] Vetinari's progressive and peaceful autocratic rule is presented as something valuable, and in several books its preservation indicates a happy ending. If there are some jibes at Vetinari's tyranny, there are plenty of jibes at democratic alternatives to tyranny. Pratchett's considerable genius at maxim-making is devoted to zingers such as, 'people only think for themselves if you tell them to';[28] likewise, Sam Vimes can 'see the flaw' in democracy: 'while he, Vimes, would have a vote, there was no way in the rules that anyone could prevent Nobby Nobbs from having one as well.'[29]

Against this background, this chapter examines the two Ankh-Morpork books of the 2000s that most energetically engage with utopian and anti-utopian themes. In both books, there are glimpses of democratic potentials on the Discworld, which are ultimately reluctantly relinquished. In both books, we are also granted utopian glimmers of abundance, dreams which are ultimately handed over to the stewardship of the status quo. These books are *Night Watch* (2002) and *Making Money* (2007).

'Glorious Revolution': Protest, Violence, and Social Change in *Night Watch*

On the Discworld, good social change is typically guided by pragmatic leaders like Havelock Vetinari and visionary entrepreneurs like Moist von Lipwig, ably assisted by ingenious, hardworking ordinary folks, and protected by police officers like Sam Vimes and Carrot Ironfoundersson. Rapid and deep change tends to be acceptable to the degree that it is technocratic or technological, and dubious to the degree that it suggests stirrings of class consciousness or a messianic tenor. Any excessively

12 Ankh-Morpork, Anti-Utopia 251

rational vision of progress is viewed with a Popperian suspicion that it will erupt into never-ending violence.[30] If the modernisation of Ankh-Morpork implicitly abandons or brutalises the more vulnerable members of society, then this can be justified via the general celebratory atmosphere around piecemeal progress.

One partial exception is *Night Watch*, which explores the possibility of rapid, bottom-up social change. The plot features time travel and is mostly set about thirty years before the main timeline of the Ankh-Morpork books. Under the especially erratic and brutal rule of the Patrician Lord Winder, which includes a secret police force, arbitrary detention, and enforced disappearances, popular dissent is growing. Even the city's nobles are unhappy with Lord Winder. The people organise their revolution and the elite organise their coup. Finally, with Winder gone, the police state apparatus is dismantled, although the city's basic hierarchy survives intact. The worn-out tyrant is replaced by a fresh one, Lord Snapcase.

While *Night Watch* offers a somewhat sympathetic portrayal of a popular uprising, it comes with heavy caveats. Collective action may haphazardly change the course of history, but only with permission from the elite. This continues the pessimism expressed in *Feet of Clay*: 'Regimes can survive barbarian hordes, crazed terrorists and hooded secret societies, but they're in real trouble when prosperous and anonymous men sit around a big table and think thoughts like that.'[31] Placing the events of *Night Watch* in Ankh-Morpork's past also reinforces a sense of stasis: revolutions are how things got the way they *are*, not ways of making the current situation any different.

Nonetheless, the rebellious zone of the city, dubbed the Glorious People's Republic of Treacle Mine Road, is something of a temporary utopian enclave. As Fredric Jameson defines, utopian enclaves function 'as a pocket of stasis within the ferment and rushing forces of social change ... within which Utopian fantasy can operate'.[32] Pratchett's utopian enclave is characterised by implied mutual aid and explicit abundance. 'There's enough for everyone to eat themselves sick', our time traveller Sam Vimes chastises Reg Shoe, when Reg officiously tries to ensure a fair distribution of food.[33] Vimes even has some fleeting revolutionary fervour of his own, envisioning the People's Republic expanding street by street:

> let through the decent people, and push the bastards, the rich bullies, the wheelers and dealers in people's fates, the leeches, the hangers-on, the brown-nosers and courtiers and smarmy plump devils in expensive clothes who didn't know or care about the machine but stole its grease, push them into a smaller and smaller compass and then leave them in there.[34]

It is perhaps to Pratchett's credit that, in handling the subject matter of revolutionary barricades, he does not merely retell the Reign of Terror as a natural and inevitable outcome of revolutionary egalitarianism. Throughout history, many insurrections have senselessly shed blood, have foundered against the sturdy yet flexible hierarchy of wealth and power, or have failed to live up to early ideals once power has been achieved.

Given these complex histories, and given the novel's relatively positive portrayal of life behind the barricades, might we be in the realm of a critical utopia, rather than an anti-utopia? Critical utopias, in Tom Moylan's formulation, reflect upon the limitations of the literary genre of utopia, emphasise conflicts on the path to utopia and flaws within achieved utopias, but ultimately 'reject utopia as a blueprint while preserving it as dream'.[35] By contrast anti-utopias, as Gary Saul Morson argues, aim to discredit the literary genre of utopia by exposing its literary devices in order to reveal 'the danger and folly of utopian lessons, but also the duplicitous strategies by which those lessons are taught'.[36]

What makes this interpretation of *Night Watch* ultimately untenable is, as John Newsinger writes in a wonderfully lucid review, 'probably Pratchett's greatest joke ever: a revolution that is actually carried out by the police!'.[37] Under the redoubtable Sam Vimes,[38] the People's Republic does not represent any kind of counterpower or alternative vision of Ankh-Morpork, so much as a zone in which safety and normality are conflated, as the rest of the city slips into chaos. Once the coup replaces Lord Winder with Lord Snapcase, the protective bubble of the People's Republic simply pops without a trace. Earlier, Vimes muses:

> *I* just wanted to keep a few streets safe. I just wanted to keep a handful of decent, silly people away from the dumb mobs and the mindless rebels and the idiot soldiery. I really, really hoped we could get away with it.[39]

Vimes does have some egalitarian instincts, despising aristocrats as much as 'dumb mobs'. A previous novel, *Men at Arms*, memorably presents the 'Captain Samuel Vimes "Boots" theory of socioeconomic unfairness'.[40] The poor must frequently buy cheap boots, Vimes notices, whereas the wealthy can afford good boots; paradoxically, the poor person spends *more* on boots overall *and still has wet feet*. It is an undoubtedly vivid portrayal of the cost of poverty, though it also faintly resonates with the reactionary canard of poverty resulting from profligacy, and wealth from thrift.

Furthermore, it is not clear whether this system is something Vimes hopes can change, or rather grimly accepts as inevitable. If you want a picture of the future, imagine the Captain Samuel Vimes 'Boots' theory of socioeconomic unfairness stamping on a human face – forever. Fortunately, a more just system for manufacturing and distributing footwear is actually alluded to in *Night Watch*, when would-be socialist rabble-rouser Reg Shoe addresses an assembly behind the barricades.

> 'People's Declaration of the Glorious Twenty-fourth of May,' said Reg.
> 'Yeah, yeah, right ... well, it says we'll seize hold of the means of production, sort of thing, so what I want to know is, how does that work out regarding my shoe shop? I mean, I'm in it anyway, right? It's not like there's room for more'n me and my lad Garbut and maybe one customer.'
> In the dark, Vimes smiled. Reg could never see stuff coming.
> 'Ah, but after the revolution all property will be held in common by the people ... er ... that is, it'll belong to you but *also* to everyone else, you see?'
> Comrade Supple looked puzzled. 'But I'll be the one making the shoes?'[41]

Reg is the only radical intellectual in *Night Watch*, and here his flustered performance reveals him as a poser. Had Reg dipped into some Discworld equivalent of Karl Marx,[42] he might have addressed Supple not as a capitalist 'living off the sweat of the common worker',[43] but, rather, as an artisan whose livelihood will soon be squeezed by capitalist mass production. Instead, the Reg-volution is constructed as dangerous at worst, ridiculous at best. Nothing like Vimes's 'Boots' theory, let alone a vision of any alternative future, appears in this scene. It serves rather to ridicule a broad category of alternatives to the status quo, that is, where productive capital is socially owned and governed. Even Reg's suspicion that he is being spied on is framed as a dogmatic delusion, despite Captain Swing and his secret police forming a major part of the plot.[44]

> Vimes sighed. 'Mr Shoe, we don't have a file on you. We don't have a file on *anyone*, understand? Half of us can't read without using a finger. Reg, we are not *interested* in you.'
> Reg Shoe's slightly worrying eyes remained fixed on Vimes's face for a moment, and then his brain rejected the information as contrary to whatever total fantasy was going on inside.[45]

To historicise this satire, at the time *Night Watch* was written the National Public Order Intelligence Unit was infiltrating numerous social justice, anti-racist, and environmental activist communities in the United Kingdom. As Rob Evans wrote in a 2017 *Guardian* article, 'undercover police officers who adopted fake identities in deployments lasting several years spied on more than 1,000 political groups'.[46]

However, as depicted in *Night Watch*, the real risk of revolution is not being watched but being massacred. *Night Watch* is a book in which a massacre might take place at any moment. The simmering tensions and violent clashes it depicts plausibly draw in elements of the Peterloo Massacre of 1819 in Manchester, Bloody Sunday in Derry in 1972, and a number of French revolutionary conflicts, including the Revolution of 1789, the June Rebellion of 1832, the Revolution of 1848 and subsequent Springtime of the Peoples across Europe, and the Paris Commune with its Bloody Week of 1871. It is instructive to glance over some of these events, to clarify how they have been fantastically reimagined on the Discworld. For example, the 1819 Peterloo Massacre began when cavalry charged through a crowd toward the speakers' platform, in order to arrest the organisers of the rally. A child was first trampled to death.[47] Other cavalry then killed seventeen others, and injured hundreds, attempting to disperse the crowd. No cavalrymen were killed, although two Special Constables were among those killed by the cavalry, and one Special Constable was killed by rioters the next day.[48] By contrast, in *Night Watch*, it is apparently cavalrymen who are killed first ('a cavalry helmet is not a lot of use against a ballistic cobblestone . . . a trooper had been pulled off his horse in Dolly Sisters, and bluntly, mobbed to death').[49] In the 1832 June Rebellion, the events that also inspired Victor Hugo's *Les Misérables* (1862), seventy-three government soldiers were killed, and ninety-three rebels. The Bloody Week of 1871 in Paris was a large and prolonged conflict, and perhaps as many as a thousand government soldiers were killed. The vast majority of the dead, however, were the socialist revolutionary communards, many thousands of whom were killed.[50] They are the dead satirised in the form of Reg Shoe. On Bloody Sunday in 1972, the British Army, deployed in support of the Royal Ulster Constabulary and on an operation to arrest rioters, shot twenty-six unarmed people, mostly protestors, fourteen of whom died.[51] Whereas *Night Watch* draws a sharp line between the peace-keeping police and the murderous military and secret police, the Troubles were characterised by a deadly blurring of these lines.

By contrast, who is killed in *Night Watch*? It is the police. Clearly, other deaths occur in the background. But only a handful of deaths are given narrative importance. Six of these are police officers: Billy Wiglet, Horace Nancyball, Dai Dickins, Cecil 'Snouty' Clapman, Ned Coates, and John Keel.[52] 'They did the job they didn't have to do, and they died doing it . . . They fought for those who'd been abandoned, they fought for one another, and they were betrayed.'[53] The rebel Reg Shoe is also killed, but survives as a zombie. In *Night Watch*, the police are not killers, but de-escalators of violence, and heroic victims of violence, who put their lives on the line to keep the peace. This is hard reading in an era in which police brutality in the United Kingdom has led to events such as the shooting of the Black British man Mark Duggan in 2011, which led to violent riots in London, Birmingham, Nottingham, Leicester, Coventry, Derby, Liverpool, and Bristol. It is like a plot lifted from a police statement in the wake of a tragedy, with the independent inquiry still pending.

Police and soldiers do die sometimes in revolutions, particularly successful revolutions; so do aristocrats. Yet in *Night Watch*, the upper classes are extraordinarily well-insulated from the armed uprising, which largely consists of ordinary people fighting among themselves. A recurring motif is the criss-crossing social relationships spanning both sides of the barricades. In contrast with the chaotic struggles on the streets, the actual coup is a genteel affair. It is engineered within the elite stratum of society, and though it results in Lord Winder's death, it is curiously bloodless. When the current tyrant is abandoned by all his friends, an assassin working for the next tyrant simply frightens him to death. What *Night Watch* appears to teach here is that politicians are impervious to popular violence, though the fates of Louis XVI of France, Tsar Nicholas II of Russia, Charles I of England, Maximilian I of Mexico, Nicolae Ceaușescu of Romania, and many others attest otherwise.

'Don't Let Me Detain You': Sovereignty, Democracy, and Financialisation in *Making Money*

The Patrician Lord Vetinari has often been seen as the quintessential Machiavellian leader.[54] It is a convincing connection, though his uncanny statecraft might also suggest the philosopher-king of Plato's *Republic*. Perhaps most strikingly of all, Vetinari is the proto-liberal anti-democratic sovereign of Thomas Hobbes. Vetinari is unlimited in his theoretical powers, and yet never abuses them. Hobbes might have preferred 'therefore' rather than 'yet': according to Hobbes, unlimited powers by definition *cannot* be abused. Hobbes thought that liberty construed as a set of natural rights, that is 'an exemption from Lawes', would be a logical absurdity.[55] Vetinari enjoys all the same powers as his predecessors Winder and Snapcase, but he employs them more sparingly. Always concise and unobtrusive, creating spaces for action rather than acting himself, Vetinari provides Ankh-Morpork with liberty 'consistent with the unlimited power of the Soveraign' and consistent with the 'Feare' that is necessary for peace and stability. Such liberty 'dependeth on the Silence of the Law'.[56] As Hobbes writes, it is whatever the sovereign omits to regulate:

such as is the Liberty to buy, and sell, and otherwise contract with one another; to choose their own aboad, their own diet, their own trade of life, and institute their children as they themselves think fit; & the like.[57]

For Hobbes, 'the greatest pressure of Soveraign Governours proceedeth not from any delight'.[58] Similarly, Vetinari appears almost without passions, except where the security of Ankh-Morpork is concerned.

'What is it you want?' said Moist.
Lord Vetinari raised an eyebrow. 'I? Nothing. What do you want?'[59]

Kevin Guilfoy is right to characterise Pratchett as 'libertarian-friendly, maybe even libertarian-curious';[60] the Libertarian Futurist Society, who are often wrong about British fiction, had a point in giving the Prometheus Award to *Night Watch*. Vetinari is the sovereign as a circumspect, unappetitive, eyebrow-cocking guardian of order. His leadership offers the stability against which his subjects can individually follow their dreams. 'People know where they stand with Lord Vetinari', says Fred Colon.[61] 'What Vetinari mostly does not do is *a lot of harm*', says William de Worde.[62]

Nevertheless, the Discworld also reflects liberal ambivalence towards the state and sometimes celebrates an expansive and energetic state as a necessary check on natural human folly and vice, or as a driver of cultural, technological, or economic modernisations. In *Making Money*, Vetinari designs a massive public works project, 'the Undertaking'.[63] First he must catalyse reform of the city's money system. His characteristically subtle approach is to engineer ex-conman Moist von Lipwig into the roles of Master of the Royal Mint and acting Chairman of the Royal Bank of Ankh-Morpork.[64] Vetinari sets Moist to his task of financial reform with these words: 'Don't let me detain you, Mr Lipwig. Remember: it's all about the city.'[65]

Before long Moist is expanding Ankh-Morpork's money supply with its first paper fiat currency, backed by nothing more than the state's insistence that it is valuable. Moist stamps his prototype banknote with Ankh-Morpork's coat of arms, and writes, in large ornate letters, 'AD URBEM PERTINET', an allusion to Vetinari's parting words, and a reminder that it is really the sovereign who set this sequence of events in motion.[66] 'It's all about the city' might hint, by way of a play on words, at a vital criterion for a well-functioning currency: these banknotes must be all *around* the city, everywhere you go. *Ad Urbem Pertinet* and 'it's all about the city' are also both modulations, one grand and one colloquial, of the primacy of *reason of state*. That is, Vetinari may be a light-touch tyrant, yet his claim to sovereignty is founded in his capacity to enslave, kill, torture, and imprison. These are the powers that ultimately ground monetary sovereignty, ensuring that Moist's banknotes are destined to circulate. The motto that insists 'it's all about the city' could just as well have read 'don't let me [the sovereign] detain you'.

In these respects, *Making Money* is mounting a critique of the commodity theory of money from the perspective of chartalism. Chartalism argues, in essence, that money comes from the state. By imposing taxes, and adjudicating debt obligations, the sovereign drives some particular means of payment into stable and reliable circulation. Pratchett writes: 'On a desert island gold is worthless.'[67] Gold may also be worthless in a city, if it fails to circulate. Through circulation, 'worthless gold', or some other means of payments, becomes generally accepted as money.[68] Chartalism is not attached to any particular 'morphic means of payment':[69] money might be pure gold coins, 'gold-ish' coins and penny stamps, unsecured banknotes, or even pickaxes.[70] Commodity theory, by contrast, sees money more like a thing that is traded for other things.[71]

Chartalism is exactly the theory of money we should expect from Pratchett. It aligns with his longstanding interest in how stories shape reality, in this case, the story that certain little bits of paper are supremely valuable. Crucially, this also enables Pratchett to return to the utopian possibilities that appeared in *Night Watch*. 'Go away and make money. Unlock the wealth of Ankh-Morpork', instructs Vetinari.[72] *Making Money* is a story about a story that, if properly embedded in law and culture, could have the power to transform material scarcity into material abundance.

Yet Pratchett also offers a distinctive twist on chartalism. Whereas chartalism insists that money is a creature of the sovereign, *Making Money* emphasises that sovereignty is a complex and often precarious thing. In Hobbes's terms, the social contract can never be an agreement between the sovereign and the people, only an agreement among the people to recognise a sovereign. When Vetinari describes Ankh-Morpork – '"A great rolling sea of evil", he said, almost proprietorially' – his *almost* is crucial.[73] It is the fulcrum of the humour, and a reminder of the precariousness of Vetinari's position. The Hobbesian sovereign by definition cannot be obliged nor entitled by contract; a sovereign is always at most *almost* a proprietor. If the sovereign is eminently well-placed to create money, by the same token (or tokens), whoever is well-placed to create money has a powerful claim to be the sovereign. Throughout *Making Money*, Vetinari is shadowed by various quasi-sovereigns or counter-sovereigns, figures in whom sovereignty appears in an estranged fashion.[74]

Moist even finds himself, quite accidentally, a pretender to Vetinari's sovereignty when he gains control of an army of golden golems.[75] The most prominent figure of estranged sovereignty, however, is Cosmo Lavish, head of a family of powerful aristocrats. Cosmo obsessively mimics Vetinari. Cosmo dresses like Vetinari. He has his carriage fitted out like Vetinari's. Cosmo frets that things which work for Vetinari – a *bon mot* before a hostile audience, for instance – somehow never quite work for him.[76] He reflects enviously:

> Don't let me detain you. What a wonderful phrase Vetinari had devised. The jangling double meaning set up undercurrents of uneasiness in the most innocent of minds. The man had found ways of bloodless tyranny that put the rack to shame.[77]

Cosmo's rivalry with Vetinari represents sovereignty as constitutively up for grabs, associated not only with literal borders, but also with borderline cases, attended by the permanent possibility that any rule, routine or regularity may turn out to be inapplicable *this* time.[78]

The corollary of sovereignty as the power to determine the exception is sovereignty as the power to determine the *non*-exception: to preside over the border where the vast realm of calculable and commensurable value begins. The chief accountant Mavolio Bent is another counter-sovereign figure, who like Vetinari and Moist seeks to control the definition of value in the city. Bent is a tireless champion of the commodity theory of money, specifically metallism, believing that the only 'true' money is gold. Bent initially resembles Vetinari in his imperturbability. As the nature of value in Ankh-Morpork shifts, the accountant experiences a melt-down, eventually attacking Vetinari with a pineapple custard pie. This is an intriguing moment, which echoes the humiliation of Bent's near-namesake Malvolio in Shakespeare's *Twelfth Night*, as well as the bloodless assassination of Lord Winder in *Night Watch*. It could be read as a reflection on the role of satire in holding sovereign power to account, and the utopian potential of such critique: as Bloch writes in his 1956 essay 'On the Present in Literature', only satire and utopia are capable of uncovering 'the *economic, causal analysis of the situation and the tendency*'.[79] At any rate, this is no innocuous pie, since 'a picture of an encustarded Patrician on the front page of the *Times* would rock the power-politics of the city'.[80] Moist manages to dive in the way of the delicious missile, and when the custard has settled, Vetinari, as befits the Hobbesian sovereign, 'had not moved'.[81]

The more enduring threat to Vetinari's sovereignty emerges from the economist Hubert Turvy and his 'Glooper' experiment. Hubert's

12 Ankh-Morpork, Anti-Utopia 259

'Glooper' device is the Discworld equivalent of an economic model, loosely inspired by Bill Phillips's MONIAC analogue computer. Pratchett takes great interest in the agency of narrative models, and how they may reshape reality in their own likenesses. In *Making Money*, this interest is extended to economic modelling. In the novel's closing pages, a kind of technologised chrysopoeia – that is, creating gold from nothing, by adding a representation of gold to the Glooper model – implies a new rival to the monetary sovereignty of the Patrician.[82] More allegorically, the Glooper may suggest the emergence of global financial markets enabled by digital infrastructure from the 1980s onwards.[83]

Making Money also hints at popular sovereignty. The novel often emphasises that real value is derived from 'the city', and the key case study is the pie, sausage, and rat-on-a-stick salesman, Cut-Me-Own-Throat Dibbler. The opportunistic Dibbler, who appears in many Discworld books, is described by one critic as 'representing Ankh-Morpork's spirit'.[84] Dibbler is a 'purveyor of absolutely anything that ... was guaranteed to have fallen off the back of an oxcart'.[85] His attempts at socio-economic mobility are usually portrayed with a mixture of affection and contempt. In *Making Money*, Dibbler's typical bit part is subtly altered. Although Moist's financial revolution is exactly the kind of civic upheaval Dibbler usually exploits, for once he is not looking for loopholes. Instead, he comes to the Bank to borrow, intending to buy a barrow for his core business. Moist muses, 'there were times when a Dibbler sausage in a bun was just what you wanted. Sad, yet true.'[86]

Through the figures such as Cosmo, Bent, Hubert, and Dibbler, *Making Money* investigates sovereignty and monetary value: two sides of the same coin, stamped with the city and with the head of its esteemed tyrant. But even as *Making Money* allows its financial institutions to be radically redesigned, it takes care to preserve the city's basic social hierarchy intact. If *Night Watch* proposes that the upper classes are beneficiaries of popular armed uprising, then *Making Money* proposes that the lower classes are the beneficiaries of key capitalist financial institutions. It imagines improved social mobility through hard work, entrepreneurship, and financialisation, all with an anti-utopian, 'radical centrist' flavour.[87]

Here it is worth noting that Vimes's 'Boots' theory is wrong. At least it is overstated: 'The reason that the rich were so rich, Vimes reasoned, was because they managed to spend less money.'[88] This is not *the* reason but *a* reason, and a minor one at that. Vimes leaves out the basics: primitive accumulation, extraction of surplus value, return on capital. Put simply, the poor are so poor because their great-great-great-etc.-grandparents were told by men with swords that the fields, forests, and pastures where they had always grown, gathered, and hunted were actually somebody else's property. Nowadays, no matter how hard they work on the land, or in the mill, or at the factory, it never pays as well as merely owning it.

However, if Vimes's theory *were* to have captured the main reason for poverty, then neoliberalism would have an easy and effective solution: improved financial inclusion. This is precisely what Vetinari and Moist oversee in *Making Money*. New paper fiat currency is inserted into the money supply as micro-loans. In this respect, the idea that 'to back the currency ... you just needed the city' is slyly equivocal.[89] On the one hand, 'the city' suggests the people of the city, workers and entrepreneurs like Dibbler, as well as the communities and material infrastructures in which they are embedded. Ankh-Morpork is a city-state, and 'the city' also suggests the government: Vetinari backing the currency with his sovereign power to detain. Finally, the City is also the colloquial term for the United Kingdom's financial services sector, including investment banks like JPMorgan Chase, Goldman Sachs, Barclays, and HSBC. Dibbler may be free to participate in the city that 'turns worthless gold into ... everything',[90] but his freedom depends upon 'the Silence of the Law', and that silence depends on his usefulness to the Discworld version of financialisation.[91]

Once again, it might be helpful to dwell on how *Making Money* re-imagines specific historical events. The novel reflects the 2000s, including New Labour's efforts to improve financial inclusion, in order to soften the 'protection, consolidation and enhancement of the City's position as a major global financial centre ... as the centrepiece of New Labour growth strategy', as British de-industrialisation accelerated.[92] The novel also borrows a little from the Nixon Shock, the last gasp of the gold standard in 1971. These modern moments are blended with an early modern one: the re-negotiation of English sovereignty around the time of the Glorious Revolution in 1688, and subsequent emergence of the Bank of England, an arrangement whereby 'fresh money [was] brought into the nation'.[93] Just as in Ankh-Morpork, the nature of this new English money was unprecedented. The crown's coinage and bonds were effectively merged with the mercantile networks and institutions that facilitated the liquidity of private bills of exchange. Because of this 'fusion of the two moneys', banknotes could enjoy the legitimacy and depersonalisation associated with the state's tax-raising powers.[94]

In *Making Money*, fresh money derives from 'the city', an amalgam of the benign Hobbesian sovereign with the hardworking and ingenious commoners. There is of course no king, but the Lavishes's loss of influence is an approximate proxy for the constraints on crown powers that emerged around this time. The divergence from historical events is again telling. *Making Money* effectively positions the sovereign as the lender, a benevolent and progressive provider of financial inclusion.[95] As Moist reflects, 'some of the people waiting hopefully to see him about a loan were thinking in terms of a couple of dollars until Friday.'[96] On the Roundworld, by contrast, the Bank of England was founded to allow the crown to *borrow*, in order to finance war against France.[97] As for the long-term beneficiaries? The original 1,500 odd investors in the Bank of England did include a few tradespeople – cooks, drapers, dyers, ironmongers – but by far the greatest amount of capital was raised from men who were gentry, merchants, or both.[98] These were no Dibblers. If anything, they were Lavishes.

Conclusion: The Democracy to Come

With indefatigable optimism, the Ankh-Morpork books accelerate a medieval city-state into liberal industrial modernity, in an array of fantastically estranged forms. Nonetheless Ankh-Morpork does not become a space for lucidly perceiving the histories that inspire it, let alone cultivating radical alternatives. Rather, the series articulates a deep suspicion of the kind of political radicalism often associated with utopian thinking. In true centrist fashion, such suspicion seldom distinguishes sharply between left and right radicalisms.

The Discworld does offer some variation around these core politics, as should be expected from any vast series of satirical novels, populated with myriad characters, and written over several decades. But every political ideology contains multitudes. In this chapter I have sought to show how the heteroglossic, dialogic, and contradictory character of the Discworld is on the whole remarkably consistent with British centrism of the late twentieth and early twenty-first centuries. Utopia forms an indispensable part of such ideology, the arch antagonist from which it borrows a sense of burning purpose. By opposing utopia, Pratchett's Discworld can comfortably lament structural violence while also lampooning reasonable remedies to such violence: such as democratic elections; or unions and industrial actions; or networks of consciousness raising and movement building; or innovations in value beyond the confined imaginaries of capitalism; or insurrections of the oppressed.

The temptation is to cherry-pick evidence to patch up Pratchett into a writer whose satirical critiques across the vast Discworld series might be said to construct a properly utopian negation of their particular sociohistorical moment, and the size and variety of his work offers plenty of opportunities. For instance, *Making Money* grows fruitfully strange in its final pages, as the new fiat currency morphs once more, into a golem-backed currency – might this also be celebrated as a moment of generative self-criticism? When *Night Watch* withholds democracy from the Discworld, might it implicitly demand a democracy that would be worthy of the name? Does it demand we imagine the utopian 'democracy to come', as Jacques Derrida termed it?[99] Ernst Bloch usefully distinguishes between *concrete* and *abstract* utopia. Briefly, concrete utopia is grounded in materially existing desires and forces with potential to realise its aspirations, abstract utopia is not. A similar distinction might be introduced to anti-utopia. The concrete anti-utopia is grounded in material dynamics that are poised to defeat whatever positive future visions it denounces, the abstract anti-utopia is not.[100] Any cultural artefact as complex as the Discworld is likely to combine utopian and anti-utopian aspects, and the critic's quest may partly lie in distinguishing these, and in evaluating or even reshaping their abstraction or concreteness. The Discworld's anti-utopian satire feels impressively concrete, well-integrated with the discourse that shaped financialisation in the 2000s, and, in the wake of the 2008 financial crisis, effectively defused and deflected desires for radical change. Whenever the Discworld reminds us what not to risk, what might go wrong, how things always work, or whom not to trust, it strongly resonates with such discourse. By contrast, whilst the Discworld is achingly alive with vivid utopian impulses, the concreteness of these impulses – that is, their connectivity with material forces pressing for positive change today and tomorrow – is far more questionable.

It can take great effort to see the politics of works that delight and console us for what they are, not for what we would like them to be. Cervantes's *Don Quixote*, which, like the Discworld, blends together the medieval with the contemporary moment of its composition, offers a suitable concluding comparison. Bloch notes how Don Quixote becomes the doer of things he has read, and how Cervantes portrays his knight-errant's madness so movingly as to practically undo all his patent mockery. But Bloch continues:

> The heroic feat of goodness, the gigantic dream of a future world, was layered into the superstructure of the Middle Ages, into a fixed, simply prevented, other world. The result was a caricature of utopia – a pathos to itself, a comedy to others, in practice a history of the thrashings suffered by the abstractly unconditional.[101]

12 Ankh-Morpork, Anti-Utopia 263

Bloch's phrase 'caricature of utopia' resonates with the Discworld. Perhaps at its best the Discworld invites us to imagine a world in which its satire would be adequate. We might even suppose that the Discworld is not satire, so much as it is a *satire on satire*: a vivid, silly costume party, attended not by actual jokes, jibes, allegories, parodies, caricatures, burlesques, pastiches, serious moral lessons, educated hopes, solaces and consolations, and so on, but by some strange order of beings, dressed up as those things to inspire our delight and our delirium.

Notes

1. A thought of Samuel Vimes, in *Night Watch* (London: Corgi, 2014 [2002]), 301. Special thanks to Christopher Churches-Lindsay, Caroline Edwards, Tony Williams, Ian Davidson, and the Pennyred Discord for support and feedback in writing this chapter.
2. *Lampshading* is a term used on the website TV Tropes (tvtropes.org). It means making use of a far-fetched genre trope whilst also signalling self-awareness to the audience.
3. Just for example, *Night Watch* plausibly references Rembrandt's artwork *The Night Watch* (1642), Victor Hugo's novel *Les Misérables* (1862), and the movies *Horsefeathers* (1932) and *Men in Black* (1997). Some of the novel's historical inspirations are discussed later in this chapter.
4. Ruth Levitas, *Utopia As Method: The Imaginary Reconstitution of Society* (Basingstoke: Palgrave Macmillan, 2013), p. 75.
5. The co-authored Long Earth series (2012–16) also features prominent utopian and post-scarcity themes. It is not covered in this chapter. See Terry Pratchett and Stephen Baxter, *The Long Earth* (London: Doubleday, 2012).
6. Mark Fisher, 'Indie Reactionaries', *New Statesman & Society*, 8(360) (1995), p. 31.
7. Jacques Derrida, *Spectres of Marx: The State of the Debt, the Work of Mourning and the New International*, trans. Peggy Kamuf (London: Routledge, 1994), p. 106.
8. Levitas, *Utopia As Method*, p. 75.
9. See Janet Brennan Croft, 'The Golempunk Manifesto: Ownership of the Means of Production in Pratchett's Discworld' in *Terry Pratchett's Ethical Worlds*, ed. Kristin Noone and Emily Lavin Leverett (Jefferson, NC: McFarland 2020), pp. 110–23.
10. John Gardner and Terry Pratchett, 'Interview: Discworld Author Terry Pratchett', *New Zealand Herald*, 25 October 2002. www.nzherald.co.nz/lifestyle/interview-discworld-author-terry-pratchett/KRKI TTNHWJOCH4VP4TQQ3RRHOI/ (Last accessed 29 February 2024).
11. Bertolt Brecht, 'Alienation Effects in Chinese Acting' in John Willett (trans.), *Brecht on Theatre: The Development of an Aesthetic* [1936] (London: Eyre

Methuen, 1987), pp. 91–99; Samuel R. Delany, *Starboard Wine: More Notes on the Language of Science Fiction: Revised Edition* (Hanover, New Hampshire: Wesleyan University Press, 2012); Ursula K. Le Guin, 'Introduction' to *The Left Hand of Darkness* in *The Language of the Night: Essays on Fantasy and Science Fiction*, ed. Susan Wood (New York: G.P. Putnam's Sons, 1979), pp. 155–9; Darko Suvin, *Metamorphoses of Science Fiction: On the Poetics and History of a Literary Genre* (New Haven, CT: Yale University Press, 1979); Fredric Jameson, 'Utopia and Its Antinomies' in *Archaeologies of the Future: The Desire Called Utopia and Other Science Fictions* (London: Verso, 2004), pp. 142–70; Tom Moylan, *Scraps of the Untainted Sky* (Boulder, CO: Westview Press, 2000); Seo-Young Chu, *Do Metaphors Dream of Literal Sleep?: A Science-Fictional Theory of Representation* (Cambridge, MA: Harvard University Press, 2010).
12. G. K. Chesterton, 'The Ethics of Elfland' in *Orthodoxy* (New York: Dodd, Mead & Co., 1908), pp. 76–116.
13. *Grimdark* is a loose label for 'fantasies that turn their backs on the more uplifting, Pre-Raphaelite visions of idealized medievaliana, and instead stress how nasty, brutish, short and, er, dark life back then "really" was'. Adam Roberts, *Get Started in Writing Science Fiction and Fantasy* (London: Hachette, 2014), p. 42. Roberts emphasises the scare quotes around 'really': grimdark owes more to a cynical inversion of chivalric aspects of the Tolkienian tradition than a concern with historical accuracy.
14. Well, not *young* so much as *living*. Getting killed is what really gives Reg Shoe a new lease of life.
15. Terry Pratchett, *Night Watch* [2002] (London: Corgi, 2014), 266.
16. Terry Pratchett, *The Fifth Elephant* [1999] (London: Penguin, 2023), p. 364. Cf. *Night Watch*, pp. 368–9.
17. Anne Hiebert Alton and William C. Spruiell (eds.), *Discworld and the Disciplines: Critical Approaches to the Terry Pratchett Works* (Jefferson, NC: McFarland & Company, 2014); Kristin Noone and Emily Lavin Leverett (eds.), *Terry Pratchett's Ethical Worlds: Essays on Identity and Narrative in Discworld and Beyond* (Jefferson, NC: McFarland & Company, 2020).
18. Brennan Croft, 'The Golempunk Manifesto', p. 146.
19. Edward James, 'The City Watch' in *Terry Pratchett: Guilty of Literature*, 2nd ed., ed. Andrew M. Butler, Edward James, and Farah Mendlesohn (Baltimore, MD: Old Earth Books, 2004), pp. 193–216 (p. 203).
20. Farah Mendlesohn, 'Faith and Ethics' in *Terry Pratchett: Guilty of Literature*, 2nd ed., ed. Andrew M. Butler, Edward James, and Farah Mendlesohn (Baltimore, MD: Old Earth Books, 2004), pp. 239–60 (p. 243).
21. Note also that most of the essays were written for the 2000 first edition, though some were updated for the 2004 edition. The period that this chapter focuses on comes mostly after the first edition.
22. Ernst Bloch, *The Principle of Hope*, vol. 3, trans. Neville Plaice, Stephen Plaice, and Paul Knight (Cambridge, MA: The MIT Press, 1986), pp. 1369–70.

23. The website *Political Compass*, for example, situated the Liberal Democrats slightly to the left of Labour on economic issues, also noting 'considerable distance from both the main parties on the social scale'. *Political Compass* (2010). www.politicalcompass.org/ukparties2010 (Last accessed 7 February 2024).
24. Philip Alston, 'Statement on Visit to the United Kingdom', *Office of the High Commissioner for Human Rights*, 16 November 2018. www.ohchr.org/en/statements/2018/11/statement-visit-united-kingdom-professor-philip-alston-united-nations-special (Last accessed 7 February 2024).
25. Terry Pratchett, *Jingo* [1997] (London: Penguin, 2023), p. 19.
26. The presence of Carrot Ironfoundersson (Kzad-bhat), a 6'6" Dwarf, is an admirable corrective to the bioessentialism of the vast majority of Tolkien-influenced contemporary fantasy.
27. Terry Pratchett, *Mort* [1987] (New York: HarperTorch, 2001), p. 137. Technically, as we gather across *Jingo*, *Night Watch*, and *The Truth* especially, Ankh-Morpork has certain statutes which provide for the election of a Patrician. The electors appear to be the heads of the Guilds, who are also predominantly the powerful nobles of the city, and the elected person holds the office for life. The way to recall a Patrician is assassination.
28. Terry Pratchett, *Men at Arms* [1993] (London: Corgi, 1994), p. 309. The speaker is Fred Colon, apparently quoting Vimes.
29. Pratchett, *The Fifth Elephant*, p. 207.
30. Karl Popper, 'Utopia and Violence', *World Affairs*, 149(1) (1986), pp. 3–9. Available at: www.jstor.org/stable/20672078 (Last accessed 30 July 2024).
31. Terry Pratchett, *Men at Arms* [1993] (London: Corgi, 1994), p. 309.
32. Fredric Jameson, *Archaeologies of the Future: The Desire Called Utopia and Other Science Fictions* (London; Verso, 2007), p. 15.
33. Pratchett, *Night Watch*, p. 389.
34. Ibid., p. 392.
35. Tom Moylan, *Demand the Impossible: Science Fiction and the Utopian Imagination* [1986] (Bern: Peter Lang, 2014), p. 10.
36. Gary Saul Morson, *The Boundaries of Genre: Dostoevsky's* Diary of a Writer *and the Traditions of Literary Utopia* (Austin, TX: University of Texas Press, 1981), pp. 115–16.
37. John Newsinger, 'The People's Republic of Treacle Mine Road Betrayed: Terry Pratchett's *Night Watch*', *Vector*, 232 (2003), pp. 15–16 (p. 16).
38. The old, grizzled Sam Vimes, not the pipsqueak Sam Vimes. At least, not that Sam *yet*. This is a time travel novel, after all.
39. Pratchett, *Night Watch*, p. 359.
40. Pratchett, *Men at Arms*, p. 29. Cf. Mikaela Springsteen, '"Lies to Children": From Folk to Formal Science in Terry Pratchett's Discworld', *Vector*, 16 March 2021. https://vector-bsfa.com/2021/03/16/lies-to-children-from-folk-to-formal-science-in-terry-pratchetts-discworld/ (Last accessed 14 February 2024).
41. Pratchett, *Night Watch*, pp. 343–4.
42. Cf. this apparent allusion to Marx, from *The Last Continent*. 'A man sits in some museum somewhere and writes a harmless book about political

economy and suddenly thousands of people who haven't even read it are dying because the ones who did haven't got the joke. Knowledge is dangerous, which is why governments often clamp down on people who can think thoughts above a certain calibre.' Terry Pratchett, *The Last Continent* [1998] (London: Penguin, 2022), p. 21.
43. Pratchett, *Night Watch*, p. 344.
44. Captain Swing is an especially nasty villain. The allusion to the Captain Swing of the 1830 Swing Riots, in which English agricultural workers protested the increasing mechanisation of their labour, is presumably unintentional.
45. Pratchett, *Night Watch*, p. 317.
46. Rob Evans, 'Undercover Police Spied on More than 1000 Political Groups in UK', *The Guardian*, 27 July 2017. www.theguardian.com/uk-news/2017/jul/27/undercover-police-spied-on-more-than-1000-political-groups-in-uk (Last accessed 7 February 2024).
47. Robert William Reid, *The Peterloo Massacre* (London: Heinemann, 1989), p. 168.
48. Anon., 'Names of Fatalities at Peterloo 1819', *The Peterloo Memorial Campaign*. www.peterloomassacre.org/deaths.html (Last accessed 3 March 2024).
49. Pratchett, *Night Watch*, p. 347.
50. Estimates of the numbers of communards killed range from 5,700 to 30,000 or even more. See Robert Tombs, 'How Bloody was *La Semaine Sanglante* of 1871? A Revision', *The Historical Journal*, 55(3) (2012), pp. 679–704.
51. House of Commons, *Report of the Bloody Sunday Inquiry*, 15 June 2010, vol. 1, pp. 99–100. Available at: www.gov.uk/government/publications/report-of-the-bloody-sunday-inquiry (Last accessed 10 February 2024). Thirteen were killed on the day, and one victim died four months later.
52. Ned Coates is both rebel and police officer. Keel's death is complicated by time travel shenanigans.
53. Pratchett, *Night Watch*, pp. 470–71. These police die at the hands of the military of a totalitarian state, after having sided (somewhat ambiguously) with an insurrection against that state. They also die at the hands of the secret police, protecting Vimes/Keel from extrajudicial execution (at the instruction of the new regime).
54. Vetinari is revealed to have written a book called *The Servant*, an ambiguous allusion to Machiavelli's *The Prince*. Terry Pratchett and Stephen Briggs, *The Ultimate Discworld Companion* (London: Gollancz, 2021), p. 50. Elsewhere, Edward James comments, 'In many ways Vetinari reminds the reader of Machiavelli's hypothetical Prince, but he has rather more scruples.' James, 'The City Watch', pp. 209–10.
55. Thomas Hobbes, *Leviathan* [1651] (Cambridge: Cambridge University Press, 2000), p. 147.
56. Ibid., pp. 148, 146, 152.
57. Ibid. p. 148.
58. Ibid. p. 128.
59. Pratchett, *Making Money*, p. 33.

60. Kevin Guilfoy, 'Capitalism, Socialism, and Democracy on the Discworld' in *Philosophy and Terry Pratchett*, ed. Jacob M. Held and James B. South (New York: Palgrave-MacMillan, 2015), pp. 105–31 (p. 105).
61. Pratchett, *Jingo*, p. 352.
62. Terry Pratchett, *The Truth* [2000] (London: Corgi, 2001), p. 290.
63. Terry Pratchett, *Making Money* [2007] (London: Penguin, 2023) p. 126. Pratchett was rumoured to have been considering a Moist von Lipwig book focused on reforming Ankh-Morpork's taxes, so perhaps this was to have been funded through taxation rather than borrowing. 'Book: Raising Taxes', *L-Space Wiki*, n. dat. https://wiki.lspace.org/Book:Raising_Taxes (Last accessed 7 February 2024).
64. The actual Chair is a little dog called Mr Fusspot.
65. Pratchett, *Making Money*, p. 127.
66. Ibid., p. 147.
67. Pratchett, *Making Money*, p. 145.
68. Ibid., p. 146.
69. Georg Friedrich Knapp, *The State Theory of Money* [1905/1923] (London: Macmillan & Company, 1924), p. 27.
70. Cf. Pratchett, *Making Money*, pp. 50, 45–6, 145.
71. Cf. Geoffrey Ingham, *The Nature of Money* (Cambridge: Polity Press, 2004), pp. 15–36.
72. Ibid., p. 126.
73. Pratchett, *Guards! Guards!*, p. 220.
74. Also worth mentioning is Captain Carrot Ironfoundersson; it is an open secret that Carrot is true heir to the throne of Ankh-Morpork. However, Carrot's role in *Making Money* is relatively minor.
75. These golems, who ambiguously allegorise a blend of automation, slave labour, and the surplus value of waged labour, complicate and perhaps subvert the novel's chartalism when Moist declares them to be backing the city's currency. Cf. Pratchett, *Making Money*, pp. 401, 463.
76. He uses an intriguing financial metaphor to describe this difference: '[i]t would have worked for Vetinari, he knew it. It would have ... raised Cosmo's stock in the room' (ibid., p. 160). Cosmo's name probably alludes to the Florentine banker Cosimo de' Medici, with extra lavishness. For a bit more on Cosmo, see my essay 'Estranged Entrepreneurs and the Meaning of Money in Cory Doctorow's *Down and Out in the Magic Kingdom*', *Foundation*, 137 (2020), pp. 62–80.
77. Pratchett, *Making Money*, p. 168.
78. Cf. e.g. Giorgio Agamben, *State of Exception* (Chicago: University of Chicago Press, 2005); and Achille Mbembe, *Necropolitics* (Durham, NC: Duke University Press, 2019).
79. Ernst Bloch, 'On the Present in Literature' in *The Utopian Function of Art and Literature: Selected Essays*, trans. Jack Zipes and Frank Mecklenburg (Cambridge, MA: The MIT Press, 1988), pp. 207–23 (p. 214).

80. Pratchett, *Making Money*, p. 430.
81. Ibid.
82. See for example Susan Strange, *Mad Money: When Markets Outgrow Governments* (Manchester: Manchester University Press, 1998).
83. For more on the performativity of financial and economic models, see for example Donald MacKenzie, *An Engine, Not a Camera: How Financial Models Shape Markets* (Cambridge, MA: MIT Press, 2006).
84. Dorota Guttfeld, 'Us and Them in Terry Pratchett's Pre- and Post-9/11 Discworld Novels' in *Ideological Battles: Constructions of Us and Them Before and After 9/11*, ed. Joanna Witkowska and Uwe Zagratzki (Newcastle-upon-Tyne: Cambridge Scholars, 2014), pp. 99–122 (p. 103).
85. Pratchett, *Guards! Guards!*, p. 80.
86. Pratchett, *Making Money*, p. 196.
87. Moist does make the intriguingly wild suggestion of talking money, which has the spirit of a variety of real-world experiments with alternative and complementary currencies. We don't see it come to fruition in the book. See Pratchett, *Making Money*, p. 464.
88. Pratchett, *Men at Arms*, p. 29.
89. Ibid., p. 146.
90. Ibid.
91. Hobbes, *Leviathan*, p. 152. Cf. Alan Haworth, *Anti-Libertarianism: Markets, Philosophy, and Myth* [1994] (London: Routledge, 2006), p. 17.
92. Eric Shaw, 'New Labour's Faustian Pact?' *British Politics*, 7 (2012), pp. 224–49.
93. William Paterson, *A Brief Account of the Intended Bank of England* [1694] (Ann Arbor, MI: Text Creation Partnership, 2011), p. 14. https://quod.lib.umich.edu/e/eebo/A56581.0001.001/1:1 (Last accessed 7 February 2024).
94. Ingham, *The Nature of Money*, p. 128.
95. Technically 51 per cent of the bank is owned by the little doggie Mr Fusspot, on whose death it will revert to the Lavish family. Mr Fusspot does end up trotting after Vetinari with promises of cake, and we can imagine that the creature may turn out every bit as resilient as Vetinari himself. The equivocation is characteristic: the bank is not quite nationalised, but it is not quite *not*.
96. Pratchett, *Making Money*, p. 195.
97. The Roundworld is a parodic name for the reader's own reality, appearing in a variety of Discworld books. See e.g. Terry Pratchett, Ian Stewart, and Jack Cohen, *The Science of Discworld* (London: Penguin, 1999).
98. Bank of England, 'Index to Original Subscribers to Bank Stock 1694', n. dat. www.bankofengland.co.uk/archive/index-to-original-subscribers-to-bank-stock-1694 (Last accessed 27 February 2024).
99. Jacques Derrida, *Rogues: Two Essays on Reason* (Stanford, CA: Stanford University Press, 2002).

100. For a helpful discussion of Bloch's writings on concrete and abstract utopia, see Ruth Levitas, 'Educated Hope: Ernst Bloch on Abstract and Concrete Utopia' in *Not Yet: Reconsidering Ernst Bloch*, ed. Jamie Owen Daniel and Tom Moylan (London: Verso, 1997), pp. 65–79.
101. Ernst Bloch, trans. Neville Plaice, Stephen Plaice, and Paul Knight, *The Principle of Hope, Vol. 3* [1959] (Cambridge, MA.: The MIT Press, 1986), p. 1042.

CHAPTER 13

Some Dialectics of Utopia in China Miéville's Bas-Lag Trilogy

Carl Freedman

China Miéville's three novels set in the imaginary world of Bas-Lag – *Perdido Street Station* (2000), *The Scar* (2002), and *Iron Council* (2004) – are widely recognised as providing an extraordinarily detailed and imaginatively solid instance of world-building. Indeed, Bas-Lag is arguably the most plausible and three-dimensional invented world in modern fantastic literature.[1] What is less often discussed is that Bas-Lag functions as (inter alia) the site of much complex dialectical play of positive and negative utopian elements. Never content with the comparatively simple positive or negative visions of more straightforwardly utopian and dystopian novels such as Edward Bellamy's *Looking Backward* (1888) or George Orwell's *Nineteen Eighty-Four* (1949), Miéville's trilogy presents a range of potential social formations more complex and dialectical. *Perdido Street Station* is set in the city-state of New Crobuzon, whose semi-Victorian and semi-fascist capitalist oppressiveness displays many of the worst possibilities that social organisation can offer. Yet, within this largely negative terrain, moments of utopian positivity can nonetheless flourish – perhaps most memorably in the love affair between the scientist protagonist and his artist partner. *The Scar* is set mostly in the floating city-state of Armada, a fundamentally positive utopian space partly modelled on the social organisation of the real-world pirate ships of the eighteenth-century Atlantic. Armada is, however, not only contrasted with the negations of freedom and equality for which New Crobuzon stands, but it is also shown to be (to employ Ursula Le Guin's phrase) an *ambiguous* utopia, which contains counter-utopian (but also counter-counter-utopian) tendencies within it. *Iron Council* displays, in considerable detail, a positive space of utopian communism in the 'perpetual train' named in the novel's title. Far more than *The Scar*, it focuses on the *construction* of revolutionary utopianism, and does not overlook the inevitable ambiguities and false starts along the way. The Iron Council's potential for success is also contrasted with the eventually defeated utopian communist space of the Collective

13 Dialectics of Utopia in China Miéville's Bas-Lag Trilogy

(itself largely modelled after the Paris Commune). It is certain aspects of the dialectic of these (and other) positive and negative utopian tendencies that I will trace in the following pages.

New Crubuzon is a negative utopian space[2] in that it is an imaginary lifeworld that the text presents as significantly worse than the society in which the text was produced and which forms the mundane status quo for at least the first generation of the text's readers. Drawing partly on the grossly undemocratic parliamentary capitalism of Victorian Britain and partly on the even more undemocratic fascist capitalism of Europe during the 1930s, the depiction of New Crobuzon, in which nearly all the action of the novel is set, presents a society in which dominant policies work almost exclusively to preserve the interests of the capitalist class. Those who set themselves against this order with sufficient resolution live highly precarious lives that may at any point end in imprisonment, torture, and death. Especially notable in this regard is the practice of the 'Remaking' of prisoners (whether common or political) that takes place in the 'punishment factories' of New Crobuzon. Remaking is a form of torture and mutilation that involves the surgical refashioning of the body by various sorts of amputations, alterations, and additions of organic and mechanical parts. Often Remaking amounts to a grotesquely cruel practical joke of the sort familiar in Dante's Hell, as when one prisoner who has refused to 'talk', that is, to inform on his associates, is deprived of his mouth, the area between his chin and his nose being refashioned into a smooth unbroken expanse of skin. It is a bit of inspired sadism that Orwell might have been glad to include as a practice of (or a threat by) the torturers in the Ministry of Love in *Nineteen Eighty-Four*.

Yet New Crobuzon is very different from Orwell's Oceania, or from such of its direct successors as the Republic of Gilead in Margaret Atwood's *The Handmaid's Tale* (1985). Orwell and Atwood both offer highly satiric projections of tendencies that the authors believed they saw in the actual world around them: projections that are extended to a *ne plus ultra* so as to produce negative utopian lifeworlds in which ordinary human life is rendered virtually intolerable. The Orwellian and Atwoodian texts are generally and rightly understood as *warnings* against totalitarian tendencies, not as plausible representations of truly viable societies (which Oceania and Gilead plainly are not). By contrast, New Crobuzon – though formally cut off completely from the actual world as Oceania and Gilead, technically, are not – seems all too viable. The unmatched three-dimensionality of Miéville's invented city-state encompasses an extraordinary range of closely delineated common activities – politics, science, art, sexuality, religion, law and law enforcement, petty and organised crime, energy production, education, commerce, manufacturing, housing, communication, transportation, and much more – and the overall effect is not of a satiric projection in the Orwellian or Atwoodian way but of a 'realistic' society in which the sheer complexity and heterogeneity of social life means that ordinary everyday experience cannot be completely defined or exhausted by the overarching political tyranny.[3] Those lacking any special concern with politics – like, for most of his life thus far, the scientist Isaac Dan der Grimnebulin, the novel's protagonist – can, indeed, sometimes even pursue their own interests for a long time without thinking much about the dictator Mayor Bentham Rudgutter, his ruling Fat Sun party, or the armed Militia that violently enforces socio-economic order. New Crobuzon is (unlike Oceania or Gilead) so *thickly* and 'realistically' delineated that its social system inevitably contains a significant amount of 'air' or elbow-room: and, even in specifically political terms, some radical opposition and even labour strikes are possible.[4]

On the allegorical level, however, *Perdido Street Station* does contain an important negative utopian element that amounts to a vision of absolute and 'airless' capitalist totalitarianism: those 'capitalist monsters', the slake-moths. They are huge flying creatures that terrorise the population of New Crobuzon; the fight against them constitutes the central narrative strand of the novel.[5] The slake-moths are physically powerful and thus physically dangerous; but the most frightening danger they pose is psychic. Mind is the nourishment they crave, and their immense slavering tongues are capable of reaching into individuals' brains in order to drain the latter dry of 'the fine wine of sapience and sentience itself, the subconscious':[6] thus leaving their victims in a quasi-lobotomised condition. The slake-moths represent complete domination and the utter levelling of all distinctness among various individuals. All consciousness (and 'subconsciousness') is food for the slake-moths, and individuals who have had their minds stolen by the giant monsters become husks of their former selves, essentially interchangeable with one another. Accordingly, in their – literal – alienation of sentience, the slake-moths perform what Marx famously describes as the vampiric function of capital, sucking the creative powers and ultimately the life out of the wage-earning proletariat.[7] The ruthless transformation by capital of labour into labour-power – that is, the transformation of the free productive capacities of the worker into a mere commodity to be bought and sold for wages – is not just formal, but, more usually, deeply substantive as well: as when, for instance, a skilled artisanal craftsman who organises and implements an entire creative process is transformed into an industrial proletarian who 'mindlessly' repeats, hour after hour and day after day, a single tiny chore within the operations of production (like pulling a lever). The tendency of the capitalist wage-relation is toward total (and totalitarian) exploitation by a monstrously inhuman rapaciousness that is allegorically figured, in *Perdido Street Station*, by the slake-moths.

Furthermore, that the slake-moths are thoroughly capitalist monsters is indicated on the narrative as well as on the allegorical level. The point is made clear when we learn that the slake-moths were originally imported into New Crobuzon by Rudgutter's bureaucrats, who were intrigued by the possibilities that the creatures' strange psychic powers might hold for mental control of the city's population in the interests of the capitalist ruling class. It is also made clear when we learn that the crime boss Motley and his mafiosi are interested in the creatures because their excrement can be processed into an extremely lucrative (and addictive) drug to be sold on the illegal (and, in the capitalist sense, 'free') market. Rudgutter and Motley think that they may have their uses for the slake-moths, until it becomes clear to them that the creatures are so radically destabilising as to threaten even their own enterprises. In this way, the monsters enact the logic of the capitalist mode of production, whose ever-expansionist drive to remake the world in its own image cannot ultimately be managed or contained from within the limits of the capitalist system, which is of course where Rudgutter and Motley operate. The slake-moths enact the principle that capitalism's 'gale of creative destruction' (Joseph Schumpeter's term) is in the end overwhelmingly more destructive than creative *even from the capitalist point of view.*

The organised forces of Rudgutter and Motley eventually attempt to defeat the slake-moths but fail to do so: appropriately enough, since, as we have seen, Rudgutter, Motley, and the slake-moths are fundamentally all on the same (capitalist) side. The monsters *are* defeated, however: by a small, irregular, and somewhat implicitly but essentially anti-capitalist band led by Isaac. This victory may be taken to qualify the negative utopianism of *Perdido Street Station*, but does not really constitute a moment of positive utopianism: for it brings about no liberating revolutionary rupture, but only the restoration of a pre-slake-moth (and highly oppressive) status quo ante, with the flying monsters gone but Rudgutter, Motley, and their associates still where they were (and with Isaac and his allies now harried fugitives from the capitalist state). For true positive utopianism we must look elsewhere in the novel.

Probably the most memorably positive moment is found in the description of sexual love between Isaac and his female lover, the artist Lin. Sexuality (and not only heterosexuality) always involves the negotiation of difference; but in this case difference is accentuated by the fact that Isaac and Lin are not only of opposite sexes but of different species. Humans are only one of the intelligent species in New Crobuzon and Bas-Lag, and Lin is a khepri: a species that appears to bear much the same sort of evolutionary relationship to insects that humans do to subhuman primates. Miéville works within, and significantly develops, a tradition of erotic representation perhaps founded – and certainly most centrally instanced – by D. H. Lawrence. For Lawrence, heterosexual coupling not only provides a privileged figure for the 'interinanimation' (John Donne's convenient term, coined in an explicitly erotic context) of two persons – irreducibly separate yet connected with maximum intimacy – but can also suggest in more general terms a dynamic utopian equilibrium of difference and identity. In *Women in Love* (1921), this equilibrium is figured on one level by the sexual love between Rupert Birkin and Ursula Brangwen, on another by Birkin's famous metaphor that represents the two lovers as two stars circling one another, distinct and separate yet always bound together. Similarly, but with much more detailed representation of the sexual act itself, the love between Oliver Mellors and Constance Chatterley in *Lady Chatterley's Lover* (1928) describes a balanced state of erotic fulfillment that the text terms 'the peace that comes of fucking'.[8] Peace here means very much the same thing that the identical term means in perhaps the most important single moment of utopian positivity in the philosophical writings of Theodor Adorno: his definition of peace as 'distinctness without domination, with the distinct participating in each other'.[9]

To evoke a Laurentian and Adornian peace – a true distinctness with interinanimation and without domination – in the lovemaking of Isaac and Lin, is extremely difficult: because Lin's quasi-insectoid alienness must somehow be synthesised with what the reader can recognise – and *feel* – as actual sexual attraction and excitement. In order to demonstrate Miéville's success here, it is useful to quote at some length:

> She pulled his hand towards [her wings] gently, invited him to stroke the fragile things, totally vulnerable, an expression of trust and love unparalleled for the khepri.
> The air between them charged. Isaac's cock stiffened.
> He traced the branching veins in her gently vibrating wings with his fingers, watched the light that passed through them refract into mother-of-pearl shadows.
> He rucked up her skirt with his other hand, slid his fingers up her thigh. Her legs opened around his hand and closed, trapped it. He whispered at her, filthy and loving invitations.

> The sun shifted above them, sending shadows of the window-pane and clouds moving uneasily through the room. The lovers did not notice the day move. (p. 14)

Isaac is a male human (a dark-skinned one, as it happens, something that the text mentions in passing and never stresses), Lin a female khepri whose head, though human-sized, resembles an earthly insect's head more than anything mammalian: a physical conjunction that the reader has never actually encountered and, it seems safe to guess, has never even imagined in a specifically sexual context. Yet the quoted passage not only informs us that Isaac and Lin are having sexual relations but produces a concrete sense of what human-khepri sexual excitement and fulfillment might feel like. The erotic value of the writing inheres partly in physical details likely to be familiar to the reader: 'Isaac's cock stiffened', and 'He rucked up her skirt with his other hand, slid his fingers up her thigh'. Such particulars that overlap with real-world human sexual experience are synthesised with the apparently quite alien description of the role that Lin's wings play in the lovemaking. Though the reader presumably has no sexual acquaintance with insectoid wings, Isaac's caressing of these delicate, fragile structures is made to seem authentically sexual: in large part because shared physical vulnerability *is* a component of actual human sex, so that the role that the wings play for Isaac and Lin is not, in the end, completely alien after all. The final sentence just quoted – 'The lovers did not notice the day move' – powerfully recalls, without exactly echoing, the whole tradition of the erotic aubade exemplified in the love poetry of Petrarch, Shakespeare, and Donne. The collective and ongoing equivalent of this shared sexual peace would be a very positively utopian society indeed.

But no such society is in view in *Perdido Street Station*. To find an invented social formation that even approaches something of the sort, we must turn to the novel's sequel, *The Scar*. This novel focuses not on New Crobuzon (though the powerful and repressive capitalist city-state remains an important offstage presence) but on the floating city of Armada, a pirate society composed of hundreds of ships joined together. As New Crobuzon draws on both Victorian and fascist capitalism, Armada draws on the illegal mercantilism of actual pirate societies in the eighteenth-century Atlantic: particularly as these societies have been reconstructed in the 'revisionist' pirate scholarship of the past several decades, a body of work that appears to have strongly influenced the writing of *The Scar*.[10]

It is worthwhile to recall in a little detail some of the salient features of 'golden age' piracy that, despite the new pirate scholarship, remain too little known. Perhaps the central point here is that the pirates are best understood neither as bloodthirsty villains nor as swashbuckling romantics but as *workers*. The labour of the eighteenth-century merchant seamen was essential to the Atlantic trade that generated gigantic profits in such commodities as sugar, tobacco, furs, gold, and silver (not to mention slaves). Yet to say that the common sailors were meagrely recompensed for their toil is a gross understatement. They worked punishingly long hours for extremely poor wages under miserable conditions; and they were subjected to discipline that generally ranged from harsh to lethal. It is unsurprising that many sailors deserted their posts in order to join the pirate ships in the hope of a freer, more pleasant, more interesting, and more rewarding life, even though one that was unlikely to last very long.

What is perhaps more surprising is the extent to which the pirates self-consciously made their ships into little oppositional societies whose norms and procedures constituted a fairly detailed utopian critique of the savagely hierarchical, authoritarian world that the pirates had left behind – and against which they had declared a war that was both armed and ideological. Pirate captains were democratically elected by their crews; and a pirate captain's authority was strictly limited (except during actual battle) by the collective will of those under his command. Life aboard the pirate ships was relaxed enough to allow for frequent bouts of feasting, drinking, and general merry-making. When discipline did need to be enforced, it was accomplished more through a spirit of collectivist solidarity than through degrading punishments. Profits went not to distant merchants who had done nothing to earn them, but were divided fairly among the pirates themselves. Though the division was not mathematically quite equal – the senior officers and those who did certain especially difficult or specialised jobs got a larger share – the ratio of the highest pay to the lowest was seldom greater than two to one (in sharp contrast to normal practices in contemporary naval and merchant-marine ships). Some pirate ships even put aside a portion of their booty in a fund to care for older and disabled colleagues – surely one of the earliest forms of social security in world history.

Amazingly for the times, the proto-socialist egalitarianism of the pirate ships seems even to have crossed all national and racial barriers. African, African Caribbean, and African American pirates who could demonstrate the requisite knowledge and prowess were normally accepted on equal terms with the Caucasian majority: perhaps the only social context in the eighteenth-century Atlantic where such racial equality existed. In some cases even female pirates were welcomed aboard, though women were

13 Dialectics of Utopia in China Miéville's Bas-Lag Trilogy

otherwise strictly excluded from all the seafaring trades.[11] Pirates were not, of course, pacific flower-children *avant la lettre*. Violence was after all integral to their professional practice of armed plunder. Still, when one considers the enormous amount of murderous violence perpetrated by the eighteenth-century bourgeois state – which, for instance, typically treated petty theft as a hanging offence – and the even greater contemporary violence integral to the process of capital accumulation, the violence of the pirates looks almost negligible by comparison. It certainly does little to qualify the notion that the pirates constructed perhaps the most humane forms of social organisation that existed in their time.

Armada, in *The Scar*, is a positive utopia that incorporates most of the attractive qualities of real-world eighteenth-century Atlantic piracy. Its comparative egalitarianism is based in an economy that is mercantilist rather than completely capitalist. Armada, indeed, practices mercantilism in an especially pure form, since – despite a modest amount of economic production that takes place within the floating city – the vast majority of Armadan wealth derives from mere exchange. Armed plunder, after all, is a form of exchange, involving the transfer of exchange-value from one owner to another; it is not actual value-creation. The economic egalitarianism of the pirate utopia is thus in large part a function of the fact that little surplus-value is created or extracted among the Armadans. Armada, though certainly involved with capital through its mercantilist transfers of value, is not itself fully capitalist, and very little economic exploitation takes place within the floating city.[12] All inhabitants work at a useful job in Armada, and all receive decent but not extravagant compensation for their labour. There are no extremes of wealth and poverty such as the reader of *Perdido Street Station* knows to be all too common in New Crobuzon (and in the world in which Miéville's novels were composed).

The relative material equality of Armada is matched by its atmosphere of relative freedom. Admittedly, an important element of coercion is (in contrast to the almost entirely voluntary composition of the actual eighteenth-century Atlantic pirate crews) integral to the city's make-up. Most Armadans arrive at the floating city when the ships on which they happened to be travelling are seized by the pirates (and the ships themselves are generally made part of the Armadan physical infrastructure). Those thus forcibly brought to Armada are (with very rare exceptions) not allowed to leave; for the Armadans reasonably fear the consequences if a major power like New Crobuzon were to learn too much about the location and workings of the floating city. Most of those thus forcibly recruited to the pirate utopia welcome (often enthusiastically) the opportunity to live in Armada; but the novel, interestingly, is told from the viewpoint of its homesick New Crobuzoner protagonist Bellis, who is never completely happy with Armada (she was on a ship because she was forced to flee New Crobuzon shortly after the defeat of the slake-moths, when the Militia was arresting those in any way associated with her ex-lover Isaac). Still, she cannot deny the justice of the point made by an Armadan acquaintance, who alludes to the enormous oppressiveness and violence of the 'legitimate' powers of Bas-Lag:

> You know what would happen if they got home and let out the wrong sort of information, and your lot [the New Crobuzon authorities] got hold of Armada? Just ask any of the Remade who made it out of the New Crobuzon slave ships, see how loyal they feel about the Crobuzoner navy. Ask some of those who've been to Nova Esperium [a colony of New Crobuzon] and seen what happened to the natives.... You think *we're* pirates, Bellis?[13]

Especially, moreover, for those accustomed to life under the terroristic capitalist regime of the New Crobuzon Militia, the way that liberty seems the default value of everyday Armadan life is impressive: 'In New Crobuzon, what was not regulated was illicit. In Armada, things were different. It was, after all, a pirate city. What did not directly threaten the city did not concern its authorities.'[14] Few real-world social orders have ever enjoyed more actual liberty.

The most spectacularly positive aspect of Armada – which directly recalls the racial egalitarianism of real-world piracy – is the strict practice of equality between humans and xenians (the generic term for non-human intelligent species): and above all the treatment of the Remade. In New Crobuzon, as *Perdido Street Station* makes clear, there is a quasi-racial hierarchy whereby humans are dominant and the various xenians (like the khepri) lead more-or-less ghettoised lives. The Remade are the lowest of the low: not only because they have usually been convicted of some (political or ordinary) crime, not only because most of them spend their lives doing the most gruelling and degrading sort of slave labour, but also because non-Remade are successfully indoctrinated to regard the Remade with intense *physical* disgust. In this context, the words are utterly astounding with which the Lover – a woman who occupies one of the most powerful political positions in Armada – welcomes the crew and passengers of the ship on which Bellis was travelling: '"Human, cactacae, hotchi, cray...*Remade*", the woman had said. "In Armada you are all sailors and citizens. In Armada you are not distinguished. Here you are free. And equal."''¹⁵ Sex between Remade and non-Remade individuals, which in New Crobuzon is the most unspeakable obscenity, can in Armada be the expression of free, reciprocal love; and the text at one point¹⁶ represents it with something of the same tender Laurentian and Adornian peace with which the inter-species lovemaking of Isaac and Lin is so memorably described in *Perdido Street Station.*

Yet Armada is – in the now canonical phrase that Ursula Le Guin coined to describe her great utopian novel *The Dispossessed* (1974) – an *ambiguous* utopia. Despite the high degree of freedom and equality that prevails in the floating city, Armada, as it gradually becomes clear, is rather less impressive in terms of democracy. The most negative element in Armadan society is without doubt the creeping despotism of the Lovers: the man and woman, never identified by actual name, who rule the Garwater section of Armada and (since Garwater is the most prosperous and powerful of the varied components of the city) to some degree the *de facto* commanders of Armada as a whole. Towards the end of the novel, it becomes clear that the Lovers are leading Armada towards the Scar, a kind of rupture in the fabric of reality itself: and that the Lovers are doing so for reasons that they refuse to make clear, in spite of mortal dangers that they have carefully concealed, and against what have long been the clear wishes of at least a significant minority of Armada's citizens. Eventually it transpires that what the Lovers hope to gain from the Scar are, apparently, powers that will enable them to transform Armada into an aggressive imperialist power like New Crobuzon: a development that would surely put paid to the floating city's egalitarian mercantilism and most of its other positive utopian characteristics. Eventually the minority opposed to the Lovers becomes an overwhelming majority, and a rebellion against their growing dictatorship takes form.

The rebellion is led by one Tanner Sack, a Remade who came to Armada on the same captured ship on which Bellis arrived. Unlike Bellis, Tanner falls in love with his new home almost at once, and soon becomes the most fervent and devoted of Armadan patriots. Tanner and those who follow his lead take their stand against the Lovers' betrayal of Armada's own utopian values; and the text makes clear that only someone of Tanner's unimpeachable loyalty to Armada could credibly lead the Armadan masses against Armada's despotic duo. '*We* say what happens now', Tanner tells the Lovers. 'We're taking control. We're turning around; we're heading home. Your orders to proceed...are *in-fucking-validated*. You can't jail or kill us all.'¹⁷

Unlike an earlier (and unsuccessful) *coup* against the Lovers by Armada's vampires, this is a genuinely democratic insurrection; and it attains a significant measure of success, halting and cancelling the city's journey towards the Scar. If Armada represents a revolution in values and social organisation within the overall context of Bas-Lag, Tanner Sack stands for a 'revolution in the revolution' (Régis Debray's phrase) that opposes the ossification of the Lovers' increasingly arbitrary rule from a stance more radically and more authentically Armadan. If the Lovers' undemocratic rule and imperialist ambitions are a counter- or negative utopian element within the positive utopia of Armada, Tanner and his comrades introduce a counter-counter-utopian tendency. Such is the necessarily dialectical and progressive nature of the utopian spirit in all its genuine manifestations. The rebellion led by Tanner nicely illustrates Oscar Wilde's famous statement on utopia in his great essay, 'The Soul of Man Under Socialism' (1891), a statement that anticipates much of the major utopian thought of the twentieth century, from Ernst Bloch to Fredric Jameson — and a statement that might deserve to be described as definitive were it not for the fact that the impossibility of true definitiveness is precisely the point: 'A map of the world that does not include Utopia is not worth even glancing at, for it leaves out the one country at which Humanity is always landing. And when Humanity lands there, it looks out, and, seeing a better country, sets sail. Progress is the realisation of Utopias.'[18] Like all true utopias, Armada is a work in progress.

The same is true of the two revolutionary societies — the Collective and the Iron Council — featured in the final novel of the Bas-Lag trilogy, *Iron Council*. In both cases, the complexity of Bas-Lag and the 'thick' descriptiveness with which it is realised allow Miéville to convey with particular force and clarity the material *overdetermination* (in the Freudian meaning as recomplicated by Louis Althusser)[19] that is crucial to a socialist revolution and the construction of a utopian communist society. Probably more than any other sort of historical event, socialist revolution is based on overdetermination in the Freudian-Althusserian sense: that is, on the conjuncture of a multiplicity of material determinations, all of them relatively autonomous of one another and none of them reducible to any of the others.

The precise overdeterminations of utopia constitute one of the major concerns of the novel. The Collective, which temporarily seizes power in New Crobuzon in somewhat the same way that the Paris Commune did in the real world of 1871, is partly the work of the Caucus, a broad coalition of socialist and quasi-Marxist parties and of underground newspapers (the best known and most influential of which is the *Runagate Rampant*, whose heroic martyred editor, Benjamin Flex – an important secondary character in *Perdido Street Station* – appears, during the time present of *Iron Council*, to have a stature for the Caucus somewhat similar to that of Karl Marx for many real-world revolutionaries of the late nineteenth and early twentieth centuries). Within the Collective, the Caucus competes with the more sensational and quasi-Narodnik terrorism of the followers of the mysterious Toro, who succeed in assassinating the Mayor of New Crobuzon. Whether this political killing makes a genuine revolutionary contribution is dubious. Reflecting the traditional Marxist hostility to violent adventurism, the novel seems to endorse the viewpoint of Ori (a former Caucus militant who leaves to join, temporarily, the anarchic terrorism of the Toroans) when, after the Collective comes into being, he finds 'in himself a drab certainty that the killing of the Mayor had done nothing at all'[20] towards the goal of revolution. Whatever the ultimate political significance of the Toroans, however, there is no doubt that the building of the Collective is due in large part not only to the Caucus but also to a great many citizens affiliated neither with the Caucus nor the Toroans, whose rage has been building over decades marked not only by grinding poverty but also by the (literally) fantastically cruel repression with which the Mayor's government has attempted to crush all stirrings of dissidence. In a further instance of overdetermination, it nonetheless seems unlikely that this rage would have risen to the level of effective political action without the additional toll taken on New Crobuzon's stability by the exhausting foreign war that New Crobuzon has been fighting with the faraway Tesh – and by the consequently increasing disaffection of the city's soldiers. There is doubtless an allusion here to the exhaustion of the Czarist state by World War I and the important role played by the Russian soldiers who, in Lenin's famous phrase, 'voted with their feet' to desert the Czarist Army and (in many cases) to join the October Revolution.

The Collective brings to birth a genuine dual-power situation in New Crobuzon, enabling a limited but authentically utopian zone of popular democracy in (parts of) the city; and the characteristic military heroism of proletarian revolution flourishes. Ultimately, though, the Collective meets much the same fate as its chief real-world model, the Paris Commune (though other historical precedents could also be cited, including such defeated attempts at revolutionary socialist democracy as the Munich Soviet Republic of 1919 and revolutionary Barcelona in 1936).[21] As it turns out, support for the Collective is neither widespread nor well organised enough to resist the massive physical power of the apparatuses of state repression – most importantly the New Crobuzon Militia, which gradually but decisively regains control of the city in atrociously bloody fighting. The golem-maker Judah Low, who is probably the most far-seeing theorist of revolution within the text (and the single most important character in the novel, though not exactly its protagonist), presciently warns that the time present of the novel is the 'wrong time' for revolution.[22]

The text's attitude towards the heartbreakingly brief triumph of the Collective recalls the attitude that Marx displays in his writings on the Paris Commune itself. On the one hand, there is an unbounded admiration for the courage and sacrifice of the revolutionaries, just as Marx, in *The Civil War in France* (1871), describes the Commune as 'the glorious harbinger of a new society' and the murdered Communards as 'enshrined in the great heart of the working class'.[23] On the other hand, such esteem is combined with a grim calculation that the objective balance of forces does not yet permit the overthrow of the repressive state followed by a popular seizure of the means of economic production. The Militia smashes the Collective but has to wreck New Crobuzon itself in order to do it. The capitalist boast – 'Order reigns in New Crobuzon!'[24] – thus rings rather hollow, especially since the slogan echoes (unwittingly, of course, as far as the New Crobuzon authorities are concerned) its real-life source in Rosa Luxemburg's final political broadside, in which the great Polish-German revolutionary jeers at the notion that any victory won by the bourgeoisie through mass slaughter can possibly be secure or lasting.[25] *Runagate Rampant* continues to publish, and revolutionary hope is not completely extinguished.

The utopian principle of hope – *das Prinzip Hoffnung* in the Blochian phrase, and best translated, I think, as 'the hope principle', on the analogy (fully intended by Bloch) with the Freudian pleasure and reality principles – endures perhaps more vibrantly, and certainly more complexly, in the Iron Council. As with the Collective, the novel stresses the overdeterminations by which the Council is constructed. The Council has its origins in a great railway project that traverses a vast continental land mass of Bas-Lag. A full generation prior to the organisation of the Collective's insurrection in New Crobuzon, the workers employed on the line have seized control of the train and maintained it ever since as a perpetually moving utopian space of proletarian democracy. The revolutionary seizure of the train is in part a straightforward labour struggle; and an essential contribution to the formation of the Iron Council is (ultimately) made by the free male workers employed by the TRT (Transcontinental Railroad Trust). But this group of workers does not actually take the lead in the uprising that leads to the Iron Council, and even displays, at first, some conservative tendencies in comparison to two other distinct elements in the ultimate revolutionary coalition. One is the contingent of female sex workers, who refuse to extend credit to their male customers and strike on the simple slogan, *No pay no lay*. At first the men respond with a myopic hostility fuelled by the sexual frustration that has, of course, provided a market for the striking women's services in the first place. Not without difficulty, the women do, however, succeed in convincing the men (whose own wages are being withheld by the TRT) that class solidarity between them is more important than the gender differences; and the women's slogan assumes a more general significance, as the strike widens to include the male workers and *lay*, in addition to its sexual meaning, comes also to signify the laying of railroad track.

But there is also a third distinct group in the uprising, and one that, unlike the free male labourers, supports and joins the women's strike without delay or hesitation: namely, the slave-labour force of Remade, both male and female. Typically looked upon with intense disgust by those who have not suffered the same fate, the Remade serve, in part, to figure the situation of any group regarded as inferior and degraded in specifically *racial* ways; and, as ever, sexual taboos play a large role in enforcing such bigotry. A crucial point in the formation of the Iron Council is reached when Ann-Hari, the principal leader of the female strikers, grips a leading Remade militant and (to the spontaneous horror of many non-Remade men) kisses him squarely on the mouth. Sexual contact between Remade and non-Remade, an obscenity in New Crobuzon, is accepted as a matter of course in racially egalitarian Armada; but here, in *Iron Council*, we see how such acceptance is forged as part of the revolutionary process. There is not necessarily any 'natural' affinity among the sex workers, the Remade, and the free male labourers. But the novel vividly illustrates how such revolutionary coalitions are formed in concrete political practice.

For a full generation, then, the perpetual train of the Iron Council maintains itself as a fairly stable (though never static) zone of utopian positivity. Its citizens successfully fight back (sometimes with the help of Judah's extraordinary golems) against attempts to crush their republic by the violent capitalist authorities of New Crobuzon; and a new generation is raised on the train who have never known anything but classlessness, freedom, and equality. When the Collective is formed, however, the Iron Council – which the Collective regards as a faraway model and inspiration for their own communist struggle – is faced with a difficult decision: Should they travel to New Crobuzon in order to place their resources and experience at the service of the Collective's struggle? The majority decide to do so, but Judah remains opposed. The Collective, he believes, is so weak that any attempt to join its revolutionary project is bound to fail: so that the Iron Council, if it entered New Crobuzon, would be committing collective suicide. Unable to convince his fellow Iron Councillors on this point, Judah takes matters into his own hands and violates democratic decision-making. In a supreme and unprecedented golemetric feat, he constructs a golem out of time itself, and uses it to suspend the perpetual train in a kind of temporal limbo. At a stroke, the Iron Council's progress towards New Crobuzon is halted, and it is also rendered invulnerable to any retaliatory action by the Militia. Most of the Iron Councillors are put into what seems to be some sort of suspended animation, there to remain until an entirely uncertain future: 'perhaps till things are ready [i.e., for revolution]', as Judah himself puts it.[26]

The text's attitude towards Judah's *coup* is complex. His unilateral action is plainly undemocratic and thus amounts, in one way, to a counter- or negative utopian action within the positivity of the Iron Council: as the dictatorial tendency of the Lovers does within Armada. Ann-Hari – perhaps Judah's only true peer among the Iron Council's revolutionary leaders as well as, at various times, his lover – is persuasive when she points out that Judah could not possibly *know*, with absolute certainty, that the revolutionary cause of the Collective was hopeless in the near term. Even more importantly, Ann-Hari maintains that Judah simply had no right to take the decision away from a collective democratic process and to arrogate it to himself alone: 'You don't get to choose. You don't decide when is the right time, when it fits your story. *This was the time we were here.*'[27] It seems that Judah (in sharp contrast to the Lovers) does not really disagree. For when Ann-Hari decides – with deep sadness but with full determination – that Judah's betrayal of democracy deserves the punishment of death and fires her gun at him, Judah makes no attempt to evade the bullet: even though his golemetric skills would have easily enabled him to do so.

Yet the text does, after all, seem to consider that Judah's estimation of the balance of political forces in New Crobuzon is probably correct. In that case, Judah's golemetric suspension of the Iron Council in an invulnerable state outside of time – however undemocratic – might have been the most effective way of preserving the utopian hope contained in the perpetual train. 'Marxist reality means: reality plus the future within it', wrote Ernst Bloch two years after his own nation had been overwhelmed by Nazism.[28] The principal image with which *Iron Council* leaves us, that of the suspended perpetual train – unable to effect immediate practical change but still charged with revolutionary energy that is, one hopes, to be discharged another day – is a powerful figure of a Blochian future that transcends the horrors and limitations of the present. The novel's final words certainly seem to stress that hope has indeed been kept alive:

> Years might pass and we will tell the story of the Iron Council and how it was made, how it made itself and went, and how it came back, and is coming, is still coming. Women and men cut a line across the dirtland and dragged history out and back across the world. They are still with shouts setting their mouths and we usher them in. They are coming out of the trenches of rock toward the brick shadows. They are always coming.²⁹

They are always coming: The final sentence might well stand as a motto of the utopian spirit itself.

Notes

1. I have made this argument in Carl Freedman, *Art and Idea in the Novels of China Miéville* (Canterbury: Gylphi, 2015), pp. 19–83.
2. Since the term 'dystopia' is often used in this context, I should explain why I consider it to be potentially somewhat misleading and hence avoid it. It literally means 'bad place' and is generally taken in that way to be the opposite of 'utopia'. But Thomas More's neo-Greek coinage does not simply mean 'good place'. It is a pun meant to suggest *both* 'eutopia' (good place) *and* 'outopia' (no place). The latter meaning is at least as important as the former – I would argue a good deal more so – and so, in order to distinguish between good and bad invented places, it is preferable to refer to positive and negative utopias, respectively.
3. A somewhat similar (though not identical) point is made in Raphael Zähringer, '"Strange Tricks of Cartography": The Map(s) of *Perdido Street Station*', in *China Miéville: Critical Essays*, ed. Caroline Edwards and Tony Venezia (Canterbury: Gylphi, 2015), pp. 61–87. Zähringer argues that New Crobuzon, as presented in the novel, cannot be mapped in a completely clear or definitive way.
4. For a more extended consideration of how *Perdido Street Station* might be considered a realistic – or 'realistic' – novel, Sherryl Vint's concept of 'ab-realism' could be pertinent. See Sherryl Vint, 'Ab-realism: Fractal Language and Social Change' in *China Miéville: Critical Essays*, ed. Caroline Edwards and Tony Venezia (Canterbury: Gylphi, 2015), pp. 39–59.
5. For the term 'capitalist monsters', and for some of the argument that follows, I am indebted to Steven Shaviro's important analyses of *Perdido Street Station*. Steven Shaviro, 'Capitalist Monsters', *Historical Materialism*, 10(4) (2002), pp. 281–90; and Steven Shaviro, *Connected, Or, What It Means to Live in the Network Society* (Minneapolis: University of Minnesota Press, 2003), pp. 168–71.
6. China Miéville, *Perdido Street Station* (New York: Ballantine, 2000), p. 375. A further reference will be given parenthetically.

7. See, for example, Karl Marx, *Capital: A Critique of Political Economy*, vol. 1, trans. Ben Fowkes (Harmondsworth: Penguin, 1976), p. 342: 'Capital is dead labour which, vampire-like, lives only by sucking living labour, and lives the more, the more labour it sucks.'
8. D. H. Lawrence, *Lady Chatterley's Lover* (New York: New American Library, 1959), p. 282. On the same page the phrase is varied as 'the peace of fucking'.
9. Theodor W. Adorno, 'Subject and Object' in *The Essential Frankfurt School Reader*, ed. Andrew Arato and Eike Gebhardt (New York: Urizen, 1978), p. 500.
10. The scholarly literature here is immense, but a convenient synthesis of much of it is provided in Marcus Rediker, *Villains of All Nations: Atlantic Pirates in the Golden Age* (Boston: Beacon Press, 2004), a work to which I am much indebted in the following three paragraphs.
11. The exclusion was based largely on a widespread superstition that the presence of women on a ship would anger the sea gods and result in bad luck for the voyage. Only the pirates, it seems, were (sometimes) intelligent and enlightened enough to resist such nonsense.
12. Cf. Christopher Kendrick, who writes that: '[T]he opposition between mercantilism and capitalism is a basic, animating referent of [*The Scar*].' Christopher Kendrick, 'Monster Realism and Uneven Development in China Miéville's *The Scar*', *Extrapolation*, 50(2) (2009), pp. 258–75 (p. 266).
13. China Miéville, *The Scar* (New York: Ballantine, 2002), pp. 219–220 (emphasis in the original).
14. Ibid., p. 395.
15. Ibid., p. 79; emphasis and ellipsis in original.
16. Ibid., pp. 120–2.
17. Ibid., p. 616; emphasis and ellipsis in original.
18. *The Artist as Critic: Critical Writings of Oscar Wilde*, ed. Richard Ellmann (Chicago: University of Chicago Press, 1982), pp. 269–70.
19. The chief reference here is to Louis Althusser, *For Marx*, trans. Ben Brewster (London: NLB, 1977), pp. 87–116 and 161–218; see also Sigmund Freud, *The Interpretation of Dreams*, ed. and trans. James Strachey (New York: Avon, 1965), *passim*. In the current context it is especially relevant to note that the October Revolution is Althusser's privileged instance of overdetermination (see pp. 99–101).
20. China Miéville, *Iron Council* (New York: Ballantine, 2004), p. 455.
21. The classic account (in English) of the positive utopian elements of revolutionary Barcelona remains George Orwell's *Homage to Catalonia* (1938).
22. Miéville, *Iron Council*, p. 548.
23. Karl Marx, *The First International and After: Political Writings*, vol. 3, ed. David Fernbach (New York: Random House, 1974), p. 233.
24. Miéville, *Iron Council*, p. 561.
25. The editorial referred to is generally believed to have been Luxemburg's last piece of writing, composed just after the defeat of the 1919 Spartacist revolt in Germany, of which she was the leading figure, and only hours before the authorities arrested and murdered her and her colleague Karl Liebknecht. In

it, Luxemburg writes, '"Order reigns in Warsaw!" "Order reigns in Paris!" "Order reigns in Berlin!" Every half-century that is what the bulletins from the guardians of "order" proclaim from one center of the world-historic struggle to the next. And the jubilant "victors" fail to notice that any "order" that needs to be regularly maintained through bloody slaughter heads inexorably toward its historic destiny; its own demise. . . . "Order reigns in Berlin!" You foolish lackeys! Your "order" is built on sand. Tomorrow the revolution will "rise up again, clashing its weapons", and to your horror it will proclaim with trumpets blazing: I was, I am, I shall be!"' The editorial was originally published in *Rote Fahne*, 14 January 1919. I have quoted it (with some modifications of the translation from the original German) from the vast and vastly useful marxists.org archive: www.marxists.org/archive/luxemburg/1919/01/14.htm (Last accessed 14 October 2021).
26. Miéville, *Iron Council*, p. 543.
27. Ibid, p. 552; emphasis in the original.
28. Ernst Bloch, 'Marxism and Poetry', in *The Utopian Function of Art and Literature: Selected Essays*, trans. Jack Zipes and Frank Mecklenburg (Cambridge, MA.: MIT Press, 1988), p. 162.
29. Miéville, *Iron Council*, p. 564.

Index

Aboulela, Leila, 25
   Bird Summons, 139, 152–3
Abraham, Karl, 78
abstract utopias, 190, 262
Adebayo, Mojisola, 25, 122–3, 128–32, 133
   Moj of the Antarctic, 129–30, 131
   STARS, 130–2
Adlard, Charlie
   Playing the Game, 166
Adorno, Theodor, 2, 13, 123–4, 128, 133, 181, 274
   Negative Dialektik, 124
Africa, 49, 50, 57
African Diaspora, 22, 129, 130
Afrofuturism, 18, 132
aftermath society, 48
Agamben, Giorgio, 48
Ahmed, Sara, 67, 126, 182
Akomfrah, John, 22
   Handsworth Songs, 209–10
Albertine, Viv, 12, 91
Albion, 74, 75, 91
Alderson, David, 112
Aldiss, Brian, 11, 24, 37, 39, 57, 63, 64–5, 80
   Acid Head War stories, 63, 64–5, **72**
   Barefoot in the Head, 64
   'Drake-Man Route', 65
   'Just Passing Through', **72**
Ali, Monica
   Brick Lane, 199
Ali, Muhammed, 133
alien beings, 76, 228, 236, 237, 238
Allan, Lucy, 186
Allen, Donald
   The New American Poetry, **192**
allyship, 112
alternate history, 78–83
Althusser, Louis, 280, **286**
Altman, Rick, 224
ambiguous utopia, 27, 270, 279
Americanisation, 57, 63

Anderson, Benedict, 6
Anderson, Perry, 100
Andi, Su, 202
Ankh-Morpork. *see* Pratchett, Terry
Ant, Adam, 30, 73
Antarctic Collective, 129
Anthropocene, 39, 43–4
anti-chivalric satire, 26, 247
anti-colonialism, 49, 50, 57–8, 61, 63, 228, 249
anti-fascism, 192
anti-utopianism
   Lessing's discovery of Sufism, 25, 168, 170
   Pratchett and anti-utopia, 26–7, 244, 246, 248, 249, 250, 252, 262
apartheid, 10, 201
apocalypse, 38–9, **52**, 162–3
apocalyptic imagery, 12–13
apocalyptic writing in England, 37–9
Apple records, 60
Aquifer, 25, 180
Arnheim, Rudolf, 56
   Entropy and Art, 58, 67, **71**
Arnold, Matthew, 7
art
   Bhabha on, 199
   Bloch on, 3
   Jameson on, 180
   Marcuse on, 10, 180, 181
   and science, 60, 66
art schools, 11, **30**
Arthurian legends, 104
Asimov, Isaac, 60
Astaire, Fred, 211, 212, 214
Astounding Science Fiction, 41
atomic weapons, 41, 42
Atwood, Margaret, 89
   The Handmaid's Tale, 271
Augé, Marc, 150
austerity, 18, 21, 181, 183, 186, 187, 191
autobiography, 166, 169, 170
automobility, 15, **31**

Baccolini, Raffaella, 18, 87
Ballard, J. G.
  beyond colonial literary utopia in 1970s science fiction, 14, 15–16
  disaster novels, 40, 44
  inner space, 31
  literary sensibility, 11
  New Wave and *New Worlds*, 24, 57, 60, 63–4
  utopian impulse in 1970s critical dystopia, 86–7
  The Burning World, 15–16, 40
  Concrete Island, 15, 16, 75, 86–7
  Crash, 15, 75, 86
  The Crystal World, 16, 40, 63–4
  The Drought, 15–16, 40, 44, 63
  The Drowned World, 15, 16, 40, 44, 63, 64
  High-Rise, 15, 75, 86, 87
  'The Terminal Beach', 42
  The Wind from Nowhere, 40
Bank of England, 260, 261
Banks, Iain, 142, 144
  The Bridge, 142, 144, 145
  Whit, 139, 143, 144, 145
Banks, Iain M.
  Culture series, 139, 143, 144
Banks, Spencer, 110
Barcelona, 281, **286**
Barnett, Corelli, 51
Barthelme, Donald, 59
Baucom, Ian, 76–7
Baudelaire, Charles, 19
Baxter, Stephen
  Long Earth series (with Pratchett), **263**
BBC (British Broadcasting Corporation), 17, 75, 82
  An Englishman's Castle, 75, 81
  1990 (TV series), 75, 83–4
  Penda's Fen, 102
  Play for Today, 102
Beat authors, 8–9
The Beatles, 10, 59, 60, 61
Bell, Eleanor, 142
Bellamy, Edward
  Looking Backward, 270
Bellow, Saul, 164
Benjamin, Walter, 2, 7, 22, 185
  'Theses on the Philosophy of History', 9
Benn, Tony, 114
Bennett, Andy, **116**
Berlant, Lauren, 46
Bertagna, Julie
  Exodus, 154
Bevan, Aneurin, 84, 85
Bhabha, Homi K., 56, 67
  The Location of Culture, 59, 197–8, 199, 207, 215

Bible, 39, 42
Bicât, Tony, 120
bildungsroman, 204, 212
binary sex, 234–5
biological determinism, 236
biology, 233
Birmingham, 13
Birmingham Centre for Contemporary Cultural Studies (CCCS), 7, 8, 13, 98, 100–1, 206
Black arts movement, 202, 203, 205, 207
Black Audio Film Collective, 209–10
Black British activism, 203
Black British *bildungsroman*, 204
Black British culture, 13, 21–3, 214
Black British theatre
  debbie tucker green's dramaturgy of refusal, 124–8
  theatre as utopian laboratory, 25, 122–3
  transformative energies of Mojisola Adebayo's theatre, 128–32
Black experience
  Carty-Williams's *Queenie* and Black and White experience, 200–2
  Carty-Williams's *Queenie* and Black belonging, 203–4
  Evaristo's *Girl, Woman, Other* and Black British *bildungsroman*, 204–6
  Evaristo's *Girl, Woman, Other* and design fiction, 207–10
  towards Black justice, 215
  utopian realism and race overview, 26, 197–8, 199, 200
Black fantastic, 22
Black feminism, 206, 208, 209–10
Black futurity, 21–2
Black justice, 26, 215
Black Lives Matter, 197–8, 200, 201, 208
Black Mime Theatre, 129
Black novel, 199
Black Power, 21
Black rage, **135**
Black Sabbath, 12
Black subjectivity, 22, 198, 202
Black utopia, 212
Black Women's Group, 202
blackface, 211, 212
Blackness, 201, 202, 206, 215
Blair, Tony, 111, 113
Blake, William, 74, 103
Blanchot, Maurice, 39
Blanqui, Louis-August
  Eternity by the Stars, 184
Bletchley Park, 77
Bloch, Ernst
  abstract and concrete utopias, 190, 262, **269**

Bloch, Ernst (cont.)
  and Adorno, 13, 123–4
  on Cervantes' *Don Quixote*, 26–7, 184, 262–3
  counterculture, utopia and class, 98
  on daydreams, 68, 99
  'forward dreaming', 104, 114
  function of utopia, 128
  future and utopia, 98–9
  on hope, 98–9, 133, 282, 284
  Noch Nicht ('not yet'), 3, 8, **29**
  No-Longer Conscious, 185
  Not-Yet-Conscious, 99
  'real venturing beyond', 59
  satire and utopia, 258
  'Thomas More variety' of utopia, 26, 224–5
  utopia's critique, 7
  utopian longing, 123–4, 127–8
  utopian rupture, 8
  'warm stream' of utopian thinking, 248
  Wilde on utopia, 280
  'Art and Society', 3
  Heritage of Our Times, 17
  'Marxism and Poetry', 284
  'On the Present in Literature', 258
  The Principle of Hope, 59, 68, 99, 123, 184, 185, 190, 224–5, 248, 262–3
  'Something's Missing', 127–8
Bloody Sunday (1971), 254, **266**
Bloody Week (1871), 254
B-movies, 37, 41
Boal, Augusto, 120, 129
body, 121, 131, 132, 153, 187–8, 189
Boltanski, Luc, 107
Bolton, Jacqueline, 127
Bond films, 5–6, 8, 16
Bonney, Sean, 25, 178, 181–6, 189, 190, 191
  'The Kidnap and Murder of David Cameron', 184
  'Letter on Poetics', 181, 183, 186
  Letters Against the Firmament, 183, 184–5, 186, 191, 192
Booker, M. Keith, 42
Boorman, John, 1, 3, 4
Borges, Jorge Louis, 60
botany, 227
Boulanga, Fabien Eboussi, 209
Bould, Mark, 43
Bowie, David, 11, **30**
  'Space Oddity', 11
Boxer, David, 129
Boycott, Rosie, 21
Boyle, Danny
  28 Days Later . . ., 52
Bradbury, Ray
  'There Will Come Soft Rains', 41

Bradshaw, Alan, 87
Branson, Richard, 97
Brazil (1985 film), 92
Brecht, Bertolt, 119, 246
  The Rise and Fall of the City of Mahoganny, 123
Brenton, Howard, 120
Brexit, 6, 51–2, 113
Brians, Paul, 42
Brigadoon (1947 musical), 146
Britain
  dystopias of lost Britain, 83–6
  nuclear imagination, 42
  post-imperial melancholy, 75–7
  Scottish utopia on British periphery, 138–9
Britannia, 74
British alternate history, 24, 75, 78–83
'British Boom', 18
British counterculture, utopia and class, 97–115
  overview, 24, 97–8
  class, counterculture and utopia, 100–2
  explosive potential of utopian surplus, 7–13
  Penda's Fen and countercultural utopianism in the present, 111–15
  Penda's Fen and utopian form, 102–5
  Penda's Fen, counterculture, and class, 105–10
  thinking about utopia, 98–100
British Empire, 45, **53**, 85, 227
British exceptionalism, 6
British national identity, 73–5, 82, 83
British nationalism, 14, 78, 81
British New Weird, 18–19
British poetry. see poetry
British Poetry Revival, 178, **192**
British theatre. see theatre
British utopian literature
  British counterculture, utopia and class, 97–115
  China Miéville's Bas-Lag Trilogy and dialectics of utopia, 284–5
  contemporary British theatre, 119–33
  cosy catastrophes and ambivalent utopias, 37–52
  Doris Lessing: surviving utopia, 159–73
  Naomi Mitchison's *Memoirs of a Spacewoman* as critical feminist utopia, 223–39
  New Wave and *New Worlds* in 1960s, 55–70
  outline of volume, 23–7
  post-imperial melancholy in the long 1970s, 73–92
  Terry Pratchett's *Night Watch* and *Making Money* and anti-utopia, 244–63
  utopian articulations in experimental British poetry, 178–92
  utopian communities in Scottish fiction, 138–54

utopian impulse in British literature and
culture since 1945, 1
utopian realism and race, 197–215
Brixton, 201–2
Brixton Black Women's Group, 21
Brockway, Lucile H., 227, **240**
Brooker, Peter, 7
Brown, Ford Madox, 91
Brown, George Mackay
Greenvoe, 139, 145, 147–8
Brown, Jayna
Black Utopias, 212
Brown, Stephen, 87
Brutalism, 87
Buchan, John
Sick Heart River, 139, 148, 149
Bunyan, John, 103
Burford, Barbara
The Threshing Floor, 207
Burgess, Anthony
A Clockwork Orange, 89
1985, 75, 83, 84–6, 91
Burke, Edmund, 25, 168
Burnett, Elizabeth-Jane, 180
Burns, Alan, 60
Burnside, John
Havergey, 154
Burris, Val, 106
Burroughs, William S., 12
Bush Women's Theatre Group, 209
Butler, Octavia E., 223, 232
Earthseed novels, 169–70
Lilith's Brood, 234
Parable of the Sower, 169
Parable of the Talents, 169
Byrne, Aoife, 80

Cage, John, 59, 60
Cahn, Sarah, 129
Calder, Jenni, 226–7
Callaghan, James, 79, 84
Callinicos, Alex, 105, 114
Cameron, David, 184
Campaign for Homosexual Equality, 104
Campt, Tina, 22
Canavan, Gerry, 170
Capildeo, Anthony (Vahni)
Measures of Expatriation, 190
capitalism
community building in poetry, 180
counterculture and *Penda's Fen*, 107, 110, 112
counterculture, utopia and class, 99
Marcuse on, 9, 99
Marx on, 99
Miéville's *Perdido Street Station*, 271, 272–3, 275

Moylan on, 17
care, 186–9, 190, 191
Caribbean, 7
Carmichael, Stokely, 9
Carter, Angela, 51, 59, 60, 88–9
The Bloody Chamber, 88
The Fairy Tales of Charles Perrault, 88
Heroes and Villains, 40, 51
The Passion of New Eve, 51, 75, 88–9
Cartmill, Cleve
'Deadline', 41
Carty-Williams, Candace, 26
Queenie, 199, 200–4
catastrophes, 38, 63–4. *see also* cosy catastrophes
Cavendish, Margaret, 230
The Description of the New World, Called the Blazing World, 230
Celtic identity, 81
Centre for Contemporary Cultural Studies (CCCS), Birmingham, 7, 8, 13, 98, 100–1, 206
centrism, 185, 244, 247, 259, 261
Cervantes, Miguel de
Don Quixote, 26, 184, 247, 262
Chambers, Ross, 48
Chandler, John, 55
The Changes (TV series), 40
Chapman, James, 6
Charles, Bradley, 131
Charles, Prince
'Vision of Britain', 77, 86
Charnas, Suzy McKee, 223, 227, 230
Motherlines, 88
chartalism, 257
Chesterton, G. K., 246
Chiapello, Eve, 107
Christ, 104–5
Christianity, 103
Christopher, John (aka Sam Youd), 24, 37–8, 47–9, 80
Babel Itself, 47–8
Bad Dream, 38
The Death of Grass, 38, 43, 48–9, 64
Pendulum, 38, 50–1
'Tripods' series, 38
The World in Winter, 44, 49–50
A Wrinkle in the Skin, 38, 43, 44
chrononormativity, 208
Churchill, Caryl, 108, 120
Churchill, Winston, 45, 61, 83, 89
civil rights, 58, 203
The Clangers (TV animation), **93**
Clapton, Eric, **30**
Clarke, Alan, 102, 103, 105, 109–10, 111
Clarke, Arthur C., 11

The Clash, 12, 90
class
  Benjamin on historiography, 185
  British counterculture, utopia, and class, 10, 12, 98, 100–2, 103
  and gender, 283
  Penda's Fen and countercultural utopianism in the present, 111–13, 114
  Penda's Fen, counterculture, and class, 105–10
  and race, 14
Clayton, Jay, 161
Cleese, John, 10
Clegg, Nick, 248
Clements, James, 164
climate change, 43, 153, 171–2, 173
climate fiction (cli-fi), 44, **53**
Cold War, 6, 39, 41
collectivity, 119, 128, 190–2, 205
Collins, Cornelius, 166, 168
Colon, Fred, 256
colonialism
  Ballard's catastrophe fiction, 15, 16, 63–4
  Christopher's catastrophe fiction, 49, 50
  entropy and empire, 57–8
  literary utopian enclaves to utopian impulse, 3–4
  Mitchison's *Memoirs* and colonial expansion, 227–8, 229–30
  New Wave and *New Worlds*, 56–8, 62–4
  postcolonial melancholia, 13, 75–6, 91
  post-imperial affect, 44–5, 49
  post-imperial melancholy, 75–6, 91
  Pratchett and anti-utopia, 249–50
  science fiction beyond colonial literary utopia, 13–14, 16
Colston, Edward, 21, 22, 198
commodity theory of money, 257, 258
Communards, **266**, 282
communications, 226, 227–8, 233–4, 235–6
communism, 14, 164, 168
communism, utopian, 270, 280
communities
  Frestonia and communal living, 209
  Scottish communal life and utopian homosociality, 145–6, 147, 148–9
  Scottish fiction overview, 25
  Scottish fiction, utopia and death, 140, 143, 144, 145
  Scottish fiction, utopian storytelling and queer futures, 150, 151, 153–4
  Zarf and community building in experimental poetry, 179–81, 191
concrete utopias, 189–90, 191, 262
Connery, Sean, 4–5, 8, **28**
Conservative Party, 51, 183, 248

consumerism, 100–1, 106, 180
contemporary British theatre. *see* theatre
Cooke, Jennifer
  Apocalypse Dreams, 190
Corbyn, Jeremy, 21
Cornwall, 80–1
cosy catastrophes, 37–52
  overview, 24, 37
  apocalyptic writing in England, 37–9
  coining by Aldiss, 37, 64, 80
  in era of decolonisation, 49–52
  genre of post-imperial affect, 43–9
  nuclear imagination, 40–3
counterculture
  British counterculture, utopia and class, 24, 97–115
  British countercultures and potential of utopian surplus, 7–13
  countercultural utopianism, 111–15
country house tradition, 4, 77–8, 84
Cousins, Norman
  'Modern Man is Obsolete', 41
Covid-19 pandemic, 21, 23, 27, 43, 113, 131, 191, 197
Cowper, Richard, 85
Cox, Jo, 6
cozies (cozy crime), 37
Craft, Ellen, 129
Craig, Cairns, 138, 145
critical dystopias, 18, 87–8, 163
critical utopias
  and literary utopias, 1
  Mitchison's *Memoirs* and feminist utopianism, 26, 223, 224, 227, 230, 232, 239
  Moylan on, 61, **155**, 161, 223, 252
  Pratchett and anti-utopia, 244, 252
Croft, Janet Brennan, 248
Crouch, Tim, **134**
cruel optimism, 46, 50, 51, 52
cruel pessimism, 172
Crumey, Andrew, 142, 145
  Sputnik Caledonia, 142
Crummell, Alexander, 208
Crutzen, Paul, 43
cult cinema, **116**
cultural formations, 100, 101
cultural identity, 7–8
cultural materialism, 6, 98, 100
cultural studies, 13, 100
culture
  Anderson on, 100
  Arnheim on, 58
  Bhabha on, 59–60
  British counterculture, 7–8, 100–2, 105
  British postwar culture and imaginary past, 6–7

defining, 6–7
Thatcher's suspicion of, 18
Williams on, 6–7, 100, 101
cyborgs, 132, 210, 232–3, 234–5

Dadaist movement, 68–9
dance, 211, 212–13, 214–15
dance music, 18
Dante, 271
Davies, Angela, 209
Davies, Ray, 30
daydreams, 67–9, 99
De'Ath, Amy
   ON MY LOVE FOR gender abolition, 190
death, 139, 140, 141, 145, 150, 153, 183, 188
death parties, 184–5, 190
DeboA, DJ, 131
decline, 39, 40, 57, 61, 65, 70, 75, 78
declinism, 13, 24, 40, 51
decolonisation, 6, 39, 49, 56, 57, 60
Defoe, Daniel
   Robinson Crusoe, 15, 16
Deighton, Len
   SS-GB, 75, 82–3
Delany, Samuel R., 11, 12, 223, 232, 246
   Triton, 1, 224
Delgado-García, Cristina, **134**
democracy, 250, 261–2, 284
Derrida, Jacques, **52**, 245
design fictions, 199–200, 211, 213, 215
desire, 206–7
determinism, 236
devolution, 79, 138
Dialectics of Liberation conference, 9, 99
Dick, Philip K., 41
   Dr Bloodmoney, 41
   The Man Who Japed, 41
Dickinson, Peter, 40
disaster fiction, 37, 38, 39, 40, 42–3
disavowal, 46
Disch, Thomas M., 12, 56
Discworld. *see* Pratchett, Terry
Dixie, Lady Florence, **243**
   Gloriana, 239
Doctor Who, 76, 78, 79, 92
Dolan, Jill
   Utopia in Performance, 121
domestic labour, 66–9
Donawerth, Jane, 228, 230
Donne, John, 16, 274, 275
Douglas, Christopher, 110
Doyle, Arthur Conan
   The Poisoned Cloud, 38
Dragon School, 226
drama, 121–2. *see also* theatre

dreams, 67–9, 99, 205–6
Dreyer, Carl Theodor, 107
Du Bois, W. E. B., 13
du Maurier, Daphne
   Rule Britannia, 24, 57, 75, 80–1
Duchamp, Marcel
   'The Bride Stripped Bare by Her Bachelors, Even', 68
Duggan, Mark, 19
Duncan Smith, Iain, 183–4, 186
Duncan, Hal, 18
Duncombe, Stephen, 18
dystopias, 12–13, 18, 24, 75, 83–6, 87–8, **285**

Eco, Umberto, 5–6
ecocatastrophe, 15, 39, 43, 63–4, 171–3
ecological changes, 43–4, 113–14
ecological imperialism, **241**
Edelman, Lee
   No Future: Queer Theory and the Death Drive, 121
Edelmann, Heinz, 10
Eden, Anthony, 45
Education Act (1944), 102
Edwards, Caroline, 23, 40
Edwards, Ken, 179
Elgar, Edward, 104, 105, 113
   'The Dream of Gerontius', 102, 105
Eliot, T. S., 46, 146
   Notes Towards a Definition of Culture, 46
Elizabeth II, Queen, 73, 74
Elphinstone, Margaret
   The Incomer, 139, 145, 146–7, 154
Emecheta, Buchi, 14
   In the Ditch, 14
   The Joys of Motherhood, 209
   The Rape of Shavi, 14
   Second-Class Citizen, 14
empire
   Brexit, 52
   British Empire, 45, **53**, 85, 227
   Christopher's catastrophe fiction, 49, 50
   and entropy, 57
   era of decolonisation, 50, 52
   Gilroy on, 14
   Jubilee and Britannia, 74
   Mitchison's *Memoirs* and colonialism, 227
   post-imperial affect, 45, 46, 49
   post-imperial melancholy, 74, 77, 85
   Pratchett and anti-utopia, 249
enclave, utopian, 2
the end, 39, 41
England
   nuclear imagination, 40, 42–3
   pastoral ideal, 4

England (cont.)
  post-imperial melancholy, 77, 78–9
  rural life, 47
  Scottish utopia on British periphery, 138–9, 142
English declinism, 13, 24, 40, 51
An Englishman's Castle (TV series), 75, 81–3
Englishness, 78, 245
enlightened colonialism, 4, 31
entropy
  emerging hope, 70
  entropy and empire, 57–9
  entropy as catalyst for utopian anticipation, 66–9
  New Wave and *New Worlds*, 24, 55–7, 61–2, 63, 65
environmental crises, 63–4, 113–14, 115, 154
Epstein, Stephen, 111
equality, 22
erotic representation, 274
erotohistoriography, 208
Eshun, Ekow, 22, 33
Eshun, Kodwo, 133
essentialism, 233–5, 236–7, 238–9
eugenics, 238–9, **240**
European Economic Community (EEC), 79, 80, 82
European Union (EU), 6, 51, 52, 113, 249
Evans, Diana, 200
  26a, 199
Evans, Rebecca, 70
Evans, Rob, 253
Evaristo, Bernadine, 26, 200
  Girl, Woman, Other, 199, 204–8, 209–11, 213, 214
experimental British poetry
  overview, 25, 178
  Sean Bonney's insurrectionary poetry, 181–6
  utopian articulations in experimental British poetry, 178–92
  Verity Spott's utopian praxis of care and response, 186–9
  Zarf and community building in experimental poetry, 178–81
experimental theatre, 122. *see also* theatre
Extinction Rebellion (XR), 21
extraterrestrials, 228

Fabian, Johannes, 208
Fagan, Jenni, 25
  The Sunlight Pilgrims, 139, 152, 153, 154
fairytales, 5, 88–9, 248
Falkland Islands, 91
Fanon, Frantz, 50, 202, 207, 209, 215
fantasy, 78, 244, 245, 246, 247, 249
femininity, 225, 231–4, 237, 239

feminism
  debbie tucker green's dramaturgy of refusal, 126
  Evaristo's *Girl, Woman, Other*, 206, 208, 209–10, 211
  Lessing on, 168
  Mitchison's *Memoirs*, 227–8, 229–30, 231, 232–4, 236, 237–9
  Second Wave Feminism, 58
  Tennant's satire, 88
  theatre, 120, 126
  utopian turn in 2010s and 2020s, 21
feminist utopianism, 223–6, 227, 232–3, 234
Ferns, Chris, 145, 153
Festival of Light movement, 103
films
  B-movies, 37, 41
  cult cinema, **116**
  monster films, 41–2
financialisation, 259–61, 262
First World War. *see* World War I
Fisher, Mark, 18, 19, 20, 59, 69, **118**, 245
Fitt, Matthew
  But N Ben A-Go-Go, 154
Fleming, Ian, 5–6, 16
Fletcher, John
  Bonduca, or the British Heroine, 82
Floyd, George, 21, 197
fluidarity, 133
folk politics, 114
folklore, 102, 141, 167
Forced Entertainment, 122
Ford, Laura Oldfield (aka Laura Grace Ford), 19, 20
foreign invasion genre, 38
Forest, Jean-Claude
  Barbarella, 224
formations, cultural, 100, 101
Forster, E. M.
  Howards End, 77
  A Room With a View, 77
forward dreaming, 99–100, 104, 114
Frank, Pat
  Alas, Babylon, 42
Franklin, H. Bruce, 41
Freeman, Elizabeth, 208
French revolutionary conflicts, 168, 254
Frestonia, 209
Freud, Sigmund, 46
  'Mourning and Melancholia', 78
Freudianism, 280, 282
Friends (TV show), 201
Fukuyama, Francis, 245
future, 99, 161–2
futurity, Black, 21–2, 23

Galford, Ellen
  The Fires of Bride, 146
Gardiner, Michael, 6
Gardner, Callie, 25, 178, 179–80, 181, 189–92
  Naturally It Is Not, 189–91, 192
Garland, Judy, 212
Gay, Roxanne, 205
gay liberation, 21, 58, 104, 109, 114
gay male subculture, 112
Gearhart, Sally Miller, 223
  The Wanderground, 88
Gee, Maggie
  The Flood, 40
gender
  British countercultures and Bowie, 11
  gendered identities, 112
  Miéville's Bas-Lag Trilogy, 276, 283
  Mitchison's critique of utopianism and feminism, 224, 225
  Mitchison's *Memoirs*, 226, 227, 228, 230–1, 232–5, 236–7, 238–9
  Scottish fiction, 143, 148, 151
  sex and gender, 234–5
  utopian realism and race, 200, 202, 205, 206
genetics, 43, 226, 236, 237–9
gentrification, 19, 20, 202
ghosts, 19, 105, 141, 150
gift exchange, 180
Gilliam, Terry
  Brazil, 92
Gilroy, Paul
  postcolonial melancholia, 13–14, 75–6, 91
  post-imperial melancholy, 24, 39, 45, 57, 75–6, 91, 92
  The Empire Strikes Back, 14
  There Ain't No Black in the Union Jack, 13, 206
Ginsburg, Allen, 9
Glass, Philip
  The Making of the Representative for Planet 8, 166, **175**
Gleichzeitigkeit (simultaneity), 17
globalisation, 113, 201
Glorious Revolution, 260
Goddard, Lynette, 130, 131
Godzilla, King of the Monsters! (1954 film), 41
Goethe, J. W. von
  Faust, 123
gold, 257, 258, 259, 260
Goldfinger, Ernő, 87
Golding, William, 164
  The Lord of the Flies, 48
Goldmann, Lucien, 9
Gothic fiction, 150
Gramsci, Antonio, 7, 9
Gray, Alasdair, 142, 144–5, 146, 154

  Lanark, 138–9, 141–2, 146
Great Refusal, 124, 127, 133
Greatorex, Wilfred, 83–4
Greenham Common, 20
Greenidge, Kaitlyn, 211
Greenland, Colin, 70
  The Entropy Exhibition, 56
Greer, Germaine, 88
Griffiths, Trevor, 108
grimdark fantasy, 247, **264**
Guilfoy, Kevin, 256
Gunn, Neil M., 144, 145
  The Green Isle of the Great Deep, 139, 140–1, 151
  Young Art and Old Hector, 140

Hakluyt, Richard
  Discourse of Western Planting, 4
Haldane, J. B. S. ('Jack'), 226–7
Hall, Lesley A., 238
Hall, Stuart, 7–8, 13, 98, 100, 206, 210
  'Cultural Identity and Diaspora', 7
Hamilton, Edward, 60
Handsworth Songs (1986 film), 209–10
happy housewife figure, 67
Haraway, Donna, 188, 228, 232–3, 234–5
  'A Cyborg Manifesto', 232
Hardy, Robin
  The Wicker Man, 143
Hare, David, 108, 120
Harle, Matthew, 103, 104
Harris, Wilson, 207
Harrison, M. John, 18
  The Centauri Device, 78
  The Committed Men, 40, 78
  'Running Down', 40, 43
Hart, Francis Russell, 140, 145
Harvey, David, 55
hauntology, 19, 114, **118**
Hayward, Danny, 187
Hazlitt, William, 27
Head, Bessie, 239, **243**
Healey, Denis, 79
heat death of the universe, 66, 69
Heath, Edward, 4, 79, 104
heavy metal, 12–13
Hebdige, Dick
  Subculture: The Meaning of Style, 8
hegemony, 7
Heinlein, Robert, 41, 60
Henry VIII, 4
Hepburn, Allan, 164
heroes, 247
hexes, 186
high and low art, 59–60
high-rises, 87

Hillegas, Mark R., 65
Hiroshima, 41
Hobbes, Thomas, 255–6, 257
Hodgson, William Hope, 18
Hoggart, Richard, 6, 7, 13, 98, 100
holocaust, 39
homophobia, 85, 89
homosexuality, 104, 106, 109, 112, 114
Homotopia Festival, 131
hooks, bell, 209
hope
   Black futurity, 21–2
   Black utopian tradition, 206
   Bloch on, 98–9, 282, 284
   debbie tucker green's dramaturgy of refusal, 127
   Gardner and poetry, 191
   Lessing's ecocatastrophe fiction, 172, 173
   Miéville's *Iron Council*, 282, 284–5
   New Wave and *New Worlds*, 70
   Scottish fiction, 151–2
   theatre as utopian laboratory, 121, 127, 133
   utopian turn in 2010s and 2020s, 20–2
Horwood, Joel
   This Changes Everything, 122
Hoskins, W. G.
   The Making of the English Landscape, 47
housewife figure, 67
housework, 66–9
Howard, Maureen, 167, **176**
Howe, Darcus, 210
Hudson, Wayne, **29**
Hugo, Victor
   Les Misérables, 254
Humphrey, Daniel, 91
Hunter, Megan
   The End We Start From, 41
Huxley, Aldous, 25, 100, 168, 224, **240**
   Brave New World, 140
   Island, 65
Huxley, Julian
   The Science of Life, 235–6

ice age, 49, 153, 171
identity. *see also* national identity
   Adebayo's theatre, 123
   British counterculture, 7–8, 103, 111–12
   cultural identity, 7–8
   An Englishman's Castle, 82
   gendered identities, 112
   identity politics, 111–12
   local and regional identity, 81
   Scottish fiction, 142
Idle Women project, 130
imagined communities, 6

immigration, 104, 113, 249
imperialism
   British feminist literature, **240**
   dream of imperial ruins overview, 23–4
   ecological imperialism, **241**
   entropy and empire, 57–8
   genre of post-imperial affect, 44–6
   Mitchison's *Memoirs*, 228, 229, 239
   More's *Utopia*, 3, 6
   post-imperial melancholy, 75, 81
   Pratchett and anti-utopia, 249
   Scottish utopia on British periphery, 138
Inchley, Maggie, 126
India, 45
individualism, 106–7, 119, 248
inner space, 14, **31**, 164
Institute of Contemporary Arts (ICA), 131
intellectuals, 7, 9
International Times (*IT*), 8
intersectionality, 112, 206
intersubjectivity, 128, 130, 132, 133
invasion narratives, 80, 81–3
Islamophobia, 131
islands, 149
It Happened Here (1964 film), 80, 82

Jackson, Brian
   Education and the Working Class, 102
Jackson, Michael, 213, 214
Jagger, Mick, 102
James, C. L. R., 13
James, Clive, 85, 86
James, Edward, 248, **266**
James, Henry, 38, **52**
James, M. R., 18
James Bond character, 5–6, 8, 16
Jameson, Fredric
   British counterculture, 100, 101, 112
   decolonisation, 57
   history and narrative, 174
   individual and collective dialectic, **176**
   Lessing's writing, 159, 162
   on Marcuse, 180
   Pratchett and anti-utopia, 246
   utopia's critique, 7
   utopian enclave, 251
   Wilde on utopia, 280
   Archaeologies of the Future, 2, 251
   'Cognitive Mapping', 100
   Marxism and Form, 180
   'Periodizing the 60s', 57
   Postmodernism or, the Cultural Logic of Late Capitalism, 98, 112
   'Progress Versus Utopia; Or, Can We Imagine the Future?', 32

Signatures of the Visible, 101
Jarman, Derek
  Jubilee, 24, 73–5, 86, 89–91
  The Last of England, 91
Jay, Martin, 46
Jenkins, Robin, 145
  The Missionaries, 139, 143, 149
Jesus Christ, 104–5
Joint Stock Theatre Company, 120
Jubilee (1978 film), 73–5, 78, 79, 85, 86, 89–91
June Rebellion (1832), 254

Kafer, Alison, 239
Kane, Sarah, **134**
Kavan, Anna, 12
  Ice, 12
Kay, Jackie, 202
Kendrick, Christopher, **286**
Kennedy, Charles, 248
Kermode, Frank
  The Sense of an Ending, 39
King, Jeanette, **173**
Kipling, Rudyard, 46
Kisuule, Vanessa
  'Hollow', 22–3
Klaić, Dragan, **134**
  The Plot of the Future, 121
Knight, Diana, 119
Kristeva, Julia, 187–8, 209
Kubrick, Stanley, 11, 89
Kumar, Krishan, 168–9

labour, domestic, 66–9
labour movement, 111
Labour Party, 111, 113, **265**
Laing, R. D., 65, 87, 88, 164
  The Divided Self, 67
lampshading, 244, **263**
Larkin, Philip, **192**
The Last of England (1987 film), 91
Lavery, Bryony, 120
Lawrence, D. H., 274
  Lady Chatterley's Lover, 274
  Women in Love, 274
Lawrence, Stephen, 75
Le Corbusier, 87
Le Guin, Ursula
  ambiguous utopia, 27, 270, 279
  British counterculture, 11, 100
  Mitchison's *Memoirs*, 223, 224
  Pratchett and anti-utopia, 246
  review of Lessing's *Shikasta*, 165
  Always Coming Home, 146
  The Dispossessed, 1, 162, 165, 279
Lee, Dennis, 139

LeFanu, Sarah, 226
Lenin, Vladimir, 281
Lennon, John, **30**
Lerner, Alan Jay
  Brigadoon (Lerner and Loewe), 146
Lessing, Doris
  beyond colonial literary utopia, 14–15
  discovery of Sufism, 163–71
  ecocatastrophe in later fiction, 171–3
  inner space, 14, **31**, 164
  Mitchison's *Memoirs*, 239
  role of houses, **177**
  surviving utopia, 159–73
  surviving utopia overview, 25, 159–60
  utopian future, beyond narrative representation and time, 160–3
  Briefing for a Descent into Hell, 14, 162, 170, **175**
  Canopus in Argos sequence, 14, 165, 166, 171
  Children of Violence series, 159–60
  The Four-Gated City, 160–2, 163, 166, 167, 170, 173
  The Golden Notebook, 159–60, **175**
  The Good Terrorist, **173**
  Landlocked, 160, 163, 170
  The Making of the Representative of Planet 8, 162, 166, **175**
  Mara and Dann, 171
  Martha Quest, 160
  The Memoirs of a Survivor, 14–15, 25, 40, 166–8, 169, 170
  Playing the Game (with Adlard), 166
  A Proper Marriage, 160
  A Ripple from the Storm, 160
  Shikasta, 162, 164–5, 170
  The Sweetest Dream, 25, 166, 168–9, 170–2, **173**
  Walking in the Shade, 169, 170
Levitas, Ruth, 7, 98, 146, 151, 159, 245, 246
Lewis, Sinclair, 80
Lewis, Sophie, 238
LGBTQIA movement, 104, 131
Liberal Democrats, 248–9, **265**
liberalism, 244, 245–6, 248–9
Liberia, 22
libertarianism, 256
liberty, 255–6, 278
Lieber, Fritz
  The Swords of Lankhmar, 245
Liebknecht, Karl, **286**
Lippard, Lucy, 55
literary postmodernism, 59
literary utopias, 1, 2, 20, 26, 75, 245, 252
local identity, 81
Loewe, Frederick
  Brigadoon (Lerner and Loewe), 146
London, 8, 9–10, 19–20, 21, 201–2, 209, 245

London Illustrated News, 12
London School of Economics (LSE), 9–10
lone survivor genre, 38
longing, 123, 127
Lorde, Audre, 127, 128, **135**
love, 139, 150, 152, 192, 273–5, 279
love poetry, 275
lovemaking, 273–5, 279
Löwy, Michael, 22
Luckhurst, Roger, 17, 24, 60, 78, 106, 111
Lunar Society of Birmingham, 77
Luxemburg, Rosa, 282, **286**
Lyall, Scott, 146
Lysenkoism, 43

Macaulay, Rose
   The Pleasure of Ruins, 38
Machen, Arthur, 19, 103
Machin, James, 103, 104
Mackie, Peter, 81
MacLeod, Ken
   Fall Revolution Quartet, 139
   Intrusion, 153
Macmillan, Harold, 82
MacNeil, Kevin, 149
Macpherson Report, 75
madness, 65, 87
Maher, Ashley, 239
Maine, Charles Eric
   Thirst!, 44
Malagardis, Maria, 204
mania, 46
Manson, Peter
   Adjunct: An Undigest, 190
Marcuse, Herbert
   British counterculture, utopia and class, 98, 99–100, 104
   Dialectics of Liberation conference, 9, 99
   Great Refusal, 124, 127, 133
   utopia's critique, 7
   utopian impulse, 2–3
   The Aesthetic Dimension, 3, 10
   The Dialectics of Liberation, 9
   Eros and Civilisation, 65
   An Essay on Liberation, 99, 180, 181
   'Liberation from the Affluent Society' lecture, 9
   One Dimensional Man, 100
Marsden, Dennis
   Education and the Working Class, 102
Marx, Karl, 108, 114, 146, 253, **265**, 272, 281, 282
   Grundrisse, 17
   The Civil War in France, 282
Marxism, 13, 14, 98, 99, 168, 284
masculinity, 225, 231, 232–3, 236

Mason-John, Valerie, 202
Matheson, Richard
   I Am Legend, 38
Mathijs, Ernest, **116**
Matless, David, 47
Mbembe, Achille
   A Critique of Black Reason, 198, 199, 201, 202–3, 204, 206, 208–9, 211, 214–15
McCarthy, Cormac
   The Road, 170
McCracken-Flesher, Caroline, 25, 138
McDonald, Dwight, 41
McFarlane, Anna, 232
McLaren, Malcolm, 73
McLuhan, Marshall, 62
Mebyon Kernow, 81
melancholy, 45–6, 47, 51, 75–8, 91
Memoirs of a Spacewoman (Mitchison)
   as critical feminist utopia, 26, 224–39
   critique of utopianism and feminism, 224–6
   feminism and utopianism, 237–9
   sea urchins and femininity, 226–33
   starfish and essentialism, 233–7
memory, 208–9, 210, 211, 214–15
Mendlesohn, Farah, 248
mercantilism, 276, 277
Merchant-Ivory, 77
Mercury, Freddie, 30
Merril, Judith
   Shadow on the Hearth, 41
   'That Only A Mother', 41
metal bands, 12–13
metallism, 258
#MeToo movement, 201
Michaels, Debra, 131
middle class, 100, 101–2, 105–8, 109, 111–12, 113, 114
Middle England, 77, 111
Miéville, China
   Bas-Lag Trilogy, 18–19, 27, 284–5
   'British Boom', 18
   psychogeographical dérive, 19–20
   Iron Council, 27, 270, 284–5
   Perdido Street Station, 27, 270, 271–5, 277, 278–9, 281
   The Scar, 27, 270, 275–80
Mill, John Stuart
   Principles of Political Economy, 77
Miller, Gavin, 233–4, 235
Millett, Kate, 88
Milner, Andrew, 112
Minimalism, 55
misogyny, 85, 226, 228, 230
Mitchison, Naomi, 26, 140
   The Bull Calves, 26

Memoirs of a Spacewoman, 26, 224–39
modernism, 60, 69
money, 256–8, 259–61
Monstrous Regiment, 120
Monty Python's Flying Circus (TV series), 10
moon landing, 11
Mooney, Jordan, 73
Moorcock, Michael, 11–12, 24, 40, 56–7, 60–3
  The Condition of Muzak, 40
  A Cure for Cancer, 40, 61–3
  The English Assassin, 40
  The Final Programme, 40, 61, 62
More, Kenneth, 82
More, Thomas, 16, 26, 224
  Utopia, 3–4, 16, 20, 168, **285**
Morrison, Ewan, 143–5, 146
  Close Your Eyes, 143
  How to Survive Everything, 144
  Nina X, 139, 144
Morson, Gary Saul, 252
motherhood, 231–2, 238
mourning, 78, 85, 150
Movement poets, **192**
Moylan, Tom
  anti-utopian tradition, 168
  critical dystopias, 18, 87–8, 163
  critical utopias, 61, **155**, 161, 223, 252
  Mitchison's *Memoirs* as critical feminist utopia, 26, 223, 236
  Pratchett and anti-utopia, 246, 252
  utopia's critique, 7
  Becoming Utopian, 17
  Demand the Impossible, 1, **33**, 151, 223, 236
Muggeridge, Malcolm, 103
multiculturalism, 26, 113
Muñoz, José Esteban
  Cruising Utopia, 121, 151, 188, 190, 212
Murdoch, Iris, 164
music, 11, 18, 91, 129–30, 212, 215
Muslims, 85, 208
mysticism, 160–1, 164
myth, 104–5, 140, 145, 150, 151, 153–4

Nadkarni, Asha, 239
Nairn, Tom, 90
  'The Twilight of the British State', 78–9
Nation, Terry
  Survivors TV series, 40
national identity
  British counterculture and *Penda's Fen*, 103, 114
  imagined communities, 6
  post-imperial melancholy, 74, 76, 80, 81, 83, 91
  Scottish fiction, 142
  utopian realism and race, 198

National Public Order Intelligence Unit, 253
National Trust, 78
nationalism, 14, 74, 78, 81, 138–9
Nazism, 76, 80, 81–2, 83, 284
negation, 124, 125, 126, 127, 133
negative dialectics, 124, 133
neoliberalism, 113, 201, 248
New Labour, 19, 111, 248, 260
New Lanark, 146, 150
New Left, 51, 58
new middle class, 105–8, 109, 111–12, 113, 114
New Sincerity, 122
New Wave science fiction
  overview, 24, 55–7, 70
  British countercultures and utopian surplus, 11
  critical utopias, 61
  dystopias, 70
  entropy and empire, 57–60
  entropy as catalyst for utopian anticipation, 66–9
  New Wave and *New Worlds*, 55–70
  new worlds for old, 60–5
  nuclear imagination, 40
  post-imperial melancholy, 78
New Weird writers, 18–19
New Worlds magazine
  entropy as catalyst for utopian anticipation, 66–9
  hope emerging, 70
  Moorcock as editor, 11, 56–7, 60–3
  New Wave and *New Worlds*, 55–70
  New Wave overview, 24, 55–7
  new worlds for old, 60–5
Newman, John Henry
  'The Dream of Gerontius', 105
Newman, Kim, 18
Newsinger, John, 252
newspaper form, 62
9/11, 208
1984 (1984 film), 92
1990 (TV series), 75, 83–4, 91
Nkrumah, Kwame, 50
Noch Nicht ('not yet' or 'still not'), 3, 8, **29**
No-Longer-Conscious, 185
non-contemporaneity, 17, 18, 19, 22
Noon, Jeff, 18
nostalgia, 76, 81–2
'Not-Yet-Conscious', 99, 104, 185
novels, 199, 204–6
nuclear power, 44
nuclear war, 39, 41–2, 115

O'Brien, Richard, 74
O'Toole, Fintan, 51
Occupy movement, 19, 20

The Octagon Press, 166
October Revolution, 281, **286**
Ofili, Chris, 22
Olufemi, Lola, 27
optimism, 21, 46, 50, 51, 52, 173
oral literature, 167
organic intellectuals, 7
Orwell, George, 25, 85, 100, 168
   Homage to Catalonia, **286**
   'The Moon Under Water', 84
   Nineteen Eighty-Four, 75, 83, 85, 270, 271
Osborne, Deirdre, 131, 132
Osborne, George, 184, 186, 187
Ott, Michael R., 128
Out of the Woods, 132, **137**
overdetermination, 280, 281, **286**
Ovid, 151
Owen, Robert, 146, 150

paganism, 102, 105, 113
Palestine, 21
Palmer, Christopher, 39
pandemics, 42, 43, 113. *see also* Covid-19 pandemic
pansexual characters, 152
Paolozzi, Eduardo, 60
Paris Commune, 9, 11, 254, 271, 280, 281, 282
Paris student-worker protests, 11
Parmar, Pratibha, 209
patriarchy, 24, 26, 205, 215, 225
peace, 274
Pearce, Michael, **135**
Penda's Fen (TV play)
   overview, 24, 98
   countercultural utopianism in the present, 111–15
   counterculture, and class, 105–10
   utopian form, 102–5
performance, 121–2
Performance (1970 film), 102
Periyan, Natasha, 238
pessimism, 169, 172
Peterloo Massacre, 254
Petrarch, 275
Phillips, Bill, 259
Piercy, Marge, 223, 224
   Woman on the Edge of Time, 1, 88, 162
pirate radio, 10
pirates, 27, 270, 275–8
plagues, 43
planetary humanism, 200, 206
Plato
   Republic, 255
Play for Today (TV series), 102
poetry
   British Poetry Revival, 178, **192**

experimental British poetry overview, 25, 178
love poetry, 275
Sean Bonney's insurrectionary poetry, 181–6
utopian articulations in experimental British poetry, 178–92
Verity Spott's utopian praxis of care and response, 186–9
Zarf and community building in experimental poetry, 178–81
Poets' Hardship Fund (PHF), 191–2
police, 210, 247, 253, 254–5
politics
   alternate history and hope of British resistance, 79
   Bonney's insurrectionary poetry, 181–2, 183–4, 185–6, 189
   British counterculture and *Penda's Fen*, 111–12, 114
   identity politics, 111–12
   Pratchett and anti-utopia, 248–9
   Spott's poetry, 186
   theatre as utopian laboratory, 119–20
Pop Art, 59, 60
Popular Modernism, 60, 69
populism, 99, 249
Portable Theatre Company, 120
post-colonial melancholia, 13–14, 75–6, 91
post-colonialism, 56–7, 58, 62–3
post-imperial melancholy, 73–92
   overview, 24, 73–5
   alternate history and hope of British resistance, 78–83
   declinism, 39, 52
   dystopias of lost Britain, 83–6
   entropy and empire, 57
   genre of post-imperial affect, 44, 45–6, 47
   post-imperial melancholy in long 1970s, 75–8
   punk changing the world, 89–92
   utopian impulse in 1970s critical dystopia, 86–9
postmodernism, 59, 108
post-punk movement, 24, 98
post-racialism, 26, 206
poststructuralism, 119
post-subcultural turn, 101
poverty, 252, 259–60
Powell, Enoch, 49
Pratchett, Terry
   anti-utopia overview, 26–7, 244–6
   death of, 249
   democracy to come, 261–3
   Pratchett's *Night Watch* and *Making Money* and anti-utopia, 244–63
   utopian villains, anti-utopian heroes, 246–50
   The Colour of Magic, 245

Discworld series, 26, 244–5, 246–8, 249, 250, 253, 254, 256, 259, 261–3
Feet of Clay, 245, 251
The Fifth Elephant, 246, 247
Going Postal, 246
Guards! Guards!, 245, 246
Interesting Times, 249
Jingo, 245, 246, 248, 249, **265**
The Last Continent, **266**
Long Earth series (with Baxter), **263**
Making Money, 244, 246, 249, 250, 255–61, 262
Men at Arms, 245, 252
Mort, **265**
Nation, 249
Night Watch, 244, 246, 247, 250–5, 256, 257, 258, 259, 262, **265**
Small Gods, 245
Snuff, 246, 249
Soul Music, 245
Thud!, 246, 250
The Truth, 246, **265**
Unseen Academicals, 246, 249
presses, 25, 179, 180
Priest, Christopher, 80, 86
 A Dream of Wessex, 78
 Fugue for a Darkening Isle, 78
primitivism, 64
Pritchard, Sam, **134**
Private Eye (publication), 10
protests, 20, 181–2
psychic transformation, 64–5
publishers, 25, 179, 180
Puig de la Bellacasa, María, 153
punk, 9, 12, 19, 73–4, 89–92
Purcell, Henry
 'Lillibullero', 82
Pynchon, Thomas, 55, 59
 The Crying of Lot 49, 55
 'Entropy', 55–6

Quatermass serials, 76
queer feminism, 233
queer utopias, 140, 151–2, 212, 234
queerness, 121, 200, 208
Quinn, Marc
 'A Surge of Power (Jen Reid) 2020', 21

race
 British counterculture and *Penda's Fen*, 113
 Carty-Williams's *Queenie* and Black belonging, 203–4
 Carty-Williams's *Queenie* and Black/White experience, 200–3
 Christopher's catastrophe fiction, 49–50
 Evaristo's *Girl, Woman, Other* and Black British *bildungsroman*, 204–7
 Evaristo's *Girl, Woman, Other* and design fiction, 207–11
 Gilroy on Black British culture, 13–14
 Gilroy on post-imperial melancholy, 75–6
 Miéville's Bas-Lag Trilogy, 276, 278, 283
 Mitchison's *Memoirs* and essentialism, 236–7
 Smith's *Swing Time*, 211–15
 towards Black justice, 215
 utopian realism and race, 197–215
 utopian realism and race overview, 25–6, 197–200
race riots, 14, 19
racial capitalism, 124, 126, 130
racism
 Carty-Williams's *Queenie* and Black/White experience, 201, 202–3
 Christopher's catastrophe fiction, 49
 debbie tucker green's dramaturgy of refusal, 126
 du Maurier's *Rule Britannia*, 81
 Evaristo's *Girl, Woman, Other* and Black British *bildungsroman*, 204, 205
 Evaristo's *Girl, Woman, Other* and design fiction, 207–8, 210
 Fleming and James Bond, 5
 Gilroy on postcolonial melancholy, 14
 Mitchison's *Memoirs*, 239
 Moorcock's Jerry Cornelius novels, 63
 punk and *Jubilee*, 89–90
 Smith's *Swing Time*, 212, 213, 214
 Sutherland's *Venus as a Boy*, 152
 utopian realism and race overview, 197, 198
Radford, Michael
 1984, 92
Radical Bookshop History Project, **29**
radical care, 191
radical theatre, 120–1
Radio Caroline, 10
Raha, Nat
 Of Sirens, Body & Faultlines, 190, 192
Ramírez-Blanco, Julia, 20
Randhawa, Ravinder
 Wicked Old Woman, 207
rave movement, 20
Reagan, Ronald, 17
realism. *see also* utopian realism
 Lessing's writings, 160, 164–5
 utopian realism and race, 25–6, 199–200, 203, 213, 214
reality, 203–4, 213–15
Reballato, Dan, 122
Reclaim the Streets, 19

refusal, 124, 125, 126, 127, 133
regional identity, 81
Reich, James, 63
Reid, Jen, 21
Reid, Trish, 126
religion, 143
religious writing, 103–4
Rembrandt
    The Night Watch, **263**
reproduction, 238
reproductive futurism, 132, 153
revolution
    Bonney's insurrectionary poetry, 181, 182, 184
    Miéville's Bas-Lag Trilogy, 27, 270, 280, 284–5
    Pratchett's *Night Watch* and social change, 251–2, 253–5
Rieder, John, 229–30
Riley, Joan, 202
riots, 14, 19, 90
Roberts, Adam, **264**
Roberts, Keith
    The Furies, 40
Roberts, Luke, 186
Roberts, Michèle, 21
Robinson, Bill 'Bojangles', 212
Robinson, Brian, 103
Robinson, Kim Stanley, 172–3
    New York 2140, 162
Robson, Justina, 18
Rosenblatt, Rand K., **29**
Roundhouse, London, 8–9, 99
Rowe, Marsha, 21
Rowe, William, 184
Royal Society, **177**, 230
Rudkin, David, 102, 103, 105, 106, 107, 108, 109, 111, 112
ruin literature, 38
rural life, 47
Rushdie, Salman, 210
Russ, Joanna, 223, 230, 232
    The Female Man, 1, 88
Russia, 281

Said, Edward
    'Jane Austen and Empire', 77
Salah, Trish, 239
same sex desire, 109
Samuel, Raphael, 106–7, 111
Sánchez-Palencia, Carolina, 208
satire
    British countercultures, 10
    Gardner's *Naturally It Is Not*, 190
    Pratchett and anti-utopia, 26–7, 244, 248, 249, 258, 261, 262, 263
'Savage '70s', 12

Savage Messiah zines, 19
Sawyer, Miranda, 74
Scafe, Suzanne, 129
Scanlan, Margaret, **173**
scars, 182–3
scepticism, 169
Schumpeter, Joseph, 273
science
    and art, 60, 66
    Mitchison's *Memoirs* and femininity, 226–8, 229–30, 232–3, 236
science fiction (SF)
    beyond the colonial literary utopia in 1970s SF, 13–16
    B-movies, 37
    British countercultures in 1960s, 11–12
    Lessing and utopian future, 160, 161, 162, 163
    Lessing's discovery of Sufism, 164, 165
    Mitchison's *Memoirs* and feminism, 224, 225, 226, 227, 229–30, 232, 234
    New Wave and *New Worlds* magazine, 56, 60–5, 66
    nuclear imagination, 41
    post-imperial melancholy, 76, 78, 92
    Scottish utopia on British periphery, 138
Scottish fiction
    Mitchison's writings, 26, 225
    Scottish communal life and utopian homosociality, 145–9
    Scottish utopia on British periphery, 138–40
    utopia, death and the promised land, 140–5
    utopian communities in Scottish fiction, 138–54
    utopian communities in Scottish fiction overview, 25
    utopian storytelling and queer futures, 149–54
Scottish independence movement, 26, 79, 138–9, 225
Scranton, Roy
    Learning to Die in the Anthropocene, 172, **177**
    We're Doomed. Now What?, 172
sea urchins, 229, 230, 234–5, 236
Second Law of Thermodynamics, 55, 56
Second Wave Feminism, 58
Second World War. *see* World War II
Secret Army (TV series), 84
Sedgwick, Helen
    The Growing Season, 153
Segal, Lynne, 21, **173**
selfhood, 122, 131
Selvon, Samuel, 207
senses, 215
Seo-Young Chu, 246

sex
    Miéville's Bas-Lag Trilogy, 273–5, 279, 283
    Mitchison's *Memoirs*, 234–5, 236–7
    Sutherland's *Venus as a Boy*, 152
Sex Pistols, 12, 90
Sexton, Jamie, **116**
sexuality
    Ballard's *Crash*, 86
    British counterculture and Bowie, 11
    British counterculture and *Penda's Fen*, 106, 108–9, 112, 114
    Evaristo's *Girl, Woman, Other*, 207
    Scottish fiction, 148, 152
SF. *see* science fiction (SF)
Shah, Idries, 163–4, 165, 166, 167, 170–1, **175**
    'The Garden', 164
    Reflections, **175**
    Seeker After Truth, 171
    The Sufis, 163–4
    The Way of the Sufi, 164
Shakespeare, William
    love poetry, 275
    The Tempest, 16
    Troilus and Cressida, 247
    Twelfth Night, 258
Sharpe, Christina, 23, 208
Shaviro, Steven, **285**
Shaw, Kristian, 210
Shelley, Mary
    Frankenstein, 233, 234, **242**
    The Last Man, 38
Sheppard, Robert, **193**
Shute, Nevil
    On the Beach, 42
Sigal, Clancy, **175**
Sinclair, Iain, 19
Sinfield, Alan, 48, 109
Singh, Julietta, 231
skin, 187, 188
Skoulding, Zoe, 183
slavery
    Adebayo's Moj of the *Antarctic*, 129
    Black British poetry, 23
    country-house economy, 78
    Miéville's Bas-Lag Trilogy, 283
    More's *Utopia*, 3
    Pratchett and anti-utopia, 250
    statue removal, 21
    utopian realism and race, 198, 201, 203, 206, 208–9, 212, 214
small presses, 25, 179, 180
Smartt, Dorothea, 202
Smith, Ali, 23, 25
    Girl meets boy, 139, 151
    Hotel World, 146, 149–51
Smith, Andy
    'Plays for the People', 122, **134**
Smith, Zadie, 26
    NW, 199
    Swing Time, 199, 211–15
Smithson, Robert, 55, 71
Snow, C. P., 66
    The New Men, 42
    'Two Cultures' lecture, 42, 55, 60
social change, 250–1
social contract, 257
social Darwinism, 38
social realism, 109
social relationality, 119–20, 122
socialism, 51, 108, 146, 205, 280, 281
sociological turn, 245, 246
solidarity, 111, 112, 126, 133, 186, 191
Sontag, Susan, 42, 61
    'The Imagination of Disaster', 37
    'One Culture and the New Sensibility', 60
Soong, Jennifer, 186
sovereignty, 255–9, 260–1
space exploration, 11
Spare Rib magazine, 21
'spect-actor', 120
spectators, 120, 122, 123, 130
Sperlinger, Tom, 172
Spoliar, Fred, **195**
Spott, Verity, 25, 178, 186–90
    Click Away Close Door Say, 186–9, 190, 191, 192
    Gideon, 186
    Hopelessness, 191
    We Will Bury You, 186
squatters' movement, 19, 20, 21, 209
Squier, Susan Merrill, 227, 232, 235–6
Srnicek, Nick, 114
Stallybrass, Peter, 109
Stapledon, Olaf, 224
starfish, 235–7, 238
statues, 21, 197–8, 201, 207, 215
Stein, Mark, 204
Stewart, George
    The Earth Abides, 42
Stoermer, Eugene, 43
storytelling, 140, 141, 150–1, 153–4
structure of feeling, 39, 44, 106
student protests, 9–10, 11, 181–2
subcultures, 7–8
subjectivity
    Adebayo's theatre, 128, 130, 132
    Carty-Williams's *Queenie* and race, 202
    contemporary British theatre, 122, 133
    debbie tucker green's dramaturgy of refusal, 124, 126, 127

subjectivity (cont.)
  Evaristo's *Girl, Woman, Other* and sexuality, 207
Sufism, 14, 163–5, 166, 170–1
surplus, utopian, 8
Survivors TV series, 40
Suspect Culture, 122
Sutherland, John, 82
Sutherland, Luke, 25
  Venus as a Boy, 139, 152, 153
Sutton, Trevor, 12
Suvin, Darko, 246
Swainston, Steph, 18
Swing Riots, **266**
Swing Time (1936 film), 211, 212
Szilard, Leo, 41

Taylor, Laura Wiebe, 13
telepathy, 161
television, 40, 75, 81–3, 201. see also *Penda's Fen* (TV play)
Tennant, Emma
  The Time of the Crack, 40, 43, 75, 88
Tey, Josephine
  The Singing Sands, 139, 148–9, 150
That Was the Week that Was (TV show), 10
Thatcher, Margaret, 17–18, 19, 51, 79, 84, 90, 184–5, 205
Thatcherism, 17, 18, 90–1, 111, 185
theatre
  contemporary British theatre, 119–33
  contemporary British theatre overview, 24–5, 132–3
  debbie tucker green's dramaturgy of refusal, 123–8
  theatre as utopian laboratory, 119–23
  transformative energies of Mojisola Adebayo's theatre, 128–32
  utopian potential, **134**
Theatre of Black Women, 205
Theatre of the Oppressed, 120, 129
theatre studies, 121, **134**
the87press, 25, 180
thermodynamics, 55, 56, 66, 69
Thomas, Ed, **134**
Thompson, Dorothy, 6
Thompson, E. P., 6, 13
Thunderball (1965 film), 5
time, 9, 162
Tiptree, James, Jr., 223, 232
totalitarianism, 140, 271, 272, 273
tower blocks, 87
Townsend, Pete, **30**
trans identity, 152, 153
transglossic literatures, 210

transphobia, 239, **240**
Trellick Tower, 87
Tricoire, Damian, 4
tucker green, debbie
  Adebayo's theatre, 128
  contemporary British theatre overview, 25, 132–3
  dramaturgy of refusal, 124–8
  theatre as utopian laboratory, 122–3
  ear for eye, 124–5, 127
  hang, 125, 127
  stoning mary, 125–6, 127
  The Two Ronnies (TV series), **94**
  28 Days Later . . . (2002 film), 52
  2001: A Space Odyssey (1968 film), 11

ubuntu, 133
ultraviolence, 183–4
Ungleichzeitigkeit (non-simultaneity), 17
Uninvited Guest
  It is Like It Ought to Be: A Pastoral, 122
unions, 83, 84–6, 91
United Kingdom (UK)
  alternate history and hope of British resistance, 78–9
  dystopias of lost Britain, 83
  Scottish utopia on British periphery, 138–9
Urry, John, **31**
utopia. see also critical utopias
  abstract and concrete utopias, 189–90, 191, 262
  British counterculture and thinking about utopia, 98–100
  British counterculture, utopia and class overview, 97–8
  coinage of term, 3
  defining, 98, **285**
  Lessing's writings, 159, 166, 168–9
  from literary utopian enclaves to the utopian impulse, 2–4
  Pratchett and anti-utopia, 252
  Scottish fiction, utopia and death, 140–5
  Scottish utopia on British periphery, 138–9
  utopian realism and race, 205, 212, 213–14, 215
  in *Zardoz*, 1
utopian communities
  Scottish communal life and utopian homosociality, 147, 148–9
  in Scottish fiction, 138–54
  Scottish fiction overview, 25
  Scottish utopia on British periphery, 138–40
  utopia and death, 140, 143, 144, 145
  utopian storytelling and queer futures, 150, 151, 153–4
utopian critique, 2, 3, 5
utopian enclave, 2
utopian hope, 127, 172, 173, 206, 284–5

utopian impulse in British literature and culture since 1945, 1
  overview, 2–3, 23–7
  beyond the colonial literary utopia in 1970s SF, 13–16
  British countercultures and utopian surplus in 1960s, 7–13
  British postwar culture and imaginary past, 4–7
  from literary utopian enclaves to the utopian impulse, 2–4
  utopian anachronism as a weapon, 1980s-2000s, 17–20
  utopian turn in 2010s and 2020s, 20–3
utopian literature
  British counterculture, utopia and class, 97–115
  China Miéville's Bas-Lag Trilogy and dialectics of utopia, 284–5
  contemporary British theatre, 119–33
  cosy catastrophes and ambivalent utopias, 37–52
  Doris Lessing: surviving utopia, 159–73
  Naomi Mitchison's *Memoirs of a Spacewoman* as critical feminist utopia, 223–39
  New Wave and *New Worlds* in 1960s, 55–70
  outline of volume, 23–7
  post-imperial melancholy in the long 1970s, 73–92
  Terry Pratchett's *Night Watch* and *Making Money* and anti-utopia, 244–63
  utopian articulations in experimental British poetry, 178–92
  utopian communities in Scottish fiction, 138–54
  utopian impulse in British literature and culture since 1945, 1
  utopian realism and race, 197–215
utopian longing, 123, 127
utopian realism, 25–6, 199–200, 203, 212, 213
utopian studies, 121
utopian surplus, 8

Vietnam war, 10, 61, 62–3, 81
Viktor, Lina Iris, 22
villains, 247
Vint, Sherryl, 70, **285**
violence, 48–9, 182–4, 186, 191, 251, 254–5, 261
visionary tradition, 103–5
Viz comic, 97
Voltaire
  Candide, 247
Vorschein (forward-dawning), 8

the wake, 208, 211, 215
Wales, 79, 81
Walker, John A., 12

Walker, Nancy A., 89
Wallace, Craig, 104
Wallace, Gavin, 138
war, 38, 41, 261
Ward, Stuart, 10, **28**
Warner, Alan, 145
  These Demented Lands, 141
Watson, Gray, 74
Wegner, Phillip E., 139, 159, 162, 165
Wells, G. P.
  The Science of Life, 235
Wells, H. G., 229–30
  First Men in the Moon, 230
  The Science of Life, 235
  The War of the Worlds, 38, 76
  The World Set Free, 41
Westway flyover, 15, **31**
Westwood, Vivienne, 12, 73
White, Allon, 109
White, Patrick, 164
White experience, 124–5, 126, 198, 200–1, 202, 214
Whitehouse, Mary, 101, 103
Whyte, Jerry, 102
The Wicker Man (1973 film), 143
Wiener, Martin, 51
Wilde, Oscar
  'The Soul of Man Under Socialism', 280
Wilkinson, David, 13
Willett, Joanie, 81
Williams, Alex, 114
Williams, Charles, 103
Williams, Heathcote, 209
Williams, Raymond
  British counterculture, 8, 98, 100
  British cultural studies, 7, 13
  cultural formations, 101
  cultural materialism, 6, 98, 100
  defining culture, 6–7
  the dominant, 8, 114
  Le Guin review, 1
  structure of feeling, 39, 44, 106
  working class culture, 110
  Marxism and Literature, 7, 44
  'Utopia and Science Fiction', 1, 100
Wilson, Harold, 79
Windrush generation, 202, 203, 207
Winters, Joseph R., 16
Winterson, Jeanette, 168
women
  British theatre, 120, 130
  Carter and fairy tales, 89
  Mitchison's *Memoirs* and essentialism, 233–4, 236
  Mitchison's *Memoirs* and femininity, 226–8, 232
  pirates, 277

women (cont.)
  writers, 26, 40–1, 199, 203, 207
women's movement, 85, 88, 202
Women's Press, 226
Wong, Denise, 129
Woods, Sarah
  The Ruff Tuff Cream Puff Estate Agency, 209
working class, 7, 20, 101–2, 107, 109–10, 111
World War I, 38, 281
World War II, 38, 41, 51, 57, 63, 80, 83, 91
World War III, 42
Worpole, Ken, 19
Wright, Richard, 13
Wymer, Rowland, 47
Wyndham, John, 24, 37–8, 46–7, 80
  The Chrysalids, 42, 46
  The Day of the Triffids, 37, 38, 43, 46, 47, 52, 64
  The Kraken Wakes, 43, 44, 46
  The Midwich Cuckoos, 46

Yellow Submarine (1968 animated film), 10
Youd, Sam. *see* Christopher, John (aka Sam Youd)
youth cultures, 8, 101

Zähringer, Raphael, **285**
Zamalin, Alex
  Black Utopia, 132, 206
Zamyatin, Yevgeny
  We, 162, 231
Zardoz (1974 film), 1, 3–5
Zarf magazine, 25, 179–81, 191
zimZalla, 25, 180
zines, 18
Zipes, Jack, 7, 89
Žižek, Slavoj, 97
Zoline, Pamela, 12, 24
  'The Heat Death of the Universe', 57, 66–9, 224

Cambridge Companions To . . .

AUTHORS

Edward Albee edited by Stephen J. Bottoms

Margaret Atwood edited by Coral Ann Howells (second edition)

W. H. Auden edited by Stan Smith

Jane Austen edited by Edward Copeland and Juliet McMaster (second edition)

James Baldwin edited by Michele Elam

Balzac edited by Owen Heathcote and Andrew Watts

Beckett edited by John Pilling

Bede edited by Scott DeGregorio

Aphra Behn edited by Derek Hughes and Janet Todd

Saul Bellow edited by Victoria Aarons

Walter Benjamin edited by David S. Ferris

William Blake edited by Morris Eaves

Boccaccio edited by Guyda Armstrong, Rhiannon Daniels, and Stephen J. Milner

Jorge Luis Borges edited by Edwin Williamson

Brecht edited by Peter Thomson and Glendyr Sacks (second edition)

The Brontës edited by Heather Glen

Bunyan edited by Anne Dunan-Page

Frances Burney edited by Peter Sabor

Byron edited by Drummond Bone (second edition)

Albert Camus edited by Edward J. Hughes

Willa Cather edited by Marilee Lindemann

Catullus edited by Ian Du Quesnay and Tony Woodman

Cervantes edited by Anthony J. Cascardi

Chaucer edited by Piero Boitani and Jill Mann (second edition)

Chekhov edited by Vera Gottlieb and Paul Allain

Kate Chopin edited by Janet Beer

Caryl Churchill edited by Elaine Aston and Elin Diamond

Cicero edited by Catherine Steel

John Clare edited by Sarah Houghton-Walker

J. M. Coetzee edited by Jarad Zimbler

Coleridge edited by Lucy Newlyn

Coleridge edited by Tim Fulford (new edition)

Wilkie Collins edited by Jenny Bourne Taylor

Joseph Conrad edited by J. H. Stape

H. D. edited by Nephie J. Christodoulides and Polina Mackay

Dante edited by Rachel Jacoff (second edition)

Daniel Defoe edited by John Richetti

Don DeLillo edited by John N. Duvall

Charles Dickens edited by John O. Jordan

Emily Dickinson edited by Wendy Martin

John Donne edited by Achsah Guibbory

Dostoevskii edited by W. J. Leatherbarrow

Theodore Dreiser edited by Leonard Cassuto and Claire Virginia Eby

John Dryden edited by Steven N. Zwicker

W. E. B. Du Bois edited by Shamoon Zamir

George Eliot edited by George Levine and Nancy Henry (second edition)

T. S. Eliot edited by A. David Moody

Ralph Ellison edited by Ross Posnock

Ralph Waldo Emerson edited by Joel Porte and Saundra Morris

William Faulkner edited by Philip M. Weinstein

Henry Fielding edited by Claude Rawson

F. Scott Fitzgerald edited by Ruth Prigozy

F. Scott Fitzgerald edited by Michael Nowlin (second edition)

Flaubert edited by Timothy Unwin

E. M. Forster edited by David Bradshaw

Benjamin Franklin edited by Carla Mulford

Brian Friel edited by Anthony Roche

Robert Frost edited by Robert Faggen

Gabriel García Márquez edited by Philip Swanson

Elizabeth Gaskell edited by Jill L. Matus

Edward Gibbon edited by Karen O'Brien and Brian Young

Goethe edited by Lesley Sharpe

Günter Grass edited by Stuart Taberner

Thomas Hardy edited by Dale Kramer

David Hare edited by Richard Boon

Nathaniel Hawthorne edited by Richard Millington

Seamus Heaney edited by Bernard O'Donoghue

Ernest Hemingway edited by Scott Donaldson

Hildegard of Bingen edited by Jennifer Bain

Homer edited by Robert Fowler

Horace edited by Stephen Harrison
Ted Hughes edited by Terry Gifford
Ibsen edited by James McFarlane
Kazuo Ishiguro edited by Andrew Bennett
Henry James edited by Jonathan Freedman
Samuel Johnson edited by Greg Clingham
Ben Jonson edited by Richard Harp and Stanley Stewart
James Joyce edited by John Nash (third edition)
Kafka edited by Julian Preece
Keats edited by Susan J. Wolfson
Rudyard Kipling edited by Howard J. Booth
Lacan edited by Jean-Michel Rabaté
D. H. Lawrence edited by Anne Fernihough
Primo Levi edited by Robert Gordon
Lucian edited by Simon Goldhill
Lucretius edited by Stuart Gillespie and Philip Hardie
Machiavelli edited by John M. Najemy
David Mamet edited by Christopher Bigsby
Thomas Mann edited by Ritchie Robertson
Christopher Marlowe edited by Patrick Cheney
Andrew Marvell edited by Derek Hirst and Steven N. Zwicker
Ian McEwan edited by Dominic Head
Herman Melville edited by Robert S. Levine
Arthur Miller edited by Christopher Bigsby (second edition)
Milton edited by Dennis Danielson (second edition)
Molière edited by David Bradby and Andrew Calder
William Morris edited by Marcus Waithe
Toni Morrison edited by Justine Tally
Alice Munro edited by David Staines
Nabokov edited by Julian W. Connolly
Eugene O'Neill edited by Michael Manheim
George Orwell edited by John Rodden
Ovid edited by Philip Hardie
Petrarch edited by Albert Russell Ascoli and Unn Falkeid
Harold Pinter edited by Peter Raby (second edition)
Sylvia Plath edited by Jo Gill
Plutarch edited by Frances B. Titchener and Alexei Zadorojnyi

Edgar Allan Poe edited by Kevin J. Hayes
Alexander Pope edited by Pat Rogers
Ezra Pound edited by Ira B. Nadel
Mary Prince edited by Nicole N. Aljoe
Proust edited by Richard Bales
Pushkin edited by Andrew Kahn
Thomas Pynchon edited by Inger H. Dalsgaard, Luc Herman and Brian McHale
Rabelais edited by John O'Brien
Rilke edited by Karen Leeder and Robert Vilain
Philip Roth edited by Timothy Parrish
Salman Rushdie edited by Abdulrazak Gurnah
John Ruskin edited by Francis O'Gorman
Sappho edited by P. J. Finglass and Adrian Kelly
Seneca edited by Shadi Bartsch and Alessandro Schiesaro
Shakespeare edited by Margareta de Grazia and Stanley Wells (second edition)
George Bernard Shaw edited by Christopher Innes
Shelley edited by Timothy Morton
Mary Shelley edited by Esther Schor
Sam Shepard edited by Matthew C. Roudané
Spenser edited by Andrew Hadfield
Laurence Sterne edited by Thomas Keymer
Wallace Stevens edited by John N. Serio
Tom Stoppard edited by Katherine E. Kelly
Harriet Beecher Stowe edited by Cindy Weinstein
August Strindberg edited by Michael Robinson
Jonathan Swift edited by Christopher Fox
J. M. Synge edited by P. J. Mathews
Tacitus edited by A. J. Woodman
Henry David Thoreau edited by Joel Myerson
Thucydides edited by Polly Low
Tolstoy edited by Donna Tussing Orwin
Anthony Trollope edited by Carolyn Dever and Lisa Niles
Mark Twain edited by Forrest G. Robinson
John Updike edited by Stacey Olster
Mario Vargas Llosa edited by Efrain Kristal and John King
Virgil edited by Fiachra Mac Góráin and Charles Martindale (second edition)
Voltaire edited by Nicholas Cronk

David Foster Wallace edited by Ralph Clare
Edith Wharton edited by Millicent Bell
Walt Whitman edited by Ezra Greenspan
Oscar Wilde edited by Peter Raby
Tennessee Williams edited by Matthew C. Roudané
William Carlos Williams edited by Christopher MacGowan
August Wilson edited by Christopher Bigsby
Mary Wollstonecraft edited by Claudia L. Johnson
Virginia Woolf edited by Susan Sellers (second edition)
Wordsworth edited by Stephen Gill
Richard Wright edited by Glenda R. Carpio
W. B. Yeats edited by Marjorie Howes and John Kelly
Xenophon edited by Michael A. Flower
Zola edited by Brian Nelson

TOPICS

The Actress edited by Maggie B. Gale and John Stokes
The African American Novel edited by Maryemma Graham
The African American Slave Narrative edited by Audrey A. Fisch
African American Theatre edited by Harvey Young
Allegory edited by Rita Copeland and Peter Struck
American Crime Fiction edited by Catherine Ross Nickerson
American Gothic edited by Jeffrey Andrew Weinstock
The American Graphic Novel edited by Jan Baetens, Hugo Frey and Fabrice Leroy
American Horror edited by Stephen Shapiro and Mark Storey
American Literature and the Body edited by Travis M. Foster
American Literature and the Environment edited by Sarah Ensor and Susan Scott Parrish
American Literature of the 1930s edited by William Solomon
American Modernism edited by Walter Kalaidjian
American Poetry since 1945 edited by Jennifer Ashton
American Prison Literature and Mass Incarceration edited by David Coogan
American Realism and Naturalism edited by Donald Pizer
American Short Story edited by Michael J. Collins and Gavin Jones
American Travel Writing edited by Alfred Bendixen and Judith Hamera
American Utopian Literature and Culture since 1945 edited by Sherryl Vint
American Women Playwrights edited by Brenda Murphy
Ancient Rhetoric edited by Erik Gunderson
Arthurian Legend edited by Elizabeth Archibald and Ad Putter
Australian Literature edited by Elizabeth Webby
The Australian Novel edited by Nicholas Birns and Louis Klee
The Beats edited by Stephen Belletto
The Black Body in American Literature edited by Cherene Sherrard-Johnson
Boxing edited by Gerald Early
British Black and Asian Literature (1945–2010) edited by Deirdre Osborne
British Fiction: 1980–2018 edited by Peter Boxall
British Fiction since 1945 edited by David James
British Literature of the 1930s edited by James Smith
British Literature of the French Revolution edited by Pamela Clemit
British Postmodern Fiction edited by Bran Nicol
British Romantic Poetry edited by James Chandler and Maureen N. McLane
British Romanticism edited by Stuart Curran (second edition)
British Romanticism and Religion edited by Jeffrey Barbeau
British Theatre, 1730–1830 edited by Jane Moody and Daniel O'Quinn
British Utopian Literature and Culture since 1945 edited by Caroline Edwards

Canadian Literature edited by Eva-Marie Kröller (second edition)

The Canterbury Tales edited by Frank Grady

Children's Literature edited by M. O. Grenby and Andrea Immel

The City in World Literature edited by Ato Quayson and Jini Kim Watson

The Classic Russian Novel edited by Malcolm V. Jones and Robin Feuer Miller

Comics edited by Maaheen Ahmed

Contemporary African American Literature edited by Yogita Goyal

Contemporary Irish Poetry edited by Matthew Campbell

Creative Writing edited by David Morley and Philip Neilsen

Crime Fiction edited by Martin Priestman

Dante's 'Commedia' edited by Zygmunt G. Barański and Simon Gilson

Dracula edited by Roger Luckhurst

Early American Literature edited by Bryce Traister

Early Modern Women's Writing edited by Laura Lunger Knoppers

The Eighteenth-Century Novel edited by John Richetti

Eighteenth-Century Poetry edited by John Sitter

Eighteenth-Century Thought edited by Frans De Bruyn

Emma edited by Peter Sabor

English Dictionaries edited by Sarah Ogilvie

English Literature, 1500–1600 edited by Arthur F. Kinney

English Literature, 1650–1740 edited by Steven N. Zwicker

English Literature, 1740–1830 edited by Thomas Keymer and Jon Mee

English Literature, 1830–1914 edited by Joanne Shattock

English Melodrama edited by Carolyn Williams

English Novelists edited by Adrian Poole

English Poetry, Donne to Marvell edited by Thomas N. Corns

English Poets edited by Claude Rawson

English Renaissance Drama edited by A. R. Braunmuller and Michael Hattaway (second edition)

English Renaissance Tragedy edited by Emma Smith and Garrett A. Sullivan Jr.

English Restoration Theatre edited by Deborah C. Payne Fisk

Environmental Humanities edited by Jeffrey Cohen and Stephanie Foote

The Epic edited by Catherine Bates

Erotic Literature edited by Bradford Mudge

The Essay edited by Kara Wittman and Evan Kindley

European Modernism edited by Pericles Lewis

European Novelists edited by Michael Bell

Fairy Tales edited by Maria Tatar

Fantasy Literature edited by Edward James and Farah Mendlesohn

Feminist Literary Theory edited by Ellen Rooney

Fiction in the Romantic Period edited by Richard Maxwell and Katie Trumpener

The Fin de Siècle edited by Gail Marshall

Frankenstein edited by Andrew Smith

The French Enlightenment edited by Daniel Brewer

French Literature edited by John D. Lyons

The French Novel: from 1800 to the Present edited by Timothy Unwin

Gay and Lesbian Writing edited by Hugh Stevens

German Romanticism edited by Nicholas Saul

Global Literature and Slavery edited by Laura T. Murphy

Gothic Fiction edited by Jerrold E. Hogle

The Graphic Novel edited by Stephen Tabachnick

The Greek and Roman Novel edited by Tim Whitmarsh

Greek and Roman Theatre edited by Marianne McDonald and J. Michael Walton

Greek Comedy edited by Martin Revermann

Greek Lyric edited by Felix Budelmann

Greek Mythology edited by Roger D. Woodard

Greek Tragedy edited by P. E. Easterling

The Harlem Renaissance edited by George Hutchinson

The History of the Book edited by Leslie Howsam

Human Rights and Literature edited by Crystal Parikh

The Irish Novel edited by John Wilson Foster

Irish Poets edited by Gerald Dawe

The Italian Novel edited by Peter Bondanella and Andrea Ciccarelli

The Italian Renaissance edited by Michael Wyatt

Jewish American Literature edited by Hana Wirth-Nesher and Michael P. Kramer

The Latin American Novel edited by Efraín Kristal

Latin American Poetry edited by Stephen Hart

Latina/o American Literature edited by John Morán González

Latin Love Elegy edited by Thea S. Thorsen

Literature and Animals edited by Derek Ryan

Literature and the Anthropocene edited by John Parham

Literature and Climate edited by Adeline Johns-Putra and Kelly Sultzbach

Literature and Disability edited by Clare Barker and Stuart Murray

Literature and Food edited by J. Michelle Coghlan

Literature and the Posthuman edited by Bruce Clarke and Manuela Rossini

Literature and Religion edited by Susan M. Felch

Literature and Science edited by Steven Meyer

The Literature of the American Civil War and Reconstruction edited by Kathleen Diffley and Coleman Hutchison

The Literature of the American Renaissance edited by Christopher N. Phillips

The Literature of Berlin edited by Andrew J. Webber

The Literature of the Crusades edited by Anthony Bale

The Literature of the First World War edited by Vincent Sherry

The Literature of London edited by Lawrence Manley

The Literature of Los Angeles edited by Kevin R. McNamara

The Literature of New York edited by Cyrus Patell and Bryan Waterman

The Literature of Paris edited by Anna-Louise Milne

The Literature of World War II edited by Marina MacKay

Literature on Screen edited by Deborah Cartmell and Imelda Whelehan

Lyrical Ballads edited by Sally Bushell

Manga and Anime edited by Jaqueline Berndt

Medieval British Manuscripts edited by Orietta Da Rold and Elaine Treharne

Medieval English Culture edited by Andrew Galloway

Medieval English Law and Literature edited by Candace Barrington and Sebastian Sobecki

Medieval English Literature edited by Larry Scanlon

Medieval English Mysticism edited by Samuel Fanous and Vincent Gillespie

Medieval English Theatre edited by Richard Beadle and Alan J. Fletcher (second edition)

Medieval French Literature edited by Simon Gaunt and Sarah Kay

Medieval Romance edited by Roberta L. Krueger

Medieval Romance edited by Roberta L. Krueger (new edition)

Medieval Women's Writing edited by Carolyn Dinshaw and David Wallace

Modern American Culture edited by Christopher Bigsby

Modern British Women Playwrights edited by Elaine Aston and Janelle Reinelt

Modern French Culture edited by Nicholas Hewitt

Modern German Culture edited by Eva Kolinsky and Wilfried van der Will

The Modern German Novel edited by Graham Bartram

The Modern Gothic edited by Jerrold E. Hogle

Modern Irish Culture edited by Joe Cleary and Claire Connolly

Modern Italian Culture edited by Zygmunt G. Baranski and Rebecca J. West

Modern Latin American Culture edited by John King

Modern Russian Culture edited by Nicholas Rzhevsky

Modern Spanish Culture edited by David T. Gies

Modernism edited by Michael Levenson (second edition)

The Modernist Novel edited by Morag Shiach

Modernist Poetry edited by Alex Davis and Lee M. Jenkins

Modernist Women Writers edited by Maren Tova Linett

Narrative edited by David Herman

Narrative Theory edited by Matthew Garrett

Native American Literature edited by Joy Porter and Kenneth M. Roemer

Nineteen Eighty-Four edited by Nathan Waddell

Nineteenth-Century American Literature and Politics edited by John Kerkering

Nineteenth-Century American Poetry edited by Kerry Larson

Nineteenth-Century American Women's Writing edited by Dale M. Bauer and Philip Gould

Nineteenth-Century Thought edited by Gregory Claeys

The Novel edited by Eric Bulson

Old English Literature edited by Malcolm Godden and Michael Lapidge (second edition)

Performance Studies edited by Tracy C. Davis

Piers Plowman edited by Andrew Cole and Andrew Galloway

The Poetry of the First World War edited by Santanu Das

Popular Fiction edited by David Glover and Scott McCracken

Postcolonial Literary Studies edited by Neil Lazarus

Postcolonial Poetry edited by Jahan Ramazani

Postcolonial Travel Writing edited by Robert Clarke

Postmodern American Fiction edited by Paula Geyh

Postmodernism edited by Steven Connor

Prose edited by Daniel Tyler

The Pre-Raphaelites edited by Elizabeth Prettejohn

Pride and Prejudice edited by Janet Todd

Queer Studies edited by Siobhan B. Somerville

Renaissance Humanism edited by Jill Kraye

Robinson Crusoe edited by John Richetti

Roman Comedy edited by Martin T. Dinter

The Roman Historians edited by Andrew Feldherr

Roman Satire edited by Kirk Freudenburg

The Romantic Sublime edited by Cian Duffy

Romanticism and Race edited by Manu Samriti Chander

Science Fiction edited by Edward James and Farah Mendlesohn

Scottish Literature edited by Gerald Carruthers and Liam McIlvanney

Sensation Fiction edited by Andrew Mangham

Shakespeare and Contemporary Dramatists edited by Ton Hoenselaars

Shakespeare and Popular Culture edited by Robert Shaughnessy

Shakespeare and Race edited by Ayanna Thompson

Shakespeare and Religion edited by Hannibal Hamlin

Shakespeare and War edited by David Loewenstein and Paul Stevens

Shakespeare on Film edited by Russell Jackson (second edition)

Shakespeare on Screen edited by Russell Jackson

Shakespeare on Stage edited by Stanley Wells and Sarah Stanton

Shakespearean Comedy edited by Alexander Leggatt

Shakespearean Tragedy edited by Claire McEachern (second edition)

Shakespeare's First Folio edited by Emma Smith

Shakespeare's History Plays edited by Michael Hattaway

Shakespeare's Language edited by Lynne Magnusson with David Schalkwyk

Shakespeare's Last Plays edited by Catherine M. S. Alexander

Shakespeare's Poetry edited by Patrick Cheney

Sherlock Holmes edited by Janice M. Allan and Christopher Pittard

The Sonnet edited by A. D. Cousins and Peter Howarth

The Spanish Novel: from 1600 to the Present edited by Harriet Turner and Adelaida López de Martínez

Textual Scholarship edited by Neil Fraistat and Julia Flanders

Theatre and Science edited by Kristen E. Shepherd-Barr

Theatre History edited by David Wiles and Christine Dymkowski

Transnational American Literature edited by Yogita Goyal

Travel Writing edited by Peter Hulme and Tim Youngs

The Twentieth-Century American Novel and Politics edited by Bryan Santin

Twentieth-Century American Poetry and Politics edited by Daniel Morris

Twentieth-Century British and Irish Women's Poetry edited by Jane Dowson

The Twentieth-Century English Novel edited by Robert L. Caserio

Twentieth-Century English Poetry edited by Neil Corcoran

Twentieth-Century Irish Drama edited by Shaun Richards

Twentieth-Century Literature and Politics edited by Christos Hadjiyiannis and Rachel Potter

Twentieth-Century Russian Literature edited by Marina Balina and Evgeny Dobrenko

Utopian Literature edited by Gregory Claeys

Victorian and Edwardian Theatre edited by Kerry Powell

The Victorian Novel edited by Deirdre David (second edition)

Victorian Poetry edited by Joseph Bristow

Victorian Women's Poetry edited by Linda K. Hughes

Victorian Women's Writing edited by Linda H. Peterson

War Writing edited by Kate McLoughlin

Women's Writing in Britain, 1660–1789 edited by Catherine Ingrassia

Women's Writing in the Romantic Period edited by Devoney Looser

World Literature edited by Ben Etherington and Jarad Zimbler

World Crime Fiction edited by Jesper Gulddal, Stewart King and Alistair Rolls

Writing of the English Revolution edited by N. H. Keeble

The Writings of Julius Caesar edited by Christopher Krebs and Luca Grillo

For EU product safety concerns, contact us at Calle de José Abascal, 56–1°,
28003 Madrid, Spain or eugpsr@cambridge.org.

www.ingramcontent.com/pod-product-compliance
Ingram Content Group UK Ltd.
Pitfield, Milton Keynes, MK11 3LW, UK
UKHW022229230426
12048UKWH00016BA/1143